DATE DUE

B 1 4 2000

PRINTED IN U.S.A.

Anglo-American Media Interactions, 1850–2000

Anglo-American Media Interactions, 1850–2000

Edited by

Joel H. Wiener and Mark Hampton

palgrave
macmillan

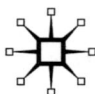

First published 2007 by
PALGRAVE MACMILLAN
Houndmills, Basingstoke, Hampshire RG21 6XS and
175 Fifth Avenue, New York, N.Y. 10010
Companies and representatives throughout the world

PALGRAVE MACMILLAN is the global academic imprint of the Palgrave Macmillan division of St. Martin's Press, LLC and of Palgrave Macmillan Ltd. Macmillan® is a registered trademark in the United States, United Kingdom and other countries. Palgrave is a registered trademark in the European Union and other countries.

ISBN-13: 978–0–230–52125–4   hardback
ISBN-10: 0–230–52125–8   hardback

This book is printed on paper suitable for recycling and made from fully managed and sustained forest sources. Logging, pulping and manufacturing processes are expected to conform to the environmental regulations of the country of origin.

A catalogue record for this book is available from the British Library.

A catalogue record for this book is available from the Library of Congress.

10   9   8   7   6   5   4   3   2   1
16   15   14   13   12   11   10   09   08   07

Printed and bound in Great Britain by
Antony Rowe Ltd, Chippenham and Eastbourne

For Suzanne and Ring

Contents

List of Illustrations

Acknowledgements

The following institutions have kindly given permission to reproduce materials from their collections: the BBC Written Archives Centre; the Reuters Archive; the History of Advertising Trust Archive; Duke University's Hartman Center for Sales, Advertising & Marketing History; Warwick University's Modern Records Centre; Ball State University (the Norman Angell archive); Boston University's Howard Gotlieb Archival Research Center on behalf of Mrs. Vera Fairbanks (the Douglas Fairbanks, Jr. papers); and Vanderbilt University (illustrations from *Punch*).

We are grateful to Simon Potter and an anonymous referee for their close readings of the entire manuscript and their valuable suggestions for revision. Kelly Boyd, Rohan McWilliam, and Stefan Schwarzkopf all helped us track down sources in London, and Ring Mei Han Low shared her computer expertise when formatting and other technical problems proved beyond our abilities. We also profited greatly from the advice of Lawrence Black, W. Joseph Campbell, Jim Epstein, Bob Franklin, David Karr, and Michael Schudson. At Palgrave, Michael Strang and Ruth Ireland have made the process of getting a book to press as smooth as we could have imagined.

Notes on Contributors

Christine Becker is an Assistant Professor in the Department of Film, Television, and Theatre at the University of Notre Dame, where she teaches film and television history. She is the author of *It's the Pictures That Got Small: Hollywood Film Stars on 1950s Television* (2007).

Jessica Bennett received a Masters of Public Administration from the University of Maryland University College-Europe, and plans to pursue a law degree in 2007.

Michael de Nie is Assistant Professor of History at the University of West Georgia. He is the author of *The Eternal Paddy: Irish Identity and the British Press, 1798–1882* (2004) and *Lives of the Victorian Political Figures: Charles Stewart Parnell* (2007).

Richard Fulton is Vice President for Instruction at Whatcom Community College. He is the former president of the Research Society for Victorian Periodicals and the Victorian Interdisciplinary Studies Association of the Western US, and editor of the *Union List of Victorian Serials* (1984).

Thomas Hajkowski is Assistant Professor of History at College Misericordia in Dallas, Pennsylvania. He is currently completing a book on the BBC and national identity in Britain, 1923–1953.

Mark Hampton is Associate Professor of History at Lingnan University in Hong Kong. He is the author of *Visions of the Press in Britain, 1850–1950* (2004) and a co-editor of *Media History*.

Christopher Kent is a Professor of History at the University of Saskatchewan. He has published numerous essays in his fields of interest, which include Victorian journalism and the arts, Victorian Bohemia, and the relations between the novel and history. He is currently finishing a book on clubs in Victorian London.

Fred Leventhal is Professor Emeritus of History at Boston University. His publications include *The Last Dissenter: H.N. Brailsford and His*

World and *Twentieth-Century Britain: An Encyclopedia*. He is a former President of the North American Conference on British Studies and former co-editor of the journal *Twentieth Century British History*.

Matt McIntire earned his PhD at the City University of New York (CUNY) Graduate Center. He has taught European history courses at Cleveland State University and at various schools in the CUNY system.

Peter Miskell is a Lecturer in Business History at the University of Reading. He has researched various aspects of multinational activity in the film, and consumer products industries. He is also author of *A Social History of the Cinema in Wales: Pulpits, Coalpits and Fleapits* (2006).

Siân Nicholas is Senior Lecturer in History at the University of Wales Aberystwyth. She is the author of *The Echo of War: Home Front Propaganda and the Wartime BBC 1939–45* (Manchester, Manchester University Press, 1996) and has published widely on aspects of the inter-war and wartime mass media in Britain.

Tom O'Malley, Professor of Media Studies at the University of Wales, Aberystwyth, is co-editor of *Media History*, and author of *Closedown: the BBC and Government Broadcasting Policy 1979–92* (1994); with Clive Soley of *Regulating the Press* (2001); and, with David Barlow and Philip Mitchell, *The Media in Wales* (2005).

Stefan Schwarzkopf is Lecturer in Marketing at Queen Mary College, University of London. His PhD (Birkbeck College) charted the rise of a service-oriented advertising industry in the United Kingdom in the twentieth-century. He has published widely on the history of advertising, marketing and political propaganda in modern Europe.

James D. Startt is Senior Research Professor in History at Valparaiso University and a former president of the American Journalism Historians Association. Among his publications are *Journalists for Empire: The Imperial Debate in the Edwardian Stately Press, 1903–1913* (1991) and *Woodrow Wilson and the Press: Prelude to the Presidency* (2004).

Joel H. Wiener is Professor Emeritus of History at The City University of New York. He has published and edited several books on British press history including *The War of the Unstamped* (1969) and *Papers for the Millions* (1988). He is a former president of the Research Society for Victorian Periodicals.

Introduction[1]: Anglo-American Media Interactions, 1850–2000

Joel H. Wiener and Mark Hampton

This book presents some of the best new research on Anglo-American media interactions in the nineteenth and twentieth centuries, a topic of strong and increasing concern to both British and American scholars. Yet, given that the countries share a common political and cultural heritage and that, in recent years, "British" media empires such as those of Rupert Murdoch and Conrad Black have thrust their way into the United States, it is surprising that the media dimension in transatlantic relations has been insufficiently examined.[2] This collection of essays seeks to rectify this gap and, among other things, to raise important questions about the transatlantic media's role in the construction of national identities and the emergence of global cultures.

Until recently, the prevailing focus of British and American media studies has been within national contexts. As Benedict Anderson, Thomas Leonard, Hannah Barker, and many others have shown, newspapers developed in the framework of emerging nation-states, and were constitutive of national identities.[3] Even with the invention of the telegraph, which made it possible to transmit news rapidly around the globe, newspaper culture continued to operate largely within national parameters; indeed, if anything, the British and American "national" press in the nineteenth century was rivaled by local papers, not by a global media culture.[4] Scholars of twentieth-century electronic media have generally followed this national tendency by studying the media in relative isolation from global or comparative frameworks. The essays in this book, by focusing on Anglo-American comparisons and making clear transatlantic cross-influences, reveal the broader context in which both the British and American media developed, as well as the transatlantic basis of the development of many aspects of national identity.

Until recent years, more attention has been given to Irish, French, and imperial influences in the construction of British identity than to the role of American culture.[5] This is not surprising because from the early nineteenth century, the image of "America" has generated ambivalent sentiments in Britain. Many Britons were attracted to the dynamism and perceived democratic foundations of American culture; at the same time, they were repelled by its crude informality, powerful commercial tendencies, and seeming bias against rigorous intellectual standards.[6] More recently, the uncertainty about American culture has been influenced in conflicting ways by the increased popularity of American pop culture, the articulation of an Anglo-American "special relationship," and in a broader sense, the general problem of imperial decline. Recent debates within Britain about that nation's degree of participation in the workings of the European Union, as well as its involvement in the wars in Iraq and Afghanistan, have merely exacerbated the ambivalence.

Given a shared transatlantic heritage, and the perception by many people throughout the world that the United States is Britain's successor empire and therefore largely indistinguishable from it, it is unclear exactly where Britain stands in relation to the paradigms of "Americanization" or "globalization," which have been put forth by scholars. Is Britain, like other European countries, chiefly a passive recipient of American culture?[7] Is it an active participant in the broad, swelling process of Westernization? Or, in less obvious ways, is it a powerful agent in the shaping of an Anglo-American culture that, in turn, is continually interacting with and remaking other national cultures?

These are important questions and, not surprisingly, it is the mass media that sits at the center of these globalization/ Americanization debates.[8] This is inevitable because the communications industries are among those that have benefited the most from the expansion of global markets, and because they are the most influential in conveying cultures across national borders. No other industries are better suited for transmitting "soft power," the ability to purvey cultural influence by indirect or agreeable means, or conversely for provoking resentment among those who resist the decline of national influence. While debate has centered on whether to see the development of a global media environment as facilitating a culturally neutral but homogenous "modernization," or as evidence of "cultural imperialism," few have doubted that the media cultural landscape is narrowing in many national contexts.[9]

As the essays in this book demonstrate, "Americanization" is a complex process involving multiple interactions. For one thing, it is evident that British and American culture, though not identical, overlap to a considerable degree. In their recent taxonomy of media systems within democratic nations, Daniel Hallin and Paolo Mancini place Britain and the United States within the same North Atlantic, or Liberal model, which is characterized by market domination, medium newspaper circulation, a strong professional feeling among journalists, and a politically neutral commercial press.[10] Meanwhile, Jeremy Tunstall's classic study, *The Media are American,* is tellingly subtitled "Anglo-American Media in the World," indicating heavy British involvement in what is commonly regarded as American global media dominance.[11] Nor is this shared cultural inheritance a recent development. Martin Conboy has traced a populist journalistic culture back and forth across the Atlantic, from John Wilkes, Thomas Paine, and William Cobbett, to W. T. Stead and Lincoln Steffens. And in a recent book Jean Chalaby contends that journalism is a nineteenth-century Anglo-American invention.[12] On a more popular level, the shared Anglo-American media inheritance is illustrated by Hollywood's Academy Awards treating British films as a domestic product, while the national provenance of numerous "transatlantic" films has become increasingly obscure.

Certainly there have been substantial differences between British and American journalistic and media practices, and some of these continue to this day. Even while broadly subsuming Britain within a North Atlantic model, Hallin and Mancini see it as sharing some characteristics with the North/Central European or Democratic Corporatist model – for example in its somewhat higher degree of newspaper partisanship and the enhanced role of public broadcasting.[13] As early as the nineteenth century, the British were more willing than Americans to countenance state intervention in communication technologies, such as telegraph ownership.[14] Later in the 1920s and 1930s, the commercial and public service models of broadcasting developed as competing "global paradigms" that were defined in opposition to each other, with BBC advocates demonizing American commercial "chaos" and American broadcasters lambasting British public service "elitism."[15] At the same time, there have been important cultural differences between the two nations which have helped to shape the media, including the fact that British journalists have not embraced "objectivity" to the same extent as their American counterparts and, for the most part, have not been as addicted to the speedy collection and transmission of news. Furthermore, the nature of Anglo-American media interactions has often been complicated, with both personal and impersonal factors playing decisive roles in culturally specific settings which frequently involve a reciprocal flow of influence.

The 15 scholars from both sides of the Atlantic survey different media interactions throughout the nineteenth and twentieth centuries, employing a variety of methodologies, including textual analysis of media content and archival research into transatlantic relations and policy decisions. Many of the essays reflect early stages of larger research projects, so that there is in these pages a glimpse of the kind of scholarship that will dominate this field in coming years, as well as suggesting additional avenues for research.

The book is organized into four thematic sections. Part I makes explicit comparisons between British and American media, revealing that commonality sometimes trumped difference. Richard Fulton compares war coverage in the American and British press during the Spanish-American and Sudan Wars, illustrating a common style of war reporting and questioning the distinction between elite and popular forms of journalism. Matt McIntire examines late nineteenth-century newspaper coverage of baseball and cricket, and shows how it influenced the development of these two very different "national" sports in a variety of ways. Joel H. Wiener analyzes how cultural preferences like speed and informality affected similarities and differences in journalistic practices on both sides of the Atlantic during the nineteenth century, particularly in the critical areas of "beat" reporting and interviewing.

Part II focuses on individual British and American media figures, demonstrating at the ground level the means by which a transatlantic media culture was created. Christopher Kent explores the career of an important but overlooked nineteenth-century cartoonist, Matt Morgan, who worked on both sides of the Atlantic. Kent's essay not only provides an insight into journalists' working conditions, but also reveals some of the ways in which British journalism shaped the American product. James Startt traces the evolving understanding of the American press in the writings of Britain's leading interpreter of American culture, James Bryce, over more than three decades in the late nineteenth and early twentieth centuries. This essay provides insight into cultural borrowings, for Bryce's writings were a key means of transmitting knowledge about the American press to British observers, and also shows the tensions between Bryce's desire to build an Anglo-American cultural identity and his recognition of cultural differences as exemplified in the American press. Fred Leventhal reveals the World War II-era propaganda activities of two major transatlantic film stars, English-born Leslie Howard and American-born Douglas Fairbanks, Jr., showing that, both in the themes of their propagandist films and in their cultivation of celebrity images, they were emblematic of an emerging transatlantic cultural identity.

Part III examines the uses of the media in creating national and transatlantic identities. Michael de Nie's study of British newspaper coverage of the American Civil War illuminates British ambivalence about the relationship between American culture and British identity. On the one hand, Americans were portrayed as sharing England's martial and other positive traits, though corrupted by geography and miscegenation; on the other hand, English national character was affirmed in opposition to American defects. Jessica Bennett and Mark Hampton's examination of the language used in British World War I propaganda and in the increasingly pro-British American press suggests the construction of a common Anglo-American identity defined against German barbarism. Thomas Hajkowski shows the role of empire in the projection of British identity in BBC radio programming in the 1940s. For Hajkowski, imperially themed programming was a way of projecting British values that were opposed to American qualities, thus defining Britishness in opposition to Americanness. At the same time, such programming reflected the desire to support empire as a means of ensuring that Britain remained a true partner, and not merely a junior partner, to the United States.

Part IV directly tackles the notion of Americanization in twentieth-century British media. Siân Nicholas investigates the negotiations among the BBC and various news agencies in the 1930s over who would supply the BBC. While this was largely a business dispute among vested interests attempting to defend their profits, it was negotiated in terms of British versus American news values, thus revealing the central place that fears of Americanization held within political discourse during this period of feared imperial decline. Peter Miskell interrogates the concept of Americanization in the British film industry of the 1930s and 1940s. He shows that while on the surface American films predominated and British cinemas were dependent on American products, the reality was more complicated. Hollywood was not a monolithic entity but a series of individual companies and British decision-makers, presiding over America's most important foreign market, were able to exercise a great deal of leverage over American studios. Tom O'Malley shows that the British Left in the 1950s participated in a sophisticated debate about the American media; he rejects the notion that the Left was uniformly anti-American in its discussion of the media. Stefan Schwarzkopf demonstrates the inadequacy of "Americanization" as a description of the British advertising industry in the second half of the twentieth century, showing that cultural influences went in both directions. Finally, Christine Becker's chapter makes clear the possibility for reversing the flow of transatlantic influence by revealing the early success of BBC America. Whereas BBC programming on PBS a few decades ago tended to present the English as particular and quaint, BBC America projects British culture as global and Becker's essay shows Americans on the receiving end of globalization.

While by no means discounting the value of media history from a strictly national perspective,[16] these essays reiterate the powerful additional insights that can be gained by examining transatlantic media interactions. What they make clear at the very least is that no unitary concept, such as "Americanization," is adequate to characterize this complex set of relationships. Perhaps above all, the essays in this book underscore that this is a new and exciting field in which many questions remain to be answered.

Notes

1   We are grateful to Regina Oost and David Karr for their helpful comments on this introduction.

2   The broader links between American and British culture are explored, for example, in Daniel Snowman, *Kissing Cousins: An Interpretation of British and American Culture, 1945–1975* (Temple Smith, 1977); Christopher Hitchens, *Blood, Class, and Nostalgia: Anglo-American Ironies* (London: Farrar Straus Giroux, 1990); David Hackett Fischer, *Albion's Seed: Four British Folkways in America* (New York: Oxford University Press, 1989); Fred M. Leventhal and Roland Quinault, eds., *Anglo-American Attitudes: From Revolution to Partnership* (Aldershot: Ashgate, 2000); Jonathan Hollowell, ed., *Twentieth-Century Anglo-American Relations* (London: Palgrave, 2001); John Dumbrell, *A Special Relationship: Anglo-American Relations From The Cold War to Iraq*, 2nd ed. (London: Palgrave, 2006).

3   Benedict Anderson, *Imagined Communities: Reflections on the Origin and Spread of Nationalism* (London and New York: Verso, 1991); Thomas Leonard, *News For All: America's Coming of Age with the Press* (New York: Oxford University Press, 1995); Hannah Barker, *Newspapers, Politics and English Society, 1695–1855* (New York: Oxford University Press, 1999).

4   Aled Jones, "Local Journalism in Victorian Political Culture," in *Investigating Victorian Journalism*, ed. Laurel Brake, Aled Jones, and Lionel Madden (London: Palgrave Macmillan, 1990); Jones, "The Dart and the Damning of the Sylvan Stream: Journalism and Political Culture in the Late-Victorian City," in *Encounters in the Victorian Press: Editors, Authors, Readers* (London:

Palgrave, 2005), 177–94; Richard Kaplan, *Politics and the American Press: the Rise of Objectivity, 1865–1920* (New York: Cambridge University Press, 2002). Recent scholarship, however, has explored the imperial context of late nineteenth-and early twentieth-century British journalism. See Chandrika Kaul, *Reporting the Raj: The British Press and India, c. 1880–1922* (Manchester: Manchester University Press, 2003); Simon J. Potter, *News and the British World: The Emergence of an Imperial Press System, 1876–1922* (Oxford: Clarendon Press, 2003); Potter, ed., *Newspapers and Empire in Ireland and Britain: Reporting the British Empire c. 1857–1921* (Dublin: Four Courts Press, 2004).

5   To take just two classic examples in a rapidly expanding literature: Linda Colley, *Britons: Forging the Nation 1707–1837* (New Haven and London: Yale University Press, 1992); L. Perry Curtis, Jr., *Apes and Angels: the Irishman in Victorian Caricature* (Washington: Smithsonian Books, 1997).

6   James Epstein, "'America' in the Victorian Cultural Imagination," in *Anglo-American Attitudes*, eds. Leventhal and Quinault, 107–23; John Humphrys, *Devil's Advocate* (London: Arrow Books, 2000), 27–8.

7   This is not to say that Europeans have uniformly experienced themselves as victims. Rather, scholars repeatedly point to ambivalent European responses. See, for example, Richard Kuisel, *Seducing the French: the Dilemma of Americanization* (Berkeley, Los Angeles, and London: the University of California Press, 1993); Jeffrey H. Jackson, *Making Jazz French: Music and Modern Life in Interwar Paris* (Durham and London: Duke University Press, 2003), 71–103; Reinhold Wagnleitner, *Coca-Colonization and the Cold War: the Cultural Mission of the United States in Austria after the Second World War* (Chapel Hill and London: the University of North Carolina Press, 1994); Victoria de Grazia, *Irresistible Empire: America's Advance through Twentieth Century Europe* (Cambridge, MA: Harvard University Press, 2005).

8   Globalization and Americanization are often conflated, perhaps reflecting the experience of developing countries for which American culture is the specific manifestation of threats to indigenous cultures. However, this elision fails to consider whether a specifically American culture is being transmitted, or whether American institutions are conveying values that are not strictly "American." As James Curran has noted, proponents of the "cultural imperialism" thesis often elide "American," "western," and "capitalist." Curran, *Media and Power* (London and New York: Routledge, 2002), 170. See also Ralph Negrine and Stylianos Papathanassopoulos, "The 'Americanization' of Political Communication: a Critique," *Harvard Journal of Press/ Politics* 1:2 (1996), 45–62. From an American perspective, this distinction is, perhaps, more easily seen, as writers as diverse as Michael Lind, Christopher Lasch, and Samuel Huntington have argued that American elites have become denationalized, switching their loyalties instead to the global economy and cosmopolitan values. See Lind, *The Next American Nation: the New Nationalism and the Fourth American Revolution* (New York: Free Press, 1995), 139–80; Lasch, *The Revolt of the Elites and the Betrayal of Democracy* (New York: Norton, 1996), 25–49; Huntington, *Who are We? The Challenges to America's National Identity* (New York: Simon and Schuster, 2004), 264–73.

9   On "cultural imperialism" see James Curran, *Media and Power*, 166–83; Anthony Smith, *The Geopolitics of Information: How Western Culture*

Dominates the World (Oxford and New York: Oxford University Press, 1980); Jeremy Tunstall, *The Media are American: Anglo-American Media in the World* (New York: Columbia University Press, 1977), 38–63.

10   Daniel C. Hallin and Paolo Mancini, *Comparing Media Systems: Three Models of Media and Politics* (Cambridge: Cambridge University Press, 2004).

11   Jeremy Tunstall, *The Media are American*.

12   Martin Conboy, *The Press and Popular Culture* (London: Sage Publications, 2002); Jean Chalaby, "Journalism as an Anglo-American Invention," *European Journal of Communication* 11 (1996): 303–26; Chalaby, *The Invention of Journalism* (London: Macmillan, 1998).

13   Hallin and Mancini, *Comparing Media Systems*, 210–5, 246–7.

14   Paul Starr, *The Creation of the Media: Political Origins of Modern Communications* (New York: Basic Books, 2004), 176–9.

15   And yet, as Michele Hilmes points out, this discourse should not be taken at face value. In her words, "both countries used the example of the other as a containment device: to limit the options available to a duality of extremes, in which differences were emphasized, similarities usually played down, and specific aspects enlarged to suit the strategic interests of each." See "Who We Are, Who We Are Not: Battle of the Global Paradigms," in Lisa Parks and Shanti Kumar, eds., *Planet TV: A Global Television Reader* (New York and London: New York University Press, 2003), 53–73 (quotation from page 69). See also Valeria Camporesi, *Mass Culture and National Traditions: The B.B.C. and American Broadcasting* (Fucecchio: European Press Academic Publishing, 2002).

16   Indeed, Martin Conboy makes a persuasive case that notwithstanding its situation in a global media ownership structure, Britain's popular press at the start of the twenty-first century remains culturally a nationalist medium. Conboy, *Tabloid Britain: Constructing a Community through Language* (London and New York: Routledge, 2005).

Part I
Comparisons

1

Sensational War Reporting and the Quality Press in Late Victorian Britain and America

Richard D. Fulton

In the decade after Matthew Arnold noticed the sea change taking place in newspaper journalism and anointed the result "the New Journalism," the so-called quality press continued to metamorphize from the staid Victorian Educator of the People to the more modern institution of People's Representative (and not so incidentally, People's Entertainer).[1] In the 1890s quality journalism still officially emphasized reason and argument in its treatment of events, while the New Journalism emphasized sensation as opposed to reason – curious, bizarre, exciting, often personal, violent, outrageous news that was never meant to teach anybody anything, but managed to incite the reader's wonder, laughter, anger, pity, horror, and other emotions. Yet even though the quality papers – the likes of New York's *Times*, *Tribune* and *Sun* and Boston's *Herald*, and London's *Morning Chronicle*, *Times*, and *Standard*, and the *Manchester Guardian* – protested their purity, a significant number of elements of sensational journalism penetrated most quality newspapers by the late 1890s and helped blur the boundaries between the sensational press (typically in Britain evening or Sunday papers, by the mid-90s generally costing a halfpenny; in the United States the widely recognized "yellow press" dailies) and the quality press (typically in Britain morning papers or Saturday weeklies costing a penny or more: in the United States three-penny dailies with more subdued front pages and headlines than the yellow dailies).

Creeping sensationalism mattered greatly to nineteenth-century cultural critics, sparking a significant number of attacks on newspaper press morality by newly emerging, self-styled media critics, especially in the magazine periodical press.[2] But the insistent demand for readable, interesting newspapers by the rapidly growing newspaper readership in England and America led to demonstrable sensational elements appearing with increasing regularity in the quality press: human interest stories, crime stories, unusual narratives that occasionally included shocking descriptions of a physical nature (blood, body parts, sex, animal-like behavior), exciting narratives with no apparent moral or intellectual point, gossip – at times accompanied by sketches, photographs, and screaming headlines stacked and crossed and imposing.[3] Contributing significantly to the importation of sensationalism to the quality press were the dispatches of war correspondents reporting real-life adventure stories of life and death from all over the globe. As practiced in the 1890s, war correspondence generally consisted of thrilling, picturesque narratives appealing to a range of emotions; war correspondents rarely considered analyzing the global political implications of their particular conflict (the conventional appeal to reason) to be part of their responsibility.

No incidents offer better examples of the sensational nature of the rhetoric and discourse of war reporting than two immensely popular and well-covered wars in 1898: the Spanish-American and the Anglo-Dervish. Thrilling accounts of the seminal battles of Omdurman in the Sudan and Santiago in Cuba appeared in virtually every newspaper in both countries. Examining those accounts in the context of the sensationalism that alarmed so many contemporary media critics reveals the depth of sensational rhetoric and discourse that made up war correspondence. A close examination also reveals how important the closely connected "isms" – patriotism, nationalism, militarism, jingoism, all central to reporting the wars of one's own nation – were to the newspapers as well as the reporters.[4] The isms, not so incidentally, provide direction for the more emotional sensational elements. As I will discuss below, the reports from Santiago that appeared in the American quality press were far more sensational than those that appeared in their British counterparts. The reverse held true for accounts from Omdurman: while the American press reported significant details of the battle, the sensational elements that appeared in the British press were for the most part edited out in the United States.

I should note here too, that the small fraternity of experienced British and American war correspondents shared most of the same values and wrote a remarkably similar discourse. American newspapers often published the accounts of British correspondents, and vice versa. Thus, despite their protestations to the contrary – British correspondents regularly denigrated their American counterparts as amateurish, sensationalist fiction writers while the Americans derided the British for lacking independence and being dull – the discourse of American and British war correspondence was virtually indistinguishable, in large part because the correspondence was being printed in newspapers undergoing the same transformation from nineteenth to twentieth-century journalistic rhetoric and values.[5]

The rhetoric and discourse of war reporting

Whether they were amateurs or professionals writing for the quality press, the popular press, or one of the news services, the newspaper war reporters shared a number of common characteristics in their dispatches. I do not claim that all combat dispatches shared all of the following characteristics, but in a wide range of articles, these characteristics, which in large part also defined sensational journalism, became the most important elements of the news report. Thus, as battle accounts made their way (often unedited) into the quality press, they injected those columns, at least, with a significant dose of sensationalism. The sensational elements of most concern to nineteenth-century media critics fell into three categories:

Typographical: Sensational typography included bold, often misleading headlines that crossed several columns and were supplemented by stacked subheads; and exciting, occasionally tasteless illustrations, often crudely rendered and carrying a misleading message. This chapter will focus primarily on the other two categories.

Rhetorical: Sensational rhetoric included descriptions of injuries, activities, or individuals that were either too detailed or that in some other way violated the standards of good taste.[6] It introduced specialist language or slang that invited the reader into the account as an "insider." It emphasized the "I" and "we" in reporting, which both reinforced the authority of the narrator and further made the reader a confidante, and thus a participant. As noted above, accounts of British battles printed in the British press, or American battles in the American press, tended to be patriotic to the point of jingoistic. Narratives were expressed in oversimplified sentences (reflecting, presumably, an oversimplification of reasoning). Sensational rhetoric made use of questionable (if colorful) metaphors, especially sporting metaphors which tended to diminish the true significance of warfare, both politically and in human terms, by reducing it to a game.[7] It inflated rather routine incidents excessively through lavish use of exemplary adjectives and action verbs. It manufactured false emotions through the creation of sentimental icons like "the Rough Riders" or "the good old Lancashire Fusiliers," and sentimental situations like the death of a young man. As contemporary critics complained, these rhetorical devices were in effect an effort to sway the reader through emotion rather than teach him through reason.

Discursive: The discourse of war reporting that overlapped sensationalism was the larger story being told in a battle narrative, the story that emphasized the noble nature of our soldiers, their invincibility, their righteousness in the face of an alien, often uncivilized foe.[8] It was grounded in essentially masculine values emphasizing personal honor, which was simply the national honor reduced to an individual scale, and the necessity of fighting successfully to prove oneself to be honorable. This discourse depends on the selection of appropriate spotless heroes (who are us) and quintessentially evil villains. The discourse invariably contains an element of the initiation of boys into manhood, which is why the designated romantic combat heroes are invariably young men led by older heroes, commanding officers who are exemplars of wisdom, sternness, coolness in the face of adversity, and chivalric virtues, and who provide role models of manhood for the young initiates. Like the danger of sensational rhetoric, the danger of the sensational discourse of war correspondence lay in the fact that it was designed to mislead readers by skewing the narrative to a particular story.

Thus, contemporary conservative journalists criticized many of the war reports as being little more than sensational trash because of the correspondents' apparent attempt to provide an entertaining, often emotional description of factual events rather than a critical examination of the events proper. In a larger sense, many of the reports were nationalistic, patriotic (or jingoistic, depending on the point of view), militaristic narratives that reinforced the sensationalism of the articles themselves.[9]

For the sake of brevity, I am limiting my discussion to an examination of two representative quality newspapers from Britain and the United States: The *Manchester Guardian* and the *New York Times*. Both were outspoken proponents of decency (read anti-sensationalism) in journalism. Adolph Ochs, the *Times* editor, believed in his catch-phrase "all the news that's fit to print," as well as in its opposite: he would print no news *not* fit to print, that is, news likely to make a young lady blush. *Guardian* readers were quick to complain to the editor when they detected sensationalism, and to his credit, the editor published their concerns. In addition, both papers printed extensive coverage of the battles at Santiago and Omdurman, and thus provide a reasonable volume of material for comparison. Finally, both papers are generally accepted examples of the quality press in their respective countries.[10] Because of the volume of published accounts in the two papers, I will necessarily have to be selective and unfortunately can only reproduce excerpts that illustrate the rhetorical and discursive sensationalism I am examining.

Reporting the Battle of Santiago

On Friday, July 1, 1898, General William Shafter, the commander of the American army in Cuba, began his assault on Santiago where the Spanish navy was anchored and the bulk of the Spanish army was dug in. The Americans had landed in Cuba in the middle of June, but much to the disgust of the well over 600 war correspondents, no fighting on a major scale had yet occurred. However, most observers agreed that the Americans would eventually overrun Santiago, and that when Santiago fell, the Spanish resistance in Cuba would collapse and the war would be over.

For a variety of reasons, the American public had generally responded enthusiastically to the war. A sizeable segment of the country's political, business, and cultural leadership (including both the popular and quality press) supported American intervention in the Cuban uprising against Spanish colonial government. Both political parties included Free Cuba planks in their platforms for the 1896 elections. The most outspoken interventionists portrayed the Spanish sensationally as cruel, lustful degenerates who butchered brave Cuban men, raped virtuous Cuban women, and starved innocent Cuban children. Beyond Imperialist politics and capitalist ambitions, beyond the Monroe Doctrine and the desire of some to thrust the United States onto the world stage as a major player, was the basic appeal to Americans, especially American men, to use their strength and their righteousness to deliver the benefits of freedom to the oppressed Cuban people, and to save helpless Cuban women and children from the ravages of the Spanish beasts. Fundamentally, interventionists appealed to American men's sense of honor, to help the weak, to right wrongs, to act, in effect, like nineteenth-century knights. The sinking of the *Maine* on 15 February 1898 provided yet another appeal to American honor: since the common wisdom was that the Spanish had somehow blown up the American battleship, Americans must retaliate or lose their manhood (note that the concept of "American" was equated with "man" and "manhood"). That vast throng of American men whose first identity was with their nation joined the sensationalist press in demanding revenge; they also voted with their bodies, lining up to volunteer in militia regiments in such numbers that the army simply did not have room for all of them.[11] Thus, the nature of the discourse that would be used to describe upcoming combats had been defined to a great extent by a dominant culture that characterized the ideal American male as young, strong, innocent, brave, and idealistic, a righter of wrongs, a shield for the weak, Christian (Protestant, of course), and morally superior to the rest of the world, the honored citizens of the City on the Hill.

Most studies of the American press coverage of the war focus on Hearst's *New York Journal* and Pulitzer's *New York World*, both poster children for the sensational press, dubbed the yellow press, in the United States. Both papers hired dozens of correspondents, chartered or bought boats, and committed themselves to overwhelming (and sometimes factual) coverage of every aspect of the war from Cuba to the Philippines, from Florida to the militia halls of New York. While both Hearst and Pulitzer believed that the war would serve to prove the moral and martial superiority of Americans to the rest of the world, they also saw the war as an ongoing, exciting, inexhaustible source of news and thus, a sure-fire stimulus for circulation. The *Daily Mail* and its sensationalist ilk in Britain used similar rhetoric in their war reporting, although the discourse tended to project the British view of Americans, not the American view of themselves.

However, most of the 600 or so correspondents in Cuba who represented directly or indirectly virtually every newspaper in the United States and a host of others in the rest of the world did not report the war in the same way that the *Mail*, *World* and *Journal* did. Most of the quality press in both Britain and the United States still insisted on news as both factual reports and critical discussions, not as entertainment, and saw their role as critical leaders of the great public debate. *Guardian* editor C. P. Scott employed sub-editors whose job it was to rewrite reporters' copy to ensure the finished copy met the paper's standards of taste.[12] Adolph Ochs, aspired to the same lofty reputation for taste and accuracy as his *Times*'s London namesake. Ochs "prized straightforward news content in abundance rather than showy style as the chief commodity he had to sell," and insisted at all times on maintaining the "dignity" of his newspaper.[13]

Although the *Times* did have its own correspondent in Cuba, most of the published news from the front came from Associated Press stringers or official dispatches released in Washington (where Ochs also assigned a reporter); some news was quoted from other newspapers, or was supplied by freelance reporters. Most of the *Times*'s initial reports of the fighting around Santiago were supplied by the Associated Press. The *Guardian* had its "own correspondent" in New York, but for combat reports from Cuba depended on reports from Reuters or from correspondents identified only as "Another Correspondent."

It should be emphasized here that both Reuters and AP reports were valued for their accuracy and their lack of, for want of a better term, flair. As the famed *World* war correspondent Richard Harding Davis said, the AP correspondents "entered into the work in the same impersonal spirit with which they would have handled an annual encampment of the G.A.R., or the first night of a new play."[14] Thus, wire service subscribers felt relatively safe in terms of taste, at least, in printing dispatches unedited. Reuters and the Associated Press provided most British and American newspapers with most of their war news. Even papers that had assigned a special correspondent to Cuba, or bought the services of a special employed by another newspaper, used wire service stories, and used them almost verbatim as they came over the wire. Rarely were the stories marked up by a subeditor, although portions of them may have been cut to fit the space available for the story. As a result, the rhetoric and discourse of the wire service war correspondents by and large became the rhetoric and discourse of the quality press, and as the following shows, in Cuba, at least, the AP reports were infected to a substantial degree with the same sensational rhetoric and the same sensational discourse as the yellow reports. Probably because the Reuters correspondent was *not* an American, the Reuters reports from Cuba were not nearly as sensational as the AP reports.

The initial accounts of the fierce fighting of July 1 consisted of General Shafter's brief dispatch to the War Department and a few fragmentary press telegrams sent from the cable station at Guantanamo Bay on July 2. The delay between the battle and the time needed to get stories by boat to cable stations in Jamaica and Tampa assured that on Saturday, at least, the only dispatches that made it back to newspaper offices in the United States simply reported a battle in progress.[15] On Sunday the first significant dispatches made their way to New York, AP reports exclusively, all of which had been written on Friday and delayed in transmission. The reports included some initial casualty lists and a summary of Friday's fighting composed at 4:00 pm on Friday. None of the reports to this point purported to be eyewitness accounts; none reported the kind of startling individual acts and incidents that characterize sensationalism. The AP mentioned that "many dramatic incidents occurred during the day, with numerous evidences of splendid personal bravery of the American officers and men in their work of continuous and intense physical strain," but didn't cite any except the Twenty-first Infantry's singing of the "Star Spangled Banner" in the heat of battle. The nature of the reports would change with the next day's dispatch.

On Monday, Independence Day, the *Times* ran a series of front page articles on the destruction of the Spanish fleet and the string of army victories at Santiago. Included among the articles presented in traditional *Times* discourse was an eyewitness AP account of the Friday battles around the city which utilized many of the typical characteristics of sensational journalism. The dispatch was relegated to column seven near the top of the page and bore a rather quiet headline in small print and a modest stack of summary heads (STORY OF FRIDAY'S BATTLE. An Artillery Duel – Our Men Charge the Enemy – How Caney Was Taken). The dispatch is a rather long one, taking up most of that seventh column on page one and all of column seven and a quarter of column eight on page two.

The AP correspondent leaned heavily on sensational rhetoric to describe what he saw: our soldiers were "daring," "gallant," "skillful," "tenacious"; our worthy enemy were "gallant," and "showed spirit and nerve." The correspondent invited his reader into the action by using the insider language of the military: the account is replete with the movements of specific units (Captain Grimes' Battery, Captain Capron's Battery, General Duffield's Michigan Volunteers) on the right and center, with flanking and enfilading, Mausers and machine guns and smokeless powder, and the technicalities of artillery fire ("Bates sent the first shell, which went whizzing down the line of intrenchments, enfilading the enemy murderously"). A passing critique of tactics represented a little insider comment with which the reader/confidante must naturally agree: "The chief error was in placing the infantry behind the artillery in position to receive all the shells of the enemy which failed to hit the mark at which they were aimed. Many needless casualties were thus caused." The correspondent drew the reader in further by assuring him that he was participating in a significant world event: "No finer work," the reader was told, "has ever been done by soldiers than was performed by the brigades of Gen. Ludlow... ." And in his description of "An Awful Charge," of "our men" being annihilated, but still charging, "on, on, up, up, they went, until with a cheer they sprang over the trenches dividing the sides of the hill checkered with their fallen comrades," he immersed himself and his reader/confidante in the sheer excitement of the charge, the desperation, exultation, terror – the sensation. His sentimental national icons included the American regulars, those Hawkeyes and Leatherstockings who used the Cuban landscape "with all the skill acquired on the Western plains of America." War as sport was implicit in the description of the charge up that hill, ending with a spring and a cheer, which bears an uncanny resemblance to a typical nineteenth-century account of a college football game. The correspondent and his reader together cheered the men "on, on, up, up" to ultimate victory. While for a variety of reasons he didn't single out individuals, naming only the commanding officers in the time-honored tradition, he did hold his gaze repeatedly to focus on a balloonist, an officer of the Twenty-fourth macheted in hand-to-hand combat, two men dead from an exploding Spanish shell. He leavened his sensationalism by abstaining from an unwholesome description of the dead and dying, or a too-naturalistic depiction of the slaughter in that captured Spanish trench (the *Journal*'s accounts of the trench epitomized yellow journalism at its most lurid).

The sensationalist discourse of this account, grounded in patriotic pride, celebrated the bravery and physical prowess of the American men through the use of all those rhetorical tools and through telling a story of "our" superior manhood. The story is clearest in the two paragraphs describing the "Awful Charge": Our men in the open, theirs under cover; our men staggering, falling, but always getting up again; our men springing over the trenches, theirs scrambling away; our men winning the day with an audience composed chiefly of their fallen comrades, whose bodies checker the hillside. Throughout the article our men must move against a "murderous hail" of rifle fire. Our men crawl through that fire and fire back at such close range as to see "the whites of their eyes" (a phrase loaded with patriotic references to another hill in another war). The correspondent emphasized that this action was basically about the initiation into, and proof of, manhood. Our troops proved their manhood by fighting through awful odds, against a skillful, obstinate enemy (who wouldn't come out in the open and fight, by the way), charging repeatedly through machine gun and Mauser fire, and cheering in victory like solid young men would. The Spanish proved to be a worthy foe for these young "American heroes": they "stuck to their work like men, and this…may well cause Spain to feel proud… ."

What is significant about this account is not so much that the AP correspondent abandoned his objectivity, but that the *Times* printed the sensational account without editing it for propriety, thus subverting the paper's staunchly conservative standards. Meanwhile, the *Guardian* carried about a page and a half in coverage of the fighting in its July 4 second edition, including summaries edited together from several sources, Reuter's telegrams, accounts from the "Reuter's Special Service" originating from the "Despatch-Boat Dandy off Juagua, via Port Antonia and Kingston, Jamaica," reports from "Our Own Correspondent" stationed in New York, reports copied from other newspapers (*Herald*, *Evening World* and others unnamed), War Department telegrams, and reports "From a Correspondent," some unnamed but presumably reliable source located in New York, Washington, or Cuba. Intriguingly, one of the reports reprinted by the *Guardian* and accredited to "A Correspondent" is the AP report printed in the *Times*. Unlike the *Times*, the *Guardian* edited the report, removing much of the sensational discourse and rhetoric to make it correspond with C. P. Scott's anti-sensational philosophy. For example, the *Times* described part of the action in this way:

> Clark's Brigade and the right of Kent's division made a gallant charge up the knoll to the north of the extreme left of the Spanish line and took possession of the hacienda in the shelter of an orange grove. This marked the beginning of a magnificent charge through the first line of intrenchments [sic]. The cavalry division and Gen. Hawkins's Brigade charged up the slope against a storm of death.

What appeared in the *Guardian* was simply: "Clark's Brigade and the right flank of Kent's division participated."

In an excellent example of sensational discourse referred to earlier, the *Times* described an extension of the action thus:

> It was in this awful charge that our men were so badly cut up that they started on a double-quick, but no troops could face such a terrific fire without annihilation. Our men staggered; they threw themselves on the ground. Again they started; again they prostrated themselves; but on, on, up, up, they went, until with a cheer they sprang over the trenches dividing the sides of the hill checkered with their fallen comrades.

The *Guardian* reported:

> It was in the awful charge that the Americans were so badly cut up. They started at the double, but no troops could face such terrible

annihilation. They staggered, threw themselves on the ground, and started, again fell, but, persisting in the face of a withering fire...they kept steadily onward until, with a cheer, they sprang over the trenches leaving behind them a hillside covered with fallen comrades.

Guardian editing eliminated the eyewitness feel transmitted by references to "our men," and thus significantly reduced the reader's personal identification with the action. The narrator/reader's cheer of "on, on, up, up" also disappeared. As might be expected, *Guardian* subeditors also eliminated the patriotic rhetoric and much of the discourse associated with American manhood, and the proof of manhood that the initiation rites of combat had provided. The *Guardian* account did not include either the comment "The Spanish soldiers stuck to their work like men, and this, the first land fight of the war, may well cause Spain to feel proud of her men" or the lines "No finer work has ever been done by soldiers than was performed by the brigades of Gen. Ludlow and Col. Miles as they closed in on the town. The Spaniards blazed at them with Mausers and machine guns, but without effect."

Clearly, national war reporting carried a somewhat different set of standards associated with sensationalism than did international war reporting. At least in the case of the reporting out of Santiago, the *Times* shucked any sensational restraints in its decision not to rewrite the sensational rhetoric and discourse of the AP reports. The *Guardian*, apparently true to its conservative approach, rewrote the AP reports extensively, stripping much of the sensationalism from them. However, as the following example from a significant British military action shows, the *Guardian*'s restraint apparently applied only to "foreign" wars; the case of Omdurman also indicates that the *Times'* sensationalism only embraced American combat correspondence.

Reporting the Battle of Omdurman

On Thursday, Sept. 1, 1898, Lord Kitchener, the British Sirdar (Commander in Chief) of the Egyptian army, moved his 25,000-man Anglo-Egyptian-Sudanese forces into place a few miles down the Nile River from the Dervish capital of Omdurman, near the ruins of the ancient capital of Khartoum. Opposing him was a Dervish force numbering perhaps 60,000. The impending battle would be the culmination of some 16 years of British conflict with the Dervishes, a Moslem sect led initially by the self-proclaimed Mahdi, and now by his successor the Khalifa, that had gained independence for the Sudan by defeating a succession of British-led Egyptian expeditions. In 1884 the Mahdi captured Khartoum and turned himself into an icon of evil in Britain by executing the British hero General Charles Gordon.

Kitchener had begun his invasion of the Sudan in 1896 and slowly moved south, fighting two or three battles a year, carefully consolidating his gains, and building a railroad as he went to keep his army plentifully supplied in the desert. War correspondents representing most of the quality British press and a few of the sensational papers joined up with the army during the spring and again in the late summer when weather and the rising river allowed offensive operations. Dispatches from early battles whetted the public appetite for the final showdown, generally projected for late September, 1898. While the public was bound to be interested in this enormous enterprise involving some of the most storied units of the British army, a railroad, a desolate, picturesque landscape, and an old enemy made famous by Kipling in his 1890 poem "Fuzzy-Wuzzy," Kitchener inadvertently fanned the flames of public interest in a widely reported incident when he exhorted his troops before the April battle on the Atbara to "Remember Gordon." Much as the sensational American press adopted "Remember the Maine" as the battle cry of the Spanish-American War, the sensational British press adopted "Remember Gordon"; the British public were handed yet another reason to hang on every word transmitted from the desert – Gordon was to be avenged. Judging by the sale of newspapers from August to October, the public certainly bought into the excitement generated by the war dispatches.

Kitchener's men were armed with modern magazine rifles, Maxim machine guns, and breach-loading artillery firing powerful lyddite shells; his infantry brigades were supported by a British cavalry regiment (the 21st Lancers), Egyptian cavalry and a camel corps, irregular forces composed of Sudanese tribesmen opposed to Dervish rule, and nine heavily armed gunboats. The Dervishes were mostly armed with swords and spears, although perhaps a quarter of them carried a variety of firearms: some old flintlocks, some Remingtons obtained from Abyssinian traders, some old Martini-Henry rifles captured from various Anglo-Egyptian expeditions. The Dervish army was supported by cavalry units and a few old muzzle-loading cannons. Outgunned, the Dervishes might have held the Anglo-Egyptians at bay for weeks or even defeated them had they stayed within the walls of Omdurman. Instead, early on the morning of September 2 they attacked the entrenched, fortified Anglo-Egyptians *en masse*. The resulting slaughter should have been predictable: lightly armed swordsmen charging an entrenched enemy over open ground – an enemy armed with machine guns, modern artillery, and repeating rifles – stood no chance whatsoever. A series of Dervish human wave rushes never approached within 800 yards of the Anglo-Egyptian squares. Somewhere between 8,000–10,000 Dervishes died in four hours of constant fighting. When Kitchener's forces counter-attacked, the remaining disorganized Dervishes offered little resistance, though thousands more were slaughtered. Kitchener entered Omdurman around noon; the Khalifa had fled south with a few hundred loyal supporters, pursued by the Egyptian Camel Corps. At the end of the day, the British suffered 28 men killed (including *Times* and *New York Herald* correspondent Hubert Howard); the Egyptian/Sudanese forces 20. Most estimates placed the final Dervish casualty toll at around 11,000 dead and perhaps another 16,000 wounded.[16]

The single telegraph line that had followed the army south from Egypt mysteriously went inoperable the night of August 31 and was not restored until September 3.[17] As a result, the sensational nature of the battle was heightened by an agonizing five days of suspense; newspaper readers in Great Britain knew that the Anglo-Egyptian army was camped virtually on the outskirts of Omdurman and preparing for a fight, but were left speculating as to the outcome until Monday, September 5.[18] Meanwhile back at Omdurman the correspondents were reduced to writing short cables and sending them by runner to the telegraph office several miles north at Nasri, to be sent as soon as the cable once again was up and running. Lionel James, the Reuters man, both dated and chronologized his cables so that the client newspapers could keep the action straight when they finally received his dispatches.

On September 5, the *Guardian* carried a three-column map of Omdurman on page 5, three and a quarter columns of Lionel James's reporting for Reuters, Kitchener's dispatch, and a few bits of Omdurman-related news on the wounded, congratulations from elsewhere, the entire coverage spanning about four and a quarter columns. The initial reporting was fairly linear, leaning on facts, and simply informing the reader that the Anglo-Egyptian army had destroyed the Dervish army and entered Omdurman. It wasn't until the next day that the *Guardian*, like most of the other quality dailies, could pick up reports from a variety of correspondents published in other newspapers. Most of the reporting could be characterized as colorful, but not particularly sensational. However, *Daily Telegraph* special Bennett Burleigh's summary of the battle and James's account of the picturesque charge of the 21st Lancers which constituted the meat of the

Guardian's September 5 reports reveal in condensed form the same aspects of sensational discourse and rhetoric that informed the *New York Times*-published accounts of Santiago.

Both of these accounts are at first stories of a battle. Both also exhibit most of the key qualities of the sensational discourse of war correspondence. Like the American AP correspondent, both James and Burleigh used sensational descriptions, narratives, and rhetoric, a discourse not normally associated with the staid, quality *Guardian*. By opening his narrative of the Lancers' famous charge with the ominous orders familiar to the readers of any military adventure story: "prevent the enemy from returning to Omdurman" (all that is left out is the even more ominous phrase "at all costs"), James tipped his reader to the British pluck to come. He also informed the reader that this action would somehow be key to the battle. James invited the reader to become confidante/participant through his knowing employment of insider military terminology – "columns of troops;" "deployed into line for the attack," "magazine and carbine fire" – and local color – "ensconced in a wallah." Like all of the correspondents, he highlighted the Lancers because of the chivalric virtues they represented as modern-day knights; though facing "enormous odds," the Lancers "charged gallantly home," phrases designed to elicit echoes of Tennyson's famous poem. Some of James's narrative was "unnecessarily" sensational, especially his description of the wounded being "hacked to pieces by the swords of the fanatic foe," and the survivors gathering "bleeding and blown, on the far side of the lanes which they had cut for themselves in the enemy's ranks." The corporal "covered in blood and reeling in his saddle" contributed nothing to the narrative of the battle, but everything to the sensational vignette James was describing (had the corporal been important to the news story rather than the story James was really narrating, surely James would have at least discovered his name). The discourse emphasized the noble, indomitable nature of the British people as exemplified by the exhausted, bloody horsemen, showing "admirable fortitude," who "reformed as coolly as if they had been on parade."

The rest of this narrative lacked the sensational nature of the first portion, but continued to indulge in references to patriotic manliness that is central to the discourse of war correspondence. James discovered his heroes – young heroes, a lieutenant and a corporal – in De Montmorency and Swarbeck, and the perhaps somewhat wiser Captain Kenna. These young heroes attempted the reckless but admirable task of rescuing the body of "young Grenfell," yet another hero by virtue of the fact that he died in the charge and was young and a lieutenant. They failed, but in their failure exhibited the best qualities of British manliness. After all, the battle had become three plucky British army youngsters armed with revolvers and off on a desperate but doomed rescue mission against three *thousand* savages who were earlier described as being "wild with excitement" and who desired nothing more than to hack young Englishmen to pieces. The meaning of this discourse is that by working together with pluck, courage, discipline, and superior weapons, the British demonstrated their overwhelming superiority over the savage Other. James emphasized the rite of passage these young men endured by proclaiming their "maiden charge...an extremely brilliant affair."[19]

While Burleigh's discourse emphasizing honor, manliness and initiation rites, physical strength and courage, and the supremacy of the national warrior corresponded to the discourse of his American and British colleagues, his rhetoric was more sensational, marked by inflated language, invocation of sensory images, and chivalric imagery. Like the AP correspondent who reminded his reader/confidante that this event transcended mere battle, Burleigh opened his account by informing his readers that they were about to witness a milestone in the glorious history of the British army: "The supreme and greatest victory ever achieved by British arms in the Soudan has been won by the Sirdar's ever-victorious forces, after one of the most picturesque battles of the century." Throughout his account he repeated adjectives like "splendid" and "brilliant" and "plucky." He kept his sentences short and his verbs active. He, too, invited his reader to participate by using the insider military language of Maxims and Martinis, the special local slang of "zareba'd" and "Gippies." He avoided typical graphic descriptions of combat gore, but made certain that the portion of his discourse dealing with the inevitable triumph of civilization over barbarism was reinforced by his reference to the Dervishes' fanaticism and his introduction of the Khalifa's harem to his narrative. Like his colleague in Cuba, he screened his descriptions with sports metaphors, announcing that "the Egyptian brigades may fairly be said to have won the honours of the day by their magnificent pluck" as if they'd just won the school rugby championship playing shorthanded.

The Dervishes, like the Spanish to the Americans, were a worthy foe, brave to the point of foolhardiness; however, they could be no match for the British and their loyal followers, the Egyptians and Sudanese. In the third paragraph of the article Burleigh implied that the Dervish had no stomach for attacking the British square, and instead hurled themselves at the less potent Sudanese and, later, the Egyptians. Through successful combat, the Sudanese – the "dark battalions" – and the Egyptians "quitted themselves like men" and were thus initiated successfully into the manhood represented by the British regiments. The fanatical bravery of the Dervishes validated the "supreme and greatest victory ever achieved by British arms in the Soudan" and helped draw attention away from the horrible slaughter that characterized this particular battle. While Burleigh was unable to dwell on the exploits of heroes who exemplified his story of honor and manliness, he managed at least to provide the name of the commander of an artillery battery that caused "fearful execution," and he also cited young dead hero Lieutenant Robert Grenfell. His regular use of "we" and "they" and his pronouncements reinforcing "our" military superiority and control of the situation like "the tactics displayed by the enemy…really played into our hands," helped further draw the reader into the battle as Burleigh's confidante, like him an observer of and thus a participant in the battle.

Burleigh's almost irrational sensationalism becomes all the more evident in light of the sober editorial on page 4 of the same issue that reminded readers that "Eight thousand dervish dead make too grim an offering on the altar of humanity" to wax eloquent on the battle as a "victory of civilization." On the editorial page, the *Guardian*, reacting not just to Burleigh's but to all of the sensational accounts of the battle in other papers and the unrestrained joy of the British public, was quick to attempt to break the sensational spell that seemed to have fallen over the entire country. Editorials in other newspapers also cautioned against the sensational nature of the press's discourse on Omdurman while carrying unedited battle narratives.[20] Clearly, however, the "damage" was already done and the *Guardian*'s editors themselves had (probably) unwittingly contributed to it.

The *New York Times* coverage of Omdurman began with the Sunday edition, with the publication of telegrams from Kitchener and a correspondent that in stark telegraphese announced the victory, followed by several columns of rumor and speculation. On Monday, the paper carried three columns on the front page, mostly compilations from the several correspondents accompanying Kitchener. As the *Guardian* had done with its coverage of Santiago, the *Times* did in its battle descriptions from Omdurman, eschewing the sensational discourse produced by James and Burleigh and toning down the rhetoric in other quotes. The charge of the 21st Lancers, for example, was encapsulated in a brief two sentences:

Galloping down on a detached body of the enemy, they found the dervish swordsmen massed behind, and were forced to charge home against appalling odds. The Lancers hacked through the mass, rallied, and kept the dervish horde at bay. Lieut. Grenfell, nephew of Gen Sir Frances Grenfell, was killed, four other officers were wounded, twenty-one men were killed, and twenty wounded.

However, the *Times* did quote the insider language of the military at length, citing Maxim guns and Zarebas as the *Guardian* had. And the *Times* paid tribute to the bravery of the Dervishes (as the press almost universally had done for the losing Spanish) summarizing the war correspondents' sentiments in two brief declarative sentences: "The bravery of the dervishes can hardly be overstated. Those who carried the flags struggled to within a few hundred yards of the British fighting line, while the mounted Emirs absolutely threw their live away in bold charges." The *Times* never participated in the initiation discourse for either the British or Egyptian soldiers; in an odd parallel to its own coverage of the fighting around Santiago the Dervishes were described in several cases as marvelously brave, but they were juxtaposed with the British troops who showed "desperate gallantry" in the face of overwhelming numbers, and who "awaited...without flinching" the Dervish assault. A careful review of the editing (the *Times* carried a few Burleigh excerpts, but nothing like the famous opening line beginning "The supreme and greatest victory..." carried in the *Guardian* and hundreds of other British newspapers) indicates that the *Times*, like the *Guardian*, was prepared to indulge in sensational rhetoric and discourse – or, at least, allow it to happen – in describing American military exploits, but to approach the narratives of foreign military exploits much more judiciously.

Conclusion

Drawing sweeping conclusions from these two admittedly limited samples would be problematic. However, a wider review of the initial reporting of these two engagements in the quality press indicates that, in general, one can conclude that battle descriptions were allowed to be considerably more sensational than accounts of other dramatic events.[21] Such a review also indicates that British accounts of British engagements were considerably more sensational than British accounts of American engagements, and vice versa. Finally, such a review indicates the remarkable similarity of British and American war correspondents' rhetoric and discourse.

I do not wish to imply that the accounts of these two engagements constituted some kind of first in sensational war reporting. Especially in Britain, where professional war correspondents had reported colonial conflicts for decades, accounts of battles had always had their sensational side. It should also be noted that, as militarism and patriotism became more embedded in the cultures of both countries, sensational war reporting generally got an exception from the concern that sensational accounts might provoke the public into committing unrestrained, irrational deeds. I selected these two particular battles for three reasons. First, they occurred at a time when journalists in both Britain and America were debating the role of journalism and the nature of sensational journalism. Second, because the battles occurred within a few months of each other, they provide an opportunity to examine how the press in both countries reported similarly sensational national events in the same historical context. Finally, much of the public in both countries seemed to consider these two battles as both sensational events in themselves and as some kind of key to their national character and culture. I find it interesting that the overwhelming national reaction in both countries to both the events and the reporting of the events was so similar.

As a postscript, in the months following these two battles the public treated both of them like any other sensation. Reporters and participants drew packed houses on the lecture circuit. At least a dozen instant books by correspondents and other participants appeared before the end of the year. Regiments returning from Cuba paraded down Broadway in New York. More Londoners turned out to view the return of the Grenadier Guards than had turned out for Gladstone's funeral six months earlier. Buffalo Bill replaced his "Custer's Last Stand" act with a "Rough Riders Charge" act. The *Illustrated London News* carried an advertisement for a Boxing Day performance of Barnum and Bailey's Greatest Show on Earth that included "A GIGANTIC TANK CONSTRUCTED, CONTAINING UPWARDS OF 400,000 GALLONS OF WATER, 375 FEET LONG BY 40 FEET WIDE, FOR THE PRESENTATION OF THE TWO NEW AQUATIC ATTRACTIONS, AMERICA'S GREAT NAVAL VICTORY AT SANTIAGO, AND DESTRUCTION OF ADMIRAL CERVERA'S FLEET." The British press launched a successful fund-raising campaign to build a college in Gordon's name in Khartoum. Kitchener's victory was used to sell Pattison's Scotch Whiskey, Pimm's No. One Cup, carpets, cigarettes, Bovril, plays, music hall acts, and public pageants. Sensational discourse led quickly to commodification, at least.

Phillip Knightley concludes his chapter on what he called "The Golden Age" of war correspondence with the comment: "To readers in London or New York, distant battles in strange places must have seemed unreal, and the Golden Age style of war reporting – where guns flash, cannons thunder, the struggle rages, the general is brave, the soldiers are gallant, and their bayonets make short work of the enemy – only added to the illusion that it was all a thrilling adventure story."[22] "Thrilling adventure story" is simply another description of sensational journalism; the fact that these thrilling adventure stories appeared in the quality press and were for the most part uncritically accepted – indeed, devoured – by most of the readers contributed significantly to an adjustment of what might be acceptably produced in a quality newspaper. Yet another transition from Victorian to modern journalism quietly occurred in the midst of the clamor of two very popular wars.

Notes

1 For an incisive discussion on the press's evolution, see Mark Hampton, *Visions of the Press in Britain, 1850–1950* (Champaign IL: University of Illinois Press, 2004).
2 See, for example, Aline Gorren, "The Ethics of Modern Journalism," *Scribner's Magazine*, 19 (1896), 507–13; George W. Smalley, "Notes on Journalism," *Harper's New Monthly Magazine*, 97 (July 1898), 213–23; "Journalists and Newsmongers Again," *Century*, 42 (July 1891), 470–1; T. H. S. Escott, "Thirty Years of the Periodical Press," *Blackwood's*, 156 (October 1894), 532–42; Elizabeth Banks, "American 'Yellow Journalism,'" *Nineteenth Century*, 44 (August 1898), 328–40; Wemyss Reid, "The Newspapers," *Nineteenth Century*, 46 (November 1899), 1848–64. Of course, the most influential of the comments came from Matthew Arnold in "Up to Easter," *Nineteenth Century*, 21 (May, 1887), 629–43 in which the great sage created the term "the New Journalism."
3 For accounts of the intrusion of sensationalism, or new journalism, into the quality press see especially Jean K. Chalaby, *The Invention of Journalism* (London: Macmillan, 1998); L. Perry Curtis, *Jack the Ripper and the London Press* (New Haven: Yale University Press, 2001); Joel H. Wiener, ed., *Papers for the Millions* (Westport, CT: Greenwood, 1988); Kate Jackson, *George Newnes and the New Journalism in Britain, 1880–1910* (Aldershot: Ashgate, 2001).
4 For a comprehensive account of the war correspondent as patriot, see chapters 4–6 of Robert Wilkinson-Latham, *From Our Special Correspondent: Victorian War Correspondents and Their Campaigns* (London: Hodder and Stoughton, 1979).
5 Representative of the many contemporary articles comparing British and American correspondents are Jonathan Gilmer Speed's "War Correspondents," *North American Review*, 168 (March 1899), 381–4, and Richard Harding Davis, "Our War Correspondents in Cuba and Puerto Rico," *Harper's New Monthly Magazine*, 98 (May 1899), 938–48.

6   A little blood was acceptable, but detailed descriptions of dismemberments would not be. Reporters were not expected to discuss (or even refer to) such subjects as prostitutes, sex, or human waste, or the defiling of women and children. Reporting that women and children died was acceptable; describing in detail how they died was not.

7   See Glenn R. Wilkinson, *Depictions and Images of War in Edwardian Newspapers, 1899–1914* (Basingstoke: Palgrave Macmillan, 2003), ch. 4.

8   As Kristin L. Hoganson points out, the discourse of war is always gendered male, and thus assumes a worldview that bases all human action on the necessity of physical violence to defend one's honor. See her *Fighting for American Manhood, How Gender Politics Provoked the Spanish-American and Philippine-American Wars* (New Haven: Yale University Press, 1998).

9   I have divided rhetoric (which includes signs) from discourse (signs plus signifiers) to simplify the impact of these elements on sensational journalism. This paper does not pretend to use discourse theory to analyze war reporting. It does recognize nineteenth-century concerns that sensational descriptions and their freighted meanings could seriously affect both the reasoning and actions of the readers. For an excellent discussion of public discourse and war reporting, see Steve Attridge, *Nationalism, Imperialism, and Identity in Late Victorian Culture, Civil and Military Worlds* (Basingstoke: Palgrave Macmillan, 2003).

10 Both papers also had specials, who knew their papers' policies, posted to their respective national encounters: the veteran Stanhope Sams in Cuba for the *Times,* and rookie reporter Henry Cross in the Sudan for the *Guardian.* Sams's first reports on Santiago were not published in the *Times* until July 18; Cross had been hospitalized with enteric fever the day before the Battle of Omdurman, and died a few weeks later. His only dispatch describing the battle itself was published posthumously, and included bitter descriptions of atrocities committed by the Sudanese troops against the Dervish wounded.

11 See especially Hoganson, but also Amy Kaplan, "Black and Blue on San Juan Hill," in Amy Kaplan and Donald E. Pease, eds., *Cultures of United States Imperialism* (Durham: Duke University Press, 1993); and Richard Slotkin, *Gunfighter Nation* (New York: Athenaeum, 1992). In the context of the constant appeal to *Americans'* honor, it is interesting to note that of the 289 casualties on the *Maine* listed by the *New York Times,* 117 were foreign born (see *Times,* February 17, 1898).

12 Lucy Brown, *Victorian News and Newspapers* (Oxford: Clarendon Press, 1985), 85–6.

13 Richard Kluger, *The Paper: The Life and Death of the New York Herald Tribune* (New York: Knopf, 1986), 164.

14 Davis, 944.

15 Charles H. Brown, *The Correspondents' War: Journalists in the Spanish-American War* (New York: Scribner's, 1967), 374.

16 Estimates of Dervish dead range from 6,000 to 16,000. The discrepancy is a result of the necessity of burying the dead quickly in mass graves or dumping them in the river and thus losing any remote chance of attaining a reasonable count. In addition, thousands of Dervish wounded dragged themselves off to the desert to die undisturbed by infidels. Certainly an

accurate body count didn't seem to be particularly important to anyone in light of the huge disparity in casualties.

17 Winston Churchill reported that a heavy rain had shorted it out (*The River War*, New York: Award Books, 1964, first published 1899), 236. The more cynical *Saturday Review*, accustomed to Kitchener's harsh censorship, speculated "an obliging sand-storm having apparently done the handsome thing by the Sirdar" (3 September 1898, p. 289).

18 A bare telegram that Kitchener had defeated the Khalifa was received in London on Sunday, sparking some late news extras and much speculation and anticipation (see 4 September NY *Times*).

19 It was far from brilliant, of course, and Colonel Martin came in for some warm criticism in later discussions for committing a dreadful military blunder that rendered his unit useless for the rest of the day's fighting.

20 See especially the radical *Weekly Times and Echo*, which carried Burleigh's narrative on September 11, and on September 18, an editorial deploring the public sensation aroused by reports from Omdurman. One of the *Guardian*'s readers wrote a letter protesting the *Guardian*'s discourse.

21 Peter Harrington discusses the published pictures and photos from Omdurman in "Images and Perceptions: Visualizing the Sudan Campaign," 82–102; Hugh Cecil discusses the reporters and the nature of their reporting in "British Correspondents and the Sudan Campaign of 1896–98," 102–28, both in Edward M. Spiers, ed., *Sudan: The Reconquest Reappraised* (London: Frank Cass, 1998).

22 Phillip Knightley, *The First Casualty: The War Correspondent as Hero and Mythmaker from the Crimea to Kosovo* (London: Prion, 2000), 66.

2
Embracing Sporting News in England and America: Nineteenth-century Cricket and Baseball News

Matt McIntire

During the nineteenth century the established game of English cricket and the fledgling game of American baseball were two summer sports promoted by the press as newspapers embraced sporting news. Periodicals in the United States, which had looked to the English model of sporting news early in the century, surpassed their brethren across the Atlantic after mid-century and, by the 1880s, the English press followed the American lead on sporting news. Baseball and cricket news offer excellent illustrations of the "symbiotic relationship" which provided benefits for the press and sports on both sides of the Atlantic.[1] In addition, the incorporation of baseball and cricket news also demonstrates the tension in the transatlantic press between the weakening liberal ideal of instruction and education and the growing dominance of the commercial imperative.[2]

From mid-century onwards, the press was integral to both cricket's and baseball's development as it fashioned and supported these sports which it exploited for summer news. The publicity and advocacy by sporting journals for these games shaped their development and their coverage in the press. While sporting papers provided the most extensive coverage of baseball from the 1840s to the present, daily newspapers, led by the *New York Herald*, realized the significance of baseball as a news subject in the 1860s.[3] Baseball remained, however, a sporadic subject in the daily press because it lacked a regular schedule until the 1870s when a professional league was founded.[4] As professional baseball established itself as a source of entertainment and civic pride in the 1870s after spreading to other cities, games received more extensive and regular coverage in daily newspapers. By the turn of the century, baseball had become a central feature of the New Journalism, which championed the consumer by emphasizing exposés and entertainment over political news and comment.[5] In England, the development of cricket followed a similar pattern as sporting papers not only offered the most thorough reports but also created the county championship in the early 1870s. The sporting press inaugurated this competition before county clubs had arranged regular, reciprocal schedules, which remained elusive until the 1890s. Cricket news played an important role in the New Journalism, even as its coverage in the daily press remained sparse compared to the exposure of baseball in the American press.[6]

Although discovering direct connections between English and American sporting news remains elusive, many contemporaries identified the cross-Atlantic impact. Especially after 1850, the press offered results and descriptions of play while also advocating the lessons and virtues of sport for the individual and society.[7] At the close of the century popular newspapers on both sides of the Atlantic offered readers news of baseball and cricket as a component of the New Journalism.[8] Commentators were critical of the developments in the American press, especially as they began to gauge and fear their influence in England. Their "representative" model of the press suggested that newspapers catered to the interests of their readers, instead of trying to influence them.[9] Thus, the American press of 1885 was perceived as "trivial, sensational, and essentially vulgar" with its "slangy and verbose reports of pugilism, dog fights, slugging matches, [and] baseball matches," and the main culprit was the *New York World*.[10] A few years later Matthew Arnold remarked with disappointment that "the newspaper is the direct product of the want felt; the supply answers closely and inevitably to the demand."[11] Although newspapers sought to "represent" the masses and attract readers by offering news of popular interest, the educational ethos never was abandoned.[12]

The first American sporting publications took their inspiration from their English forerunners. After its establishment in 1822, *Bell's Life in London and Sporting Chronicle* quickly became the pre-eminent sporting journal in the English-speaking world. By 1828 the weekly boasted sales of 25,000 copies as it flourished under the editorship of Vincent George Dowling from 1824, and his son Frank, who succeeded him and edited the paper until 1867.[13] *Bell's Life* was a unique institution in Anglo-American publishing with its coverage of prizefighting, pedestrianism, horse racing, police intelligence, and theater reviews. It appealed to the aristocracy and the working class as well as across the

Atlantic to American readers; in pubs, it was revered as "The Poor Man's Bible," and subscribers could be found at exclusive schools and clubs like Rugby and London's New University Club.[14] The paper served as a nexus for gambling on sport by publishing challenges offered and accepted by sportsmen, acting as a stakeholder for the contests it covered, and printing contest results for bookmakers and gamblers.[15] As horse racing emerged as the first national sport *Bell's Life* was the leader in publishing racing intelligence.[16]

Throughout the first third of the nineteenth-century sporting journalism in the United States sought to "catch-up" to the British model it copied. The most significant early American sporting journal devoted to sport was William T. Porter's *Spirit of the Times*, established in 1831. Porter's publication took inspiration from across the Atlantic, beginning as an imitator of *Bell's Life* and it was called the "*Bell's Life* of the New World."[17] Soon *Spirit* included sketches and tall tales from the American frontier and the weekly emerged from the 1830s as an American original, reporting on American events in its signature style. *Spirit* was the dominant sporting journal in the country from the 1830s to the 1850s when new papers began to challenge its superiority.[18]

Although one historian has implicated *Spirit* as a model for the first successful penny daily, the *Sun*, established in New York in 1833, most recent histories have ignored the role of sporting news in the development of the press as a commercial enterprise.[19] The most successful exponent of the commercial use of news was the Scottish-born proprietor and editor of the *New York Herald*, James Gordon Bennett.[20] The *Herald* began life in 1835 and it broadened the range of news published in the daily press by including political, financial, society, local, foreign, criminal, and sporting news aimed at New York's growing working class and lower-middle class.[21] As part of this transformation, the *Herald* and other papers offered new attention to the sporadic, but significant sporting events of the ante-bellum era, including the still evolving urban sport of baseball. The development of baseball and the press' coverage of it were intricately intertwined, illustrating the "symbiotic" nature of their relationship.[22] Newspapers provided the game with publicity and they also advocated for change in the game and, in return, the press received news about the organized baseball played intermittently in the New York area by private clubs.[23] Before the 1870s, much longer reports appeared in *Wilkes' Spirit of the Times* and the *New York Clipper*, journals which dedicated themselves to baseball. In America, journalism had diversified and specialized with its variety of penny and sporting papers sooner than in Britain where newspaper taxes limited these developments before 1855.

Early reports of baseball contests consisted of a few sentences and, perhaps, an accompanying score which might include the batting order of each side, a list of runs and outs made by each participant, and inning-by-inning scores for each team.[24] Still, prior to 1855 when a handful of clubs existed, the press coverage paled compared to what would come only a few years later.[25] Prominent New York clubs attempted to organize the game on a larger basis and create a standard code of baseball rules which culminated in the establishment of the National Association of Base Ball Players (NABBP) in 1858. Baseball was now a nine-inning game (rather than one which ended when a side scored 21 runs), and by 1864, after years of debate, and pressure in the press by respected journalists like Henry Chadwick, the NABBP adopted the rule that fielders retired the batter if they caught the ball on the fly, instead of on the first bounce.[26] The organization of baseball far out-paced English cricket, which, while governed by the rules of the Marylebone Cricket Club, lacked any centralized body to arrange contests until the 1890s.

The *Herald* took up the cause of baseball news in earnest beginning in 1862 by hiring Chadwick as its baseball correspondent. Chadwick's career in journalism blossomed as he promoted the game in print and behind the scenes, acquiring the moniker, the "Father of Baseball." Henry, the brother of Edwin Chadwick, the English health reformer, immigrated to the United States in the 1830s and, following in the footsteps of his father, began a career as a journalist. During the 1850s, he published free accounts of cricket matches in the *New York Times*, the *New York Tribune*, and other papers to attract interest in his writing about ball games. Chadwick also published baseball reports in New York's *Sunday Mercury*, beginning about 1858, the same year the *Clipper* named him baseball editor, a position he held until 1879.[27] In 1862, Chadwick began his important reports for the *Herald* covering New York clubs and the Philadelphia Athletics, whose contests he claimed sparked baseball's popularity.[28] As a testament to his influence on the game the league voted him an honorary membership and a lifetime pension of 50 dollars a month.[29]

Along with his baseball reports, Chadwick also authored and edited books and annuals devoted to baseball and cricket which promoted baseball as a quintessentially American game in an emerging urban-industrial society. In an attempt to measure individual performance on the field, Chadwick devised a scoring system for baseball inspired by the model used in cricket annuals in England. By using a "uniform" method of measurement "to obtain an accurate estimate of a player's skill" the feats of players could be quantified, analyzed, and compared.[30]

By 1870, other New York newspapers began to incorporate baseball news as a regular topic in their columns. The *Tribune* included detailed images of the action as well as box scores, and its "OUT-DOOR SPORTS" column which contained baseball and turf news, was front-page material. Baseball reports had become more sophisticated, listing some combination of runs, hits, putouts, total bases, assists, and errors. Although baseball had replaced cricket as the number one ball game in the States, cricket reports in the American press remained significant if judged by the space devoted to the respective stories.[31]

The overt emphasis on commercialism and its ties to civic pride in baseball contrasted with the unique situation of first-class cricket with its amateur and professional cricketers and its geographical base in the county clubs. Civic pride drove the popularity of baseball to new heights after the Civil War as cities and towns, and their newspapers, competed for victories over their rivals long before similar developments affected English cricket.[32] The *New York Clipper* encouraged such competition with the "Silver Ball Match" which it began sponsoring in 1861.[33] Important matches between New York clubs and those pitting New York's best teams against out-of-town clubs received extensive descriptions of play.[34] The Cincinnati Red Stockings began their 1869 season as the first acknowledged professional team, and the first professional league, the National Association of Professional Base Ball Players (NAPBBP), soon followed in 1871, with support from Henry Chadwick, in the *Clipper*, and Alfred Wright, in the *Philadelphia Mercury*.[35] Chadwick also served on the rules committee of the NAPBBP, the same committee position he had held under the first National Association of Baseball Players.[36] The National League of Professional Base Ball Clubs, established by club owners, replaced the NAPBBP in 1876.

Newspapers in the major midwestern cities of Cincinnati, Chicago, and St Louis offered substantial column inches of coverage of their major clubs. The presentation was impressive as these papers used new typographical styles, including extensive lower-case subheadings to draw attention to their news.[37] While these papers focused on their local clubs, they also realized the lure of comparisons to rival clubs and extended their coverage with scores from other games and lists of club standings. The *Chicago Tribune* advertised itself as "the Western Sporting Authority" which provided "accurate, reliable, and comprehensive base ball [*sic*] records and reports."[38]

Unlike the English press, which did not adopt sports departments until the 1890s and 1900s, the 1880s saw further American innovations in the coverage of baseball as Joseph Pulitzer brought the New Journalism to New York by purchasing the *World* in 1883. He created one of the first sports departments with H. G. Crickmore as editor, and published evening editions and Sunday supplements, perfect vehicles for sporting news, to boost interest in his new publication.[39] The paper argued in an early editorial that "in the matter of turf and sporting news the *World* is without equal in daily journalism. It is the authority."[40] Over the next decade most of the leading papers in large cities retained "sporting editors" with "a corps of trained specialists to describe and write of sporting events" and in New York, the *Herald*, the *World*, and the *Sun* often devoted a page or more to sporting news.[41]

When William Randolph Hearst bought the *New York Journal* in 1895 he challenged Pulitzer's *World*, with, among other innovations, the first separate sports section. He had expanded on the New Journalism formula first in his *San Francisco Examiner*, arguing that smaller newspapers "must have articles to suit the different classes," because such a strategy was a "necessity" to survive with adequate circulation.[42] This strategy included printing baseball scores on page one and when Hearst entered the New York market he continued to seek a wider audience.[43] While most New York papers included anywhere from three to seven columns of sporting news, Hearst decided the *Journal* needed more. The *Journal*, like its competitor, Pulitzer's *World*, also published Sunday supplements on sport and included banner headlines.[44]

In England, the press lacked the diversity of American newspaper publishing until the 1860s, when cheap newspapers became available, after the repeal of the "taxes on knowledge."[45] While the *Sunday Times* included a racing column in the 1850s there was no weekly sporting rival to *Bell's Life* until 1859 when the first penny newspaper to concentrate on sport was established. The new weekly publication, *Penny Bell's Life and Sporting News*, which soon changed its name to the *Sporting Life*, took advantage of the repeal of the duties on newspapers. Horse racing was its main topic, a development which meant that "the narratives of the turf are no longer confined to old-fashioned journals, the circulations of which limited them to the bar of a tavern or the trainer's table."[46] Within ten years *Bell's Life* had lowered its price to one penny because of growing competition from the *Sporting Life*, and another penny upstart, the *Sportsman*, which began publication twice a week. In 1876, the *Sportsman* became the first daily sporting paper in the world, arguing that "it has seemed to us that the time was ripe for the experiment."[47]

Cricket enjoyed a public following prior to the emergence of penny papers and it found its first forum in *Bell's Life*, as the journal preached the virtues of the game and spread cricket news throughout Britain.[48] Many professional sides toured England between 1846 and 1882, and up until the late 1860s these tours drew the most public interest.[49] The game underwent a striking surge in popularity during the "great cricket explosion" of the 1880s as popular contests drew attendances in excess of 10,000. Cricket clubs were formed in nearly every community, the classifications in county cricket emerged, international competitions began between teams from England and teams from Australia, Canada, and the United States, and professional cricket leagues developed in northern England.[50]

The press was critical to these developments as it promoted and publicized "the universal English summer game" from the 1860s on.[51] Cricket developed very differently than baseball as it retained a system employing professionals and amateurs for the county game which dominated English cricket from the 1870s onward. Like baseball coverage, however, the press encouraged the growth in cricket's popularity by keeping readers apprised of the latest results and statistics.[52]

During the same period, newspapers also documented the exploits of "the single most influential figure in the history of cricket."[53] With his batting performances W. G. Grace became a celebrity, a "Victorian Hero" whose familiarity equaled or exceeded that of prime ministers.[54] No individual has had more of an impact on the game before or since.[55] He was a complete player displaying skills as a bowler and a batsman; and with Grace as their captain Gloucestershire was a threat to defeat any county eleven for parts of five decades during the Victorian era.[56] Baseball lacked such a towering figure until Babe Ruth transformed the game in the 1920s.

Grace's celebrity coincided with the creation of the championship competition between county clubs by the press. The competition provided a context which fostered a growth in the popularity of cricket as well as publicizing Grace's exploits as his Gloucestershire side battled for the county championship. The reports of the matches played during the summer between the top county elevens in England were the core of cricket journalism. As early as 1870, the *Sporting Life* had argued that "county cricket, of course, takes precedence of all other, both with regard to the interest it excites and its own importance."[57] While eight American professional baseball clubs established the

National League in 1876, agreeing to a 70-game schedule, the county clubs had no organization to oversee their contests. As a result, the counties played entirely different schedules with some clubs playing more often than others, which meant that the winner of the unofficial county championship for many years was the county with the smallest number of defeats. The championship criteria would change in 1890, again in 1896, and numerous times during the twentieth century.

While the conventional view of the county cricket competition dates its beginnings from 1873, cricket periodicals had chosen victors during the 1860s. Such a policy suggests that an acknowledged contest between the counties existed. During the 1860s the four principal cricket annuals, *Fred Lillywhite's Guide, John and James Lillywhite's Companion, James Lillywhite's Annual,* and *Wisden Cricketers' Almanack* chose the top team in some years, sometimes disagreeing on the best team.[58] In 1873, a meeting of county secretaries, led by C. W. Alcock of Surrey County Cricket Club, established qualification rules for county amateurs and professionals which limited their participation to only one county per season.[59]

As early as 1869 *Bell's Life* had offered readers a "retrospect of county cricket" which listed all the matches of the respective sides. This description of the season did not include any tables ranking the participating counties.[60] The following year, however, *Bell's Life* listed the results of the county cricket season in a more comprehensive manner and included the Marylebone Cricket Club in its results. Each county and its matches were listed with the results and the grounds where they had competed. It also placed the results in "tabular form" according to the number of matches a side had played.[61] While *Bell's Life* did not name a champion in the report, the obvious choice was Yorkshire with six victories, no losses, and one draw, as the *Sporting Life* and the *Sportsman* both noted.[62]

Because of cricket's growing popularity and its significance as a social and cultural institution, as early as 1875 *The Times* began publishing a sporadic feature article on cricket to accompany its concise reports on matches.[63] Cricket news had become a staple of a newspaper's overall coverage by 1885 whether it was a sporting paper or a general interest paper. Prior to 1885 cricket news usually consisted of short, descriptive summaries of important matches and, perhaps, the scores of less significant encounters. If cricket fans could not play or watch a match then they could read about it, because:

> the next best thing to playing cricket is to see it played; and next after that, at a long interval, doubtless, but still not without a strong

clash of excitement, comes the hurried glance in the morning at the scores of the day before. What new surprises have they in store for us? To whatever pitch of dullness the rest of the morning's news may descend, in the cricket intelligence we are tolerably sure to find some 'century,' some wonderful bowling, some unexpected result, some exciting finish.[64]

Readers who sought more extensive accounts of play looked to papers which specialized in sporting news, like *Bell's Life*, the *Sportsman*, the *Sporting Life*, and the *Athletic News*.

While American dailies first viewed baseball as a subject to exploit systematically, in England halfpenny evening papers led the dailies in using cricket as a daily news feature in the 1880s. By the 1890s newspapers had to provide the most up-to-date coverage possible because "there are very few newspaper readers who do not turn to the cricket column first when the morning journal comes; who do not buy a halfpenny evening paper to find out how many runs W.G. [Grace] or Bobby Abel has made."[65] In popular daily papers like the *Daily Telegraph*, sports coverage remained low until the 1890s when it rose from roughly 2 percent to 7.5 percent of its contents.[66] Evening papers were the first to develop a sporting consciousness and to capitalize on the rise of sport, especially football during the 1880s.[67]

For cricket, the evenings began offering readers the latest match results and statistics, often up to the close of play, in special cricket editions. In 1884 the publishers of the Bolton *Evening News* produced the *Football Field and Sports Telegram*, which became the *Cricket and Football Field* in 1887. The London evening, the *Star*, aspired to a mass readership at its launch in 1888 and its founding editor, T. P. O'Connor, included a sporting editor, E. C. Mitchell, better known as "Captain Coe."[68] The *Star* included a "SPORTING CHAT" column of one to three sentence notes, written in a crisp, economical style and format. Coverage of sport was also important in the *Star*'s sibling, the *Morning Leader*, which had extensive coverage of cricket from its beginnings in 1894, including one page each on Saturdays and Mondays. Important matches received more prominent attention from the editors, with larger headlines and longer reports, whether the match was a county match or a test match from Australia. By the 1890s, in the *Evening News*, "CRICKET CHRONICLES" appeared on page one, with summaries of the day's play by the metropolitan counties, the M.C.C., and the "Varsities". Longer reports of play with less extensive statistics than the daily papers ran in the "TO-DAY'S CRICKET" column on the inside pages along with up-to-the minute scores under "LATEST RESULTS". Often a table of the first-class standings and the batting and bowling averages accompanied the summaries.[69]

Much of the preceding material illustrates the commercial relationship of the press to baseball and cricket, as they became an increasingly important part of the leisure culture of the late nineteenth century. While many newspapers sought to increase their circulation with the inclusion of sporting news, the press also argued that baseball and cricket were significant to their respective cultures. Newspaper advocacy for sport began in the New York press in the 1830s to promote a healthy mind, body, morality, and character. The press endorsed baseball, in particular, by the 1860s, as a manly sport because it "affords a field for the development of the manly attributes of courage, nerve, pluck [and] endurance."[70] *Porter's Spirit of the Times* supported the game with a series of articles chronicling the historical development of baseball and the *Clipper* featured columns on creating a baseball club and playing the game.[71] The press appealed to readers to share in the baseball experience because "participation in the rituals of baseball contributed to both individual self-improvement and national betterment."[72]

Newspaper support continued as baseball became part of the commercial entertainment industry from the late 1860s on. Baseball content increased enough during the 1870s and 1880s, so that, by 1890, all major metropolitan papers included a sporting editor and baseball reporter.[73] Local teams provided publicity and prominence for their city and encouraged a type of civic participation among fans.[74] Even amongst this spread of "representative" news, the press continued its liberal practice of extolling the virtues of sport. The daily press "merely followed the public demand for news" during the early years of baseball but "soon assumed the lead, and to-day is foremost in helping the development of sport." Sporting news, as a liberal agent of education, was critical to the continued evolution of baseball because its oversight would keep the game "healthy" and "honorable."[75]

Like baseball in American culture, cricket was a vital ingredient of English culture during the nineteenth century. The press imbued cricket with a reverent quality over the course of the nineteenth century, much like the teachers and schoolboys in the novel *Tom Brown's School-Days*. It was "a noble game," "an institution," and "the birth right of British boys young and old," which taught selflessness and the importance of playing for a side.[76] On the field cricket was a course in ethics, morality, justice, and the superiority of English culture.[77] The sport was central to the educational curriculum in

England, both formal and informal; cricket was "a pastime healthy alike for mind and muscle," and it promoted the strength, vitality, and courage necessary for a virtuous society.[78]

Cricket propagandists claimed that the game fostered social peace in England and united England and its colony, Australia. Long before the popular press had discovered the game, the *Field* had explained that cricket united the diverse classes of England and the press continued to promote this view of cricket as the century drew to a close.[79] "Incorruptible" amateurs had a leavening effect on the roughness of the professionals and the interactive play on the field not only reconciled the classes, but also resulted in "much more interesting" cricket.[80] The English also exported cricket to the British empire to enlighten colonists and natives in the colonies. As *Bell's Life* argued, "the missionaries of cricket must seek their heathen on foreign shores; our own pagans are all clothed (in flannels), and in their right minds."[81] Cricket was an integral component of the shared culture of the British empire and the language of nationalism suffused the literature of cricket.[82] Even when the myth of class unity came under attack during incidents like the professionals' demand for more pay during the last 1896 test match against Australia, the press criticized their actions as unpatriotic.[83]

In the twentieth century, the media coverage of these two ball games has risen to extraordinary levels of importance around the globe. Cricket remains the sport linking England with the West Indies, Pakistan, India, South Africa, and Australia, the states that succeeded the British colonies. Likewise professional baseball, while still dominated by Americans from the United States, now connects the Americas and the Pacific rim. The popular press of the nineteenth century shaped the multifaceted and, oftentimes, contradictory meanings of the games. Newspapers on both sides of the Atlantic celebrated virtues like selflessness and teamwork that baseball and cricket were claimed to embody. These explanations appeared within the same columns as the tables ranking clubs and the individual batting statistics. One journalist has presciently labeled this cultural web encompassing sport and the modern media, "SportsWorld."[84] The first strands of this web were the creation of the nineteenth-century press as it promoted sport as both an educational recreation and a commercial news subject.

Notes

1 Tony Mason, *Association Football and English Society, 1863–1915* (Atlantic Highlands, NJ: Humanities Press, 1980), 187; Tony Mason, "Sporting News,

1860–1914," in *The Press in English Society from the Seventeenth to Nineteenth Centuries*, eds. Michael Harris and Alan Lee (Rutherford, NJ: Farleigh Dickinson University Press, 1986), 168–86; Robert W. McChesney, "Media Made Sport: A History of Sports Coverage in the United States," in *Media, Sports, and Society*, ed. Lawrence A. Wenner (Newbury Park, CA: Sage Publications, 1989), 49.

2 Mark Hampton, *Visions of the Press in Britain, 1850–1950* (Urbana: University of Illinois Press, 2004); Ted Curtis Smythe, *The Gilded Age Press, 1865–1900* (Westport, CT: Praeger, 2003); William Huntzicker, *The Popular Press, 1835–1865* (Westport, CT: Greenwood Press, 1999), 163–76; Alan J. Lee, *The Origins of the Popular Press in England, 1855–1914* (London: Croom Helm, 1976).

3 Melvin L. Adelman, *A Sporting Time: New York City and the Rise of Modern Athletics, 1820–70* (Urbana: University of Illinois Press, 1986), 121–83, chronicles the emergence of baseball. One of his key sources was the *New York Herald*.

4 John Rickard Betts, "Sporting Journalism in Nineteenth-Century America," *American Quarterly*, 5 (1953): 45.

5 Smythe, *Gilded Age Press*, 72. Smythe does not address sporting news directly, but lumps it into the entertainment category of news.

6 Lee, *Origins*, 127–8.

7 There is a large literature dealing with the subject of sport as an educational tool. For a start, see J. A. Mangan, *Athleticism in the Victorian and Edwardian Public School*, new ed. (London: Frank Cass, 2000).

8 Smythe, *Gilded Age Press*; Joel H. Wiener, "How New was the New Journalism?" in *Papers for the Millions: The New Journalism in Britain, 1850s to 1914*, ed. Joel H. Wiener (Westport, CT: Greenwood Press, 1988), 54; John Goodbody, "The *Star*: Its Role in the Rise of the New Journalism," in *Papers for the Millions*, 148–9.

9 Hampton, *Visions*, 106–8.

10 Theodore Child, "The American Newspaper Press," *Fortnightly Review*, 44 (1885): 829, 835.

11 "Civilization in the United States," *Nineteenth Century*, 23 (April 1888): 489–90. Also see Evelyn March Phillipps, "The New Journalism," *New Review*, 13 (August 1895): 182.

12 Edward Dicey, "Journalism New and Old," *Fortnightly Review*, 77 (1905): 916.

13 For most of the next 20 years *Bell's Life* never seemed to exceed sales of much more than 30,000. Adrian Harvey, "The Evolution of Modern British Sporting Culture 1793–1850" (Ph. D. thesis, Oxford University, 1995), 107–8, 113; *Bell's Life*, 23 May 1847. On Vincent Dowling, see *Illustrated London News*, 13 November 1852.

14 Robert Patrick Watson, *Memoirs of Robert Patrick Watson: A Journalist's Experience of a Mixed Society* (London: Smith, Ainslie, 1899), 343–4; Thomas Hughes, *Tom Brown's School-Days* (first published, 1857; Reprint: Ware, 1993); Stephen Koss, *The Rise and Fall of the Political Press in Britain*, vol. 1 (London: Hamish Hamilton, 1981), 159.

15 See *Bell's Life*, 23 May 1847; Harvey, "Evolution," 94; Mason, "Sporting News," 169; Watson, *Memoirs*, 343.

16   *Sporting Mirror*, 1 (July 1881): 188.
17   Jack W. Berryman, "The Tenuous Attempts of Americans to 'Catch-up with "John Bull"': Specialty Magazines and Sporting Journalism, 1800–1835," *Canadian Journal of History of Sport and Physical Education*, 10 (May 1979): 55.
18   Betts, "Sporting Journalism," 41; Norris W. Yates, *William T. Porter and the Spirit of the Times: A Study of the BIG BEAR School of Humor* (Baton Rouge: University of Louisiana Press, 1957), 3, 18, 22; Berryman, "Tenuous Attempts," 54–7.
19   Bernard A. Weisberger, *The American Newspaperman* (Chicago: University of Chicago Press, 1961), 95. Three recent works which ignore sporting news are Smythe, *Gilded Age Press*, George H. Douglas, *The Golden Age of the Newspaper* (Westport, CT: Greenwood Press, 1999) and Huntzicker, *The Popular Press*.
20   James L. Crouthamel, *Bennett's "New York Herald" and the Rise of the Popular Press* (Syracuse: Syracuse University Press, 1989).
21   Michael Schudson, *Discovering the News: A Social History of American Newspapers* (New York: Basic Books, 1979), 18–29, 50–7. One admirer called Bennett "the Journalist of the People." *Memoirs of James Gordon Bennett and his Times* (New York: Stringer and Townsend, 1855), 428. Crouthamel, *Bennett's "World,"* 246; Weisburger, *Newspaperman*, 97–101. Also see Joel H. Wiener, "The Americanization of the British Press, 1830–1914," *Studies in Newspaper and Periodical History* (Westport, CT: Greenwood Press, 1996), 64–5.
22   Adelman, *A Sporting Time*, 121–83, examines this relationship and its role in the development of baseball.
23   Harold Seymour, *Baseball: The Early Years* (New York: Oxford University Press, 1960), 35.
24   *New York Clipper*, 16 July 1853, in Mears' Baseball Scrapbooks, v. 1a, Cleveland (Ohio) Public Library. For another example, see the report, "Base Ball Match at Buffalo," *Herald*, 6 July 1860.
25   Mears' Scrapbooks, v. 1a; Adelman, *Sporting Time*, 126–7.
26   Adelman, *Sporting Time*, 127–31. For more detail of Chadwick's advocacy of catching the ball on the fly, see Warren Goldstein, *Playing for Keeps: A History of Early Baseball* (Ithaca, NY: Cornell University Press, 1989), 49–50.
27   W. M. Rankin, "Early History of Baseball," Mears' Baseball Scrapbooks, v. 1a. See the Henry Chadwick scrapbooks, Albert Spalding Collection, New York Public Library, for stories from the *Sunday Mercury*.
28   Henry Clay Palmer, *et al.*, *Athletic Sports in America, England and Australia* (Philadelphia, 1889), 575–6; *Editor and Publisher*, 12 January 1907 (6): 3; Chadwick scrapbooks; Henry Chadwick diaries, Albert Spalding Collection, New York Public Library, v. 6, 1878, 1879.
29   *Brooklyn Daily Eagle*, 18 November 1896, 5 December 1897.
30   Henry Chadwick, ed., *Beadle's Dime Base-Ball Player* (New York: Beadle, 1861), 58–61. For an early example of a scoring system used by one newspaper, see Mears' Scrapbooks, v. 4a.
31   For example, compare the *Herald*, 4 May 1870, with the *Herald*, 6 July 1875.
32   On localism in early baseball see Goldstein, *Playing*, 101–3.
33   Mears' Scrapbooks, v. 1a; *New York Clipper Annual* (1891): 17.

34 *New York Tribune*, 5 May 1870, 5 July 1870. Also see the preview of the Chicago White Stockings before their tour of New York City, *New York Tribune*, 2 July 1870.
35 Palmer, *Athletic Sports*, 40.
36 *Sporting News*, 21 May 1936.
37 Mears' Scrapbooks, v. 5a, includes clippings from a number of midwestern newspapers, including the *Chicago Times*, the *Chicago Tribune*, the *Cincinnati Enquirer*, the *St. Louis Democrat*, and the *St. Louis Globe*.
38 *Spalding's Official Base Ball Guide* (1882).
39 Frank Luther Mott, *American Journalism, A History: 1690–1960*, 3rd ed. (New York: Macmillan, 1962), 430–45. Thomas E. Flynn was the sporting editor of the *San Francisco Chronicle*, as early as the 1870s. John P. Young, *Journalism in California* (San Francisco: Chronicle Pub. Co., 1915), 103. Elliot Gorn and Warren Goldstein, *A Brief History of American Sports* (New York: Hill and Wang, 1993), 115, have argued that Pulitzer realized the worth of sporting news from the success of the *National Police Gazette*, published by Richard Kyle Fox, who had emigrated from Belfast in 1874.
40 *New York World*, 27 May 1883, cited in George Juergens, *Joseph Pulitzer and the "New York World"*, (Princeton: Princeton University Press, 1966), 120.
41 J. B. McCormick, "The Sporting Editor," *The Making of a Newspaper*, ed. Melville Philips (New York: G. P. Putnam's Sons, 1893), 205; Mott, *American Journalism*, 443.
42 William Randolph Hearst, "Pacific Coast Journalism," *Overland Monthly* (April 1888): 403.
43 David Nasaw, *The Chief: The Life of William Randolph Hearst* (Boston: Houghton Mifflin, 2000), 76.
44 William Henry Nugent, "The Sports Section," *American Mercury*, 16 (March 1929): 336–7.
45 Lee, *Origins*, 42–9.
46 *Sporting Life*, 22 August 1866.
47 *Sportsman*, 20 March 1876.
48 *Select Committee of the House of Lords on the Laws Respecting Gaming*, Parliamentary Papers, 1844 (25), vol. 6, p. 89, Q. 234.
49 Ric Sissons, *The Players: A Social History of the Professional Cricketer* (London: Kingswood, 1988), 3–62.
50 Keith A. P. Sandiford, *Cricket and the Victorians* (Aldershot, UK: Scolar Press, 1994), 53–79.
51 Richard Holt, "Cricket and Englishness: The Batsman as Hero," in *European Heroes: Myth, Identity, Sport*, eds. Richard Holt, J. A. Mangan and Pierre Lanfranchi (London: Frank Cass, 1996), 48; Richard Holt, "Heroes of the North: Sport and the Shaping of Regional Identity," in *Sport and Identity in the North of England*, eds. Jeff Hill and Jack Williams (Keele: University of Keele Press, 1996), 144.
52 Sir Home Gordon, "The Coming Cricket Season," *Badminton Magazine*, 30 (1910): 390.
53 Derek Birley, *The Willow Wand: Some Cricket Myths Explored* (London: Queen Anne Press, 1979), 59.
54 W. F. Mandle, "W. G. Grace as a Victorian Hero," *Historical Studies*, 19 (1981): 353–68.

55 C. L. R. James, *Beyond a Boundary* (Durham, NC: Duke University Press, 1993; first published 1963), 174.
56 Holt, "Cricket and Englishness," 54.
57 *Sporting Life*, 12 October 1870.
58 Rowland Bowen, "The Early County Champions," *Wisden Cricketers' Almanack* (1959): 91–8. Also see Bowen, "The Early County Champions: A Postscript," *Wisden Cricketers' Almanack* (1960): 992–3. Bowen only consulted cricket publications, not sporting newspapers.
59 *Cricket*, October 25, 1894, 417; *Athletic News*, June 8, 1925, 8; Gordon Ross, *A History of Cricket* (London: Barker, 1972), 26, cites *The MCC Diary's* list of champions that begins in 1873; Christopher Brookes, *English Cricket: The Game and Its Players Through the Ages* (London: Weidenfeld and Nicolson, 1978), 120; Sandiford, *Cricket*, 59–60.
60 *Bell's Life*, 25 September 1869.
61 *Bell's Life*, 24 September 1870.
62 *Sporting Life*, 12 October 1870; *Sportsman*, 4 November 1870.
63 Marcus Williams, *Double Century: 200 Years of Cricket in "The Times"* (London, 1985), vii–viii.
64 *The Times*, 16 July 1883.
65 Prince Ranjitsinhji, "Cricket and the Victorian Era," *Blackwood's Edinburgh Magazine*, 162 (July 1897): 11.
66 Mason, "Sporting News," 174.
67 Mason, *Association Football*, 187–94; Matthew J. McIntire, "'The News that Sells': Sport and the Press in British Society, 1855–1914," (Ph. D. Dissertation, City University of New York, 2003), 167–211.
68 T. P. O'Connor, *Memoirs of an Old Parliamentarian*, vol. 2 (New York: Appleton, 1929), 256.
69 For example, see *Evening News*, 25 May 1894, 28 May 1894. By the turn of the century the *Evening News* had incorporated a "Late Cricket Edition"; for example, see 2 July 1901. Evening papers may have begun such editions earlier, but often there are no surviving copies available to consult.
70 *Baseball Chronicle*, 1 (27 June 1867), quoted in Adelman, *A Sporting Time*, 281–2, and also see 269–86, for a general discussion of the role of the press.
71 *Porter's Spirit* 3 (24 October 1857–23 January 1858); *New York Clipper*, 30 April 1859, 18 February 1860, 10 March 1860, 17 March 1860, 31 March 1860, 7 April 1860, cited in George B. Kirsch, *The Creation of American Team Sports* (Urbana: University of Illinois Press, 1989), 62.
72 Steven A. Riess, *Touching Base* (Westport, CT: Greenwood Press, 1980), 13–4.
73 Palmer, *Athletic Sports*, 571.
74 *New York Times*, 23 September 1887, cited in Riess, *Touching Base*, 18–21.
75 Palmer, *Athletic Sports*, 572–3.
76 Hughes, *Tom Brown's*, 313; F. G. Alfalo, "The Sportsman," *Fortnightly Review*, 80 (1907): 166–7.
77 See Sandiford, *Cricket*; Holt, "Heroes of the North," and "Cricket and Englishness."
78 *Sporting Life*, 21 December 1867. Also see the list of "manly virtues" that were essential to playing cricket in *Cricket*, 25 November 1886, 466.
79 *Field*, 17 October 1863, 381.
80 *Saturday Review*, 14 July 1883; *Times*, 24 March 1894.

81 *Bell's Life*, 21 September 1872.
82 Sandiford, *Cricket*, 144–60.
83 For example, see the *Daily Telegraph*, 10 August 1896; *Times*, 10 August 1896. For an examination of how the press influenced the controversy, see McIntire, "'The News that Sells,'" 249–67.
84 Robert Lipsyte, *SportsWorld* (New York: Quadrangle/ New York Times Book Co., 1975).

3
"Get the News! Get the News!" – Speed in Transatlantic Journalism, 1830–1914

Joel H. Wiener

On the morning of July 29, 2005 Muktar Said Ibrahim was arrested in west London on charges of attempting to detonate a bomb on a bus in Shoreditch two days earlier. This dramatic, tense confrontation between the police and a man accused of involvement in the second of London's terrorist incidents in the summer of 2005 was witnessed live on television by millions of viewers. It had the virtue and excitement of immediacy – an instant compression of time – and seemed centuries removed from the leisurely tempo of nineteenth-century print journalism when most news, even with the use of the telegraph and telephone, took more than a day to reach its audience.[1] In the July incident speed had caught up with reporting, and in a curious, almost cosmic way, transcended it.

Speed is relative to the cultural mores of a particular time and place. It has "real" meaning, to be sure, and in the words of Stephen Kern, has had "a profound impact on civilization."[2] But it is also what a society chooses to make of it and how it chooses to define it. In the context of British and American journalism in the nineteenth century it had different meanings for people living on either side of the Atlantic. For many Britons it represented superficiality: a valuing of "legs over gray matter, of attrition ... over mere book knowledge." It seemed to place in danger literary canons built up in the course of centuries. The historian Alexander Kinglake, writing in mid-century, put it this way: "Everyone now hurried to print what nobody thought it worthwhile to say." Several decades later James Bryce, an insightful critic of transatlantic culture, likewise bewailed the effects of speed in producing newspapers, which were, almost by definition, "adverse to solid thinking and dulling to the sense of beauty."[3]

Speed was generally looked upon with greater enthusiasm in nine-teenth-century America. It had the virtue of brevity and appeared to make commercial sense, with its technical advances applicable to jour-nalism such as the telegraph, the typewriter, and the telephone. To some observers it also suggested a link to a kind of democratic pop-ulism. The crudeness of the end product might be self-evident to those of solid intellectual attainment. Yet what of it, in the view of many aspiring Americans? Vigor and youthfulness (without a need for cre-dentials) were there to take its place. As Joseph Hatton, a British jour-nalist who wrote for several American newspapers, observed: "The rule in America is restlessness.... Nothing is fenced in." Another British journalist, Evelyn March Phillipps, bewailed the mediocrity of American culture. Yet, concerning its press she found sufficient to praise in its "wealth of intimate detail, and that determination to arrest, amuse, or startle."[4] And the French-born writer, Paul Blouet (writing under the pseudonym "Max O'Rell"), expressed his admiration of the American press for its "spirit of enterprise, liveliness, childishness, inquisitive-ness... indiscretion, love of gossip, (and) brightness."[5]

Numerous nineteenth-century commentators addressed the virtues and defects of American and British journalism with speed often at the core of the debate, and the controversy continues today amidst the explosion of a tabloid revolution on both sides of the Atlantic. It is not my intention to take sides in this spirited skirmish but rather to make the case for a cultural approach to journalism studies, to argue that when studying American and British journalism such an approach can best be viewed in a transatlantic setting rather than as a series of national histories, and to pinpoint the usefulness in focusing on a cul-tural construct like speed. As I have shown elsewhere, the ties among journalists working on both sides of the Atlantic during the nineteenth century were considerable. There was a constant "push and pull" of personnel, technology, editorial direction, methods of reporting, stylis-tic expression, and proprietary interaction which truly amounted to a "transatlantic revolution." This revolution had a reciprocal impact, notably in the areas of illustration and leader writing, where Britain's influence on American journalism was notably strong. But in the main the challenge to older traditions of newspaper production emanated from America, and the trick is often to decide how to measure the British response to American "aggression." Other historians have noted the importance of this kind of comparative analysis, including notably Jeremy Tunstall and Mark Hampton, but a great deal of work (too much, I would argue) is still being done in a national framework.[6]

In recent years the case for looking at journalism primarily through a cultural lens has been strongly urged by sociologists and historians such as Michael Schudson, David Copeland, and Thomas Leonard working from the American end, and by Martin Conboy, writing from a British perspective.[7] Yet, many recent journalism studies in what has become a burgeoning field of scholarship ignore factors other than the economic, or the political, or the technological, not to speak of books and articles which perceive the press exclusively from a social control model or from the point of view of producers rather than consumers.[8] During the nineteenth century, a large Anglo-American readership was coming into existence, and almost every element of what came to constitute modern journalism was becoming redefined in some way. To give insufficient weight to aspects of culture such as speed, attitudes towards privacy, and sensationalism; or, alternatively, to ignore authentic reader interest in stories about sports, crime, and sex, to use three obvious examples, however undernourished these may appear to the modern sensibility, is to miss a critical dimension of the nineteenth-century transatlantic revolution in the press. This essay focuses on speed, which was a more persistent element in America than in Britain, and it seeks to pinpoint some of the ways in which it acted as a spur to the American press and affected the interaction of journalism between the countries. The similarities between the two journalisms were and are considerable, and there is no inevitability about the shape of the end product. But I will try to show thematically how some key areas of modern reporting in particular were affected by what I believe to be a critical element of American culture.

Ever since the innovations of James Gordon Bennett and others in the 1830s American reporting appeared to be driven by speed. Reporters were often referred to as "legmen" (in contrast to the more somnolent word "correspondent," which was widely used in Britain), and tenacious reporters in the United States were sometimes called "break-in reporters." They sent "dispatches" instead of "letters," and by the final decades of the century were on the move in search of "beats" and "scoops," words of the trade which came to be used more slowly and at a somewhat later date in Britain. Competitiveness and quickness in newsgathering took priority over accuracy and the quality of writing. As Horace Greeley, the editor of the *New York Tribune*, told a British Parliamentary committee in 1851: "The quickest news is the only (one) looked to (in America)."[9] In the 1890s Theodore Dreiser worked on several newspapers in Chicago and St Louis while learning the trade of writing, and in both cities he found the pace unrelentingly brutal. Failure to produce rapid copy was regarded as unforgivable, especially if this meant being scooped by a competitor. Dreiser reported that the great cry of the editorial room was: "Get the news! Get the news! Get the news! Don't worry much over how you get it, but get it, and don't come back without it."[10]

The hunt for news gained momentum in the 1830s with the rise of a penny press, was given an enormous boost by the insatiable desire for war news in the 1860s, and in the post-Civil War period settled into a struggle to bring American urban society, with its millions of unassimilated immigrants, into some kind of cultural order. But what this comparatively young country prided itself on journalistically, above all, was its ability to outdo older and more experienced rivals, or to rephrase the puerile words of a modern advertising slogan, to be "The Fastest with the Mostest." The editor of the fictional *New York Sun* in "The Paper," Ron Howard's fine film about tabloid journalism, captured the essence of speed when he told his reporters: "We only have to be right for a day." More terrifying was the injunction given to the rookie reporter, Fred Wile, in the 1890s by his editor on the *Chicago Record*. Wile was assigned the task of covering President McKinley and told: "Stick to him like a leech. Sleep with him if you can, and eat with him, too. And the Lord have mercy on you if the *Record* is scooped."[11]

The journalistic rivalry within American cities was particularly vicious, in seeming affirmation of the disconnected, fragmented nature of its urban life. Unlike the "national" daily press in London, which remained relatively unchallenged until the emergence of a tough kind of urban journalism in Manchester at the turn of the twentieth century, and which mostly featured national and foreign news, American newspapers fought competitive battles over local news. This was especially true in New York and Chicago. In the former city, reporters from Bennett's *New York Herald* and Greeley's *Tribune* engaged in a no-holds-barred slugfest that was described colloquially as "slam-bang, (and) going-off-half-cocked." A confidential statement attributed to Frederic Hudson, who managed the *Herald* for Bennett, made the point succinctly: "Bear in mind that the *Herald* must never be beaten." John Augustus O'Shea, the famous Special Correspondent for the London *Standard* who worked briefly for the *Herald* in the 1860s, told his readers that it was considered a "mortal sin" for that paper's reporters to be "cut out in the transmission of news by rivals."[12]

Chicago was even more driven by speed. Melville E. Stone, the editor and proprietor of the *Chicago Daily News*, boasted that his leading reporter, Clarence Dresser, "prowled among the railroads, gathered what he could, betrayed confidences generously."[13] The ineffable Ben Hecht-Charles MacArthur saga of modern journalism, *The Front Page*, with its ceaseless noise and frantic obsession with news, was set in Chicago, and it became almost a literary paradigm of American big city journalism. In John McCutcheon's autobiography, based on his recollection of the pressroom of the *Daily News* in the 1890s, a picture is drawn of copy boys "rushing in to send or get stuff" and of a "continuous clatter and scurrying."[14] Martin Mayer, who has written insightfully about the American media in the late twentieth century, maintains that "the tradition of the scoop has been cultivated more jealously and singlemindedly in Chicago" than in any other city in the world.[15]

Speed is not necessarily synonymous with sloppiness and unreliability. Some of the best news stories have been written under considerable pressure; some of the least worthy have been composed in conditions of relative calm. Nonetheless, there is some correlation between the incessant pressure to find and get a story into print (the journalistic word "story" is itself a nineteenth-century American term) and the possibility of that story containing inaccuracies. All of this is by way of suggesting that widespread charges of inaccuracy in the American press have a basis in fact, and that Charles Dickens, who condemned the "rampant ignorance and base dishonesty" of American journalism during his first visit to that country in 1842, was not far off the mark.[16]

It was the push and hurry of big city journalism, its "hideous uproar," in the words of the novelist, William Dean Howells, which generated the demand for speed and was most to blame for the unsavory reputation of American journalism.[17] American reporters were known to turn up suddenly – at a police station, a city morgue, a political rally – and demand information. If they did not get what they wanted, they often wrote the story anyway, with or without the proper facts. This was increasingly common on evening papers, which were more popular in America than in Britain because they relied on impulse buying, and where news was often submitted in segments, a page or less at a time and subject to the pressure of constant deadlines. There were accounts of speeches being made up out of whole cloth and printed in American evening papers.[18] Editors sometimes overlooked inaccuracies, notably during the 1890s when William Randolph Hearst and Joseph Pulitzer fought for control of the New York market. Bonuses were offered for exclusives, or for a particularly speedy news story. One editor conjured up a vision of the ideal reporter as "a man

who knows where trouble is going to break loose and is on the spot."
Hearst himself took the idea of speed to a new level of rhetorical
urgency. Allegedly he replied to a cable from one of his illustrators,
Frederick Remington, who was stationed in Havana in 1897, in the following words: "You furnish the pictures, and I'll furnish the war."[19]
That such machinations caused difficulties for many American journalists is clear from the example of John W. Fox, a New York reporter,
who wrote: "I find I am falling into the habit of tinging things and of
trusting to my imagination. I am frequently forced to do this because I
have no time and because it is often impossible to make personal
investigation."[20]

A great many journalists endorsed the war cry of their editors and
proprietors. For example, Charles Carleton, a tireless "news-gatherer"
during the Civil War, believed that he "must keep ever in view the
thousands that are looking at the journal he represents, who expect his
account at the earliest possible moment.... His account must be first, or
among the first, or it is nothing." James Creelman, the Hearst reporter,
went even further in explicitly linking the obsession with speed to
democratic feeling. As with other journalists Creelman may have been
engaging in self-justification when he penned the following words
which nonetheless reverberate with cultural significance. Creelman
wrote: "(The modern newspaper) may be intrusive, it may be irreverent,
it may be destructive of sentiment; but it gradually breaks down the
walls of tradition and prejudice that divide the human race.... It is the
subtlest, swiftest element in the chemistry of modern civilization."[21]

In assessing the extent to which British journalism, as compared to
its American counterpart, was affected by speed it is necessary to point
out that the latter was by no means an exclusive American preserve.
Parliamentary reporting, for example, which was honed into a fine art
in Britain by the late nineteenth century, was based upon speed.
Newspapers were expected to print verbatim accounts of the evening's
debates in the next morning's editions, and to satisfy this demand
shifts of energetic young reporters, including future literary stars like
Dickens and Thackeray, took notes in shorthand before rushing their
accounts to the Fleet Street offices of *The Times* or the *Morning
Chronicle*. Parliamentary sketch writers, for which there has never been
an American equivalent, were expected to attend the debates and
produce instant "descriptive" analyses of the speeches. In a well-known
book published in 1882, Charles Pebody captured the essence of this
highly specialized world of speed, which was signified by "the constant
patter of telegraph boys all through the night, with their showers of

pink envelopes; of the rattle of machinery; of the glare of gas; of the busy scenes in the printing office...."[22]

British leader writers also worked in conditions of speed to meet harsh deadlines. In America, editorials often remained unread. Not so in Britain, where until late in the century leader writers, well educated and at the top of the social and professional hierarchy, maintained a dominant position in journalism. They worked hard to sustain it. Henry Wilkinson penned his leaders for the *Morning Post* in the early hours of the morning while debates in the House of Commons were still going on. His paragraphs were transmitted to the printing room slip by slip. Incessant speed was likewise demanded of T. P. O'Connor, when he covered the sessions of the Parnell Commission in 1888–89, which was investigating a series of forged letters by Charles Stewart Parnell that had been published in *The Times*. O'Connor was required to produce 3–5 columns of "descriptive writing" within a brief time of the body adjourning.[23] Even fakery sometimes occurred in the British press, especially among those working for "lineage money." Like American space reporters – who unlike British "penny-a-liners" were on the payroll of the newspapers they worked for – the temptation to exaggerate and invent was considerable. It was stated that many Fleet Street penny-a-liners did creative "research" in the old City newsroom in Farringdon Street rather than on site.[24]

The advent of the New Journalism in Britain in the 1880s and 1890s gave a fillip to speed, as did personal exchanges with American reporters, who began to report regularly from London after the construction of a transatlantic cable in 1866. "Beats" and "scoops" became a part of the vocabulary of British journalism. Penny-a-liners rushed about looking for stories that might earn them space in newspapers. John Passmore Edwards, the editor-proprietor of the *Echo* and a pioneer in "American-style" journalism, sent his reporters into the streets of London in pursuit of news, while Richard Whiteing, who was acclaimed for his rapid "descriptive writing," observed: "We old stagers had the sense of holiday, if we managed to get away before two in the morning, when we staggered to our cabs at the door, to take a first installment of sleep on our way home."[25] Newspapers like T. P. O'Connor's *Sun* and Alfred Harmsworth's *Daily Mail* ("the busy man's daily journal"), which was founded in 1896, gave an increased emphasis to speed. O'Connor urged clear, direct writing because "to get your ideas across through the hurried eyes into the whirling brains that are employed in the reading of a newspaper there must be no mistake about your meaning." Bernard Falk, writing at a slightly later period for the *Daily Mail*, observed: "The storm, rush and excitement, the play on the nervous system (on that newspaper), were as much as I could stand even at my age."[26]

Yet despite a shift in British journalism towards speed, cultural differences between the two countries remained significant, and it is important to keep this in mind if one is to understand fully changes in print journalism during these years. Until after 1914 an "American-style" emphasis on speed continued to be mostly regarded as socially and culturally unacceptable by those working in British journalism. The historian Bernard Weisberger has encapsulated the two respective approaches: "racy, aggressive, and independent" in the United States; "solid, careful, and slightly bent under a sense of official responsibility" in Britain.[27] William H. Russell, the Special Correspondent of *The Times*, exemplified the latter approach until the end of his career. He always took time before sending a news dispatch. He made little use of the telegraph, preferring to write leisurely accounts of events, and whenever possible he revisited the site of a battlefield or a crime scene before setting pen to paper. Another leading *Times* correspondent, Henri de Blowitz, cultivated information by confidential means and sought to convey news discreetly. He believed that access to reliable sources was more important than speed. Even after reporting from the Continent for several decades he insisted on using the word "letters" to describe his communications rather than "dispatches," which by then was the more commonly used term.[28]

As late as 1900 speed was not highly prized in many British newspaper offices. The Park Row area in lower Manhattan, where New York's leading newspapers were published, was described by a contemporary as "seething and bubbling," as was "Newspaper Row" in Washington. By comparison, Fleet Street was much quieter.[29] American city reporters were generally assigned beats, or territories, to cover, and told to "chase" news and employ personal initiative to dig for stories. They tried to outdo competitors by following up unexpected leads. Their British counterparts generally moved at a more leisurely pace. In the late nineteenth century, the practice in London and Manchester was still for reporters to be given assignments by their editors when they reported for work, or more commonly to receive assignments in advance by post. Sometimes this produced solid results, as at the time of the Ripper murders in 1888, when British reporters scoured the East End of London in pursuit of "picturesque and lurid" details of the crimes. More often than not, it made for a diminished "news sense," in the words of the press historian and journalist, Harold Herd.[30]

John Augustus O'Shea first came to London in the 1870s to work for the *Standard*, one of the more enterprising morning newspapers. Initially, he spent most of the day "killing time." When he complained to his editor he was told: "Upon my word, you are a most unreasonable fellow. Don't you get paid regularly? We cannot invent work for you." Lincoln Springfield, another famous reporter, relied exclusively on agency reports when covering the general election of 1895 for the *Pall Mall Gazette*. He reported from six northern constituencies "without setting foot in them."[31] The famous sports tipster, "Captain Coe," covered racing for the *Echo* and the *Star* in a similar fashion. He stayed in his office and awaited telegrams from "watchers" at the tracks but hardly ever went there himself. In 1902, American reporters covering the coronation of Edward the Seventh in Westminster Abbey beat their British rivals decisively by smuggling copy out of the church in segments, telephoning it to their London offices, and then having it cabled to the United States.

One cultural attribute of American journalists related to speed and much noted at the time, was their seeming informality. Their dress code at work was often considered by Britons to be vulgar; even worse, on some newspapers reporters mingled freely with editors. Such practices were barred in Fleet Street, where propriety took precedence over speed, even as traditional ways of doing things were gradually subverted by the "hurry-skurry of …modern life."[32] Police reporters in Britain, for example, still wore frock coats and top hats to work in the 1890s, and many continued to do so until after 1914. Lord Northcliffe, the chief innovator in British popular journalism, firmly rejected any derogation from a rigid dress code. He required his employees to dress formally, even when on a "hurry call" in pursuit of news. According to Philip Gibbs, he was prepared to lose "important news for the lack of this livery," a proprietary decision that it is almost impossible to conceive either Pulitzer or Hearst being called upon to make.[33] On British newspapers, speed was associated with "the rushing routines of the lower ranks of reporting," where a dress code was of little importance. True reporters (that is, those above the level of penny-a-liners) were held to a higher standard. At a reception for George the Sixth and Queen Elizabeth in New York in 1939, several British reporters admitted to feeling "half-naked in lounge suits, instead of cutaways," as they stood next to a representative of the *New York Daily News* who was comfortably attired in a green suit and white polo socks. To compound his felony this reporter stabbed his forefinger rudely in the direction of the queen while attempting to interview her.[34]

The method of journalism that most sharply differentiated American from British journalism was interviewing. In a brilliant essay by Michael Schudson, the interview has been described as "a vital, characteristic cultural invention and cultural force."[35] Schudson's point is that interviewing reflects the qualities of a particular cultural milieu, in this instance nineteenth-century America with its informality, seeming aggressiveness, and most of all, obsession with speed. The interview helped to fashion a "democratic" brew that equalized the balance between the press and authority; it also provided (in the words of the former BBC political editor Andrew Marr) "the best adrenaline-pumping entertainment you can have sometimes."[36] Interviewing was a distinctively American creation, as W. T. Stead, Edmund Yates, and other British writers who integrated it into Britain's New Journalism acknowledged, and by 1914 it had become a mainstay in the world of transatlantic print. Yet modes of interviewing were different in each country, and a closer look at these makes clear the usefulness of a cultural analysis of journalism.

The practice of interviewing began in the 1830s during the coverage of a famous murder case in New York City by Bennett's *Herald* and took hold of the American imagination in the 1870s and 1880s, as interviews of celebrities and politicians in newspapers like the *Herald* and Pulitzer's *New York World* provided a surfeit of information and entertainment. According to Pulitzer, public people were "public property," and interviews should be conducted rapidly and with little concern for privacy. "Impertinent" American interviewers stalked their prey, using a rapid crossfire technique of interrogation to elicit information that was sometimes of a highly personal nature. Speed clearly trumped privacy, as omnipresent reporters breached the levees of social reserve. A prominent Chicago lawyer, for example, gave an interview to the Chicago reporter Fred Wile, while leaning out of his window in the middle of the night attired in his pajamas.[37] Politicians, who were often on a first-name basis with American reporters, a practice unheard of in Britain, acceded to interviews in the belief that they could manipulate the news in their favor, an early form of "spinning." Actresses vied for publicity, even (as is true today) if this meant little more than some transient scuttlebutt in the next day's paper.

Literary lions also participated in this slippery journalistic terrain. When Arnold Bennett visited the United States in 1911, he feared the worst because of "the great national sport of interviewing," with its notoriously rude interlocutors. Bennett stated: "I trembled. I wanted to sit, but dared not. They stood; I stood." As it turned out, the rapid-fire questions of the interviewers were not quite as offensive as Bennett feared, although their vapidity could not be gainsaid. Hundreds of thousands of readers, for example, learned the following morning that "the most salient part of (Bennett) was (his) teeth" and that he "behaved like a school-boy." G. K. Chesterton similarly remarked that American interviewing was "always very rapid" and typified "many of the qualities of American dentistry."[38] Interviewers in America rarely used shorthand. Their aim was to extrapolate the essence of the subject quickly by means of a "personal write-up," which was direct and on the record. This abjuration of objectivity, an ideal increasingly prized in other aspects of American journalism, meant that accuracy was often sacrificed to speed. As an American writer commented in the 1890s, though with considerable overstatement, some journalists wrote interviews with "people they never saw (and) put words in the mute lips of dying men."[39]

In Britain interviewing became increasingly popular by the 1880s, which meant that the chronological gap between the journalisms of the two countries in this area was relatively narrow. Stead was the pioneer interviewer, in his *Pall Mall Gazette*, where he published about 140 interviews. He believed that interviewing was the "most interesting method for extracting the ideas of the few for the instruction of the many which has yet been devised by man," and he championed the democratic foundations which he believed underlay it.[40] Yet British interviewing, including that by Stead, remained formalized in a way alien to American culture. Partly this had to do with a sense of place; partly it was a result of traditional self-restraint. As the journalist Harold Spender observed, "The high places of English life were clothed in decorum and silence."[41] Thus it was nearly impossible to engage in rapid "door-step" interviews with politicians in Britain, as was a common practice in America. British interviews were arranged by formal appointment, sometimes as long as ten days in advance. Even in the Commons, where a lobby system was evolving, reporters were obliged to congregate in a special place and wait to be approached by members of parliament.[42]

Information derived from interviews was often passed along slowly, by confidential means or in the form of leading articles, as was the practice of mid-Victorian editors like John T. Delane of *The Times*. In the 1890s, Frank Banfield conducted more than 100 interviews with politicians, churchmen, and military figures for several London newspapers. He described these as "conversations" because he believed that they signified "the temporary alliance of two intelligent men on level terms," which was very different from the American conception of an interview. An anecdote involving the Chicago reporter, Fred Wile, points up the barriers in transferring the speedy style of American interviewing to another cultural milieu. Wile was covering Berlin for the *Daily Mail* in 1906, and as an "American-trained" journalist he sought to get an impromptu interview with Viscount Haldane, the British Secretary of State for War. This horrified the "smug, typically John Bullish correspondent" of the London *Morning Post*, since by custom ministers of the Crown were never "molested" by journalists, particularly when they were abroad. However, Wile persisted, got his interview, and was then hired on a permanent basis by Northcliffe.[43]

The formal process involved in setting up interviews in Britain was an obstacle to speed, but even more significant was the languid structure that shaped them. American reporters eschewed shorthand because it slowed them down, whereas in Britain interviewers, though not Stead, used shorthand for accuracy and because they sought to publish a verbatim transcript of the questions and answers. This desultory process meant getting approval of the text from the interviewee and making changes in it before publication. Even Stead did not publish interviews until his subjects signed off on them. By admission he also avoided questions that were "too personal or unduly intimate." Raymond Blathwayt, who specialized in celebrity interviews for several British newspapers, always sent his subjects an advance proof copy. He rationalized the practice by describing American-style interviewing as a "trade," whereas its British counterpart was a "profession." According to Blathwayt, the task of the reporter was "to raise (interviewing) out of a very slough of despond into its own legitimate place in journalism."[44]

In fairness, cultural restraints against "American-style" speed sometimes operated as a barrier on both sides of the Atlantic. The American journalist, Edward Price Bell, who did "high level" interviewing for the *Chicago Daily News* as head of its foreign news service in London, also showed his texts to his subjects before publishing them, and the *New York Times*, following upon a traditional model of journalism, published only a handful of interviews before 1914.[45] By then press conditions were being transformed as a result of wartime pressures, and the "American newspaper interview...ceased to be a shocking innovation" in Britain.[46]

Three key advances in technology in the nineteenth century gave a pronounced stimulus to the use of speed in journalism, and in each instance American cultural mores proved more receptive. These inventions were the telegraph, the typewriter, and the telephone. The telegraph was the core innovation in that it made possible a quantum leap in the collection and distribution of news. It influenced almost every aspect of journalism, including the rise of wire agencies, stylistic changes and a tendency towards more "objective" news reporting, and the use of the "inverted pyramid," beginning in the 1880s, which has been described as equivalent to serving the dessert before the main course. The first dispatches sent by wire appeared in newspapers in both countries in the mid-1840s. However, within a few years most American cities were connected by wire, whereas the process was took much more time in Britain.[47]

There were significant milestones in the development of the telegraph: the construction of a Washington-New York line in 1846, which ensured the rapid transmission of news from the nation's capital to its foremost urban center; the creation of a link between the east and west coasts of North America by wire in 1861; and perhaps most important, the completion of an underwater cable between Europe and the United States in 1866. By the 1850s, routine political news was distributed by wire in America, and in the following decade the Civil War became the first military conflict in the world to be systematically reported in this way. Although the cost of transmission by wire remained high, a factor that made its interplay with journalism problematic for a time, by the late nineteenth century the generic heading 'LATEST BY TELEGRAPH' began to appear with increasing frequency in American newspapers.[48]

London newspapers like *The Times* and the *Daily News* also made use of the telegraph, though more slowly. The construction of a Dover-Calais cable in 1851 (followed two years later by a link between London and Ostend) greatly speeded up news reporting. Yet, not until the Franco-Prussian War of 1870–71 did the British press become substantially "wired," and American press bureaus like that of the *New York Tribune*, headed by the enterprising George Smalley, were largely responsible for this. Until late in the century national news in Britain was distributed primarily by rail partly because this ensured the dominance of the London press over its provincial rivals. A seminal difference between the two countries is that the critical Washington-New York axis, linking politics to journalism, has no parallel in the latter country. London was and is the center of both politics and journalism, with Fleet Street being only about a mile from Westminster. For many years, therefore, foot messengers continued to carry parliamentary and other reports to London newspaper offices for a fraction of the cost of the telegraph.

The rise of wire agencies in both countries is too large a story to narrate here. Suffice it to say that American press agencies emerged at an earlier period than those in Britain. The New York Associated Press was established in 1848 and it preceded the founding of both the Central Press (1863) and the Press Association (1868), Britain's two chief domestic agencies. Reuters came into existence in 1851, but it did not begin to sell news directly to papers until seven years later, and not until the 1870s did it became a byword for foreign news distribution by making use of a network of international telegraphs and cables. Likewise, with a distinct chronological edge to the United States, newspapers in both countries created their own press services to complement the agencies and organized direct access to their offices by wire to beat their competitors to the latest domestic and overseas news.[49]

Many factors shaped the use of the telegraph but when taken together with the typewriter and telephone, the cultural receptivity to speed at an earlier period in the United States becomes clear. "Fast news" was especially prized in America. By the 1850s about 8 percent of American news stories were reported by wire, and within a decade this percentage was much higher. By the 1880s, the time lag for domestic news was about a half day and for foreign news no more than two days. Speed was prized even in the workings of the telegraph. In 1879 the Phillips Code was invented in the United States as a replacement for the Morse code, and by substituting 3,500 abbreviations for the full spelling of words it increased operator speed by nearly 30 percent.[50]

After mid-century, nearly every American paper trumpeted its claims to foreshortening time in the delivery of news, particularly during the Civil War when the hunger for information reached unprecedented heights. The telegraph very nearly became an obsession in America. The immense distances separating cities like New York, Chicago, San Francisco, and St Louis could only be overcome, psychologically as well as physically, by speed. As the British reporter, Bennett Burleigh, stated: "It is an age of hurry."[51] Such an age, with its slippage in standards but greatly increased efficiency, found a more secure footing in the United States.

The typewriter and the telephone affected journalism similarly, though neither invention was securely established in newspaper offices until the beginning of the twentieth century. However, both were fulsomely welcomed by Pulitzer in the 1880s and became a key element of "yellow journalism." Although some American journalists opposed the use of typewriters in the belief that they would stifle personal journalism, they came to be widely used by the Associated Press and by "rewrite" men on evening newspapers who received dispatches by telegraph and then typed rapid copy for the printers. In the 1890s, typewriting bureaus sprang up in the vicinity of Park Row, in lower Manhattan. By 1907, typewriters were commonly regarded as essential newspaper equipment in America.[52]

This was not nearly as true in Britain, where resistance to their use was considerable. The one notable exception was T. P. O'Connor, who welcomed typewriters primarily because they brought about an increase in speed. O'Connor used a typewriter when writing his political sketches in the House of Commons and also typed a weekly letter for the *New York Sun*, a practice which was regarded as daring for the time. In 1931, an authoritative textbook on British journalism declared that the typewriter was 'indispensable," even though "up to a few years ago, there was a considerable prejudice against it in reporters' rooms."[53]

The telephone followed a similar trajectory. It found a more ready home among American journalists, and according to one historian had taken a hold in that country's press by 1902.[54] As with the telegraph, which it essentially replaced, its major selling point was the enormous compression of time it brought about. The vastness of America worked in its favor as did the more ready acceptance of "intrusiveness." As with mobile phones today, early telephones were regarded as noisy and detrimental to privacy. People shouted into receivers and often had to redial before making a connection. This was less tolerated in Britain, where the word "call" signified a personal visit instead of a telephone call. Not surprisingly, a historian of the telephone has described the United States as being its "natural home."[55]

In Britain, even the commercial possibilities of the telephone were viewed as uncertain, to the extent that the Bank of England did not begin to use telephones until after 1900. And in newsrooms the practice of using telephones took root slowly. Archibald Forbes, the great war correspondent, spoke for an earlier generation when he exclaimed upon seeing his fellow journalists using telephones: "My God! What would Herodotus say to this?" *The Times* briefly established a telephone line in the Commons for its parliamentary reporters but then abandoned the practice in 1894, while in 1900 most British reporters still relied on "flimsies," or carbons, to distribute local news stories and on the telegraph for stories sent at a longer distance.[56] After the turn of the century telephones began to be used more frequently: by provincial newspapers in the collection of football and racing results and, increasingly, by reporters for evening papers who telephoned their stories to editors and "rewrite" men. As with the typewriter, O'Connor was the chief advocate of the telephone among British journalists, although he was joined by Northcliffe, who insisted that his reporters use telephones and was so obsessed with them that he wanted to be near one to his dying day.[57] By 1910, or roughly a decade after the United States, telephones were in widespread use in British newspaper offices.

In this essay I have sought to indicate some of the ways in which the cultural concept of speed took root earlier and with greater enthusiasm among American journalists. The transatlantic context in which speed came to be accepted was consequential because Anglo-American interchanges were part of a complex web in which the two journalisms paralleled and interacted with each other. The specific ways in which this intersection occurred have been only lightly touched upon in this essay, but they involved a complicated fabric of personal, technological, economic, and, above all, cultural threads. I have tried to indicate the relevance of cultural influence and to make clear that by focusing on a single construct – in this instance, the increasing resonance of the idea of speed – it is possible to shed light comparatively on two national press histories that are closely bound together by language and background.

Notes

1 Richard A. Schwarzlose, *The Nation's Newsbrokers, Vol. II; The Rush to Institution, from 1865 to 1920* (Evanston: Northwestern University Press, 1989), 121.

2 Stephen Kern, *The Culture of Time and Space, 1880–1918* (London: Weidenfeld and Nicolson, 1983), 129.

3 The quote is by the American reporter, Julius Chambers, in *News Hunting on Three Continents* (London: John Lane, The Bodley Head, 1921), 4; Kinglake's words are in T. H. S. Escott, *Masters of English Journalism: A Study of Personal Forces* (London: T. Fisher Unwin, 1911), 347; James Bryce, *The American Commonwealth* (London: Macmillan and Co., 1888), vol. III, 566.

4 Evelyn March Phillipps, "The New Journalism," *New Review*, vol. XIII (1895), 182.

5 Leon Paul Blouet, "Lively Journalism," *North American Review*, vol. CL (1890), 366.

6 Jeremy Tunstall, *The Media are American: Anglo-American Media in the World* (London: Constable, 1977); Jeremy Tunstall, *The Anglo-American Media Connection*, (Oxford: Oxford University Press, 1999); Mark Hampton, *Visions of the Press in Britain, 1850–1950* (Urbana: University of Illinois Press, 2004). See my essay entitled, "The Americanization of the British Press, 1830–1914" in *Studies in Newspaper and Periodical History*, 1994 Annual,

ed. Michael Harris and Tom O'Malley (Westport: Greenwood Press, 1996), 61–75.

7 Michael Schudson, *The Power of News* (Cambridge: Harvard University Press, 1995); David A. Copeland, *Colonial American Newspapers: Character and Content* (Newark: University of Delaware Press, 1997); Martin Conboy, *Journalism: A Critical History* (London: Sage Publications, 2004).

8 For examples of two recent studies of considerable merit, which in my judgment lean too strongly towards an economic interpretation, see Gerald J. Baldasty, *The Commercialization of News in the Nineteenth Century* (Madison: The University of Wisconsin Press, 1992) and Jean K. Chalaby, *The Invention of Journalism* (London: Macmillan Press, 1998). For social control, see James Curran, "The Press as an Agency of Social Control: an Historical Perspective" in George Boyce, James Curran and Pauline Wingate (eds.), *Newspaper History: From the 17th Century to the Present Day* (London: Constable, 1978), 51–75. Curran has modified his views in recent years and has become one of the most astute commentators on the British press. For example, see Curran, "Media and the Making of British Society, c 1700–2000" in *Media History*, vol. VIII (2002), 135–54.

9 Quoted in Frederic Hudson, *Journalism in the United States, from 1690 to 1872* (New York: Haskell House Publishers, 1968; first published in 1873), 541.

10 Theodore Dreiser, *A Book About Myself* (London: Constable, 1929), 152.

11 Frederic William Wile, *News is Where You Find It: Forty Years' Reporting at Home and Abroad* (Indianapolis: The Bobbs-Merrill Company, 1939), 43.

12 Hudson's quote is in Louis M. Starr, *Bohemian Brigade: Civil War Newsmen in Action* (New York: Alfred A. Knopf, 1954), 12; John Augustus O'Shea, *Roundabout Recollections* (London: Ward and Downey, 1892), vol. I, 233.

13 Melville E. Stone, *Fifty Years a Journalist* (London: Curtis, Brown, 1921), 117.

14 John T. McCutcheon, *Drawn From Memory* (Indianapolis: The Bobbs-Merrill Company, 1950), 63.

15 Martin Mayer, *Making News* (Garden City: Doubleday & Company, 1987), 46.

16 Charles Dickens, *American Notes for General Circulation* (Leipzig: Bernhard Tauchnitz, 1842), 301.

17 Howells referred to an "uproar so frantic that you would think they would go mad of it." (*Through the Eye of the Needle: A Romance* (London: Harper and Brothers, Publishers, 1907), 10).

18 The reference to manufactured speeches is in Laura Stedman and George M. Gould, *Life and Letters of Edmund Clarence Stedman* (New York: Moffet, Yard and Company, 1910), vol. I, 169.

19 Isaac F. Marcossen, *Adventures in Interviewing* (London: John Lane, The Bodley Head, 1920), 75; David Nasaw, *The Chief: The Life of William Randolph Hearst* (Boston: Houghton Mifflin Company, 2000), 127. Nasaw claims there is no evidence for the authenticity of this telegram.

20 The quote by Fox is in Baldasty, 90.

21 James Creelman, *On the Great Highway: The Wanderings and Adventures of a Special Correspondent* (London: Charles H. Kelly, 1901), 61–2.

22 Charles Pebody, *English Journalism and the Men Who Have Made It* (London: Cassell, Petter, Galpin & Co., 1882), 24.

23 H. W. Massingham, *The London Daily Press* (London: The Religious Tract Society), 181.
24 The reference to the Farringdon newsroom is in Charles A. Cooper, *An Editor's Retrospect: Fifty Years of Newspaper Work* (London: Macmillan and Co., 1896), 88.
25 For Edwards, see Harold Spender, *The Fire of Life: A Book of Memories* (London: Hodder and Stoughton, 1926), 22–3; Richard Whiteing, *My Harvest* (New York: Dodd, Mead & Company, 1915), 279.
26 The O'Connor quote is in Conboy, 172; Bernard Falk, *He Laughed in Fleet Street* (London: Hutchinson & Co., 1933), 91.
27 Bernard A. Weisberger, *The American Newspaperman* (Chicago: The University of Chicago Press, 1961), 3.
28 Frank Giles, *A Prince of Journalists: The Life and Times of Henri Stefan Opper de Blowitz* (London: Faber and Faber, 1962), 55–6.
29 James Edward Rogers, *The American Newspaper* (Chicago: The University of Chicago Press, 1909), 16.
30 L. Perry Curtis, Jr., *Jack the Ripper and the London Press* (New Haven: Yale University Press, 2001), 108; Harold Herd, *The Making of Modern Journalism* (London: George Allen & Unwin, 1927), 55.
31 John Augustus O'Shea, *Leaves from the Life of a Special Correspondent* (London: Ward and Downey, 1885), vol. II, 310; Lincoln Springfield, *Some Piquant People* (London: T. Fisher Unwin, 1924), 40, 129.
32 Francis Leupp, "The Waning Power of the Press," *The Atlantic Monthly*, vol. CV (1910), 146.
33 The Gibbs quote is in Cosmo Hamilton, *People Worth Talking About* (Freeport: Books for Libraries Press, 1970, first published in 1933), 110.
34 See C. V. R. Thompson, *I Lost My English Accent* (New York: G. P. Putnam's Sons, 1939), 284, 289, 294–5.
35 Schudson, 50.
36 See Andrew Marr, "Unleashing Humphrys or Paxo as a Democratic Service," *British Journalism Review*, vol. XVI (2005), 13–23.
37 Wile, 57–8.
38 Arnold Bennett, *Those United States* (Leipzig: Bernard Tauchnitz, 1912), 19–23. The Chesterton quote is taken from Christopher Silvester (ed.), *The Penguin Book of Interviews: An Anthology from 1859 to the Present Day* (London: Viking, 1993), 18.
39 Quoted in Baldasty, 90.
40 Raymond L. Schults, *Crusader in Babylon: W. T. Stead and the Pall Mall Gazette* (Lincoln: University of Nebraska Press, 1972), 86.
41 Spender, 30.
42 John Boon, *Victorians, Edwardians, and Georgians: The Impressions of a Journalist Extending Over Forty Years* (London: Hutchin & Co. (Publishers)), 1928), vol. I, 223.
43 Wile, 152.
44 Raymond Blathwayt, *Interviews* (London: A. W. Hall, 1893), 352–3.
45 James D. Startt, *Journalism's Unofficial Ambassador: A Biography of Edward Price Bell, 1869–1943* (Ohio University Press, 1979), 59.
46 Willis J. Abbot, *Watching the World Go By* (London: John Lane, The Bodley Head, 1933), 270.

47   Schwarzlose, 395; Henry R. Fox Bourne, *English Newspapers: Chapters in the History of Journalism* (London: Chatto & Windus, 1887), vol. II, 138.
48   On the expenses of sending telegrams, see George W. Smalley, *Anglo-American Memories* (London: Duckworth & Co., 1911), 145. Horace Greeley told a *Tribune* reporter in 1850: "I will thank you to send by telegraph rather than the slower way. Bear in mind that expense is no object in the matter of early advices." Quoted in Henry Luther Stoddard, *Horace Greeley: Printer, Editor, Crusader* (New York: G. P. Putnam's Sons, 1946), 144.
49   On Reuters, see Donald Read, *The Power of News: The History of Reuters, 1849–1989* (Oxford: Oxford University Press, 1992). A journalist observed in the 1890s: "Thanks to Reuter, there is not a provincial newspaper in England which does not supply better telegraphic news from abroad than could be found thirty years ago in any newspaper in the world." T. Wemyss Reid, "Some Reminiscences of English Journalism," *Nineteenth Century*, vol. XXXXII (1897), 60.
50   J. Steven Smethers, "Pounding Brass for the Associated Press: Delivering News by Telegraph in a Pre-Teletype Era," *American Journalism*, vol. XIX (2002), 18.
51   Quoted in R. J. Wilkinson-Latham, *From Our Special Correspondent: Victorian War Correspondents and Their Campaigns* (London: Hodder & Stoughton, 1979), 107.
52   In the late 1880s, James Gordon Bennett, Jr. would not allow typewriters to be used on the *Herald*. (Stephen Bonsal, *Heyday in a Vanished World* (New York, W. W. Norton & Co., 1937), 15.
53   The resistance to typewriters is mentioned in John St Loe Strachey, *The Adventure of Living: A Subjective Autobiography* (London: Hodder and Stoughton, 1922), 198; C. F. Carr and F. E. Stevens, *Modern Journalism: A Complete Guide to the Newspaper Craft* (London: Sir Isaac Pitmans & Sons, 1931), 17.
54   John L. Given, *Making a Newspaper* (London: Williams & Norgate, 1907), 204.
55   Charles R. Perry, "The British Experience 1876–1912: The Impact of the Telephone During the Years of Delay," in Ithiel de Sola Pool (ed.), *The Social Impact of the Telephone* (Cambridge: The MIT Press, 1977), 69–96; John Brooks, *The Telephone: The First Hundred Years* (New York: Harper & Row, Publishers, 1975), 118.
56   The Forbes quote is in Bonsal, 414. On the flimsies, see G. Binney Dibblee, *The Newspaper* (London: Henry Holt and Company, 1913), 51. Arnold Bennett wrote: "The European telephone is a toy, and a somewhat clumsy one, compared with the inexorable seriousness of the American telephone." *Those United States*, 91.
57   Peter Young, *Person to Person: The International Aspect of the Telephone* (Granta Editions, 1991), 111.

Part II
People

4
Matt Morgan and Transatlantic Illustrated Journalism, 1850–90

Christopher Kent

The career of the Anglo-American artist Matthew Somerville Morgan illuminates some of the connections linking developments in illustrated journalism in Britain and the United States during a period of explosive growth and technological transformation. Although popular demand for printed pictures is as old as print itself, most pictorial reproductions were produced from metal plate engravings which were not only costly but, being engraved in *intaglio*, could not be printed together with raised type. However the wooden block, engraved in relief, made it possible to print a page combining letterpress and illustration in a single operation, an essential precondition for mass-market pictorial journalism. As is well known, the first two journals to effectively cash in on this formula were *Punch* and the *Illustrated London News*, first appearing in 1841 and 1842 respectively. Imitators were quick to follow and the supply of wood engravers expanded rapidly to meet demand, as did that of illustrators to draw on the blocks. Matt Morgan had won a considerable name for himself as a commercial artist in London, when he decided to take his talents to the United States, where he was to become even better known as an unusually versatile popular artist and illustrator.

Morgan was born into London's artistic community in 1836.[1] His father was a minor actor and music teacher, his mother a minor actress and singer; an uncle was a *mezzotint* engraver and portrait artist of some reputation. At age 14 he was apprenticed to the leading London scene painting partnership of Thomas Grieve and William Telbin and was soon designing and painting for the lavish, scenery-dominated productions of Charles Kean. The gentlemanly Kean, ever mindful of the fact that he had been sent to Eton by his father, the celebrated actor Edmund Kean, was preoccupied with elevating the social status of the theater. He became a favorite of the young Queen Victoria and as a result Morgan had the opportunity to work at Windsor Castle preparing scenery for the special productions Kean staged there at the Queen's request. Morgan completed his apprenticeship at a time when London was entering a theater boom and demand for scene painters was high. Scene painters enjoyed public recognition: they were given individual credits on programs and the more successful received star billing in theater advertisements. Before age 30 Morgan would become one of London's leading theater artists. He was chief scene painter at the Theatre Royal in Covent Garden, where he enjoyed the privilege of a curtain call to acknowledge audience applause for the spectacular transformation scenes that he produced for the annual Christmas pantomime. By the time he was 30 he was at the top of a respectable and well-paid occupation. However it didn't contain his energies and ambitions. Many scene painters pursued the profitable sideline of painting small watercolor land and seascapes, utilizing their adeptness in creating picturesque atmospheric effects. Indeed some, such as Clarkson Stanfield and David Roberts, left scene painting altogether for successful careers as "high" artists. Early on Morgan pursued a course of self-education to extend his artistic skills and widen his career options.

Demand for illustrators in London during the 1850s and 1860s was even greater than for scene painters, and the field less regulated. Little training, or even talent, was needed to at least get a footing in that world. The way to employment was through the wood engravers, a tightly knit group who had learned their craft by apprenticeship to its leaders, engraving dynasties such as the Smiths, Thomases, Vizetellys, Dalziels, Whympers and Landells who largely dominated it through their family firms. To draw effectively on wood it helped to have a knowledge of engraving, as did some of the most successful artists in the medium like the extraordinarily prolific John Gilbert and the celebrated *Punch* artists John Leech and Charles Kean, all of whom received training as wood engravers. Engravers were often the dominant figures in the production of illustrated periodicals and books. Ebenezer Landells and Henry Vizetelly were the central figures in the launching of *Punch* and the *Illustrated London News*. Subsequently Vizetelly would start the *Illustrated Times* and George Luson Thomas would start the *Graphic* as successful rivals to the *Illustrated London News*. These were the men who largely controlled the commissioning of woodcut illustrations. Morgan, a young man with social and entrepreneurial as well as artistic talents, began early to make contacts in this somewhat Bohemian business. In 1856 he was living with his father in Islington in a house previously occupied and probably owned by one of the Dalziel brothers.

In 1858 Morgan's first known illustrations appeared in both the *Illustrated London News* and the *Illustrated Times*, by then co-owned sister journals. He had traveled in the previous year to Algeria, where he may have encountered another young English artist, Frederick Leighton, who was also there in 1857 searching for the mastery of the human form which ultimately brought him the Presidency of the Royal Academy. Algiers was an increasingly popular destination for the more adventurous Victorian tourist who had heard of its mysterious Casbah and sought the thrill of the alien combined with the security of European rule. English tuberculosis victims in search of a suitable climate had already begun to make it one of the chief sanitoriums of the Mediterranean. For those Britons who could not afford, or face, the real thing there was vicarious tourism. As an apprentice Morgan would have been involved in the production of the highly successful panorama "The Overland Route," painted by Grieve and Telbin and exhibited in London in 1850–51. At the Gallery of Illustration in Regent Street a quarter of a million visitors paid to see the series of 31 large scenes unroll before their eyes, depicting the route taken by the Imperial mails to India via Gibraltar, the Mediterranean and, overland to the Red Sea. Not surprisingly the *Illustrated London News* decided that Morgan's "Sketch Book of a Recent Tourist in Algeria," with its market scenes and depictions of mysterious Moorish women, would bring a suitable taste of the exotic into the living rooms of its arch-*bourgeois* readership.[2]

The Victorians' "Mediterranean Passion" also heightened popular interest in the unification of Italy, which took a step closer to realization when hostilities broke out in northern Italy between France and Austria in 1859.[3] Morgan was among the artists covering this war, and his pictures were again published in both the *Illustrated London News* and the *Illustrated Times*. Most were published under the caption "from a sketch by M. Morgan" and were drawn onto the woodblock in London by staff artists working from drawings sent in by post. This short war climaxed in the battles of Magenta and Solferino where the slaughter so appalled the French Emperor Louis Napoleon that he decided to bring it to an end, and the sight of the dead and wounded left behind on the battlefield caused a passing Swiss witness to form the International Red Cross. A few years earlier the two leading illustrated papers had covered the Crimean War with artists whose on-the-spot pictures of that bloody and ill-managed war had helped to feed public disenchantment and bring down the government. The career of war artist was born, and henceforth these adventurous illustrators sketched battlefields throughout the world until sufficiently fast camera films made them redundant in the early twentieth century.

Also in Italy covering the war for the *Illustrated Times* was Henry Vizetelly's brother Frank who would later portray the American Civil War for the *Illustrated London News* and die in action as a war artist in Sudan. Morgan however chose not to depict the fighting: His pictures include a fine marine scene with French troops landing in boats from distant troopships at Genoa, and several group scenes of Austrian and French soldiers in convivial situations behind the lines. His best illustration, appearing in the *Illustrated London News*, is a dramatic landscape showing French cavalry fording a stream by moonlight with the water splashed by the horses' hooves effectively highlighted (16 July 1859). Such theatrical moonlight effects show his training as a scene painter – not for nothing was his teacher called "Moonlight" Telbin. Interestingly this picture carries Morgan's signature in full, cut into the block – the first time the name which he would make so well known, "Matt. S. Morgan," was published on an illustration. Most illustrations published at this time bore no artist's mark; when they did it usually took the form of a cryptic colophon directed at knowing insiders – chiefly other artists. Morgan was unusual among illustrators in publicly asserting his identity. He was already determined quite literally to make a name for himself in illustrated journalism. He also managed to further publicize himself in print. The *Illustrated London News* printed an engaging despatch from Morgan which gave almost a tourist's eye view of the war, good naturedly bemoaning the tendency of large armies to deplete the supplies of decent food and accommodation. Fortunately he was not an object of public suspicion as were many future war artists who found themselves being mobbed and arrested as enemy spies.[4]

In the following year the cause of uniting Italy sparked a revolution in Sicily led by Giuseppe Garibaldi, who was greatly admired in British radical circles. One such admirer was the engraver W. J. Linton, who organized a British volunteer force to join him. Morgan however stayed in London. Yet his full signature appears on a scene of the Sicilian revolution "drawn from a sketch by our special artist, Frank Vizetelly" (*ILN* 16 June 1860). Had he gone to Sicily he would have encountered a future rival, the young German-born artist Thomas Nast, who was sketching the war for the *New York Illustrated News*.[5] Morgan did not like war, as his cartoons for a new journal called *Fun* would soon make clear. He was now a family man, having just married Caroline Smith, orphan daughter of the distinguished wood engraver John Orrin Smith and the ward of Linton who had been her father's partner. Morgan's marriage tightened his ties to the world of wood engravers and illustrators. Henry Vizetelly had been a pupil of Orrin Smith. His new brother-in-law Harvey, who took the name Orrinsmith, had succeeded to the family partnership with Linton. A contemporary guide listed Morgan among Britain's 40 "professional draughtsmen on wood," as a specialist in "figures and landscape."[6] The *Post Office Directory* lists him in 1859 and 1860 at addresses near Fleet Street shared with leading wood engravers, all of whom he was working or would soon work with, including William Luson Thomas, the future founder of the *Graphic*, which became the *Illustrated London News'* most distinguished competitor. Morgan's work regularly appeared in the latter journal, and in the *British Lion*, a new journal connected with it, but in 1861 his work as chief cartoonist for *Fun*, a comic journal established as a rival to *Punch*, became a major occupation.

Morgan's growing skill as a draftsman is evident in the greater confidence and freedom of line that can be seen in his work. Despite his lack of academic training he learned from the work of other artists and illustrators, including such contemporary continental masters as Gustave Dore and H. G. S. Gavarni, both of whom worked in Britain as illustrators, and the great German artists Adolf von Menzel and Alfred Rethel. He also paid close attention to the talented artists on wood who were working for *Punch*, John Leech, John Tenniel, and Charles Keene. Another opportunity for self-improvement was provided by the Artists' Society, a cooperative club of professional artists who met regularly to sketch from a live model and profit from each others' work and comment. The quality of English periodicals illustration was advancing dramatically at this time. The 1860s would be a golden era for woodcut art as a number of new journals came into existence publishing serial fiction of the highest quality that required illustration of an equally high standard. Between 1859 and 1862 *Once a Week*, the *Cornhill Magazine*, *Good Words*, and *London Society* were founded, and a number of others followed.

The high quality of engraving promised by such journals, employing the top quality firms like Swain's, Dalziel's, and Linton's, as well as the handsome fees they offered, attracted many of the best of the rising generation of artists. The work of Rossetti, Whistler, Holman Hunt, Leighton, Millais and Poynter (the last three would become successive Presidents of the Royal Academy) began to appear in their pages.

Morgan began to mix with some of them, socially and commercially. In 1862 he opened an art gallery on Berners Street in the heart of London's artists' quarter with the purpose of "placing before the public the works of young artists who may not have access to the ordinary galleries."[7] Among the works on view was one by James McNeill Whistler that had been rejected by the Royal Academy. It was labeled by Morgan – wrongly according to Whistler – *The Woman in White*.[8] Morgan's conviviality is noted in the letters of George du Maurier who was at this time struggling to establish his own artistic career. He entertained at his gallery and at his home in Camden Town among his fast increasing family.[9] He became a member of the Arundel Club, a Bohemian club with a mixed membership of journalists, artists and actors which further extended his social and professional network.[10] In addition to his weekly "big cut," the full-page political cartoon in *Fun*, he regularly did smaller "socials" for that journal that clearly showed the influence of John Leech's work in *Punch*. These were light-hearted views of the world with which he was becoming increasingly familiar – family life and children in particular, but also the world of smart young gentlemen, the theatre, horses, female fashions, servants and holidays abroad. Social insecurity, snobbery and mobility are constant themes. As *Fun*'s chief artist he would have been earning from three to five pounds per week, a solid income at a time when 150 pounds was the average annual income of an artist. To this could be added his earnings from theater work and other projects.

No evidence suggests that Morgan felt demeaned by working at these "lower" forms of art. Scene painting was not an art form for soloists: he was used to working with assistants. And he accepted its ephemerality: such work was destined to be painted over when the play closed or be consumed by the frequent fires that destroyed theater scenery. The compensation was a mass audience for as long as it lasted. Illustrating periodicals was similar. Pictures drawn on wood were at the mercy of the engraver and the printer. They too left behind no "original": after the press run the block would be planed down and reused, since the close-grained Turkish boxwood was expensive. But several hundred thousand readers might see the engraving. Some of Britain's top practitioners of "high" art were willing to accept such terms. Not surprisingly however, given his versatility and the circles in which he was beginning to move, Morgan tried his hand at the more prestigious easel art – portraits, seascapes, picturesque scenes – exhibiting his work at some of the secondary London galleries including his own. Ever enterprising, he was also developing yet another specialized line of work, commissioned animal portraits, taking advantage of his growing acquaintanceship among sporting gentlemen who might want a painting of a favorite horse or dog. Among his *Fun* socials is a sketch of an artist attempting to sketch a foxhound while surrounded by the rest of the pack: the artist is a recognizable self-portrait (25 Oct 1862).

By the mid-1860s Morgan's fortunes were at high tide. Few artists in Britain enjoyed greater name recognition among the general public than he did. His pantomime transformation scenes at Covent Garden were described in detail and fulsomely praised in *The Times*. His sporting and society illustrations appeared in the prestigious *London Society* and his melodramatic illustrations for Mrs Braddon's sensation fiction in the mass market *London Journal*. The special Christmas editions of the *Illustrated London News* and *Broadway*, a new journal explicitly aiming at readerships in both Britain and the United States, contained his work. But perhaps his greatest fame, or notoriety, came from his cartoons in the new satirical journal *Tomahawk*, which attracted controversy for their lightly veiled criticism of the Prince of Wales's loose life, and Queen Victoria's abstention from her ceremonial duties and close relationship with her Highland servant John Brown. The exact nature of Morgan's relationship with *Tomahawk*, which commenced publication in May 1867, is unclear. In different sources he is variously described as an employee, manager and even part-owner. What is certain is that he was its chief, virtually its sole, artist. Also certain is that the journal's success was due mainly to his big, sensational cartoons. Some were two-page center-spreads, and most were printed from two blocks – a main detail block giving the conventional black lines, and a tint block overprinting the main block in color. Where the tint block was cut it printed white, which enabled Morgan to produce cloud, moonlight, sunset, lightning flashes, spectral figures, and other lurid theatrical effects that became his trademark. His bold full signature appeared on every *Tomahawk* cartoon, instead of the modest "M" he had been confined to in his *Fun* cuts.

It caught the eye of Frank Leslie, America's biggest publisher of illustrated periodicals. Born Harry Carter, Leslie was a former *Illustrated London News* wood engraver who emigrated to the United States in 1848. He brought with him its founding principle, that in the reader's eyes an illustration confers self-authenticating truthfulness upon a news story. In 1855 he founded the weekly *Frank Leslie's Illustrated Newspaper*, departing from his London model by not avoiding unpleasant domestic issues, such as the filthy conditions in the New York City dairy industry which his artists recorded in a circulation-boosting exposé in 1858. Although on this occasion he protected his artists' identities for their own safety, he explicitly acknowledged and even made heroes of them elsewhere. While the print journalists remained anonymous, his artists received recognition, on occasion even inserting themselves in their illustrations as if to emphasize their credibility. When the Civil War broke out Leslie rose impressively to the challenge, covering it with dozens of artists, though he now faced serious competition in the form of *Harper's Weekly*, founded in 1857. By the end of the war Leslie had created a publishing empire of nearly a dozen illustrated papers selling half a million copies a week and employing 70 wood engravers. One of these was W. J. Linton, for whom he had once worked in London. Widely recognized as one of Britain's finest engravers, Linton, an ardent republican, immigrated to the land of opportunity in 1866. Within two months of arriving he was recruited by his former employee who soon named him "artistic director" of the firm. In America's booming post-war economy the demand for competent engravers and artists outstripped domestic supply, and Leslie was always on the lookout for talent. When he visited England with Linton in 1867 he would not have failed to notice the sensation caused by Morgan's cartoons in *Tomahawk*. They may well have met at this time, either through Linton or their shared tastes as men about town. Leslie was an affable and generous *bon viveur*; so was Morgan, if on a less opulent scale.

Morgan had by now moved from shabby-genteel Islington to Bloomsbury and was moving up socially as well. The young gentlemen of *Tomahawk* were even more posh than the *Fun* set. He got on "like a house on fire" with its editor, Arthur A'Beckett, who considered him "one of the most accomplished men I ever knew."[11] When A'Beckett decided to start the illustrated monthly magazine *Britannia* with financial backing from two of Morgan's rich sporting friends, Charles Hambro of the banking family, and Viscount Newry, a dashing young military bohemian, Morgan became its illustrator. This now scarce journal (the British Library has no set) survived for less than two years. Its text, particularly its rambling serialized novels by A'Beckett, is decidedly third rate. Its merit lies in Morgan's eye-catching illustrations. He did as many as five per issue, including two full-page cuts employing one or more engraved color blocks to add the atmospheric effects now characteristic of his work. The engraver, as for *Tomahawk*, was his friend Thomas Bolton. Morgan was a very fast worker. His strength lay in striking compositions and a free, bold line. He was by now a very competent draftsman when he took care, though at times his figures are a bit crude. Where the theme of the picture was comical he would use a minimally shaded style reminiscent of Leech. Where the theme was melodramatic he employed strong contrast and theatrical lighting effects. His skill in this area could save both himself and his engraver precious time, as for example by combining his favorite moonlight on water effect with a ruined mill in silhouette. Strong back-lighting eliminates the necessity of much foreground detail since it is heavily in shadow. Morgan also did a number of small insert and capital letter sketches, as well as some attractive picturesque landscape vignettes reminiscent of J. M. W. Turner's illustrations for the poems of Samuel Rogers. Interestingly several of the illustrations were produced by a new process called "Graphotype," in which the artist drew on a pressed-chalk surface using a special ink that hardens the chalk. On completing the drawing the artist brushed away the uninked chalk, leaving the drawing in high relief from which a plate could be made.[12] Some of the *Tomahawk* cartoons were also reproduced by this process. Bolton had a reputation as an innovator, and the versatile Morgan was always willing to try something new.

Morgan even wrote a short story for *Britannia*. "Owner for a Year: A Tale of a Racehorse" is the humorous tale of a naive Cockney greengrocer who strays into fast company and finds himself buying a horse in a claiming race: "I was the owner of race horses. I felt a swell. I walked different. I found myself making my arms look bandy and a-carrying my stick different." When he tries to cut a dash by riding his horse in Rotten Row, the horse bolts and throws him and he ends up being charged by the police for reckless riding. It is an engaging little tale about social pretensions and the risks of upward mobility – the theme of countless music hall songs and jokes. Read as a fable the moral is plain: keep to your station in life.[13] This was also the pervasive doctrine of *Tomahawk* – not so much Morgan's cartoons as its articles which have a decidedly top-down, snobbish air to them. Morgan's story, significantly written in the first person, is unique in its bottom-up perspective. Morgan was himself something of a Cockney upstart among many of his new acquaintances. They too were Bohemians, but public school and university-educated gentleman Bohemians, which he wasn't.[14]

Things began to go pear-shaped for Morgan sometime in the late 1860s. Precisely how and why remains unclear. In 1869 he was detained as a bankrupt but released on undertaking to pay off his creditors in full by quarterly installments.[15] It was the mark of a gentleman that tradesmen, or at least high class tailors, bootmakers, wine and tobacco merchants and the like, did not require immediate payment from him, but were happy to charge him more and extend credit for as long as they trusted his means. Morgan was probably living beyond his means, despite his considerable income as an illustrator and scene painter. Caught up in the smart world, indulging his sporting tastes, and supporting a large family, he became overextended. In the summer of 1870 *Tomahawk* mysteriously folded despite its undiminished popularity. *Britannia* expired shortly thereafter. Around this time, too, Morgan's wife, who had given him six children, disappears from view. I can find no mention of divorce, desertion or death: perhaps it was the latter. Morgan remarried. His new wife was a beautiful young actress at the Theatre Royal, Covent Garden.[16] In the late summer of 1870 he slipped off to Spain with her to escape his creditors. His life, according to one commentator, was "a general mess."[17] He needed a new one.

Happily America now beckoned, in the ample form of Frank Leslie. Morgan probably met him in London earlier in 1870 when Leslie was establishing a British edition of his most sensational publication, *Day's Doings*. It contained racy paragraphs about men and women behaving badly, heavily illustrated with spicy pictures of women in wet bathing costumes and other forms of undress. The London edition, which ran for about two years, largely shared plates with the New York edition.[18] Both carried in addition numerous illustrations acquired from French publishers, particularly high quality woodcuts of French Salon art featuring the female nude. Morgan, whose last *Britannia* illustrations were sent from Spain, provided *Day's Doings* with an illustration of Spanish Gypsies dancing at a fiesta.[19] Leslie's periodicals, like many of their increasingly numerous American rivals, used a lot of European illustrations. For example, the just-launched *Every Saturday* borrowed heavily from the London *Graphic*, as did *Harper's*. Leslie had himself drawn extensively on the *Illustrated London News* for many years but was now trying to reduce his reliance on foreign sources and was emphasizing the distinctively American character of his publications.[20] He offered Morgan lucrative employment with his journals in New York. By the autumn of 1871 Morgan was working for Leslie at the extraordinary salary of $10,000 a year. His main employment was as chief cartoonist for *Frank Leslie's Illustrated Newspaper*, where he would use his *Tomahawk* style against President Grant in the upcoming election. His opponent was Thomas Nast, the Grant-worshiping cartoonist for *Harper's Weekly*.

America was not unfamiliar to Morgan. Social and economic bonds between Britain and the U.S. were never closer than in the mid-

Victorian years, despite some diplomatic frictions. As Michael de Nie's chapter in this book shows, the Civil War was followed with intense interest in Britain. Morgan would have heard the Confederacy defended by Whistler, who enjoyed playing the Southern gentleman. His friend Lord Kilmorey had fought on the Northern side, although the British upper classes tended generally to be pro-South. The war was the biggest topic of his cartoons in *Fun*, which were fairly neutral, chiefly deploring the destructiveness of the war itself.[21] The cultural traffic between the two nations was heavy. One of Morgan's earliest commissions was to provide illustrations for an English edition of Longfellow's poems, which enjoyed great popularity in Britain. Transatlantic exchange was particularly strong in the realms of theater and popular entertainment. President Lincoln was assassinated while watching a performance of *Our American Cousin*, a play gently mocking national stereotypes both British and American that was hugely popular on both sides of the ocean. It was written by Tom Taylor, a journalist on the staff of *Punch* (a paper avidly read each week by Henry James as a young boy in Boston).[22] American minstrel shows and songs captured the British imagination. Many of Morgan's theater acquaintances would have performed in America. The stock of popular images and cultural allusions in which artists like him traded was largely common between the two nations. High and low, the white population of the U.S. was still predominantly Anglo-Saxon. Consequently, Morgan had little difficulty fitting into his new home. To further enhance his credentials, he gave his immigration story a republican spin. Cashing in on the controversy created by his *Tomahawk* cartoons critical of the Queen and the Prince of Wales, he put it about that he had driven out of his native country by royal wrath. Shrewdly, he claimed the benefit of victimhood.[23]

Morgan drew over 125 cartoons for *Leslie's* between late 1871 and the end of 1875, most of them during the election year of 1872. His candidate, Horace Greeley, not only lost, but died a month after the election and is now chiefly remembered for the deathless words, "Go West, young man!" His cartoons are largely forgotten too, although in artistic merit, if not political force, they were at least the equal of Nast's. The critic Brander Matthews made the striking claim that Morgan "never learned how to draw an American face: all his figures, good and bad, were cockneys of the purest water."[24] He was in fact quite good at drawing faces and figures, better than Nast despite the latter's genius for caricature. As for how "American" they were – that raised an interesting question at a time when New York was becoming the nation's great melting pot. After the election Morgan worked for *Leslie's* chiefly as an illustrator, and drawing faces and figures from American life became his specialty. The pool of competent illustrators in the U.S. was growing at this time, but so was demand as *Harper's* built up its art department and *Appleton's Journal*, founded in 1869, and *Scribner's Monthly*, founded in 1870, quickly developed reputations for the excellence of their illustrations. A number of able illustrators contributed to *Leslie's* – though not Winslow Homer, perhaps the finest American illustrator of this period, and Morgan's exact contemporary. Its chief artist, Albert Berghaus, had been with the journal from its start; Joseph Becker was another early recruit; John Hyde and Fernando Miranda were its other main illustrators in the 1870s.

Morgan was probably the best artist among them when he took the time – as he clearly did in most of his *Leslie's* illustrations. The quality of his work improved markedly during this period, though credit for this must also go to the journal's staff artists and engravers. Some of his sketches were redrawn onto the wood by others; sometimes he drew on wood from sketches by others, and sometimes he did his own work directly on the wood. But any illustration to which he contributed in any way bore his signature alone. He was unique among *Leslie's* artists in having this privilege, such was the prestige his name had won. However it was above all the anonymous engravers who could make or mar the final printed picture. During the 1870s the quality of American wood engraving rose dramatically to the point of being considered by the end of the decade to be the finest in the world, though ironically it reached this peak at almost the precise point when the photoengraving technologies that would quickly make it obsolete became commercially viable. Although W. J. Linton had left Leslie's employment by the time of Morgan's arrival because he was morally offended by the contents of *Day's Doings*, he had raised the firm's standard of engraving, and Morgan was among the beneficiaries.

In a recent study of *Leslie's*, Joshua Brown analyzes its illustrations and text within what he argues was the journal's admirable but ultimately unsuccessful publishing strategy. This was intended to forge a mass readership from the dynamic instability of Gilded Age America by playing a mediatory role amongst its divisions of race, class, ethnicity, religion and region. Against its competitors, with their literary pretensions and foreign borrowings, *Leslie's* proudly declared itself in 1871 "the sole purveyor of PICTORIAL NEWS in our country."[25] Its artist-reporters depicted scenes from high life and low life, town and country, North and South, employer and employed, in ways that reflected the transatlantic impact of the new social realist style pioneered by London's *Graphic* (a style that profoundly impressed the young Vincent Van Gogh who built a large personal collection of its engravings[26]). Morgan's work covered the full gamut of *Leslie's* concerns, with a particular emphasis on scenes of urban poverty and social conflict. He drew Italian child street musicians being beaten by their cruel masters (8 March 1873), German drinking in a Bowery beer hall (9 January 1872), Irish laborers at leisure (16 Aug 1873), workers striking

Figure 4.1 New York City – Among the poor – a summer evening scene at the Five Points; *Frank Leslie's Illustrated Newspaper*, 16 August 1873

Figure 4.2   New York City – The Eight-hour movement – a group of working-men on a strike in one of the up-town wards; *Frank Leslie's Illustrated Newspaper*, 8 June 1872

Figure 4.3   New York City – The Eight-hour movement – Procession of Workingmen on a 'strike,' in the Bowery, June 10th, 1872; *Frank Leslie's Illustrated Newspaper*, 29 June 1872

for an eight-hour day (8, 29 June 1872), "Riotous communist working-men" being driven out of Tompkins Square by mounted police (31 January 1874).

As Mary Cowling and L. P. Curtis have shown, Victorian artists and caricaturists employed certain conventional physiognomic signs that were widely recognized by the public to typify certain racial and social groups, often in a negative way.[27] The Irish were particularly subject to this sort of facial stereotyping in Anglo-American cartoon art and Morgan has been associated with this tendency on account of his earlier *Tomahawk* cartoons.[28] Yet the physiognomies he drew in crowd scenes for *Leslie's* tend to be fairly neutral. Though distinctly various, they avoid attributing coarse, brutal or degenerative features to working people. His treatment of African-Americans is particularly noteworthy for avoiding simianization. A striking example is his careful drawing (from a sketch by Joseph Becker) of a Southern court-room scene in which a "Negro justice reproves a disorderly white brother, and dismisses him with a fine." The black judge is dignified and fine-featured, while the white offender is physiognomically coded as somewhat degenerate (23 February 1889). Several of Morgan's pictures depict New York slum scenes of deep poverty. "A Sermon for the Hour: Suggested by the Center Street Catastrophe" shows three poor people praying at a makeshift cross erected in the rubble of a collapsed tenement where seven children died. It is accompanied by a text on the duties of the rich to the poor (18 January 1873). Some of Morgan's most effective cartoons in *Tomahawk* had also addressed this theme. In "A Lodging House on Water Street," a policeman's bull's-eye lantern starkly illuminates utter destitution. (9 March 1873). Morgan draws himself as a witness to the scene. This picture also appeared in Leslie's London *Here and There*, successor to *Days Doings*, with the title "Our Homeless Poor: An Artist's Midnight Visit to a Low Lodging House" (6 July 1872). In the London version a distinctively helmeted London Bobby holding the lantern is shown beside Morgan. In the New York version the policeman conveniently disappears into the shadows. Policemen's uniforms apart, New York and London flop houses and their inmates, were considered sufficiently transatlantic to be pictor-ially interchangeable.

Although most of Morgan's illustrations for *Leslie's* showed the darker side of America's Gilded Age, its glitter occasionally came under his pencil. Certainly Frank Leslie himself glittered: the publishing baron was a fine advertisement for the land of opportunity. Morgan enjoyed a cordial relationship with his fellow English immigrant, who

Figure 4.4   Negro justice reproves a disorderly white brother, and dismisses him with a fine; *Frank Leslie's Illustrated Newspaper*, 23 February 1889

lived in high style and was not averse to publicizing the fact in his papers. He entertained Morgan at Saratoga Springs, the chief resort of New York's rich, where he built a lavish twelve-room "cottage." Morgan duly described the pleasures of sport in the Adirondack mountains in both picture and word for *Leslie's* readers, even making his own sporting activities the subject of a front-page illustration (8 November 1873). His bond with his employer was strengthened by his unusual role in assisting Leslie's beautiful mistress and business partner to win a divorce so that they could marry. This enterprising woman set up her inconvenient husband for adultery charges by arranging a party for him with several prostitutes; Morgan was there to sketch them cavorting with him in the nude for *Day's Doings*. The threat of publishing the pictures, combined with his verbal testimony in the divorce court, apparently did the trick.[29] Mrs Frank Leslie, an adventuress who had once toured with the legendary courtesan Lola

Montez, later took over her husband's empire on his death, rescued it from financial collapse, and drove it to even greater success.

Nowhere was the smell of money – and opportunities for making, and losing it – stronger than in post-Civil War New York. Morgan knew that smell, and captured it in several illustrations. He drew the stock exchange at the height of the Erie Railroad "bubble," showing a frenzied sea of top-hatted, frock-coated traders swept by competing motives of greed and fear (13 April 1872). A sequel of sorts, "The

Figure 4.5 The Stock Exchange; *Frank Leslie's Illustrated Newspaper*, 13 April 1872

Ruined Speculator" (20 November 1875), depicts a scene at Union Square, where New York newspapers posted their latest headlines on giant billboards. Everyone is transfixed by the news of a financial disaster except Morgan himself, the figure on the right, who is more interested in the reactions of the others. The feverish spirit of competition and social mobility are captured in "The Moment of Triumph" (20 February 1873), where an aggressive one-horse upstart, cigar erect, enjoys his victory over the occupants of an opulent two-horse sleigh after an impromptu race in New York's new Central Park.

Morgan's own entrepreneurial instincts surged at this time. He decided to leave *Leslie's* and go into theater management. He had begun establishing himself in New York's theater world as soon as he arrived, taking on major scene painting commissions even while his cartoon war with Nast was raging. Several illustrations of his scenes appeared in *Leslie's*, including one for Boucicault's *The Shaughraun* that "elicited round after round of merited applause," as the caption obligingly noted (5 December 1874; 20 February 1875). When the depression of 1874–78 hit the New York stage hard, theater owners lowered their rents to attract managers. Morgan seized the opportunity and took over the Theatre Comique in 1875, and the Lyceum in 1876, putting on variety programs similar to what he had seen in London's music halls. However these ventures did not succeed.[30] Consequently Morgan went back to illustrating, but now cashed in on his expertise by specializing in theater and circus poster designs. He quickly made his name in this highly commercial form of art and in 1879 moved to Cincinnati as chief artist for the Strobridge Lithographing Company, the country's top firm in entertainment posters. He remained there for nearly seven years at a very high salary, and managed also to found an art school and an art pottery manufacturing firm. While in Cincinnati he also became, remarkably, chief cartoonist for a new English periodical. This was the *St. Stephen's Review*, a Tory Radical journal whose editor, recalling Morgan's slashing *Tomahawk* cartoons in a similar political vein, tried to get him to return to England. Morgan said he was quite happy where he was, but agreed to provide its weekly cartoons by post.[31] These were quite innovative, being reproduced by two-color lithography, a medium in which he was by now thoroughly adept. He drew the pictures in crayon on transfer paper, rolled them up and mailed them to London where they arrived within a couple of weeks to be transferred onto lithographic stone by his old partner Thomas Bolton. The arrangement worked because the cartoons were not acutely time-sensitive.

Instead of being closely tied to specific political events, they dealt in allegorical denunciations of Gladstonian policies and praise of the journal's hero, Lord Randolph Churchill. This unique transatlantic arrangement lasted from January to September 1885. Later that year he resigned from Strobridge to launch yet another venture, a series of large dioramic pictures of Civil War battles for a touring exhibition. Despite the widely acknowledged artistic merits of his paintings, the show was a financial failure.[32]

Morgan now returned to New York where he once again combined scene painting and periodicals illustration. He painted vast backdrops for "Buffalo Bill" Cody's ambitious *Drama of Civilization*, and a giant exhibition painting, *Christ Entering Jerusalem*. Working out of his studio in Union Square he also did freelance poster designs and illustrations for periodicals including *Leslie's* and the *Illustrated London News*. For the latter he did some American scenes, but also a fine scene "The Unemployed at the East End of London," which although wholly imaginary captures the look of authenticity.[33] In 1888 he became art editor and chief artist for *Collier's Once A Week*. This newly launched magazine, soon simply titled *Collier's*, would become one of the greatest mass circulation weeklies of the twentieth century. It started as a publisher's premium to buyers of cheap mail order books but soon went onto news stands at seven cents a copy, the low end of the magazine market. It appeared at a time when the world of illustrated journalism was entering a period of dramatic change. The era of wood engraving, which had produced *Leslie's* and the *Illustrated London News*, was ending. A top quality woodcut cost $300 to engrave. New technologies such as process engraving and halftone photography could produce an engraving plate nearly as good for $20. *Collier's* was part of the new generation of journals that sprang into existence in the 1880s to take advantage of a growing market, lower production costs and lucrative advertising revenues.

During its first five months, *Once A Week* contained much inferior artwork by unknown illustrators, leavened with pirated work by top British and continental artists such as Charles Keene and "Caran d'Ache" (Emmanuel Poire). Morgan's arrival in September 1888 is marked by a distinct improvement in its illustrations as the journal took on a more distinct character. Its attention to society news gave Morgan an opportunity to exercise his skill in drawing pretty women. Moralistic illustrations reminiscent of *Tomahawk* decried the prevalence of divorces in high society, as in "Ha! Ha!! Ha!!!" (10 November 1888). In others, tubercular seamstresses toiled through the night to

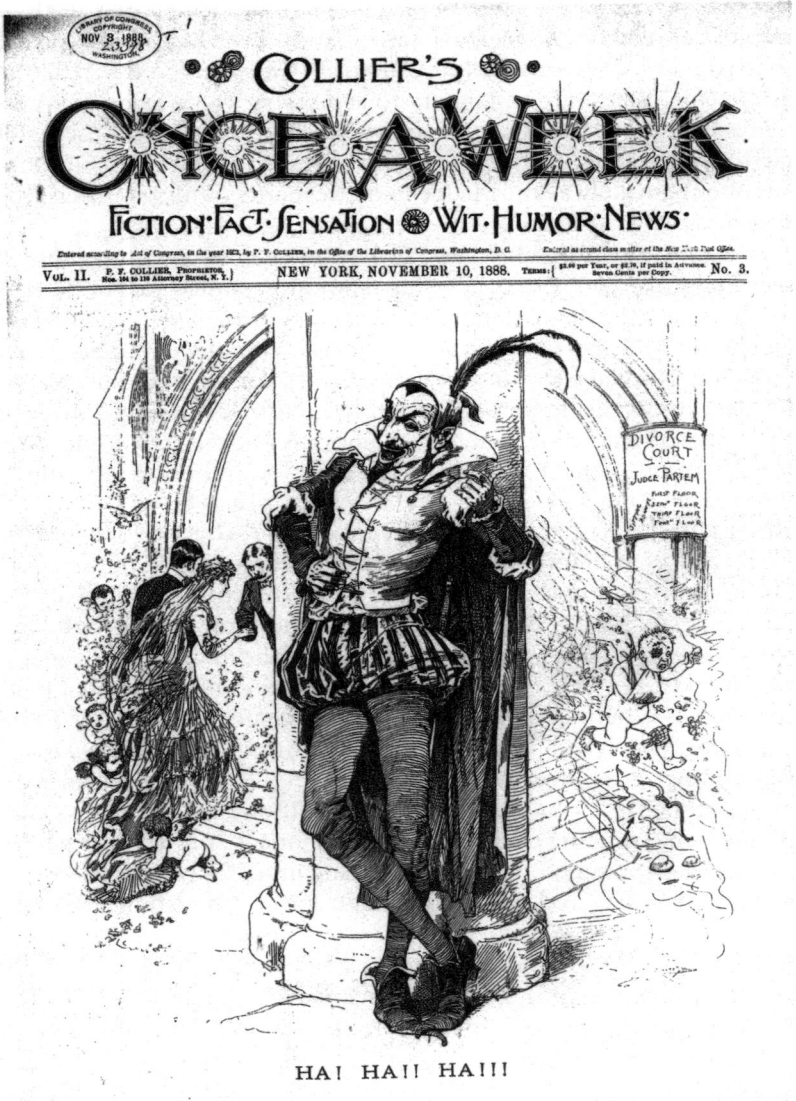

Figure 4.6   Ha! Ha! Ha!; *Collier's Once a Week*, 10 November 1888

serve the capricious demands of fashion and beautiful debutantes sacrificed their hearts on the altar of mercenary marriage. With practiced skill he rang the changes on conventional melodramatic themes, such as beauty and the beast in a cover illustration for Amelie Rives' interminable poem *Asmodeus* (29 September 1888). The journal also began to carry "cover girl" pictures, front-page portraits of society beauties drawn from photographs in the somewhat bland crayon stipple technique that he learned in the 1870s doing poster pictures of actresses. He engaged freelance illustrators, and like Frank Leslie he showed a certain preference for foreign, particularly English-born artists including Albert Sterner, a Londoner who was at the start of a long career as one of America's best illustrators. The Canadian-born Palmer Cox drew his famous Brownies for the magazine's children's page and Gray Parker, Paris-born of English parents, specialized in society pictures, particularly riding and coaching scenes. He even commissioned his old rival Thomas Nast, now fallen on hard times, to do an illustration of the great Johnstown flood. However Morgan did most of the illustrations himself until February 1889. After that his most frequent contributor was his son Fred, the only one of the children of his first marriage to follow him to the United States. Starting with smaller illustrations his contributions increased in number and quality under his father's tutelage. By the summer of 1889 Fred Morgan had taken over as *Once a Week*'s main illustrator.

During the last year of his life Matt Morgan was once again fully engaged in scene painting. On June 2, 1890, he died while hard at work on scenery for a ballet spectacular commissioned for the grand opening of Stanford White's new Madison Square Garden. Numerous obituaries appeared in the American and British press. He had succeeded in breaking out of the anonymity that surrounds most popular art to become well known in his lifetime. He died on the threshold of the great age of opportunity for illustrators. The advent of photo journalism freed them from the task of doing what the camera did better, and enabled them to do more artistic work for the proliferating popular magazines, including high quality advertising art. In this development the United States led the way, and Morgan was an important pioneer. But his work, like that of all commercial artists, was ephemeral. So too was his fame. The part of his enormous and varied output that can best be recovered today is his work in the transatlantic illustrated press.

Notes

1 Most biographical sources state that he was born in 1839, as his obituary in the *New York Times* states. However the registry entry for his first marriage on 19 January 1860 gives his age as 23, which certainly fits better. He presumably shaved three years off his age when he began his new career in the U. S.

2 Henry Vizetelly mentions publishing Morgan's Algerian sketches which appeared in both the *Illustrated London News* and the *Illustrated Times* between January and June of 1858, though without artist identification. Henry Vizetelly, *Glances Back Through Seventy Years* (London: Kegan Paul) I, 389.

3 See John Pemble, *The Mediterranean Passion: Victorians and Edwardians in the South* (Oxford: Oxford University Press, 1987).

4 *Illustrated London News*, 22 May 1859, p. 6. On the perils of being a war correspondent during this period see Mason Jackson, *The Pictorial Press* (London: Hurst & Blackett, 1885), 328–54.

5 Albert B. Paine, *Thomas Nast, His Period and Pictures* (New York: Macmillan, 1904), 34.

6 John Jackson, *A Treatise on Wood Engraving* (London: Henry Bohn, 1861), 241.

7 *Catalogue of the Pictures and Drawings Selected from the Works of the Leading Artists of the Day at the Gallery, 14 Berners Street, W.* (London: Privately Printed (1862)), "Preface."

8 Stanley Weintraub accepts Whistler's claim that Morgan invented this title without consulting him. In his reply Morgan states that Whistler had given his approval to the title. Stanley Weintraub, *Whistler: A Biography* (London: Collins, 1974), 76. I agree with Gordon Fleming that the controversy was probably cooked up by both men in collusion in order to attract publicity by linking the painting in the public mind with Wilkie Collins's best selling novel (whose artist-hero, Walter Hartright, is transformed from an ineffectual drawing-master into a manly magazine illustrator). Gordon H. Fleming, *James Abbott McNeill Whistler: A Life* (Gloucestershire: Windrush Press, 1991), 92.

9 Daphne du Maurier, *The Young George du Maurier* (London: Peter Davies, 1951), 88, 154, 177.

10 Christopher Kent, "British Bohemia and the Victorian Journalist," *Australian Victorian Studies Journal* 6 (2000), 31–3.

11 Arthur W. A. Beckett, *Green Room Recollections* (Bristol: Arrowsmith, 1896), 70.

12 *The Times*, 28 August 1869, p. 4.

13 *Britannia* I, 514; II, 258–9, 350–1.

14 Christopher Kent, "The Angry Young Gentleman of *Tomahawk*," in Barbara Garlick and Margaret Harris eds., *Victorian Journalism: Essays in Honour of P. D. Edwards* (Brisbane: University of Queensland Press: 1998), 75–94.

15 *The Times*, 8 May 1869, 4.

16 I owe this information to Morgan's granddaughter, Mrs Elizabeth Morgan Munsey.

17 H. G. Hibbert, *Fifty Years of a Londoner's Life* (London: Grant Richards, 1916), 157.

18 *Day's Doings* commenced publication as *The Last Sensation* in 1867. It was always owned by Leslie who initially concealed his connection with it. Joshua Brown, *Beyond the Lines: Pictorial Reporting, Everyday Life, and the Crisis of Gilded Age America* (Berkeley and Los Angeles: University of California Press, 2002), 43–4, 259 n.33. An upmarket version of the *Police Gazette* it attracted the attention of New York's anti-vice crusader, Anthony Comstock. Madeleine Stern, *Purple Passion: The Life of Mrs. Frank Leslie* (Norman: University of Oklahoma Press, 1953) 223–4; Helen L. Horowitz, "Victoria Woodhull, Anthony Comstock, and the Conflict Over Sex in the United States in the 1870s," *Journal of American History* 87 (September 2000): 425–6. The London edition began publication on 30 July 1870. The major newsagent W. H. Smith refused to stock it on the grounds of its alleged indecency. Its name was changed to *Here and There* on 24 February 1872 and it expired at the end of that year.

19 *Days Doings*, 12 November 1870, 9.

20 The extensive republication of British periodicals in the U. S., initially in pirate editions, but increasingly after the Civil War by arrangement, has been noted by Mott, who also notes the increasing publication in Britain of American illustrated magazines like *Scribner's* and *Harper's* from the 1870s. Frank Luther Mott, *A History of American Magazines: 1741–1930* (Cambridge: Harvard University Press, 1930–68), II, 128–30: III, 278–9. Joshua Brown documents *Leslie's* assertions of its American character in *Beyond the Lines*, 265 n.4.

21 Christopher Kent, "War Cartooned/Cartoon War: Matt Morgan and the American Civil War in *Fun* and *Frank Leslie's Illustrated Newspaper*," *Victorian Periodicals Review* 36 (Summer 2003), 153–81.

22 Elizabeth Hepworth Dixon, *As I Knew Them: Sketches of People I Have Met Along the Way* (London: Hutchinson, 1930), 69.

23 G. H. Bernasconi, a Birmingham cartoonist who shared a studio with Morgan when he worked on *Tomahawk*, attributed Morgan's departure to America to the fact that he had "incurred the displeasure of certain exalted personages moving in the highest social ranks." *Notes and Queries* Ser.2, VIII, 53. Presumably Queen Victoria was not amused by *Tomahawk*, but it was in no sense republican – quite the contrary – and its other staff members remained in Britain and prospered. His American family was apparently encouraged to think of him as having been exiled.

24 "Arthur Penn" (Brander Matthews), "The Growth of Caricature," *The Critic* (25 February 1882), 49.

25 Brown, *Beyond the Lines*, 61. J. C. Goldsmith, an editor of *Leslie's* in the early 1870s, confirms this view: Charles F. Wingate, *Views and Interviews on Journalism* (New York: F. R. Paterson, 1875), 104–50.

26 Julian Treuherz, *Hard Times: Social Realism in Victorian Art* (London: Lund Humphries, 1987), 119–20.

27 Mary C. Cowling, *The Artist as Anthropologist: The Representation of Character and Type in Victorian Art* (Cambridge: Cambridge University Press, 1989); L. P. Curtis Jr., *Apes and Angels: The Irishman in Victorian Character* (Washington, D. C.: Smithsonian Institution Press, 1971).

28 See Brown, *Beyond the Lines*, 274 n.65. I agree with Kemnitz that Morgan's Irish monsters in *Tomahawk* were Gothic representations of Fenian

terrorism. Thomas M. Kemnitz, "Matt Morgan of *Tomahawk* and English Cartooning, 1867–70," *Victorian Studies* 19 (September, 1975): 15–17, 5–34.

29   Stern, *Purple Passion*, 63–4, 206.

30   Morgan's most successful theater production was a series of *tableaux vivants* representing celebrated paintings of nude women. It encountered the opposition of Anthony Comstock on the grounds of obscenity, which Morgan vigorously rejected in the sacred name of art. Jack W. McCullough, *Living Pictures on the New York Stage* (Ann Arbor: UMI Research Press, 1984), 75. As "Matt Morgan's Living Pictures" the tableaux successfully toured the U. S. for several years.

31   William Allison, *My Kingdom for a Horse* (London: Grant Richards, 1919), 285, 288.

32   Christopher Kent, "Spectacular History as an Ocular Discipline," *Wide Angle* 18 (1996), 1–21.

33   Simon Houfe, *The Dictionary of British Book Illustrators and Caricaturists, 1800–1914* (Woodbridge, Suffolk: Antique Collectors Club, 1978), 394.

5

James Bryce and the Promise of the American Press, 1888–1921

James Startt

During his lifetime, James Bryce achieved lasting distinction as an extraordinary British interpreter of American institutions. That reputation rests mainly on his classic study, *The American Commonwealth*, published in 1888.[1] However, his interest in the United States spanned 50 years, from the time of his first visit there in 1870 to 1921. Bryce was fascinated by democratic institutions, including the press, and he made them the subject of his inquiries. Americans in and beyond journalism were engaged in an ongoing debate about the status of the nation's press during those years. As it modernized and became more commercial and politically independent, critics claimed it was losing its authority. They charged that the social, entertaining, trivial, and sensational content associated with the New Journalism was expanding in newspapers at the expense of important (i.e., political) news. Commercialization of the press, they feared, made it an object for capitalist exploitation, thus calling its trustworthiness into question. On the other hand, defenders of the modern press held that, with modernization and greater democratization, its vitality and influence was growing. Bryce's thoughts on the American press can be placed in the context of that debate.

As a jurist, veteran parliamentarian, minister of state, historian, and incurable traveler, Bryce had an uncommon background for studying American institutions.[2] He often visited the United States and traveled extensively while there, establishing friendships with many of the nation's economic, political, and intellectual leaders. Furthermore, he was a great champion of Anglo-American friendship, and by voice and action he strove to advance the movement that historian Bradford Perkins labeled "the great rapprochement" that grew between the two countries in the pre-World War I decades.[3] Bryce had a great curiosity about Americans that led him to seek out people he met everywhere – waiters, tradesmen, bankers, and editors. He was the most popular Englishman of his generation in America, and his popularity reflected the faith Americans had in him. Woodrow Wilson once observed that they appreciated him for his "point of view."[4] What then was his "point of view" of the American press?[5] Bryce first broached that topic in 1888 in his *American Commonwealth*, developed it further while ambassador to the United States from 1907 to 1913, and returned to it in his last book, *Modern Democracies*, published in 1921.

I

His treatment of the press in his classic 1888 work was generous. He argued that it was the most active one in the world, a noisy watchdog able to expose abuses and to prevent others by the "fear of publicity." Although the nation's appetite for news, and for "sensational" news, along with the way in which keen competition forced journalists to work "in unceasing haste" could lead them to take license with truth, he contended that, as narrators of news, newspapers did some harm ... but probably more good."[6] Bryce also claimed that the press could be impressive as an advocate "when it takes hold of some fact (real or supposed), and hammers it into the public mind."[7] But it was the press acting as a reflector of public opinion that most impressed him. He believed the independent or semi-independent great urban journals were the most effective disseminators of public opinion in the land.

Several practices of the American press attracted his particular attention. He found, for instance, that compared to British newspapers, those published in the United States took more notice of one another. They were more apt to quote from others of similar persuasion and to attack those of differing views. Moreover, American newspapers contained much more of the "private deliverances of prominent men" than found in newspapers elsewhere. Along with letters to the editor, which would also be found in the British press, this "deliverance" was accomplished by the publication of letters not addressed to newspapers but to a friend, who in turn gave the letter "the publicity for which it was designed." Then there was the interview, a device commonly used in American newspapers but still uncommon in the British press.[8] Many times interviews were sought by reporters; sometimes they were invited by prominent figures who wished to communicate their views to the public. "All of these devices," Bryce concluded, "serve to help the men of eminence to impress their ideas on the public, while they show that there is a part of the public which desires such guidance." Such practices also gave the American press an ability to detect, fathom, and report opinion that was "almost unknown in Europe. Taken as a whole, he concluded that the American press served "the expression, and subserved the formation, of public opinion more fully than ... [did] the press of any part of the European continent, and not less fully than that of England."[9] Having set out to analyze the press in the United States as an instrument useful in influencing and reflecting public opinion, his favorable opinion of that institution is clear.

The American Commonwealth, moreover, reflected the main professional attitudes towards the press in the 1880s. It was then considered a dynamic element of urban reform, and that fact impressed Bryce. Moreover, by that time Frederic Hudson's *Journalism in the United States, from 1690–1872* had appeared. Published in 1873, it was the first full treatment of the subject since the advent of the penny press in the 1830s. Although his history attracted some criticism, his interpretation of the press as a developing vehicle of reform whose "power and influence was widely acknowledged" became the prevailing view of the institution.[10] So Bryce was in basic accord with the most authoritative statement on the American press available at the time.

Finally, it can be noted that Bryce believed that the effectiveness of the American press was due in large measure to the reading public. In one of his most revealing passages, he wrote: "Individual newspapers and journalists altogether may enjoy less power than is the case in some countries of the Old World; but if this be so, the cause is to be found, not in the inferior capacity of editors and writers, but in the superior independence of the reading public, who regard their paper differently from the English, while finding it no less necessary a part of the mechanism of free government."[11] This liberal view of society and his confidence in public opinion as an independent force working within it for its betterment, led Bryce to describe the press in positive terms. To his credit he did so without reference to the exaggerated "Fourth Estate" rhetoric that was all too common at the time.[12]

Before long, however, he began to question the positive view of the press contained in *The American Commonwealth*. During his visits to the States, he resented being hounded by reporters, though he remained cordial to them. He deplored the sensationalism associated with Joseph Pulitzer and William Randolph Hearst in this country and with the Harmsworth press in Britain.[13] Moreover, he became apprehensive about the role of the press in international relations. At the time of the Anglo-American dispute over the Venezuela boundary in the mid-1890s, which occasioned an onslaught of anti-British and jingoistic articles in the American press, Bryce attempted to quiet the excitement by an article in the *North American Review*. "The Newspapers," he wrote, "fan every spark of annoyance into a flame and cover violence and misrepresentation with the cloak of patriotism. They are as great a danger to peace ... as the jealousies of kings and queens were in earlier centuries."[14] Between the Venezuelan crisis and Bryce's appointment to Washington in 1907, the Spanish-American and Anglo-Boer Wars occurred, and in both cases the emotional bravado characteristic of the American and British popular press respectively again disturbed him.[15] Consequently, by the time he arrived in Washington as ambassador, concern about irresponsible tendencies apparent in the press had become a matter of alarm for him.

II

The portrayal of the American press that Bryce offered in his ambassadorial correspondence and reports represents the second effort he made to understand it as a political force. Now he punctuated his *communiqués* with London with disquieting references to the press. Typical of his remarks were: "It grows more mendacious and more reckless every year," and news reports, especially when about prominent figures, were often pure "inventions" or "malicious" stories.[16] As for Hearst's and Pulitzer's New York newspapers, they were "the most unscrupulous papers in the U. S.," and "most of what they print is pure invention."[17] Just as maddening to Bryce was the failure of even educated men to "insist on having something better" from their press.[18]

Two tendencies in the press particularly troubled him. The first dealt with interviews. As he explained it: "When I refuse, as always, to talk about politics ... [the interviewers] invent statements which they put into one's mouth.... . Against these shameless falsehoods there seems to be no remedy."[19] The second tendency concerned the newspapers' tendency to inflame international relations. "Here the press has been doing its best to make trouble [between Japan and the United States]," he reported.[20] Not long after making that report, he reflected on such loose journalism: "Why the newspapers persist in trying to get up a war between the U. S. and Japan is not easy to see except as the hypothesis that it suits them to burn down houses for the sake of having paragraphs describing the fire. They have brought themselves to the point of believing their own nonsense."[21]

The performance of the press so disturbed Bryce that he assigned Herbert Grant Watson, the third secretary at the British embassy, to compose a report on the subject. Watson produced a comprehensive document surveying the history, operation, strengths, and weaknesses of the American press. Beginning by recognizing some strengths of the press, he underscored its energy and organizational genius and had many complimentary things to say about the Associated Press, which he considered the main source of stability in American journalism. Nevertheless, the overwhelming tone and content of the report was critical. Foreign news coverage was weak, most dailies were unreliable, and thanks to the license offered by freedom of the press that editors abused, newspapers produced a stream of "lies and horrors." News was slanted by reporters, who habitually quoted selected comments from speeches out of context, and by owners preoccupied with circulation. Few citizens, he said, denied that the reform of the press was "an urgent national duty."[22]

He ended with a caustic summation about both the popular press and its audience. Regarding the latter, he observed that Americans were a "news-mad people" who voiced the frequent comment that they did not "believe a word ... [they] read in the papers." This led Watson to comment, "But where, then, do they draw their opinions from? Perhaps, from their friends; but they, too, are probably biased by the dailies, for only a small proportion of the nation ... [was] in touch with its propelling forces." However, these "news-mad people" exerted considerable influence on the press, for many journalists tried to feel "the pulse of the masses" and followed the "demoralizing" habit of writing that which they wished to read. Thus, despite its superb organization and the ability of many of its practitioners, the desire to please the people "sapped" the press of "all sense of fitness and proportion and of determining the real value of events as they hurry by." The result was discouraging. "Reading each day the interminable budget of petty crimes and other horrors with no thought to any of the permanent movements of mankind," Watson concluded, "one cannot but be reminded of the dirty refuse carts which ... slowly climb the Kalorama Heights and empty their loads in the Rock Creek Valley; but it is refuse that the papers collect, and of all the many features of American life the press is the most discouraging."[23]

Given that biting conclusion, Bryce's reaction to the report was telling. He forwarded it to the Foreign Office calling it an "instructive report," and adding, "Mr. Watson couched his comments in language whose moderation I appreciate all the more because I should have felt inclined to point in darker colours the reckless irresponsibility of a large section of the American press."[24] This, in fact, was the tone that permeated Bryce's own commentaries on the press in his official annual reports on the United States.

Gone in those reports was the positive picture he drew of this nation's press in *The American Commonwealth*. No longer did he speak of it as a force of reform capable of doing more good than harm, nor as an index to public opinion, nor as an outlet for the opinion of prominent men through its interviews and public letters. Recalling that Thackeray once "humorously talked of a journal to be written by gentlemen for gentlemen," Bryce now reflected, "the exact opposite would be a fairer description of the majority of the American daily newspapers."[25] Toward the end of his ambassadorship, he began to speak of the American press as an "evil" that sensible people tolerated as a type of disease for which "no cure has been or can be discovered."[26] In his opinion, the bulk of the newspapers had become a detriment to public opinion. The only saving grace he could offer was that "among educated people at least the newspapers, especially in personal matters, have probably less weight here than in any other country."[27]

What hardened Bryce's views about the American press? The obvious explanation partly answers the question. As a public figure, he was being covered by the press and not merely observing its workings in a scholarly manner. Many champions of the press, from Thomas Jefferson to Woodrow Wilson, became cooler toward it when they engaged it in practice. There is also a good deal of contextual evidence to widen that explanation. Years before the start of his ambassadorship the New Journalism initiated by Pulitzer in the 1880s had devolved into the "yellow journalism" epitomized by the famous Pulitzer-Hearst circulation rivalry. A virtual genre of commentary about "yellow journalism" soon emerged that denounced its sensationalism, its untrustworthy reporting, its detrimental effects on private and public character, and its commercialism.[28] When the exposé journalism that Theodore Roosevelt labeled "muckraking" appeared after the turn of the century, it too drew abundant criticism from publicists.[29] They complained about how it played upon passions, aroused fears of the established form of government, disregarded facts, made reckless attacks on public figures, and offered no reasonable alternative to the existing if imperfect order. As was true of the criticism of the press in general, it was admitted in the case of the muckrakers that there were some decent elements in the movement that served the public good. Regardless, the widespread criticism of the press that appeared particularly in the nation's best journals of opinion, with which Bryce was familiar, reinforced his misgivings about the institution.

Chief among those misgivings was his apprehension of sensational journalism as a volatile force in international relations. This is not surprising. Anything that might influence Anglo-American relations deserved to be included in his reports to the Foreign Office. It is significant that, in his opinion, the American press qualified as a major problem, and he would have been remiss not to have alerted Whitehall to the recklessness of the institution and its potential for disrupting friendly relations among countries. Moreover, none other than President Theodore Roosevelt provided credence for Bryce's perceptions about the irresponsible actions of a large portion of the press. As he told Sir Edward Grey, the Foreign Secretary, in 1910: "Mr. Roosevelt, otherwise an inveterate optimist, told me three years ago that within his memory the daily press had grown worse, and ... observation continued during many years makes one fear that he is right." It is reasonable to assume that Roosevelt influenced Bryce's changing attitude toward the press, for the ambassador admired the president and placed a high value on his judgment. Despite Roosevelt's considerable skills in the art of mass communication, he had his troubles with the press. Like Bryce, he complained in private about its dishonest reporting and editorializing. The president said, along the same line echoed by Bryce, that by practicing such mendacity the press was a great force of "evil" in the country.[30] Conversations he had with various other people also confirmed Bryce's fears about the press. In one report he reflected: "I have never met a thoughtful American prepared either to palliate its [the press's] faults or to suggest a remedy for them."[31] "All sensible Americans," he wrote in another report, admitted the "turpitude" of the press. By the time he made the latter comment, he had begun to perceive "reckless mendacity of the press" as one of five main dangers threatening the United States.[32]

It is difficult to escape the idea that Bryce, whose reputation rested on his ability to collect and synthesize facts and opinions, was influenced by the people he most associated with in this country. Until his death in 1902, his closest friend among American journalists was the Irish born Edwin Lawrence Godkin, who learned his journalism in London and Belfast and went on to become the long-time editor of the New York *Evening Post*. It was the favorite newspaper among east coast, college-educated readers. Bryce had a preference for associating with others involved in this journalistic genre, men like Horace Scudder of the *Atlantic Monthly*, Albert Shaw of the *American Review of Reviews*, and

Washington Gladden of the *Independent* and *Scribner's*. It was journalists like John Bigelow, Arthur Sedgwick and Oswald Garrison Villard, all connected with the New York *Evening Post*, whom Bryce cited most often as his friends in the American press. Added to this was his fondness for association with university presidents such as Charles W. Eliot of Harvard and Andrew White of Cornell. Bryce based his evaluation of American institutions on his wide reading (including newspapers), on his own experience and observations, and on his efforts to understand the attitude of ordinary people. However, his extensive and ongoing conversations with his American friends and acquaintances, who represented the nation's cultural elite, were central to the formulation of his views.[33] His own patrician background and Victorian preferences made him comfortable in the orbit of their thought. Nowhere was this more evident than in his reflections on the American press. The newspapers he considered as proper standard bearers were those leading publications of the British political press, newspapers like *The Times* (London), the *Manchester Guardian*, and the *Westminster Gazette*. American newspapers like the *Evening Post*, which as historian Arthur J. Kaul points out, appealed to the "genteel intelligentsia," were those that most resembled the great quality dailies of Britain.[34] They were also ones that Bryce considered upholders of the proper journalistic standards in this country. His sense of Victorian propriety and, to some extent his Scottish Presbyterianism, led him naturally to this conclusion.

III

A few years later, in his *Modern Democracies*, Bryce made his last appraisal of the American press. He began that study in 1904, three years before his ambassadorship and completed it after the end of World War I in 1921. Before and during the war, the performance of the press of the belligerent countries disturbed him, and it appeared to confirm his observations about the press as a dangerous force in international relations. "The Jingoes on both sides have a lot to answer for," he wrote to a friend. The press in Germany and England, "made our people believe that Germany was working to attack us and made them believe the like of us."[35] And because of a much-cited report on German wartime atrocities, which he oversaw, he was aware of the propaganda operations of the war and the use they made of the press.[36] Consequently, wartime journalism heightened his apprehension about the press, and at the time he published *Modern Democracies*, he could be found telling an American friend that the press was "the greatest danger ahead of democracy."[37]

Moreover, during the final stages of his writing *Modern Democracies*, Anglo-American relations were undergoing a new cycle. Beginning with the peace negotiations at the end of World War I, discord appeared that threatened both the spirit of cooperation and the wartime idealism that had characterized relations between the two countries after the United States entered the conflict in 1917. The British looked askance at the huge naval construction program that the United States began during the war. As Anglo-Irish relations descended into open warfare between 1919 and 1921, the British little appreciated demands for Irish independence voiced by Irish-Americans and their newspapers. The American rejection of the Versailles Settlement and of the League of Nations that seemed to mark their withdrawal from the affairs of Europe and their descent into isolationism fed British disillusionment with the United States. Meanwhile, in the United States those newspapers that the British sometimes referred to as the chauvinistic American press did all in their power to stir up anti-British sentiment. Led once again by the outspoken anglophobe William Randolph Hearst and his newspaper empire, they were relentless in chastising the British for what they perceived as their selfish motives in the recent war and in their support of the League of Nations. Now the reemergence of tensions between the two countries imperiled Bryce's cherished idea of Anglo-American friendship, and aggressive organs in the American press had encouraged those tensions.

Consequently, he could not dismiss the anxieties he had about the press in democratic societies, anxieties which had grown during years of observation. He could, however, try to transcend them. In *Modern Democracies*, he set out to offer a balanced account of the "causes that thwart democracy and those that pull it straight again."[38] In the inquiry, he applied that standard to the mainsprings of democracy in Australia, Canada, France, New Zealand, Switzerland, and the United states. In the opinion of Walter Lippmann and Allan Nevins, the result was "one of the great Liberals of his generation testing, in balanced and penetrating fashion, a set of democracies by Liberal touchstones."[39] The sections in the study dealing with the press discussed its performance not only in the United States but also at democracies in general. Bryce used the American press as an unmistakable model for his generalizations about that institution.

In *Modern Democracies*, he delineated what he considered its three major flaws. First, he believed its growing commercialization was impairing its role as an instrument of political enlightenment. Commercialization invited "undisclosed" motives rather than "honest conviction" to influence a newspaper's position, and it also threatened to create a "dictatorship" of syndicated newspapers, as their combinations and control of markets expanded.[40] So serious was this flaw that he felt that "recourse might be needed to drastic legislation of a kind not yet tried" in order to protect freedom of the press, which he contended remained the "Ark of the Covenant in every democracy."[41] Second, he feared for truth in both news and opinion due to sloppy reporting, unfounded argumentation, misrepresentation of fact, slanted selection of facts presented, and "indiscriminate" partisanship.[42] Understanding that impartiality as a remedy for this flaw was a counsel of perfection, he settled for a lesser one, the standard of fairness. "We are satisfied," he wrote, if each newspaper "is fairly honest, neither distorting facts nor misrepresenting the position of opponents."[43] Third, the inflammatory effect on public opinion, especially as a factor in foreign relation, continued to disturb him. "The newspapers," he claimed, "exaggerate the prevailing sentiment of the moment, claiming everything for their own country, misrepresenting and disparaging the foreign antagonist."[44] Why? Not for commercial gain in war, for in war their expenditures increase, but "because it is easier and more profitable to take the path of least resistance."[45]

Nevertheless, he could not allow his critique of the press to stand alone, for he still had faith in its potential as an instrument of political life. He yet believed there were respectable newspapers and periodicals published in the United States, contending that if "the worst papers" had become worse, "the best papers ... [had] grown better." He continued to find much that was admirable in the press in general. In his opinion, it still deserved credit for its reform impulse and for its vigilance, which prevented many other shameful deeds. Most of all he felt that public opinion was the real ruler in the United States and that the gradual rise of its standard of excellence along with the continued improvement of the nation's civic and educational institutions would influence the press in time. All considered, the press was still an indispensable popular instrument that connected the government with the people and helped the people to make those who govern responsible.[46] Consequently, in *Modern Democracies* he concluded that although the problems of the press could not be wished away, it was "the newspaper press that has made democracy possible in large countries," and it was the "press alone" that could do so much of the "necessary work" in a democratic community.[47]

What led Bryce to this final positive assessment of the press? Possibly he saw no alternative to the role, imperfection included, that it played in a democracy, or perhaps he believed the major problems with the press would be mitigated in time. The question cannot be answered with certainty. It is important, however, to remember that Bryce's *American Commonwealth* was a type of source book for progressive reform.[48] It drew attention to the needed reforms in our political institutions. So it was with *Modern Democracies*. Still, the question remains: How would the reform of the press transpire? Journalists themselves would have to assume responsibility for raising the standards of their work. But that is only part of Bryce's solution. A clue to his more subtle thinking on press reform can be found in his reflections on the consumers of newspapers.

More than most reformers who focused on the press, Bryce believed that its readers had a responsibility in its reform. By explaining its problems and flaws, he hoped to raise the public's understanding of what they read in newspapers. Believing that a democracy demanded an informed public opinion, he urged people to become aware of how the media presented news and opinion. In one of his several references to this need, he warned: "The Tree of Knowledge is the Tree of Knowledge of Evil as well as of Good. On the printed page Truth has no better chance than Falsehood, except with those who read widely and have the capacity of discernment."[49] Therefore, just as he believed in the good opinion of the American people, so he maintained that they should be involved in the reform of the press. He urged them to reflect and to judge as well as to read, to read several newspapers rather than only one, and to make their opinion known.

Bryce considered their relationship with the press as a civic responsibility. Now he held that better-educated Americans were interested in the reform of the press, as was the "Average Man." However, he had less faith in those whom he called "the lower strata in city populations." Their newspaper reading habits encouraged some of the worst features of popular journalism, but those habits could be changed only by education and an improvement of their social and economic conditions. Reflecting, as it does, his own Victorian and Protestant middle-class bias, that line of thought underscored the faith in the potential of education and economic reform to advance the public well-being that Bryce held to the end of his life. It also underscores his belief in the assimilative nature of American institutions, including the press.[50]

The assimilation Bryce had in mind in the case of the press worked downwards from the top. As the best publications in the country grew in number and influence, they would become models for others to follow. Bryce always contended that there was a sense of unity between Britain and the United States, and his views on the reform of the American press underscore his contention. The standard of journalism he advocated was that practiced by the quality political press in England and its counterpart in the United States. He shared the criticism of American popular journalism that was common among the editors of those quality newspapers, which were so integral a part of the Fleet Street-Whitehall political axis. And no doubt, he also shared their view that the American journalistic practices then growing in the British press represented a potential danger to its trustworthiness and influence. Nevertheless, it remains an open question if the journalistic standard Bryce preferred was a viable one for the heterogeneous modern American press, though his commitment to it was a reflection of his progressive view of democratic life and of the indispensable role the press performed in it. Just as he believed that reason would triumph over ignorance, so until the end, he believed in the promise of the American press as an instrument of democracy.

Notes

1 Bryce. *The American Commonwealth*, 2 vols. (New York: Macmillan, 1917), 1:4. First published in 1888, this work went through many subsequent editions starting in 1891. The sections he devoted to the press in those editions only varied by a word or two from those in the original edition.

2 Bryce served as a Member of Parliament for 26 consecutive years (1880–1906) and he held positions in all of the Liberal governments during those years (i.e., those of Gladstone, Rosebery, and Campbell-Bannerman). Aside from *The American Commonwealth*, his major books were the *Holy Roman Empire* (1864), *Studies in History and Jurisprudence* (1901), and *Studies in Contemporary Biography* (1903).

3 Bradford Perkins, *The Great Rapprochement: England and the United States, 1895–1914* (New York: Athenaeum, 1968), 3–11. Various reasons are usually given to explain this rapprochement. Some are political such as the need for Britain to accommodate itself to the emergence of the United States as a world power, the sympathy the governments of the two countries showed for one another during the Spanish-American and Anglo-Boer wars, the apprehensions the two had about the specter of German power, and the growth of common international concerns about trade, China, and other problems. Some are cultural such as the strength of common traditions in the two nations, the interaction of progressive reform movements in the two countries, the growth of personal contacts especially among elites, and the increasing similarities of interests and outlooks detectable in both cases.

4 Woodrow Wilson, *"Bryce's American Commonwealth: A Review," Political Science Quarterly* 4 (March 1889): 153.

5 Neither of Bryce's major biographers considers his treatment of the press in *The American Commonwealth*. See H. A. L. Fisher, *James Bryce*, 2 vols. (New York: Macmillan, 1927), 1:222–42, and Edmund Ions, *James Bryce and American Democracy, 1870–1922* (London: Macmillan, 1968), 133–41. W. Brooke Graves provided a synopsis of how Bryce depicted the press in *The American Commonwealth* in his chapter, "American Public Opinion As Bryce Described It and As It Is," in *Bryce's American Commonwealth: Fiftieth Anniversary*, ed. Robert C. Brooks (New York: Macmillan, 1939), 87–9. Lawrence W. Mazzeno and Allen Lefcowitz cite Bryce's positive interpretation of the press in *The American Commonwealth* in contrast to Matthew Arnold's negative opinion of that institution in their "Arnold and Bryce: The Problem of American Democracy and Culture," in *Matthew Arnold in His Time and Ours: Contemporary Essays*, Clinton Machann and Forrest D. Burt (Charlottesville: Univ. of Virginia Press, 1988), 72.

6 Bryce, *American Commonwealth* (1888 edit.), 2:232–3.

7 Ibid., 236–7.

8 For the influence of the American press on British popular journalism in the late nineteenth century, see Joel H. Wiener, "The Americanization of the British Press," *Studies in Newspaper and Periodical History: 1994 Annual*, eds. Michael Harris and Tom O'Malley (Westport, CT: Greenwood Press, 1996), 61–74; see also Wiener's chapter in this book.

9 Ibid., 237.

10 Frederic Hudson, *Journalism in the United States, from 1690–1872* (1873; reprint ed., New York: Haskell House Publishers, 1968), XXVII.

11 Bryce, *American Commonwealth*, (1888 ed.) 2:237.

12 See Mark Hampton, *Visions of the Press in Britain, 1850–1950* (Urbana and Chicago: University of Illinois Press, 2004), 106–29.

13 Ions, *James Bryce*, 166–7.

14 Bryce, "British Feelings on the Venezuelan Question," *The North American Review* 162 (1896), 149.

15 See Richard Fulton's chapter in the present book. More broadly, the transition in American journalism during the 1890s is the subject of W. Joseph Campbell, *The Year That Defined American Journalism: 1897 and the Clash of Paradigms* (London and New York: Routledge, 2006).

16 Bryce to Sir Charles Hardinge, 2 August 1907, Papers of Sir Edward Grey, F. O. 800, General Series, vol. 81, fols. 224–7, Public Record Office, London. Hereafter cited as Grey Papers. Also, Bryce to Edward Grey 16 September 1907, James Bryce Papers, vol. 27, fol. 130, Bodleian Library Oxford. Hereafter cited as Bryce Papers, Bod. L. Other Bryce Papers, including his annual reports to Whitehall, are in the Public Record Office, London.

17 Bryce to Edward Grey, 18 November 1908, Grey Papers, vol. 81, fols. 407–10.

18 Bryce to A. V. Dicey, 16 February 1909, Bryce Papers, Bod. L., English Correspondence, vol. 4, fol. 7.

19 Bryce to Edward Grey, 2 August 1907, Grey Papers, vol. 81, fols. 221–2. See also Bryce to Edward Grey, 16 September 1907, Bryce Papers, Bod. L., vol. 27, fol. 130; and Beckles Willson, *Friendly Relations: A Narrative of Britain's Ministers and Ambassadors to America 1791–1930* (Boston: Little, Brown, 1934), p. 300.

20 Bryce to Sir Charles Hardinge, 2 August 1907, fols. 224–7.
21 Bryce to Sir Charles Hardinge, 21 January 1908, ibid., fols. 315–16.
22 "Report by Herbert Grant Watson on the Press of the United States and its Methods," enclosed in James Bryce to Sir Edward Grey, 13 April 1908, F. O. 371–566, p. 2, Public Record Office, London.
23 Ibid., p. 9.
24 Ibid., covering letter.
25 "United States: Annual Report, 1909," F. O. 371, Political, vol. 1022, file 10003, pp. 16 and 39, Public Record Office, London. The annual ambassadorial reports were signed by Bryce and he personally wrote the section on "Public Opinion and the Subjects that Relate to it." See B. J. C. McKercher, *Esme Howard: A Diplomatic Biography* (Cambridge: Cambridge University Press, 1989), 95–6.
26 Bryce, "United States: Annual Report, 1909," F. O. 371, Political, vol. 1022, no. 10003, p. 17, Public Record Office, London.
27 Bryce to Edward Grey, 16 September 1907, Bryce Papers, Bod. L., vol. 27, fol. 130.
28 Typical of the press criticism articles during the years of Bryce's ambassadorship were "International Hatred and the Press," *The Nation* (26 March 1908), 276, and "Offenses Against Good Journalism," *The Outlook* (29 February 1909), 479.
29 See, for instance, "After Exposure What?" *The Nation*, 22 March 1906, 234, and "President Roosevelt on Muck-Rakers," *Harper's Weekly*, 28 April 1906, 580.
30 Bryce, "Annual Report, 1910," F. O. 881, Confidential Papers, no. 9857, p. 34, Public Record Office, London. In his private correspondence, Roosevelt employed sharp language to describe certain newspapers in the country, including the ones that Bryce used for his examples of journalism harmful to the public good. See, Roosevelt to William Dudley Foulke, 24 and 30 October and 1 December 1908, William Dudley Foulke Papers, box 4, Library of Congress, Manuscript Division.
31 Bryce, "Annual Report, 1910," p. 34.
32 Bryce, "Annual Report, 1909," p. 17. The four other dangers he cited were 1) the power of great corporations, 2) the demands of organized labor, 3) the "selfish power of the machine," and 4) the weakness of the state judiciary.
33 As various Bryce scholars mention, he "claimed that five-sixths of his data came from observation and from conversation with Americans." For example, see Morton Keller, "James Bryce and America," *Wilson Quarterly* 12 (Autumn 1988): 89.
34 *Biographical Dictionary of American Journalism*, s. v. "Godkin, Edwin Lawrence," by Arthur J. Kaul.
35 Bryce to N. M. Butler, 1 October 1914, quoted in Keith Robbins, "Lord Bryce and the First World War," *The Historical Journal* 10 (December 1985): 258.
36 *Report on the Committee on Alleged German Outrages*, usually known as the Bryce Report, (New York: Macmillan, 1915). The role of one of Bryce's stature in the inquiry is puzzling, but for a reasonable interpretation of his involvement in it see Trevor Wilson, "Lord Bryce's Investigation into

Alleged German Atrocities in Belgium, 1914–1915," *Journal of Contemporary History* 14 (July 1979): 381.

37 Bryce to Dr. Charles W. Eliot, 4 March 1921, quoted in H. A. L. Fisher, *James Bryce*, 2 vols. (New York: Macmillan, 1927), 2: 259.

38 Bryce to William A. Dunning, 9 October 1919, James Bryce Correspondence, microfilm, Columbia University Special Collections, Rare Book and Manuscript Library, Columbia University Libraries, New York.

39 Walter Lippmann and Allan Nevins, eds., *A Modern Reader: Essays on Present-day Life and Culture* (Boston: D. C. Heath, 1936), 125.

40 Bryce, *Modern Democracies*, 2 vols. (London: Macmillan, 1921), 1:107–14, & 122.

41 Ibid., 1:105.

42 Ibid., 1:113, 118–19, & 127–8.

43 Ibid., 1:109.

44 Ibid., 2:406.

45 Ibid., 1:114–15.

46 Ibid., 2:129 & 611, & 1:124.

47 Ibid., 1:104–05, 109, & 124.

48 Robert C. Brooks, "American Parties and Politics, 1888 and 1938," in *Bryce's American Commonwealth: Fiftieth Anniversary*, ed. Robert C. Brooks (New York: Macmillan, 1939), 79.

49 Bryce, *Modern Democracies*, 1:82.

50 Ibid., 2:123, and E. F. Shaughnessy, "Anatomy of the Republic," *Encounter*, July–Aug., 1989, 37.

6
Leslie Howard and Douglas Fairbanks, Jr.: Promoting the Anglo-American Alliance in Wartime, 1939–43

Fred M. Leventhal

When the civilian plane transporting Leslie Howard back to England after a British Council-sponsored lecture tour to Portugal and Spain was shot down by German fighters on June 1, 1943, press reaction was effusive, even for a stage and screen actor who had become a transatlantic celebrity. Caroline Lejeune, the *Observer's* film critic, wrote:

> Probably no single war casualty has induced in the public of these islands such an acute sense of personal loss. Howard was something more than just a popular actor. Since the war he had become something of a symbol to the British people. He stood, in an odd way, for all that is most deeply rooted in the British character.[1]

Hannen Swaffer, writing in the *Daily Herald*, remarked that:

> Leslie Howard died as he would have wished it – serving his country. Really good actor though he was, film star though he became, he was proudest of the propagandist work he did in the war – on the screen, on the platform, and on the air.[2]

Anthony ("Puffin") Asquith, Howard's collaborator on the film version of *Pygmalion*, memorialized him as:

> uniquely fitted for the unofficial post of Britain's screen ambassador to the world at large.... He was the perfect embodiment of many of our national characteristics, and was able to make those characteris-

tics internationally intelligible and, what is far more important, lovable.[3]

The Second World War changed the trajectory of Howard's career, and yet his image as the quintessential Englishman was already well-burnished by 1939. His dignified charm and sensitivity, his gentle manner and ironic humor, enabled him to play the dreamy, absent-minded intellectual – the thinking man as hero, to quote Jeffrey Richards,[4] so that by the end of his career his persona seemed insepara-ble from the roles he acted.

Yet his personal background and early theatrical and cinematic career hardly portended so emblematic a role at the time of his prema-ture death at age 50. This Englishman's Englishman was the son of Ferdinand Steiner, a Hungarian-Jewish immigrant, and Lilian Blumberg, although the family was subsequently to dissociate them-selves from their Jewish origins.[5] Later garnering kudos for his perfor-mances as Professor Henry Higgins and Professor Horatio Smith, he was an indifferent student, leaving his local Dulwich school to become a bank clerk, a job for which he showed neither inclination nor apti-tude. At the beginning of the First World War he volunteered for the cavalry and served in France before suffering shell shock in 1916 and resigning his commission. Refusing to return to the bank, Leslie, who had earlier taken part in amateur theatricals, resolved to try his luck on the stage. He secured small parts in touring companies before making his London debut in 1918, and in 1920 he accepted a part in a New York play. For the next 16 years he acted primarily on the New York stage with occasional forays to the West End and, after 1930, enjoyed a lucrative film career. Most of his appearances in the 1920s were in drawing room comedies and bedroom farces, few of which were partic-ularly noteworthy. Between 1920 and 1939 Howard was steadily employed: during the 1920s he was usually in two or three plays a season, and, once his Hollywood career took off, with a featured debut in *Outward Bound*, he made films every year for the rest of his life. However, it was only during the mid- and late 1930s, in the stage and film version of *The Petrified Forest* and in movies like *Of Human Bondage, The Scarlet Pimpernel, Pygmalion*, and *Gone With the Wind* that Howard earned critical acclaim as a serious actor capable of transcend-ing light, romantic comedy.[6]

After the comparative failure of his *Hamlet* in 1936 – inevitably over-shadowed by John Gielgud's concurrent New York production – Howard abandoned the stage to concentrate on movies, but became increasingly disenchanted with the tedium of film acting, preferring instead to focus on producing and directing. When *Gone With the Wind*, in which he had played Ashley Wilkes, was completed, Howard, eager to distance himself from Hollywood, decamped for England, initially with the intention of making a film called *The Man Who Lost Himself*, an ironically self-referential title. With war looming, he resolved to place himself at the disposal of the government, convinced that he could be more useful to the British cause in a propaganda role than by cavorting in period costume on the screen. As his son later observed, even though Howard had spent most of his working life in America, "England was his real home at heart and he remained, for all his long absences, essentially English and England-loving."[7]

While fruitlessly seeking funding for his film project, he also approached Lord Halifax with a proposal to make a documentary film "depicting the last days of peace and the efforts of England to avoid war and yet remain true to her pledges." He contended that the subject was "so compelling and dramatic that it would attract an enormous public, particularly in the United States." Howard offered to "put aside all personal plans and give my services to such a project."[8] At the same time he submitted a lengthy document entitled "Notes on American Propaganda" to the Ministry of Information. In it he acknowledged that the "dogged determination never to shed American blood again in any foreign war" gave rise to the "spectacle of a great world power apparently behaving like a second-rate state in its isolation and fear of the outside world." What was needed was a "properly camouflaged message that could be carried direct to the American people." The essential message he sought to drive home for American audiences was that Britain was "engaged once more in a struggle for principles" because "we cannot stand by and see an ever increasing area of the civilised world dominated by a bully and subjected to gangster force."[9]

In addition, Howard and Anthony Asquith prepared a memorandum for the Ministry of Information on "The Film Industry in Time of War," with which Michael Powell and other film-makers associated themselves as signatories.[10] Although he was appointed to the Ideas Committee of the MOI, and attended meetings of the Anglo-French Propaganda Council in Paris in January and April 1940 with the goal of producing Anglo-French war films, he became increasingly frustrated at "the blank wall of apparent uninterest" he encountered in government circles in late 1939.[11]

Despite official inertia and initial problems in obtaining funding for his first wartime film, Howard found the BBC more receptive.

Following his first broadcast in 1938, his name resurfaced as a prospective speaker in Empire programs, but little seems to have transpired before July 1940. By then the BBC had launched the nightly program *Britain Speaks*, intended for listeners in Canada and the United States. Intermittently faulty reception and accents deemed impenetrable by North Americans made it imperative to find intelligible speakers if the service were to build an audience. The program's producers welcomed Howard's participation, and over the next six months Howard delivered commentaries, usually written by himself, almost every week – more than two dozen programs before film commitments forced him to phase out his talks in the spring of 1941.[12]

From the outset Howard sought to capitalize on his close associations with America to reinforce the Anglo-American connection. In his initial broadcast he remarked that since his arrival in the fall of 1920, the United States "has been my principal home."[13] He underscored his bifurcated personality in a broadcast two months later when he proclaimed:

> I am an Englishman and an American. I am an Englishman because I was born and raised one, and an American because I have lived the greater part of my adult life in the United States... I believe now that I understand thoroughly the American way of life and attitude of mind; in fact, to a large extent, I have made them my own.[14]

This made him the ideal culture broker, not only because he knew both countries, but because he could recognize the affinities between the two. Again and again in his broadcasts he emphasized the common sympathies and political identity of the two countries:

> Though more than forty million free people in this island are again involved in the eternal fight against European continental domination, their eyes are towards the West ... And although we and you have many superficial differences, when the world goes mad the English-speaking peoples come very close together.[15]

In an October 1940 broadcast Howard, observing that "the superficial differences between myself and family and our American friends became almost indistinguishable," went so far as to advocate that Britain and America "unite into a great Federation and a Union of Common Citizenship." His demand for a "Great Union, in War and Peace, for the benefit of the world and the safety of humanity" was the furthest he would go in calling upon Americans to involve themselves directly in the war.[16]

Americans not only needed to be reassured about their own political virtue: they must also be informed about what the British were enduring in order to wean them from their neutrality. In one of his earliest broadcasts Howard described London as "prepared to fight street by street, with habitual Cockney spleen, if our enemies have the temerity, and the luck, to penetrate so far."[17] The following week he compared the light-hearted revelry when he was a soldier during the First World War with the sandbags and shelters, the solemnity of the blackout, that marked the scene in 1940. But through the grim vistas, the British sense of invincibility shone through:

> Here is only a people facing the worst menace in their history, committed to a life or death proposition and knowing full well all the implications – a people without illusions but with a stronger ... a more profound conviction that no matter what the cost or how long the time, once again they will triumph.[18]

In November he devoted an entire talk to recounting his nights in a London air-raid shelter in the basement of his block of flats where men and women of all social backgrounds gathered nightly and where Howard "had never been so contented in my life as I am in that shelter." He found it remarkable that although most of the shelter occupants were individually scared of the bombs, "when we are all together down there, we don't get frightened." In the social mingling he discerned a foretaste of a new democratic resolve. There was, he informed his American listeners:

> a spirit abroad now, today in Britain, a better spirit of unselfish living and thinking, a spirit of sacrifice and a spirit of humility which I am convinced must endure long after this struggle is ended.[19]

An additional theme in Howard's broadcasts was denunciation of the Nazi regime, but – and this was in line with British propaganda – without stigmatizing the German people. Germans had been "hypnotised by their false gods into believing that an aggressive war [was] good not evil, and the right and only way to get what they want."[20] Frankly admitting that his weekly "transatlantic telephone calls" to all his American friends might be deemed propaganda, he declared that it was time for the British to abandon their "painstaking rectitude" and reticence and to tell Americans "openly what is in our hearts and in our minds." He blamed the government's poor showing in the war of words on the "British horror of propaganda as calculated to alienate rather than gain sympathy." After American entry into the war, Howard's tone changed. No longer wary of offending American neutralist sentiment, he argued that democracy needed to be "as militant as autocracy."[21]

During more than six months he became the most familiar British interpreter of the war for American listeners, although it was perhaps name recognition and his disarmingly informal delivery that enabled him to rival American radio journalists broadcasting from London, like Edward R. Murrow. In fact, while *Britain Speaks* was wound down, Howard continued to broadcast in the North American service, especially on *Answering You*, in which British commentators responded to questions posed by Americans.[22] He recognized that his talents as a broadcaster would be best deployed in America, where he was, if anything, more popular than in Britain.

Howard's first propaganda film appearance was in *From the Four Corners*, a 15-minute documentary prepared for the Ministry of Information in 1940, in which he escorts three Dominion servicemen around London while questioning them about their motives for enlisting.[23] More memorable was Howard's pivotal role as Philip Armstrong Scott in Michael Powell and Emeric Pressburger's hugely successful 1941 propaganda film, *The 49ᵗʰ Parallel*. Subsidized by the government, it tracked six survivors of a marauding German submarine bombed in Canadian waters who attempt to escape capture while propagating Nazi ideology among the people they encounter. With Canada as a surrogate for the United States, the film was a cautionary tale about the permeability of borders and the fanaticism of the German invaders, who murder with impunity. During their travels they meet a French Canadian trapper, a pacifist Hutterite community, a Canadian soldier who has gone AWOL, and a solitary English writer living in a tepee amid the splendor of the Canadian Rockies.

As depicted by Howard, Scott is an intellectual, who decorates his walls with a Picasso and a Matisse and who reads Hemingway and Thomas Mann. Scott is the epitome of the British pipe-smoking aesthete, gracious to the German escapees, oblivious to the war, and skeptical about his own courage. Howard deliberately cultivated the image of the effete, unworldly Englishman, readily dismissed by his German intruders as "soft and degenerate – rotten to the core." He gently chides his German guests with offhand references to Hitler and Goebbels, but when he discovers that they are brutal Nazis, he retorts, "That explains everything: your arrogance, your stupidity, your bad manners." After he goads them into tying him up, smashing his paintings, and burning his books and manuscripts, he responds with a kind of genteel hauteur: "Well, I never could have believed that grown up men could behave like spiteful little schoolboys." Yet, once he is freed by others in the camp, he beats a cowardly German into submission. Vindicated – although with his cherished possessions destroyed – he tells one of his rescuers that his German antagonist had "a fair chance: one armed superman against one unarmed decadent democrat."[24] Although his scene lasts only 15 minutes out of a two-hour film, it is the ideological fulcrum of the story – the fundamental conflict between the values of Anglo-Saxon democracy and the delusions of the Nazi supermen.

In 1938, shortly before the *Anschluss*, Howard went on a skiing holiday to Austria where he met Alfons Walde, a Jewish painter whose expressionist paintings were certain to be denounced by the Nazis. Howard felt an affinity with the professors, artists, and intellectuals who had lost their positions or faced imprisonment for heterodox views or racial impurity. By 1940 he was beginning to sketch out the idea of an escape movie, in which a celebrated anti-Nazi painter would be rescued from Hitler's clutches, the germ of what was to become his most effective propaganda exercise, the brilliant film *Pimpernel Smith*.[25] By updating his celebrated characterization as *The Scarlet Pimpernel* from the French Revolution to 1939, Howard contrived an inspired vehicle for a satirical adventure story with a political message. Serving as both producer and director of the film, he created the role of Cambridge archeologist Professor Horatio Smith, an absent-minded, superficially pompous, misogynous scholar, who conceals his secret life as a daring adventurer smuggling victims out of Germany and foiling efforts to uncover his identity. Recognized only by his whistling of "There is a Tavern in the Town" and by his calling-card message, "The mind of man is bounded only by the universe," Smith accomplishes repeated feats of daring in Germany, including disguising himself as a scarecrow in a labor camp and as the leader of the Nazi-American Bund, all the while saving scientists, journalists, and musicians who were targeted as enemies of the Nazi regime. Early in the film he tells a scientist he has rescued from the Gestapo, "I hate violence. It seems such a paradox to kill a man before you can persuade him what's right. It's so uncivilized." Using ingenuity and wit, peppering his conversation with quotations from Shakespeare and Lewis Carroll, he is able to outfox the obtuse and bullying

Propaganda Minister, General von Graum (modeled by actor Francis L. Sullivan on Hermann Goering) and to prove that the Englishman's secret weapon is his sense of humor. Rather than elude von Graum, who is slow to suspect Smith of being the "mysterious rescuer," he repeatedly confronts him to banter about whether Shakespeare was English or German and to find ways of mocking the Nazis for their humorlessness and barbarity. Having abducted six dissidents from a concentration camp while his Cambridge students posed as visiting American journalists, Smith, finally captured, is sentenced to be summarily executed, a "strange end," he muses, "for one who despises violence at the hands of those who worship it." When von Graum boasts of the ultimate Nazi victory, Smith tells him:

> You will never rule the world because you are doomed ... all of you who have demoralized and corrupted a nation. You will go on and on from one madness to another, leaving behind you a wilderness of misery and hatred.

In the movie's final scene, a momentary distraction enables Smith to escape across the borders, taunting his captors by saying "I shall be back. We shall all be back."[26]

The film was more of a triumph than Howard could have anticipated. It was not only a box-office success in Britain and the United States, but it aroused the ire of German officials, who sought to prevent its showing in neutral countries and targeted Howard as an enemy. Only *The 49th Parallel* and Chaplin's *The Great Dictator* earned more money in 1941–42 from distribution in British cinemas. Some critics have seen Pimpernel Smith as a modern Christ figure, surrounded by disciples, crucified – at least temporarily – as a scarecrow, with his bloodied hand like a stigmata, and vowing to return.[27] While it is unlikely that Howard had anything as far-fetched in mind, he clearly saw Smith as a symbol of beleaguered culture. In truth, Horatio Smith was virtually indistinguishable from Philip Armstrong Scott, the character Howard portrayed in *The 49th Parallel*. Both were sensitive intellectuals with a visionary streak, both hated the violence that underpinned Nazism, both defended civilization against the barbarians, both armed themselves with kindliness, tolerance, modesty, and an ironic sense of humor – the distinctive qualities of the stereotypical Englishman that Howard had come to embody in his screen persona.

Howard pursued several ideas in the aftermath of *Pimpernel Smith*. He planned lecture tours to Canada and the United States and contemplated a film that would "try to explain England and America to each other" by tracing a family politically divided at the time of the American Revolution to its descendants in the present who come to understand each other "in their common devotion to democracy threatened by Fascist domination."[28] None of these plans were realized, but Howard was soon enticed by the idea of a film based on the life of R. J. Mitchell, the designer of the Spitfire fighter plane. In a film entitled *The First of the Few* (released in abbreviated form in the United States as *Spitfire*), Howard, once again serving as producer, director, and star, depicted Mitchell as a quiet visionary determined to equip his nation with the aircraft needed to combat the military power of resurgent Nazism. His characterization transformed Mitchell into the now-familiar Howard screen persona – understated, gentle, pipe-smoking, sacrificing himself for his ideals. Once again the Germans are depicted as arrogant, menacing, and humorless. By his use of flashback, Howard links the heroic feats of the RAF during the Battle of Britain with Mitchell's striving to gain approval for his revolutionary airplane design against pusillanimous politicians. Dying of apparent exhaustion – Mitchell, in fact, had cancer – he learns in his (and the film's) final moments that the government had sanctioned the building of the Spitfire, which the film's 1942 viewers knew had been the salvation of the nation.

The film historian Jeffrey Richards refers to *The First of the Few* – the few being those to whom so much was owed – as Leslie Howard's "masterpiece and his monument,"[29] although my own preference is for *Pimpernel Smith*, which is tautly constructed, has a much livelier script, and is not encumbered with hagiographic pieties. If *Pimpernel Smith* is a propagandistic gem couched in the guise of traditional romantic adventure, *The First of the Few* is a testimonial to the virtues of the English character, a theme that harked back to Samuel Smiles' inspirational life histories. In its affirmation of English ingenuity and determination, it captured the spirit of the early years of the Second World War, the idea that the British underdog would prove invincible even in the face of a more powerful Germany. To friends of the British cause in America, these films confirmed the growing sense that the British might actually prevail and that they were allies worth having.

Douglas Fairbanks, Jr.'s background differed dramatically from that of his friend, Leslie Howard. Born into Hollywood royalty as the son of one of the first internationally known stars and the stepson of "America's sweetheart," Mary Pickford, Fairbanks built a career as a movie actor very much in his father's shadow and in similar swashbuckling roles. Although he never attained the pinnacle of success and Hollywood insider status of the elder Fairbanks, he appeared in more than 90 films, beginning in 1923, when he was only 14. Aside from an occasional memorable production, such as the 1930 feature, *Outward Bound,* in which he starred with Leslie Howard, he acted in a succession of second-rate melodramas, romantic comedies, and swashbuckling adventures, easily adapting to the transition from silent to speaking parts. The bulk of his films between 1926 and 1940 were standard studio fare, quickly produced for movie-crazed Anglo-American audiences, with actors, like Fairbanks, appearing in as many as eight films in a single year. In contrast to Howard, several of whose performances exploited his Englishness, Fairbanks evoked no particular national persona. His good looks and resemblance to his father meant that he had no difficulty in securing parts, and he avoided becoming typecast by appearing in hard-boiled gangster films as well as historical romances.

In 1934 Fairbanks left Warner Bros., taking up residence in England where he made several movies, while emulating the life of an English gentleman and cultivating friends in high places, including politicians like Anthony Eden, Ronald Tree, and Duff Cooper and royals like the Duke of Kent and Prince Louis Mountbatten. Among his closest British friends was Lord Tweedsmuir (the writer John Buchan), whose political views inspired the rather callow American actor, still in his 20s. Fairbanks' anglophilia was deeply rooted. Throughout his childhood he had visited England frequently and, without losing his American identity, came to regard England as his second home. He later took probably unwarranted credit for being one of the proponents of a royal visit to the United States, eventually undertaken in June 1939, two years after Fairbanks suggested the idea to the Duke of Kent.[30] In retrospect, Fairbanks also claimed that he attempted to infuse some of his films in the 1930s with a conviction about the importance of Anglo-American relationship. One of his early films, *Dawn Patrol* (1930) romanticized the Royal Flying Corps, while the remake of *Prisoner of Zenda* (1937), in which he appeared with Ronald Colman, was purportedly conceived as "a paraphrase of the abdication crisis." As early as 1938 Fairbanks was urging Hollywood producers to make anti-Nazi movies, but many of them feared that explicit hostility to Hitler would generate an anti-Semitic backlash in America.[31] Pro-British sentiment was more overt in the imperialist epic, *Gunga Din* (1939) and in the Cunard story, *Rulers of the Sea* (1939),[32] although their propagandistic intent is perhaps more apparent with hindsight than when they were produced. One might indeed question whether *Gunga Din* underscored the beneficence of the British Empire for Americans in the ways that Fairbanks imagined, notwithstanding the popularity of such films.

In contrast to Howard, Fairbanks was to restrict and later temporarily forsake his film career first for wartime propaganda work and then during active service in the Navy after American entry in the war, when he lobbied successfully to get himself assigned to Mountbatten's naval command. Before his stint in active service, Fairbanks devoted himself more or less full time to winning American support for the British war effort and trumpeting that support in broadcasts to Britain. His famous name and celebrity status made Fairbanks an effective cultural interme- diary between the two countries, and his personal ties to President Roosevelt himself, as well as to prominent Englishmen, opened doors for him which might have been closed to ordinary film stars.

In September 1939 Clark Eichelberger, the director of the League of Nations Association and the Union for Concerted Peace Efforts, per- suaded William Allen White, the respected editor of the *Emporia Gazette*, to chair a committee that would seek to build public support for President Roosevelt's "cash and carry" bill, a proposal that would have repealed the embargo on the sale of armaments to belligerents. Originally called the Non-Partisan Committee for Peace through the Revision of the Neutrality Law, its members included a broad spectrum of internationalist opinion, committed both to keeping the United States out of the war and contributing to the defeat of Hitler. Although White and other enlightened Republicans, like Frank Knox and Henry Stimson, lobbied in favor of the cash and carry bill, they failed to per- suade most Republican Congressmen to endorse it. By the spring of 1940 the White Committee was recast as the Committee to Defend America by Aiding the Allies, its roster including a veritable roll call of notable American internationalists and anglophiles among university presidents, religious leaders, businessmen, politicians, publishers, and political activists.[33] White believed that by supplying Britain with the wherewithal to continue the struggle, the United States would be able to stay out of the war. His personal preference was for an end to neu- trality, not support for intervention, but many of his collaborators increasingly came to view eventual American entry as inevitable and even desirable.

By July 1940, the White Committee, campaigning in favor of selling airplanes to Britain and France, had expanded nationally to 300 local branches. Robert E. Sherwood, playwright and speech writer for Franklin Roosevelt, invited Fairbanks to become Vice Chairman of the Southern California chapter and a national vice president, partly because he was known to enjoy the President's personal confidence. During the following months Fairbanks met with the President and Secretary of State Cordell Hull several times to discuss strategy for aiding the British. Roosevelt endorsed these efforts to rally the people, insisting that, since a democratic leader could not get too far ahead of the electorate, the Committee, by mobilizing opinion behind the President's foreign policy, might enable him to provide substantive aid to the British.

Never diffident about self-promotion, Fairbanks offered his services to the White House in the summer of 1940. As he informed a member of the President's staff:

> I feel that I could be of value in liaison and propaganda work or even in the diplomatic field. Because of unusual fortune I have been able to commute between here and Europe since childhood and have lived and worked in Britain for some years. During this time my interest in international politics gave me an intimate entree to men in public life which under less unusual circumstances would be denied to others.

In addition he claimed to have made "the first concrete suggestion" for the royal visit and that passages from his letters to Lord Stamp, the Duke of Kent, Duff Cooper, and Anthony Eden "were being used in broadcasts and statements." Although his public activities were then limited to the Committee to Defend America by Aiding the Allies and war relief charities, he did not hesitate to sound out the White House about an assignment with responsibility for Anglo-American or Canadian-American relations. "I have been so flattered by the confidences shown me by people in Britain," he concluded, "that I am most anxious to inspire the same confidence in the authorities of my own country."[34] His eagerness was eventually rewarded with invitations to Hyde Park and an appointment as a special envoy to five South American countries in 1941 to assess the role of the media in countering Nazi propaganda.

In the meantime he continued to campaign on behalf of the White Committee as it attempted to clarify the issues of the war and win over waverers by rebutting the strident message of isolationists. In a speech in Chicago in September 1940, before an audience of several thousand, Fairbanks declared:

> I am frankly pro-British. But only because I am radically pro-American. In these days the two terms are well-nigh synonymous.... Today only the British, who are now right under the guns, can fight back, and ... are doing it with all the courage which we and history expect of them... America can keep out of this war if Britain wins, and wins within a reasonably short time. The longer it lasts the more chance of our having to get in it.

If Britain was fighting to defend the political principles that Americans cherished, then America's welfare and security required a British victory. He therefore appealed to his listeners:

> Let us give – not lend – the British all possible assistance...We have the greatest material resources in the world. Let us prove that our moral resources are just as great, and give them the means to keep the conflagration away from our shores.[35]

The speech was well-publicized in the United States and in England, where Mountbatten responded by writing, "I must say that this Country owes people like yourself a great debt of gratitude for the work you are doing and few people can have done more for the Allied cause than you have."[36]

In another speech a month letter, ironically commemorating the Battle of Yorktown in 1781, he reiterated his theme:

> Whatever the original causes of the war may have been... it has developed into a struggle of such universal magnitude that there is no doubt that Britain is leading, alone, and with the bravery which only free men can show, a crusade not only for herself and her sister nations, but for all free people everywhere... .We must make known to our representatives in Washington again and again that we do not want the war to come to these shores; that inasmuch as the British can and *will* continue to fight *our* battle as well as their own, we will do *our* bit by giving, not lending, them all aid.[37]

Later in the year he told the California Women's Club Convention that:

> if the British win the war, our safety is assured. We also understand that the longer the British resist, the longer we are given to com-

plete our defenses. We understand further that if Britain is conquered, we stand alone against the combined power of Germany,
Japan, Italy, and all their satellites... . To be the one democratic
power left in a world of victorious Dictator States would be a kind of
isolation such as Americans have never dreamed of.[38]

Speaking in Miami in February 1941, he attacked isolationists in
general and targeted America First spokesman Colonel Charles
Lindbergh, who was confident that the United States would never be
attacked and whose equanimity was unshaken by "the subjugation by
force of all religious, social and political institutions or military aggres-
sions against innocent neighbors." Fairbanks acknowledged that "the
very lives of the free people of this country are in danger." Refuting
Lindbergh, who perceived little difference in the aims of belligerents,
he affirmed that "the torch of liberty is held aloft by British hands. We
must give it fuel to stay alight."[39]

Fairbanks' role as a cultural intermediary was enhanced when,
having initially rejected his overture on the grounds that "talks
Britainwards are confined to rather objective interpretations of what is
happening" in America,[40] the BBC invited him to broadcast to England
in October 1940. Much as Leslie Howard's talks were designed to culti-
vate American support for Britain, Fairbanks sought to reassure British
audiences that such support was growing. In his first broadcast he
explained the initial reluctance of Americans to become involved, the
distance having deluded many into imagining that they were not in
danger. But in the aftermath of the Blitz, isolationists were "disappear-
ing faster than the buffaloes and red Indians eighty years ago."
Westerners had come to realize that "nobody is safe in this war."
Extolling British indomitability, he exclaimed that:

> your spirit has improved our morale, has rekindled our faith in
> humanity and the idea of freedom, and has fortified our determina-
> tion to help you preserve the way of life we both cherish... . I am
> sure that most other Americans, realizing as they do that not only
> are you fighting for your self-preservation of an idea which has
> taken you over a thousand years to develop, but that you are
> fighting for us too, feel the same.[41]

Fairbanks received dozens of letters from listeners in England, expressing appreciation for his consoling words in the middle of the Blitz. The
success of his initial broadcast brought another invitation to speak to
Britain in January 1941, at which time he interpreted Roosevelt's

election to a third term as signifying "in unmistakable terms our conviction that your battle is ours too, and that we must exert all our energies to help you bring about a complete and civilized victory." He also recounted what the Hollywood community was doing to help "unify American opinion behind the British crusade" through appearances and by raising money for war relief.[42] David Niven reported that the "broadcast was a <u>screaming</u> success and you are very quickly becoming a popular hero over here."[43] In response to a suggestion made by Mountbatten, Fairbanks was himself privately furnishing funds to support three RAF hospitals in Hampshire, known as the Douglas Voluntary Hospitals.[44] His final broadcast in April 1941, hailed the passage of the Lend-Lease Act as clear indication that American policy was now completely dedicated to a British victory:

> More than a year and a half ago we Americans decided that we wanted Britain to win, not only for herself, because she was our closest of kin and because we sympathized with her cause, but for ourselves and our own security as well. As the months passed, the desire became stronger, and the American people decided to *insist* on a British victory, *come what may*. Today we have made that decision clear to the world.[45]

Fairbanks' role as a propagandist for the British war effort largely ceased once the United States entered the war, and he joined the Navy. After the war his anglophilia reached new heights, especially after being offered an honorary knighthood in 1949 for furthering Anglo-American amity and becoming a favorite of the royal family. His film career tapered off during the 1950s, and in later years Fairbanks essentially lived the life of a playboy celebrity, much of the time in England, occasionally acting or hosting a television series, or dabbling in philanthropic activities, but always maintaining his personal contacts with the high and mighty on both sides of the Atlantic.

The activities during these years of both Leslie Howard and Douglas Fairbanks, Jr. reflect the emergence of a celebrity culture in Britain and America that enabled actors to speak out politically and to influence public opinion at a time of national crisis. The growth of the cinema as the most popular medium in the inter-war period transformed its stars into popular heroes, instantly recognizable and idolized by masses of people. This notoriety could be harnessed for public purposes, as governments on both sides of the Atlantic belatedly realized. In this case, two intelligent, public-spirited actors devoted themselves wholeheartedly to reinforcing the Anglo-American connection, which they believed was instrumental in winning the war against Hitler. They proved to be more effective spokesmen for their cause than many of their contemporaries and made a distinct contribution to rallying morale and instilling patriotic sentiment in the early years of the Second World War. Although the impact of cultural propaganda is difficult to measure, there seems little reason to doubt that it played a role in the vital task of winning the hearts and minds of the American people and converting residual isolationism into genuine support for the "special relationship."

Notes

1 *New York Times*, 27 June 1943.
2 *Daily Herald*, 3 June 1943.
3 *The Cine-Technician*, No. 42 (May–June 1943), 68.
4 Jeffrey Richards, "Leslie Howard: The Thinking Man as Hero," *Focus on Film*, No. 25 (Summer–Autumn 1976), 37. Also see Anthony Aldgate and Jeffrey Richards, *Britain Can Take It*, 2nd ed. (Edinburgh: Edinburgh University Press, 1994), 44–75.
5 Leslie dropped the Steiner (or Stainer, which the family had used) and adopted his middle name – Howard – as his surname. The rest of the family – at least those who went into the theatre – followed suit, including his sister Irene, brother Arthur, and nephew Alan.
6 Information on Howard's early life and career can be gleaned from Leslie Ruth Howard, *A Quite Remarkable Father* (New York: Harcourt Brace, 1959); Ronald Howard, *In Search of My Father* (New York: St. Martin's Press, 1981); Jeffrey Richards, "Leslie Howard: The Thinking Man as Hero," *Focus on Film*, No. 25 (Summer–Autumn, 1976), 37–50; Dan Van Neste, "Leslie Howard: Unmasking the Pimpernel," *Films of the Golden Age*, No. 19 (Winter 1999/2000), 23–43.
7 Howard, *In Search of My Father*, 31.
8 Copy of letter from Leslie Howard to Lord Halifax, n.d. [8 Sept. 1939]. I am grateful to Professor Douglas Wheeler for making this letter available to me. Howard told journalist Hubert Cole that he had intended to make a film "revealing the origins of the war and the Nazi treatment of political opponents," but quickly concluded that the subject was too large for a documentary. See Hubert Cole, "What Should Leslie Howard Do Now?," *Picturegoer*, 8 Feb. 1941. The theme was later treated in Frank Capra's documentary film series, *Why We Fight*, especially in the first two episodes, *Prelude to War* and *The Nazis Strike*.
9 Copy of "Notes on American Propaganda" (8 September 1939). I am grateful to Professor Wheeler for making this document available to me. Sections of the report are quoted in Howard, *A Quite Remarkable Father*, 268–9.
10 I have been unable to find a copy of this memorandum. Ronald Howard indicates that it expanded many of Leslie's American propaganda ideas, but was more detailed and technical, covering home and overseas propaganda, training and instructional films. See Howard, *In Search of My Father*, 59.

11 Ibid., 61. The first Paris meeting is mentioned in *The Times*, 19 Jan. 1940. Howard had discussions with Jean Giraudoux, Andre Maurois, and Noel Coward, and a propaganda film starring Howard and Danielle Darrieux and directed by Rene Clair was planned, but it was never produced. See Howard, *In Search of My Father*, 59.

12 Howard was ordinarily paid 15 gns for each talk. When filming began to consume most of his time, the BBC offered to work out a system of ghost-writing to alleviate the burden of writing the scripts for the weekly talks. However, the producers were wary of letting this process go too far, telling him that "as you write much better scripts for yourself than I feel we could ever write for you, and as it is most important to preserve your own individual manner of presenting your material, I think we should be careful not to overdo this." James Ferguson to Leslie Howard, 11 Nov. 1940, BBC Written Archives Centre (henceforth BBC WAC), File 910HOW. Broadcasts on 18 Nov. and 3 and 10 Dec. 1940 were written by BBC staff members and delivered by Howard.

13 *Britain Speaks* Transcript 47a (16/17 July 1940), BBC WAC, File 910.

14 "Shopkeepers and Poets," *Britain Speaks* Transcript 137 (14/15 Oct. 1940), BBC WAC, File 910.

15 *Britain Speaks* Transcript 74a (12/13 Aug. 1940), BBC WAC, File 910.

16 "The Great Union," *Britain Speaks* Transcript (28/29 Oct. 1940), BBC WAC, File 910.

17 "London Today," BBC Overseas Transmission (20 July 1940), reprinted in Leslie Howard, *Trivial Fond Records*, ed. Ronald Howard (London, 1982), 154.

18 "Two Wars – One City," *Britain Speaks* Transcript 60 (29/30 July 1940), BBC WAC, File 910. Reprinted in *Trivial Fond Records*, 156–61.

19 *Britain Speaks* unnumbered typescript (24/25 Nov. 1940), BBC WAC, File 910.

20 "The Female of the Species," *Britain Speaks* Transcript 179 (25/26 Nov. 1940), BBC WAC, File 910. Reprinted in *Trivial Fond Records*, 165–9.

21 "The Fighting Democrat," *Britain Speaks* Transcript (13/14 Jan. 1941), BBC WAC, File 910.

22 BBC files indicate that Howard took part in ten *Answering You* programs between October 1941 and February 1943, several of them as host. BBC WAC, File 910.

23 Howard discussed the film in a broadcast in December 1940. "Three Soldiers," *Britain Speaks* Transcript (30/31 Dec. 1940), BBC WAC, File 910. Also see Howard, *In Search of My Father*, 91–2.

24 Quotations are from the film *The 49ᵗʰ Parallel* (1941). The film was released in the United States with the starker title, *The Invaders*. The cast included Laurence Olivier, Anton Walbrook, Raymond Massey, and Eric Portman. Although some of it was photographed on location, Howard never went to Canada: his scenes were filmed at the Denham studio, notwithstanding the backdrop of the Rockies.

25 See Howard, *In Search of My Father*, 63–5.

26 Quotations are from the film *Pimpernel Smith* (1941).

27 The idea of *Pimpernel Smith* as Christian allegory was suggested by two Swedish scholars, Leif Furhammer and Folke Isaksson. Their interpreta-

tion is discussed in Aldgate and Richards, 63. Raoul Wallenberg also seems to have been inspired by the film in his later efforts to rescue Hungarian Jews. See John Bierman, *Righteous Gentile: the Story of Raoul Wallenberg, Missing Hero of the Holocaust* (Harmondsworth: Penguin, 1982), 29.

28 Harold Hobson, "Leslie Howard, Anglo-American Interpreter," *Christian Science Monitor Weekly Magazine*, 18 Oct. 1941, 7.

29 Richards, "Leslie Howard: The Thinking Man as Hero," 41.

30 Lord Tweedsmuir, the Canadian governor-general, may have started the ball rolling by suggesting a royal visit to Canada to Prime Minister W. L. Mackenzie King who extended an invitation at the time of the coronation of George VI. Informed of the Mackenzie King overture, President Roosevelt instructed his personal envoy at the coronation to broach the subject of an unofficial royal visit to the United States. See Fred M. Leventhal, "Essential Democracy: The 1939 Royal Visit to the United States," in George K. Behlmer and Fred M. Leventhal, *Singular Continuities: Tradition, Nostalgia, and Identity in Modern British Culture* (Stanford: Stanford University Press, 2000), 163–77.

31 See Nicholas John Cull, *Selling War: The British Propaganda Campaign Against American "Neutrality" in World War II* (New York: Oxford University Press, 1995), 17.

32 Interview with Douglas Fairbanks, Jr., 9 March 1990. I am grateful to Professor Nicholas Cull for making his transcript of this interview available to me. Also see Leonard Maltin, *Movie Encyclopedia* (New York: Dutton, 1994).

33 Members included the Presidents of Harvard, Yale, and Columbia universities and the Union Theological Seminary, Reinhold Niebuhr, Adlai Stevenson, Robert E. Sherwood, Henry Luce, Judge Samuel Seabury, future Senator Paul H. Douglas, and banker Thomas Lamont.

34 Douglas Fairbanks, Jr. to Lowell Mellett, 3 July 1940, Box 1433, Record Group 208, National Records Center, Suitland, MD. I am grateful to Dr. Mark Glancy for making this letter available to me.

35 "Hitler or Britain," Speech for the White Committee, 18 Sept. 1940, Fairbanks Papers, Box 4, Howard Gotlieb Archival Research Center, Boston University. Also see Douglas Fairbanks, Jr., *Salad Days* (New York: Doubleday, 1988), 367–8.

36 Lord Louis Mountbatten to Douglas Fairbanks, Jr., 10 Dec. 1940, Fairbanks Papers, Box 167.

37 "Unity of English America," Speech for the White Committee, 19 Oct. 1940, Fairbanks Papers, Box 4.

38 *Give – Not Lend Unstinted Aid to the Allies,* [Nov. 1940]. Pamphlet published by the Western Office of the Committee to Defend America by Aiding the Allies. Box 1433, Record Group 208, National Records Center.

39 Speech for White Committee, Feb. 1941, Fairbanks Papers, Box 4.

40 Gerald Cook, BBC, New York, to Douglas Fairbanks, Jr., 26 July 1940, Fairbanks Papers, Box 26.

41 BBC broadcast transcript, 11 Oct. 1940, Fairbanks Papers, Box 2.

42 BBC broadcast transcript, 15 Jan. 1941, Fairbanks Papers, Box 2.

43 David Niven to Douglas Fairbanks, Jr., 24 Jan. [1941], Fairbanks Papers, Box 166.
44 Fairbanks, *Salad Days*, 365.
45 BBC broadcast transcript, 14 Apr. 1941, Fairbanks Papers, Box 2.

Part III
Anglo-American Identities

7
The London Press and the American Civil War

Michael de Nie

British opinion on the American Civil War was decidedly mixed and did not necessarily conform to traditional political or social cleavages. Scholars have explored how a variety of important issues, such as anti-slavery, democratic politics, American expansionism, and economic self-interest affected British reactions to the conflict, though not always in the manner that one might expect.[1] Older accounts of the war and Anglo-American relations offered a rather simplified dichotomy, with aristocratic and conservative groups supporting the South and radicals and members of the working classes backing the North.[2] More recent studies reveal a much more complex and shifting set of opinions on the civil war and American society. These studies persuasively argue that although sharp criticism of, or even hostility toward, the North was widespread in Britain, particularly after the winter of 1861–62, this rarely translated into genuine support for the South, primarily because of a deeply felt antipathy for slavery. In fact, as the conflict dragged on and certainly by the end of 1863 the majority of British journalists, politicians, and public intellectuals had reached the limits of their patience and simply declared a plague on both their houses.

This turn of events and British reactions to the war more generally are better understood by examining a neglected facet of British opinion and newspaper reporting – popular ideas about the character of American society. British conceptions of Americans as a grasping, violent, rash, and hypocritical people predated the war and strongly influenced how the British press reported on the events of 1861–65. These stereotypes were employed by newspapers across the political divide and informed denunciations of an imperialistic North just as readily as condemnations of an immoral slaveholding South. While these preconceptions informed popular understanding of the war, they also served to reinforce the British public's complacency and pride in their own national character. Brother Jonathan, the iconic lanky, reckless, gun-toting, slave-owning American proved a useful foil to manly, even-tempered, and honest John Bull. So, in writing about American disorder and destruction the British press was also heartily congratulating its readers on their own prosperous, stable, and patriotic nation. Drawing on over 25 London newspapers, this chapter explores how these traditional stereotypes about American and British identity informed British reporting on the causes, progress, and anticipated outcomes of the civil war. The press cited American emotionalism, violence, instability, aggressive expansionism, and bravado as contributing factors to the crisis as well as clear indicators of the superiority of the British people, whose own inherited qualities, it claimed, were the opposite of many of those attributed to America. Condemnations of the despotic President Lincoln or musings about potential racial degeneration or dilution in the United States were similarly understood as celebrations of the genius of the English parliamentary system and the preeminence of the Anglo-Saxon race.

Although some scholars have used *The Times* and other major London newspapers as if they spoke for the entire British press, most newspaper historians argue against the existence of anything like a national press until the end of the nineteenth century. Local newspapers remained the primary source of news for the majority of British readers through the Victorian era. The London papers did, however, successfully claim a privileged political position because of their location and access to and influence on the administration and the governing classes.[3] Engaged in a dialogue with their readers and their governors, the London press helped to establish the political boundaries within which the politicians felt free to act. Within British culture, the press was also the most powerful force articulating the dialogues of race, gender, class, and religion that informed popular conceptions of national identity.

This essay will explore a variety of London newspapers, some of which, such as *The Times, Morning Post,* and *Saturday Review,* were noted by contemporaries for their supposed Confederate bias. Others, such as the *Morning Star* and *Daily News,* were regarded by some as Northern mouthpieces. The majority of the London newspapers fell somewhere in between these two groups. Most were very critical of the Southern states during the prelude and outset of the war. But the North quickly lost Britain's goodwill by the confrontational tone of some of its politicians and newspapers, its failure to make emancipation a central war aim, and the *Trent* affair of November 1861–January 1862. The last of these began on 8 November 1861 when the British mail packet *Trent,* carrying two Confederate commissioners to Europe on a diplomatic mission, was stopped by the U.S. warship *San Jacinto* and the Southern agents were taken into custody. This action produced universal outrage in Britain and threatened to ignite a war between the United States and Britain until the agents were released in January 1862 and sent to Britain. While press opinion on the causes of the war, its probable consequences, and the conduct of the belligerents shifted between 1861 and 1865, there were some consistent themes. One of these was the belief that the South could not be conquered, or that even if the North could secure a military victory, it could never reestablish a truly United States. Another, almost universally shared, opinion was that Britain must not get involved in the conflict. This essay will mainly concern itself with a third common theme, a general sense that the war and the state of Anglo-American relations could be explained in large part by examining the deficiencies of the American people and their government.

Anglo-Saxons?

As was the case with much of British reporting on Ireland in the nine-teenth century, the London press sought to understand events in America by first exploring the racial identity of its people. Race was a plastic term in mid-nineteenth century Britain that was used primarily to denote a collection of supposedly inheritable character traits. Whereas Victorian commentators focused a great deal on the racial dif-ferences between the English and Irish, or Anglo-Saxon and Celt, the London press emphasized Anglo-American affinities and their common interests, at least in the opening stages of the war. The reason for this, of course, was that Britons still regarded America, a former colony settled by English people, as an Anglo-Saxon nation. These journalists thus saw the impending war as a disaster not only for America, but for the wider "Anglo-Saxon community."[4] The Americans were, in the esti-mation of the independent-Liberal *Illustrated London News*, "a great race planted in a great country" who were "imbued with the Anglo-Saxon temperament" and enjoyed "the widest scope for the perfecting of a system of political freedom."[5] Like a pleased parent, the Whig-Liberal *Daily Telegraph* noted, "We in England have watched the growth and progress of the great Transatlantic Republic with interest, with plea-sure, with affection, and with pride ... We had planted the acorn."[6]

And yet, despite these racial advantages the American nation was descending into fratricidal strife. This course of events was worrisome not only because, as the *Telegraph* noted, "America cannot suffer without the United Kingdom's suffering in every part," but also for its implicit reflection on Anglo-Saxon civilization.[7] The London press quickly determined, however, that the causes of the American war were not to be found in its Anglo-Saxon inheritance but rather a collection of uniquely American attributes and political problems.

Indeed, as the conflict dragged on and press opinion increasingly turned against the North or both sides, some newspapers began to posit that the Anglo-Saxon race had somehow degenerated in the physical and political climate of the United States. While the independent *Illustrated Times* professed its admiration for American bravery, it also expressed its belief that for some reason, perhaps "their large indulgence in alcoholic drinks, ... the Americans, as a people, have physically and morally deteriorated during the last quarter of a century."[8] The Conservative *Saturday Review*, for its part, bemoaned the "large influx of Irish, French, and German immigrants which has alone so completely changed the English physiognomy in America." The democratic *Morning Chronicle* struck a similar note in December 1861: "Possibly, the Anglo-Saxon skin has been transplanted to their soil; but it has universally deteriorated. It has blended with German, Greek, French, Muscovite, Sicilian, Irish, and Hebrew bastardy; it has been corrugated from Spain and the West Indies; it has cast off a hundred delicate sensibilities which help to inspire and dignify the English character."[9] Interestingly, the press overwhelmingly described the contaminants of American racial stock as other Europeans. Very little, if any, attention was paid to the supposed dangers or negative influence of black and white racial mixing. This should not be regarded as evidence of progressive attitudes on the part of the London newspapers, which often couched even their condemnations of slavery or pleas for abolition in extremely prejudicial and racist terms. Most likely, the newspapers' silence on black-white miscegenation reflected British assumptions that it was a rare phenomenon, particularly when compared to the massive influx of Irish, Germans, and others into the United States.

While the Anglo-Saxon nation planted in America had deteriorated from racial dilution, frontier life, the climate, or all of these, at least it had not yet lost its masculine character. Unlike the Irish or French, the Americans were widely regarded as a manly people, perhaps overly so given their reputation for violence and expansionism. The London press traced American masculinity, courage, tenacity, and stubbornness back to its Anglo-Saxon ancestry. In other words, any positive qualities that Britons could agree Americans possessed were traced directly back to the mother country. These qualities spelled trouble for both sides in the war, as Anglo-Saxons were supposedly known for their refusal to surrender. This inherited trait ensured both a long and bloody conflict and that the North would never completely subdue the South. As the *Economist* remarked in June 1861, "they are fighting, not with savage Indians, nor with feeble Mexicans, but with Anglo-Saxons, as fierce, as obstinate, and as untamable as themselves."[10] These obstinate Southerners, the prevailing wisdom ran, would never submit to the invading Yankee armies and thus the North should simply recognize reality and come to terms with the South.

One of the foundations for this argument was the notion that the North and South had become two different nations, not only culturally and politically, but also perhaps racially.[11] For example, in its review of the motivations for continued fighting in late summer 1864, the *Illustrated London News* opined that ultimately both sides were "struggling for political ascendancy," but also noted "something may be set down, also, for difference of race."[12] Opinion diverged on which, if either, of these two nations was more Anglo-Saxon. Southern sympathizers contrasted a supposedly paternal, agrarian, and Anglo-Saxon South with the industrial cities of the North, teeming with recent arrivals from Ireland and the continent. Northern supporters (or at least stern critics of the South) found Anglo-Saxon qualities best reflected in the free and egalitarian North.

Hot blood

Members of the London press might have disagreed on America's ethnic identities and racial health, but they shared a common low regard for the excesses of American behavior. Well before the political crisis began, many Britons already regarded America as a violent, unstable, and sometimes lawless society, particularly on the frontier. These impressions were provided by travel literature, newspaper reporting, and editorial cartoons which collectively portrayed the American people as impulsive, lacking wisdom and all too quick to settle problems with the bowie knife or "Judge Lynch."[13] These perceptions filtered British reporting on secession and the war. For example, in early 1861 numerous papers blamed not only slavery or other political issues, but also the rashness and volatility of Southerners for the crisis.

For example, the *Illustrated London News* suggested in January 1861 (with wonderfully mixed metaphors) that Northern triumphalism over the election of Lincoln "may have caused the hot blood of the South to kindle into a ferment."[14]

Other commentators felt that both parties in the conflict were ruled by emotion. For example, in September of 1862 the *Economist* complained that "passions have reached a pitch at which the parties themselves can neither see plainly, nor think rationally, nor feel decently – they are blinded with blood and dust, and maddened by pain and anger ... everybody in America seems to have abdicated the capacity of reflection."[15] The *Illustrated Times* criticized alike the "fiery-tempered Southerner" and the "ravage, cruelty, and destruction" wrought by Northern troops, who lacked even the "rough chivalry" of the "red-skins."[16] As in previous and subsequent reporting on the United States, the British press often used the "red Indians" as a rhetorical tool to gauge and criticize American behavior.

Not surprisingly, this theme also appeared in the comic press. *Punch*'s "Retrogression (A Very Sad Picture)" presents a lanky "I.O.U. Indian" with stars and stripes war paint performing a war dance with a *New York Herald* banner in front of sinking ships at the mouth of Charleston harbor.[17] In the accompanying text *Punch* noted that the I.O.U. Indian "was originally English," but "the deteriorating influences of climate, and still more the vast infusion of inferior animalism, in the form of convict Irish, deboshed Germans, and the accumulated scum of other nations" had deteriorated him. As a result he has "acquired the propensities but not the savage virtues of the aborigines."[18] Locked in a fratricidal struggle and spurred on to ever lower depths by his irresponsible newspaper press, the formerly Anglo-Saxon Yankee Indian appeared to have succumbed to all the negative qualities associated with native America and descended into savagery.

Perhaps the most effective symbol of American volatility was the mob, usually identified with the teeming cities of the North and their large immigrant populations and sensationalist newspapers. The British press had long harbored distrust and distaste for the rabble of Britain and Ireland, but recognized the American mob as a different animal. As the independent-Liberal *London Review* put it, "In America we have to ask, 'What will the mob think?' In the United States the mass, the majority, rule and dictate – not the sagacious, or the cool-headed, or the right-minded."[19] In their introduction to a special issue on the "American Outrage" (the Trent affair) in December 1861, the editors of *Public Opinion* bemoaned "the frightful amount of influence

PUNCH, OR THE LONDON CHARIVARI.—February 1, 1862.

RETROGRESSION (A VERY SAD PICTURE).

War-Dance of the I. O. U. Indian.

Figure 7.1   Retrogression (a Very Sad Picture); *Punch*, 1 February 1862

which the *populace*, as distinguished from the *people*, exercised over the legislature through the journalism of New York."[20] This is an interesting distinction. In this model the people were distinguished from the populace by their political rights, in particular the right to cast a ballot.

The people, then, constituted the political nation whom the press self-consciously claimed to represent as the "Fourth Estate." The people were the educated middle classes, a group that was supposedly informed, reflective, and to whom the newspaper press could address reasoned appeals. The populace included the "dangerous classes" and other groups without the vote. The problem with America, some British journalists felt, was that the populace was the people. The American mob, easily swayed, vocal, and potentially violent, was even more dangerous because it possessed the vote. As a result, the *Morning Herald* argued, "The mob is supreme; and the mob is ruled by passion and not by principle."[21] According to many British journalists, no American institution was more adept at manipulating and wielding the passions of the urban mobs than the newspaper press. The result was an impulsive and unbalanced nation that was subject to sudden volatile swings in public opinion.

One of the worst results of American emotionalism, according to many newspapers, was a complete loss of perspective by the Federal government, which refused to accept the reality of Southern separation. As the conflict continued the press sought some explanation for the North's stubborn determination to prosecute a war that could never be won no matter the cost in blood and treasure.[22] A consensus formed that the North was fighting not for principle, as was the case in the English Civil War, but for retribution and imperial ambition.[23] As the *Saturday Review* argued in August 1862, "No war has ever been prosecuted so exclusively for the avowed purpose of revenge."[24] Not surprisingly, these characterizations of Northern war aims did not begin to appear until after the *Trent* affair, which soured British opinion on the North. One of the best examples of this shift can be found in the pages of the *Daily Telegraph*. For the first half of 1861 the *Telegraph* frequently criticized the South for causing a devastating civil war out of self-interest and cupidity. But, in December 1861 the newspaper reacted angrily to the "filibuster of the San Jacinto" and began to argue "that the war of secession did not originate with the South, but with the North." In particular, the paper noted the North's attempt to claim the American territories for itself (by banning slavery) and its "military hostilities."[25]

In forwarding these characterizations of the United States and Americans, the London press was also offering an idealized conception of Britain. Whereas Brother Jonathan was rash, vengeful, and grasping, John Bull was calm, measured, and interested only in fair play and the general commonweal. When the British people were forced to act firmly with their imperial subjects, such as during the recent Indian Mutiny in 1857, they recognized the necessity of disciplining their unruly wards but proceeded with deliberation and always with an eye toward future reconciliation. In contrast, the Americans seemed at times to almost revel in the immeasurable destruction and bloodshed of their struggle while the North gave no thought to how it might move forward if and once it defeated the Confederate armies.

Slavery and hypocrisy

The press made another unfavorable comparison between British forth-rightness and American hypocrisy. The Americans were often described as braggarts full of swagger and bluster who rarely spoke or acted with sincerity. A number of journalists also pointed out on any number of occasions that the North was violating the very principle upon which their country was founded – self-determination. The most frequent and pointed critiques of American hypocrisy, however, concerned the North's position on slavery. The London press, for the most part, expressed great pride in England's history of antislavery efforts and constantly noted their distaste for the South's "peculiar institution." Because of their attitude toward slavery, and because conflict over the spread of slavery was one of the prime sparks of the American war, many members of the British press and public expected emancipation to become an immediate goal of the North. The Federals' refusal to embrace this cause brought consternation and then disgust in the pages of the London newspapers. Some journalists recognized that Lincoln's government had to tread softly on the issue to ensure the neutrality of the Border States, but nonetheless argued that an unequivocal condemnation of slavery was the surest route to winning England's sympathy.[26]

When the North refused to move on the issue this reaffirmed British suspicions over American sincerity. If the North did not intend to bury the institution of slavery, journalists reasoned, then they must be fighting for power and territory.[27] While describing the origins of the war in September 1861 as "inscrutable," *The Times* was certain of one thing – the North was not fighting to end slavery.[28] In fact, the paper soon began to offer a muted defense of slavery, arguing in December that "the slaves themselves have no wish to be liberated on the condi-tions suggested" by advocates of emancipation.[29] A letter writer to *The Times* in January 1862 echoed some of these sentiments, arguing, "The North does not fight against slavery. It fights for the profits of slavery."[30] The working-class and democratic *Reynolds's Newspaper*, which rarely if ever found itself on the same side of an issue as *The Times* and its readers, was equally skeptical of the North's war aims. In August 1861 the newspaper asserted that failing an invasion of the North by the Confederate forces, only "the deliverance of Africans from bondage" justified the war. Otherwise, the paper warned, the North fought for "no better reason than the gratification of the pride of conquest and the passion of revenge."[31] As relations between the North and Britain deteriorated after late 1861 criticisms of the North's duplicity over slavery became legion. In fact, the British press and public were so dubious of the Federals that Lincoln's Emancipation Proclamation was dismissed or downplayed as a purely political maneuver, a tattered cloak that could not conceal the Northern majority's own prejudice against the black population.

The controversy began when Lincoln issued his Preliminary Emancipation Proclamation on 22 September 1862. This document stated that all slaves living in states in rebellion against the federal government would be free as of January 1863. Those slaves living in the Border States or areas of the South under Union control would not be affected. The subtext to this threat to the South was not lost on the British press. As the working-class *Beehive* put it in October 1862, "President Lincoln offers freedom to the Negroes over whom he has no control, and keeps in slavery those other Negroes within his power. Thus he associates his Government with slavery by making slaveholding the reward to the planters of rejoining the old Union."[32] In the estimation of the *Illustrated Times*, the Proclamation demonstrated that Lincoln's government was "so insincere and hypocritical in its professions of philanthropy that towards *it* one can scarcely have any feeling but antipathy."[33] "We can have no copartnery with hypocrites," the *Standard* declared, "we can have no sympathy with the brutal ruffians who in the South are murdering old men and children to emancipate the Negro, and who in New York murder the Negro if he dares to cross the path of their drunken riot."[34] The *Standard* seemed to almost portend the New York Draft Riots, which broke out ten days after this leader appeared. Like many of its peers, the *Standard* pointed to the notorious racism of Northern cities as reason to question the Union's professed sympathy for those held in bondage.

Some newspapers also criticized the Proclamation as instigation to a slave rising. The Federal government was inciting a slave rebellion, the argument ran, without any realistic hope of assisting slaves who took the government on its word and struck a blow for their own freedom.

For critics of the North the proclamation thus proved hollow on every count. It would not truly free anyone and, in fact, could lead to the pointless death of any slave who believed in Lincoln's empty promise. One of the strongest proponents of this idea was *The Times*, which paraded the specter of servile war on frequent occasions. For example, the paper argued in September 1862 that Lincoln's plan was "a scheme for subjecting an Anglo-Saxon people to horrors equaled only by those which fell upon the English in India five years ago."[35] The *Saturday Review* was equally disapproving, arguing in October 1862 that Lincoln should be immediately impeached for exceeding his authority. A few months later the paper argued, "In verbally condemning the white population of the South to massacre, the Government of Washington regards with characteristic indifference the probable fate of the insurgent slaves."[36] Like *The Times* and the *Review*, the Sunday *Examiner* also foresaw a racial bloodbath, but it upped the ante by raising the vague specter of sexual danger as well. The Proclamation, it predicted, was "sure to carry the war of the knife to private homes where women and children are left undefended ..."[37] The supposed danger posed to Southern whites, rather than the fates of the freed or rebelling slaves, was the dominant justification for opposing emancipation. In fact, because of widespread stereotypes about black immaturity and savagery, most of the London newspapers expressed considerable unease at or outright opposition to the prospect of a sudden end to slavery.

Punch and *Fun* produced a number of cartoons that reflected this powerful undercurrent of anti-black prejudice in Britain. For example, in "Abe Lincoln's Last Card; or Rouge-Et-Noir," the President plays his last card against Jefferson Davis – an Ace of spades with an African-American face.[38] Like most British observers, *Punch*'s first instinct was to regard emancipation as a desperate and therefore insincere gesture. It also shared the widespread fear that Lincoln's policy might lead to a servile insurrection. For example, in "Brutus and Caesar (From the American Edition of Shakespeare)" an African American ghost of Caesar stands between Brutus (Lincoln) and a sleeping minstrel, informing Brutus that "I am dy ebil genus, massa Linking. Dis child is am awful Inimpressional."[39] So, a policy born of the North's need for cannon fodder and its desire to cow the rebels seemed charged with unintended consequences. Here again the London newspapers claimed to be speaking from a position of authority and experience. The regrettable and horrific experience of Mutiny in India demonstrated to Britain the need for strict control and supervision of "inferior" races taken into military service. Britain tried to relay this lesson to their

Figure 7.2   Abe Lincoln's Last Card; or, Rouge-et-Noir; *Punch*, 18 October 1862

American cousins, the press asserted, but as always they charged ahead, impulsively acting on instinct and emotion rather than reason.

Hatred and jealousy

Another frequent theme in British reporting on the conflict was American, particularly Northern, belligerence and popular animosity toward Britain. Throughout the war years the London press compared Britain's sober, moderate, and adult attitudes with America's intemperate and churlish outbursts. In this model the British honestly conceded America's strengths and good qualities while pointing out, as a friend, its shortcomings. The Americans, both Northern and Southern, responded, inexplicably, with vituperative threats and bluster. At the root of American belligerence, some London newspapers argued, was its aggressive imperialistic ambitions. While the British understood their empire as a serious moral obligation, the Americans seemed to greedily desire territory for its own sake. London journalists easily found evidence of this in the Mexican-American war, Manifest Destiny, freebooters in Cuba and America, and supposed designs on

Figure 7.3 Brutus and Caesar (From the American Edition of Shakespeare); *Punch*, 15 August 1863

Canada. As Duncan Andrew Campbell argues, British observers viewed America as "an aggressively expansionist power with an apparently insatiable appetite for territory."[40]

This image of a bellicose America predated the war, but it was continually reinforced by statements made by figures such as William Seward (the Secretary of State) and Cassius Clay (the U.S. ambassador to Russia) in addition to what Britons read in the pages of the New York and eventually Southern newspapers as well. Fully convinced of their own national rectitude and impartiality, the London newspapers quickly grew weary of American charges of partisanship. Britain's official policy of recognizing the South as a belligerent (but not an independent nation) and accepting the North's blockade only succeeded in displeasing both sides. For some Britons, this mutual discontent was probably the clearest sign that they were on the right diplomatic course. Still, the attacks in the American press stung. Writing in the midst of the *Trent* crisis, the *Economist* complained, "They have given the impression that they were not only willing but rather anxious to insult us."[41]

The *Trent* outrage was of course the biggest insult and truly marked a critical juncture in British press opinion on the North and the war. In the opinion of the London papers, the Northern government had "struck its best friend in the face," it was a "nation which has no respect for law or right," and, what "little sympathy was felt for the Federalists before, "there will be still less now."[42] The *Morning Chronicle* offered its support for the North for most of 1861, but then changed tack in December when it concluded that the Federals were "contending for power and jurisdiction, and for no principle under the sun."[43] A few days earlier the paper had noted that for some time in England there had been developing "an involuntary dislike of the being which calls itself a Yankee," which it ascribed to "the repulsive vanity of the Race, which is as yet scarcely half-bred, and nevertheless claims for itself the foremost stand in creation."[44] "The North is fighting for no sentimental cause – for no victory of a 'higher civilization',", the Conservative *Quarterly Review* concluded, "it is a struggle for empire."[45]

These critiques were not reflective of any principled stand against imperialism or territorial expansion in the abstract. Rather, they reflected British disapproval of America as an upstart nation. Certainly, the majority of London newspapers recognized that America was an ascendant nation possessed of tremendous economic and military potential. At the same time, however, they still regarded it as essentially a second-tier nation that had not yet earned a place at the table with the leading European powers. So, any bluster from the United States regarding its imperial ambitions or potential threat to the United Kingdom was described as empty posturing. This was well evidenced by the comic press, which frequently depicted "Naughty Jonathan" as

PUNCH, OR THE LONDON CHARIVARI.—December 7, 1861.

LOOK OUT FOR SQUALLS.

Jack Bull. "YOU DO WHAT'S RIGHT, MY SON, OR I'LL BLOW YOU OUT OF THE WATER."

Figure 7.4   Look out for Squalls; *Punch*, 7 December 1861

a child or midget who acted up and misbehaved in front of John Bull or Britannia. For example, in *Punch*'s "Look Out for Squalls," Jonathan strikes a defiant pose, guns in his belt, but he is dwarfed by John Bull who sternly warns him to "do what's right, my son, or I'll blow you out of the water."[46] Like Ireland or the various subjects of the empire, the Americans were infantilized in these cartoons to reinforce both their unequal status in the community of nations and their failure to convey themselves in a sober and adult manner. Only a manly and mature nation, such as Britain, could bear the responsibilities of empire without losing perspective and humility.

American belligerence and arrogance were widely accepted facts, but not all members of the press agreed that their origins lay in imperial ambition. Some traced anti-British sentiment to old jealousies of the mother country while others looked to the supposed hopes of New England mercantile interests who hoped to profit from a transatlantic war. A number of newspapers also attributed the hostility of the American governments and press to democratic politics. The *Illustrated Times*, for example, pondered in May 1862 if "the holding out of threats of war upon England may be considered advisable, in order to secure the adherence of the lower orders of American Irishry."[47] But the *Daily Telegraph* disagreed with the common assumption that Northern politicians and journalists abused England solely to appeal to the masses. The paper argued that anti-English attitudes were universal in America, noting in December 1861, "Hatred and jealousy of England are quite as common among the upper ten thousand as among the bestial ruffians of the Bowery."[48] These Irish-American "bestial ruffians," like the Fenians who left the United States after the war to participate in terroristic attacks in British cities, were widely described by the British press as mongrel creatures that combined the worst features of American society with native Irish character defects.[49]

Although they shared a common revulsion for Irish Americans, not all the newspapers accepted the image of a warmongering and petulant America but instead criticized some of their peers for their antagonistic commentary. Writing in the immediate aftermath of the *Trent* affair, the *Illustrated London News* complained, "Unhappily, we have allowed ourselves to be goaded into an unseemly display of passionate indignation."[50] A few months later the paper featured a leader entitled "Our American Brothers," which offered praise for the United States and attributed tensions between the two nations to mutual misunderstanding.[51] The *Pall Mall Gazette* also chided its peers for emphasizing anti-British sentiment in America. "We would no more take any expressions of indignation as symptoms of permanent ill-feeling," the paper argued, "than we would reckon up all the proofs of irritability of a man in a fever." The *Gazette* was particularly disapproving of *The Times*, which spun every Federal victory as a defeat and serially denied "that any good thing can come out of America."[52] So, while traditional anti-American stereotypes were fundamental to newspaper reporting on the war, they did not go unchallenged. Various newspapers expressed empathy for America, pled for mutual understanding, or admitted British prejudices. These sympathetic discourses may have challenged the dominant understandings of the United States and Anglo-American relations, but they did not successfully supplant or even substantially temper them. As a result, the London press consistently crafted their reporting on the American conflict using the traditional stereotypes and preconceptions that were ready at hand and easily recognized by their readers.

The American press

For those who believed that Americans harbored ill-will toward Britain and perhaps even desired an Anglo-American war or least an invasion of Canada evidence of these opinions was easy to find, particularly in the pages of the Northern newspapers. British journalists were quite surprised by the vitriolic tone of American reporting and commentary. Worst of all, in British opinion, were the New York papers, which reputedly played to the democratic mob by publishing endless invective and threats against England.[53] London journalists censured the American newspapers repeatedly throughout these years for appealing to the lowest orders and their base passions with melodramatic stories and prurient tales. They were also accused of being mercenaries serving as mouthpieces of demagogues or certain political or commercial interests. This contrasted sharply, of course, with the London journalists' conceptions of their own press, which supposedly stood between the educated voters and their governors, transmitting information and advice in both directions.

So, judging by the standards with which they assessed themselves, London journalists found their American cousins sorely lacking. In its hour of trial, the *Illustrated London News* concluded in February 1863, "the boasted press of the North has proven hollow and rotten."[54] For the *Economist*, the failings of the American press were a telling reflection of the people themselves. According to the paper there were "no good political newspapers" in America, and "if the people cared about politics, they would have good newspapers; and if they had good newspapers, they would care about politics. But the first is the cardinal principle."[55] The *Economist* chalked up this situation in part to the fact that "their Press, with scarcely an exception, has fallen into bad hands, and is distinguished by a vicious tone."[56] *Punch* agreed, denouncing in December 1862 a recent *New York Times* article as:

> The characteristic howl of the Yahoo, or Irishman of the baser sort, who, for the good of his own country, and for the bane of yours [the Union], has transported himself into your midst. He occupies many an Editor's writing desk, but would be much more suitably situated in your gallant army, where he would serve as food for Southern powder. The fittest position of all for him would be that of suspension at some altitude from the ground by a ligature embracing his neck with a running noose, and maintaining him in antagonism to the force of gravitation.[57]

So much for journalistic collegiality!

The New York organ that most incensed British commentators was the city's largest paper, the *New York Herald*, which was noted for both its anglophobia and proslavery stance before the war. After the fall of Fort Sumter and the appearance of an angry mob outside its offices, the *Herald* promptly adopted a solidly pro-Union editorial line.[58] It was especially noticed for its calls to invade Canada and bellicose editorials in the midst of the *Trent* affair. While it believed that all of the New York newspapers were filled with "rowdy threats" and "bunkum," *Reynolds's Newspaper* observed, "the *New York Herald* bounces and barks the loudest of all."[59] The *Morning Chronicle* was considerably more incensed, blasting the "depraved *New York Herald*" and its "unclean columns" at the height of the *Trent* crisis in December 1861.[60]

The New York papers also received the worst of the abuse from the comic press. In *Fun*'s "The Neutral Beast" a Yankee Indian with a *New York Herald* and *New York Times* cape threatens the British lion with a tomahawk and long knife.[61] Identified as the "Yankee War Party," (i.e. the New York press), the Indian declares, "What! You won't growl nor wag your tail? Well! We'll see!" Aside from openly aggressive commentary on the *Trent* affair or exhortations to seize Canada, the Union newspapers most incensed British commentators with their seemingly endless attacks on British neutrality. Britons and their newspapers were thoroughly convinced that staying out of the conflict was prudent and

Figure 7.5   The Neutral Beast; *Fun*, 12 September 1863

fair and, if any side benefited from Britain's stance, it was the North. So, condemnations of British neutrality in the New York press were chalked up as another example of American petulance and immature attempts at playing the bully.

Democracy and republicanism

Just as the London press and British society were divided over the merits or dangers of democracy and "Americanization," they also disagreed over the role that American political institutions played in bringing about secession and civil war. American democracy was one of the few issues on which British commentary split on fairly clear political lines. Conservatives were fairly unified in their belief that the United States was simply too large and diverse to survive as a democratic republic. Liberals and Radicals tended to view America in a much more sympathetic light. But even among the latter opinion was divided, as Richard Blackett argues: "To some, America was a beacon of hope, a place where the experiment in democracy had been a success; to others, it was hope betrayed."[62]

If the press could not reach a consensus on the role of American political institutions in precipitating the conflict, they could generally agree that the American system was inherently inferior to that of Britain.[63] As noted previously, the London papers frequently criticized the harmful political influence wielded by the urban mobs and "scandal press" in the United States. Many London newspapers, however, offered their most stinging criticism not for the excesses of democracy in America but rather for what they regarded as the despotic tendencies of Lincoln's government. The demands and restrictions produced by the first modern industrial war, such as conscription and the suppression of civil liberties, disturbed British observers and, as Campbell argues, "flew in the face of mid-nineteenth century ideals of progress and freedom."[64] *Fun* summed up the popular view of Lincoln's administration with "The Yankee Guy Fawkes."[65] In this cartoon Lincoln fans the flames to burn a figure resembling George Washington and consisting of "American Laws," "States Rights," and "Liberty." Lincoln exclaims, "I'll warm yer! Your old constitution won't do for U.S." while a figure in the background calls out for "a few old greenbacks ... to help burn the Constitution."

Lincoln's "despotism" was usually traced to a number of fundamental flaws in the American constitution and government. In analyzing American political shortcomings, London journalists naturally compared the qualities of the United States government with those of the most stable and free government ever devised – the British parliamentary system. The root of the problem as many British journalists saw it was the fact that the American President wielded executive power alone, separate from the people's representatives, and that he could

Figure 7.6 The Yankee Guy Fawkes; *Fun*, 7 November 1863

not be removed for at least four years. The result was a critical distance between the people and their government that allowed the latter to exercise extraordinary powers in times of crisis. As the war dragged on it seemed to many British journalists that the Federal executive loosed itself of any and all restrictions on its power, enabling the government to enact a number of legally dubious measures such as conscription, the Emancipation Proclamation, censorship, and the suspension of *habeas corpus*.[66]

It went without saying that such measures were unimaginable in Britain. "We have known war time in this country," the *Daily Telegraph* wrote, "and have heard of monstrous administrative proceedings in the days of the STUARTS, and within the shores of Ireland; but Englishmen would be rather astounded if institutions capable of being thus administered were introduced among them."[67] This statement is quite revealing of not only distaste for the infringement of liberty in the United States, but also the double standard applied within the borders of the United Kingdom. Martial law and the suspension of *habeas corpus* had already been instituted several times in Ireland by 1862, but Ireland was a singular case, a people and a land that stood simultaneously within and without the political nation.

Conclusion

Initially, at least, most British observers were astounded by the outbreak of the American Civil War. London newspapermen expressed their disbelief that a prosperous, industrialized, and mainly Anglo-Saxon nation could tear itself apart. As tensions mounted in late 1860 and early 1861 most London newspapers expressed confidence or at least sincere hope that it would not come to armed conflict. When war did finally arrive, they sought to understand how and why America had descended into fratricide. As we have seen, the press considered a number of different and sometimes complementary explanations for the American war, all of which also served to highlight British virtues. In light of the theme of this collected volume, perhaps the most interesting contrast drawn by the London newspapers was between themselves and the American press. In Britain the press supposedly fulfilled a vital and active social and political role, informing and expressing the public mind. In the process it offered a vital check to both popular misconceptions and the abuse of power. As Britons saw it, in America the newspaper press fulfilled neither of these functions and instead focused its energies on swaying the popular mob by playing on their fears and prejudices. While it was effective in mobilizing the democratic masses around election time or during certain crises, the American press did not on the whole speak for the better part of society and as a result could not effectively influence the governing classes beyond their need to win votes. For London journalists this stark difference in the role and power and the press reflected not only the superiority of Britain's Fourth Estate, but indeed its entire society and government.

Notes

1 The most important recent works include Duncan Andrew Campbell, *English Public Opinion and the American Civil War* (Woodbridge, UK and Rochester: Royal Historical Society/ Boydell Brewer, 2003); R. J. M. Blackett, *Divided Hearts: Britain and the American Civil War* (Baton Rouge: Louisiana State University Press, 2001); Martin Crawford, *The Anglo-American Crisis of the Mid-Nineteenth Century: The Times and America, 1850–1862* (Athens: University of Georgia Press, 1987); and Hugh Dubrulle, "'We are threatened with...Anarchy and Ruin': Fear of Americanization and the Emergence of an Anglo-Saxon Confederacy in England during the American Civil War," *Albion* 33:4 (Winter 2002): 583–613. See also Philip S. Foner, *British Labor and the American Civil War* (New York: Holmes & Meier, 1981); Donald Bellows, "A Study of British Conservative Reaction to the American Civil War," *Journal of Southern History* 51:4 (November 1985): 505–26; and Douglas Lorimer, "The Role of Anti-Slavery Sentiment in English Reactions to the American Civil War," *The Historical Journal* 19:2 (June 1976): 405–20.

2 The two classic works in this vein are E. D. Adams, *Great Britain and the American Civil War* (London and New York: Longmans, Green & Co., 1925), and Edwin J. Pratt, *Europe and the American Civil War* (Boston and New York: Houghton Mifflin, 1931). For a more recent study following this approach see Alfred Grant, *The American Civil War and the British Press* (Jefferson, NC: McFarland & Co., 2000).

3 For detailed discussions of relationship between the press, the reading public, and British politicians see A. Aspinall, *Politics and the Press, c.1750–1850* (London: Home & Van Thal, 1949); Alan J. Lee, *Origins of the Popular Press in England, 1855–1914* (London: Croom Helm, 1976); Stephen Koss, *The Rise and Fall of the Political Press in Britain: Volume 1 The Nineteenth Century* (London: Hamish Hamilton, 1981); Aled Jones, *Powers of the Press: Newspapers, Power and the Public in Nineteenth-Century England* (Hants, UK: Scolar, 1996); and Mark Hampton, *Visions of the Press, 1850–1950* (Urbana and Chicago: University of Illinois Press, 2004).

4 Crawford, *The Anglo-American Crisis*, 48, 107.

5 *Illustrated London News (ILN)*, 12 January 1861.

6 *Daily Telegraph*, 19 April 1861. See also 1 February 1861.

7 *Daily Telegraph*, 5 June 1861.

8 *Illustrated Times*, 4 January 1862. See also *The Times*, 17 September 1861.

9 *Morning Chronicle*, 12 December 1861. See also *The Times*, 17 September 1861.

10 *Economist*, 29 June 1861. See also 25 May, 28 September 1861, and 14 June 1862.

11 Dubrulle, "'We are threatened with...Anarchy and Ruin,'" 597–8; Blackett, *Divided Hearts*, 15–16; Bellows, "A Study of British Conservative Reaction," 518. For a contemporary example, see *Illustrated London News*, 4 October 1861.

12 *ILN*, 20 August 1864.

13 Campbell, *English Public Opinion*, 197; Dubrulle, "'We are threatened with…Anarchy and Ruin,'" 586; Crawford, *The Anglo-American Crisis*, 41. See also Oscar Maurer, "'Punch' on Slavery and Civil War in America, 1841–1865," *Victorian Studies* 1:1 (September 1957): 5–28.
14 *ILN*, 12 January 1861. See also 22 June 1861, 4 October 1862. See also *Daily Telegraph*, 1, 11, 15, 17, 18, 19 January, 4 March 1861.
15 *Economist*, 6 September 1862. See also *Reynolds's Newspaper*, 13 January, 2 June 1861; *The Times*, 21 October 1861, 6 May 1864.
16 *Illustrated Times*, 26 December 1863, 16 May 1862. See also *Morning Herald*, 29 November 1861.
17 *Punch*, February 1, 1862. This cartoon referenced the Union's attempt to block off Charleston harbor by assembling and sinking a fleet of old whaling ships loaded with granite blocks and stones. The plan was only partially successful, but nonetheless produced reams of bad press in Britain and Europe, where the "stone fleet" was condemned as vandalism and contrary to the rules of war.
18 *Punch*, February 1, 1862. See also *The Times*, 21 May 1861.
19 *London Review*, December 12, 1861.
20 *Public Opinion*, 7 December 1861. See also *Saturday Review*, 15 February 1862, 7 January 1865.
21 *Morning Herald*, 4 December 1861. See also *Economist* 17 August 1861.
22 See Campbell, *English Public Opinion*, 103.
23 See, for example, *Times*, 14 February 1863; *Morning Chronicle*, 27 December 1861. See also Bellows, "A Study of British Conservative Reaction," 524.
24 *Saturday Review*, 23 August 1862. See also 30 August 1862, 14 March, 11 July 1863; *The Times*, 10 May 1861.
25 *Daily Telegraph*, 4 December 1861.
26 See, for example, *Daily Telegraph*, 3 February 1862.
27 Bellows, "A Study of British Conservative Reaction," 523.
28 *The Times*, 9 September 1861. See also 7 December 1861.
29 *The Times*, 27 December 1861.
30 *The Times*, 21 January 1862.
31 *Reynolds's Newspaper*, 4 August 1861. See also 21 July 1861.
32 *Beehive*, 11 October 1862. Cited in Philip S. Foner, *British Labor and the American Civil War*, 29.
33 *Illustrated Times*, 24 January 1861. See also 17 January 1861.
34 *Standard*, 1 July 1863.
35 *The Times*, 19 September 1862.
36 *Saturday Review*, 18 October 1862, 17 January 1863.
37 *Examiner*, 11 October 1862.
38 *Punch*, 18 October 1862.
39 *Punch*, 15 August 1863. See also "Scene from the American 'Tempest,'" 24 January 1863 and *Fun*, "The Penny Jupiter," 18 October 1862.
40 Campbell, *English Public Opinion*, 13.
41 *Economist*, 7 December 1861.
42 *Daily News*, 29 November 1861; *Morning Herald*, 29 November 1861; *Morning Advertise*, 29 November 1861. See also *Morning Chronicle* and *Standard*, 29 November 1861.
43 *Morning Chronicle*, 14 December 1861.

44 *Morning Chronicle*, 10 December 1861.
45 "The United States as an Example," *Quarterly Review* 117:233 (January 1865): 249–86, 252.
46 *Punch*, 7 December 1861. See also "Naughty Jonathan," 6 July 1861; "The Wilful Boy," 23 November 1861; and "John Bull's Neutrality," 3 October 1863.
47 *Illustrated Times*, 2 May 1862.
48 *Daily Telegraph*, 3 December 1861. See also 4, 20 December 1861.
49 For more on this topic, see Michael de Nie, *The Eternal Paddy: Irish Identity and the British Press, 1798–1882* (Madison: University of Wisconsin Press, 2004).
50 *ILN*, 18 January 1862.
51 *ILN*, 19 April 1862.
52 *Pall Mall Gazette*, 16 February, 10 March 1865. See also *Morning Star*, 11 January 1862.
53 Campbell, *English Public Opinion*, 35–41; Crawford, *The Anglo-American Crisis*, 12–13. See also *Reynolds's Newspaper*, 14 December 1862.
54 *Illustrated London News*, 7 February 1863.
55 *Economist*, 9 August 1862.
56 *Economist*, 17 October 1863.
57 *Punch*, 13 December 1862.
58 See Campbell, *English Public Opinion*, 36–41.
59 *Reynolds's Newspaper*, 16 June 1861.
60 *Morning Chronicle*, 30 December 1861. See also 27 December 1861. See also *Daily Telegraph*, 3, 28 December 1861.
61 *Fun*, 12 September 1863. See also *Punch*, "The Latest from America," 26 July 1862.
62 Blackett, *Divided Hearts*, 17.
63 See Blackett, *Divided Hearts*, 35.
64 Campbell, *English Public Opinion*, 104.
65 *Fun*, 7 November 1863. See also *Punch*, "Extremes Meet," 24 December 1863; and "Holding a Candle to the *****. (Much the Same Thing,)" 7 November 1863, which compare Lincoln with Czar Alexander II and his suppression of the 1863 Polish rebellion.
66 See, for example, *Economist*, 30 August, 6, 12 December 1862; 10 January 1863, 10 September 1864.
67 *Daily Telegraph*, 10 April 1862.

Newspapers Consulted

Daily News	*John Bull*
Daily Telegraph	*London Review*
Economist	*Morning Advertiser*
Examiner	*Morning Chronicle*
Fun	*Morning Herald*
Globe	*Morning Post*
Illustrated London News	*Morning Star*
Illustrated Times	*Nonconformist*

Pall Mall Gazette
Public Opinion
Punch
Quarterly Review
Reynolds's Newspaper
St. James Gazette
Saturday Review

Spectator
Standard
Tablet
The Times
Watchman
Weekly Register

8

World War I and the Anglo-American Imagined Community: Civilization vs. Barbarism in British Propaganda and American Newspapers[1]

Jessica Bennett and Mark Hampton

The mythology of the Anglo-American "special relationship," often emphasizes the experience of World War II, particularly the close wartime relationship between Churchill and Roosevelt. At a cultural level, however, much groundwork was built during World War I as the American press defined Allied war aims as a natural product of Anglo-American shared values. At the war's outset in 1914, American opinion was divided. Strong commercial interests were threatened by British competition, and German-American and Irish-American communities were generally suspicious of the British cause. Against such opinion, however, were advocates of an American melting pot defined in primarily "Anglo" terms, and those who championed a pro-British foreign policy as the best guarantee of American national security.[2] The eventual entry of the United States into the war on the Allied side represented a victory for the latter groups in the United States. As these groups emerged victorious, Anglo-American ideals and identification similar to those projected in British propaganda also triumphed in the American press.

I

From the start of the war, the British state took a strong interest in American news coverage, and its manipulation was a key goal in Britain's wider propaganda efforts. Although we cannot document overt British government influence on American newspaper coverage, such influence seems likely. British documents confirm the goal and proclaim (self-servingly) its success, and a comparison of the language of British propaganda pamphlets aimed at American elites with the language increasingly found in American newspapers provides circumstantial evidence. Yet whether the convergence of themes and language in British propaganda with those in American newspapers represents direct British influence, at one extreme, or mere coincidence, at the other, for the purposes of this chapter it is the shared values, not the institutional relationships, that are most compelling.

Following the Fashoda crisis in 1898, the British War Office became increasingly concerned with censoring war-time news that could offer valuable strategic information to enemies. Although, according to a War Office report, most newspaper proprietors had seen the logic of such censorship, they had stridently resisted any regulations "which might deprive them of their rights of criticism."[3] Early in World War I, British politicians recognized the need to control the image of the British state and British war effort. In the domestic arena, such propaganda aimed initially at recruiting volunteers and, throughout the war, at keeping morale high. Such aims could be met in part through censoring news of military defeats (both in newspapers and in letters home) and through relying on newspapers' voluntary efforts to demonize the Germans. British politicians quickly recognized, however, that winning the war also required winning hearts and minds outside Britain, particularly in the United States. Initially, the chief goal was to ensure American neutrality, but as the war progressed, British politicians increasingly sought to attract American involvement on the Allied side.

This propaganda effort, which Philip M. Taylor has called "essentially the first experiment by a modern nation to target propaganda at friendly as well as enemy regimes," began haphazardly.[4] Several discrete and competing agencies were charged with overseas propaganda. The Foreign Office understandably viewed propaganda as subordinate to policy, and quickly established a news section charged with supplying British and overseas newspaper correspondents with war news. In addition, two semi-official propaganda agencies, the Neutral Press Committee and the War Propaganda Bureau, came into existence. The former belonged under the jurisdiction of the Home Office and was a close associate of the Press Bureau, the main wartime press censorship agency. The War Propaganda Bureau, located at Wellington House, was strictly autonomous but under the jurisdiction of the Foreign Office.

According to Taylor, it was the most important of the propaganda agencies between 1914 and 1917. Its main purpose was to produce and distribute overseas books, pamphlets and periodicals, as well as pictorial materials. In 1918, a Department of Information (later upgraded to a Ministry of Information) was created, headed first by Lord Northcliffe and then by Lord Beaverbrook, the two most prominent press barons. This development, ostensibly a rationalization aimed at eliminating wasteful repetition of function, signaled a shift toward influencing mass opinion. In addition, it reflected Prime Minister Lloyd George's mistrust of the Foreign Office, with its legacy of secret diplomacy, and his belief in the power of the press.

Rather than targeting mass opinion, Wellington House propaganda to the United States, presided over by Sir Gilbert Parker, aimed at influencing elites in the United States and other countries who could then guide affairs in their own country. This choice derived from a traditional preference for dealing with elites rather than the masses, but also from a perception that clumsy, heavy-handed German propaganda had produced a backlash.[5] This decision reflected prevailing British perceptions of the difference between elite and popular opinion; whereas readers from the popular classes supposedly could be easily manipulated, elite readers could be expected to weigh arguments and process facts rationally. For this reason, it was important to convey the impression of providing simple facts that American elite readers would fashion into their own opinions. Wellington House thus emphasized producing pamphlets ostensibly by private individuals with no connection to the state.[6] Almost a year into the war, in June 1915, Parker reported in a self-congratulatory assessment that "in the eyes of the American people the quiet and subterranean nature of our work has the appearance of a purely private patriotism and enterprise."[7] Besides commissioning and distributing pamphlets, Parker supplied news and columns to newspaper editors around the United States, in large part through syndication.

What themes did Wellington House pamphlets convey in defense of Britain's war aims? A brief sampling of the over 300 pamphlets and books produced under the auspices of Wellington House provides a window into this content.[8] Although the messages conveyed in these publications were diverse and multifaceted, and belong as much to the biographies of their separate authors as to the study of British propaganda, they collectively projected an image of Anglicized virtues under threat by German barbarism, aggression, and militarism. The virtues that Britain fought for were presented on a universal scale: justice, honor, humanity, and civilization were under attack. In these pamphlets such universal virtues were often Anglicized to emphasize the commonalities between Britain and the United States. These pamphlets projected such virtues as justice, law, rights, and honor onto Britain and, by extension, the budding Anglo-American partnership. These Anglo-American virtues were further reinforced by contrast with Germany's manner of waging war.

The most common theme found in the pamphlets was the German threat to humane "civilization." Germany's invasion of Belgium and its manner of conducting war involved broken promises and the violation of human rights, viewed as not only illegal and immoral but also as a threat to international peace. In his book, *Neutral Nations and the War,* Lord Bryce emphasized that the invasion of Belgium, by breaking a legally binding treaty, should trouble every country, large or small. Bryce, whose reputation as a highly respected former British ambassador to Washington lent him great credibility, headed a committee whose 1915 report (popularly known as the *Bryce Report*), unfairly confirmed for many what was, in fact, an exaggerated picture of German atrocities in Belgium.[9] In *Neutral Nations*, Bryce presented the invasion of Belgium as a violation of universal morality on the argument that world peace was not possible if treaties and obligations could be broken, an assessment with which G. K. Chesterton concurred in *The Barbarism of Berlin.*[10]

Germany's militarism and treaty-breaking stood in striking contrast to Britain's principled and reluctant entry to the war. Wellington House head Charles Masterman argued in *After Twelve Months of* War that Britain went to war, only after all other attempts to keep the peace had failed, in order to maintain commitments to European allies. Having entered the war Britain would fight "until the purposes for which she entered the war were fulfilled, and she could sheath the sword as honorably and gladly as honorably and reluctantly as she drew it."[11] Masterman acknowledged that the Cabinet's inability to find a peaceful solution constituted a "failure," and he paralleled the reluctance of Britain to enter the war to the American desire to maintain neutrality.[12] Britain's decision to go to war was necessitated by Germany's violation of Belgian neutrality, which seemed to testify to Germany's willingness to imperil civilization to serve its expansionist ends.

Britain's circumspect attitude toward war, and its insistence on rules and honor in the international arena, were contrasted sharply with German militarism. In *Neutral Nations*, Bryce attributed Germany's actions to a might-is-right mentality. According to Bryce, the disregard of rules and agreements exemplified by the Belgian invasion now dominated German policy more broadly. Although this policy, best exemplified by General Friedrich von Bernhardi, reflected the views of a minority in German society, this minority had propelled Germany to war.[13] Bryce argued that small nations were particularly threatened by such might-is-right attitudes, and that Bernhardi's doctrines threatened the very of heart of civilization, namely law and humanity.[14] In *Why Britain is at War* Sir Edward Cook similarly concluded that the German government believed "that there is no Right, but Might," an attitude that imperiled world peace. Accordingly, in Cook's words, "On the maintenance of the opposite principles, for which Britain stands in this struggle, depends every hope of saving the world from the rule of mere brute force and militarism."[15]

As the unprecedented destruction and horror of total war brought issues such as the rights of non-combatants to the forefront, these rights became central issues in Wellington House pamphlets. German treatment of Belgians not only illustrated their disregard of treaty obligations, but revealed that the Germans made no distinction between combatants and civilians, a moral failure that linked the "rape" of Belgium to unrestricted submarine warfare.[16] Violations of treaty obligations, though a serious offense, were not an immediate threat to the United States, separated from Europe by the Atlantic Ocean. Wellington House propagandists thus recognized that the United States could more easily identify with the questions of rights of non-combatants, a topic that allowed both a focus on the war's legal aspects congenial to Wellington House's interest in targeting elite opinion-makers in reasoned, non-sensationalistic language, and that provided a link between Belgium and the *Lusitania*.

One manifestation of this line of propaganda appears in an interview with Admiral Dudley de Chair, Commander of the Tenth Cruiser (Blockade) Squadron in the North Sea from 4 August 1914 to 6 March 1916. In speaking to Mr Henry Suydam, London correspondent of the *Brooklyn Daily Eagle*, de Chair explained the organization and procedures of the British blockade, emphasizing that British practices were "safer and more humane" than German submarine warfare.[17] Yet as the British blockade tightened, submarine warfare became more crucial for the Germans. Despite its necessity, submarine warfare, especially after the sinking of the *Lusitania*, struck many as a crime against humanity. In his pamphlet, *Murder at Sea*, Archibald Hurd distinguished between German methods and the rules of law and civilization. By using submarines in war the Germans broke international wartime naval law, which required signaling, warning shots, and ample care for non-combatants. Hurd's description of the sinking of the *Lusitania* illustrated that such traditional laws were not followed: "There was no vessel of any kind within view; no challenge to stop was given, no warning was made. While still submerged, the German submarine fired a torpedo, though her commander knew that it might bring the death of two thousand human beings."[18]

Wellington House staff recognized that emphasizing the virtues of honor and justice would appeal to American foreign policy idealism and help to create an image of Britain and the United States as partners in a beneficent Anglo-American world order. Even further, Wellington House encouraged writing that would be especially appealing to widely held American democratic and libertarian ideals. Parallels were drawn between the reluctance of Britain to enter the war and the American desire for neutrality. Not only did Masterman make this parallel, but Bryce took it one step further, stating that Britain had hoped that a "friendliness with Germany might enable Britain, with the cooperation of the United States (our closest friend) ... to secure the general peace of Europe."[19] Bryce emphasized the international concern for peace, especially the role that the United States and Britain could play in leading such a movement.[20]

This Anglo-American connection was reinforced in several of the pamphlets by the incorporation of evocative American quotations. Sir Edward Cook quoted Abraham Lincoln's famous "With malice toward none" speech.[21] A pseudonymous Dikaios Logos similarly claimed British defense of liberty for an Anglo-American community. In his words, "We [the British] have 'great allies' – and a determination that 'government of the people, by the people, and for the people, shall not perish from the earth.'"[22] The United States was encouraged to join the British in defending these (American) principles for the sake of the world. James Bryce invoked American ideals in asking of German policy, "Is there none of that 'decent respect to the opinion of mankind' which the framers of the Declaration of Independence recognized?"[23] These pamphlets portrayed a world in which liberty and freedom, principles as dear to Britain as to the United States, must be defended on a global level, against a Germany whose war campaign contrasted directly with Anglo-American honor and justice. H. W. Massingham, editor of Britain's radical weekly, *The Nation*, dismissed official German claims that "German troops, with their iron discipline, will respect the personal liberty and property of the individual in

Belgium, just as they did in France in 1870." Although this homage paid by German vice to virtue contrasts with its audacious scorn for a "scrap of paper," Massingham remained unconvinced:

> Let the hideous tale of burning towns, churches, and public buildings, the confiscations, the shooting of civilians, the wholesale fines, and the general looting of private property and invasion of private rights which has left a black track of ruin behind the German invasion of Belgium, supply the answer.... Let the world judge whether so wanton a crime was ever wreaked on the head of innocence."[24]

Not only was the German government uncivilized, but, in Charles Masterman's view, so were the German people. According to Masterman, when Britons heard the news of war, they responded with "a kind of awe and expectation, to know whether the world in which they had lived and moved all their lives, had ceased to exist."[25] By contrast, "the proclamation of war was cheered by delirious crowds in Berlin and Vienna."[26] Interestingly, this depiction of Germans contrasted with much of the propaganda, especially later in the war, that excoriated the German government while exempting the German people.

One of the greatest challenges for propagandists was the embarrassing alliance with Russia. How could Britain's supposed mission to save civilization from German barbarism be reconciled with Britain's alliance with a country that, in the eyes of most Americans as well as western Europeans, far surpassed Germany on the scale of barbarism? Indeed, for an initial critic of the war, *Daily News* editor A. G. Gardiner, a strong German socialist party combined with the Russian threat to render the British position quite embarrassing:

> What was to be gained, he asked, by helping Russia to achieve her 'hegemony of the Slav world'? It was unthinkable that any Englishman should 'wish the Russian civilisation to overwhelm the German civilisation', which would mean 'the triumph of blind superstition over the most enlightened intellectual life of the modern world'.[27]

Many Wellington House pamphlets ignored the question, concentrating merely on the magnitude of Germany's militarism. Several pamphleteers referred not to "Germany" but to "Prussia" with its militaristic connotations. More overtly, in his history of the Great War, Sir

Gilbert Parker focused largely on the German traditions and principles that led to war, arguing that "[t]he doctrine of frightfulness is not a new one, but its adoption by a civilised nation as a settled policy is wholly new."[28]

By contrast, G. K. Chesterton took the embarrassment of Russia head on, reconceptualizing barbarism, in an effort to demonstrate that Germany reflected a newer and more sinister kind of barbarism than did Russia. When applied to Russia, wrote Chesterton, "barbarism" implied merely a backwardness that had once been characteristic even of Britain. One could hope that Russia would grow out of such limitations. By contrast, "we, the French and English, do not mean this when we call the Prussians barbarians....For we do not mean anything that is an imperfect civilisation by accident. We mean something that is the enemy of civilisation by design. We mean something that is willfully at war with the principles by which human society has been made possible hitherto."[29] Events like the sacking of Louvain, the death sentence of English nurse Edith Cavell, and the sinking of the *Lusitania* in 1915 all contributed to the barbaric image of the Germans.[30] Unlike Russia's backwardness, German barbarism demanded punishment.[31]

Exhortations to punish the Germans for their barbaric war-making were presented in a deliberately measured tone. Even when reporting about atrocities most pamphleteers self-consciously avoided overt sensationalism. In the preface to *The Truth about Louvain*, M. Giran stated that "there will not be found in this narrative any incidents which, framed in a picture of frightfulness, are exhibited to excite the indignation of the crowd." Instead this "simple testimony" based on "trustworthy sources" had been published with the desire to awaken German conscience, which cannot be held accountable since all the true facts are concealed from her.[32] The revelation of "truth" was a commonly stated purpose in the pamphlets. Such posturing was found, for example, in J. D. Redmond's *Account of a Visit to the Front*. This pamphlet was not, for the most part, overtly or obviously propagandistic. Its overwhelming self-projection was as an account of what was "really" going on in the war, implying that people back home desired nothing more than accurate information. Similarly, the pamphlet *German Barbarians: Excerpts from Diaries of German Soldiers* illustrated, without editorial comment, that German words and deeds did not match. In this pamphlet, the Germans were allowed to proclaim, in the form of a signed protest, that their "just and good cause" had been stained by "lies and slanders. IT IS NOT TRUE that we are waging war contrary to the laws of nations. Our soldiers are guilty neither of indiscipline nor of cruelty."[33] Subsequently, however, the pamphlet presented a sampling of German soldiers' diary entries reporting occurrences of atrocities. The entries, or as the author calls them "confessions," tell of shootings, hangings, looting, burnings, etc. After the presentation of the evidence, the pamphlet closes with the injunction, "They spoke. They acted. Judge them."[34] Despite the polemical title, the pamphlet's format suggested that the reader was expected to reason to his or her own conclusions. The primary evidence was presented without comment, and the entries were purportedly verifiable since the original documents were kept at the French War Office.

This last example serves well to illustrate the singular approach of Wellington House. Taken as a whole the pamphlets were to be read by Americans as the "facts" of the war; upon a presentation of the truth, the reader was expected to form an educated opinion. These "facts" confirmed that Britain was the guarantor of civilization, while some of the pamphlets overtly extended this national character beyond Britain to an Anglo-American idealized community, by emphasizing that Americans and Britons upheld similar virtues such as justice, laws, rights, and honor. Each of the themes focused upon in the pamphlets stemmed from these virtues, which gained more power when contrasted against German barbarism, aggression, and militarism.

II

American entry to the Great War in 1917 stimulated a notoriously oppressive political atmosphere in the United States, which included censorship, lynching, tar-and-featherings, and the Sedition Act, as well as overt American government-sponsored propaganda.[35] Much of its groundwork was prepared by newspaper coverage that crystallized, even during the period of American neutrality, into a defense of the pro-British position. Initial press coverage was heavily, though not unanimously, British. According to one early study, of 367 American newspapers during the period of neutrality, 105 favored the Allies and 20 the Germans, while the remaining 242 were neutral.[36]

Despite this advantage, Britain's supporters faced considerable obstacles. Above all, much of public opinion was uninterested in European wars. For this reason, a case had to be made that Germany's purported malevolence affected Americans locally.[37] Moreover, pro-German and pro-neutrality positions were well-articulated. Until the United States entered the war, William Randolph Hearst, owner of one of the largest newspaper and magazine empires in the United States, continued to print pro-German and anti-British editorials, in an effort to keep America out of the war. While British propaganda portrayed the war as a matter of honor, Hearst "preached that the war was purely an economic struggle, that England and Japan were more menacing to American neutrality than Germany, that Americans would be dupes and gulls if they permitted a single drop of American blood to be shed upon foreign soil." Even the *Lusitania* incident, declared Hearst's *New York American* on June 6, 1915, was justified "under the accepted rules of civilized warfare" and was "of course, no cause for a declaration of war."[38]

Meanwhile, some less mainstream papers, including foreign-language papers, argued that England was the real enemy of ordinary Americans. North Dakota's two main Norwegian-language newspapers, *Fram* and *Normanden*, insisted on carrying news from Berlin as well as London, reasoning that news releases from Germany were often more reliable. Russia, not Germany, was viewed as the primary threat to Europe, particularly the small neutral countries. Both papers attacked Britain for maneuvering Japan into war against Germany, for mining the North Sea in violation of international law, for confiscating the goods of neutral countries, and finally because all of these steps drove Germany to adopt drastic measures for protecting its vital interests. President Wilson's pretensions to neutrality came in for scorn as well; his insistence on the right of Americans to travel unmolested on belligerent ships was portrayed as absurd, particularly when the duplicitous British would simply ensure that at least one American sailed on each British merchant vessel in order to provoke a confrontation between the United States and Germany. These papers insisted that Britain, not Germany, had long been the threat to American interests, and denounced the American sale of arms to Britain as a violation of neutrality and an obstacle to peace. This hostility to Britain, argues Odd S. Lovoll, stemmed from Norwegian immigrants' populist and socialist politics, for they saw Britain as the ally of the big capitalists who unfairly hindered their own economic progress.[39]

Supporters of Britain also had to contend with German-language papers and German-funded propaganda. Much of this lacked credibility, influencing Wellington House's policy of avoiding overt propaganda.[40] For example, George Sylvester Viereck's English weekly, *The Fatherland*, subsidized by the German government, justified the invasion of Belgium by positing a Belgian-led conspiracy to invade Germany along with the British and French, in order to plunder the German Empire. The invasion of Belgium was thus preemptive and defensive, and comparable to the American nineteenth-century seizures of California and Texas. In addition, *The Fatherland* emphasized the struggle between Slav and Teuton, and the necessity of defending Teutonic culture against its attack by materialistic England. The Kaiser's power was downplayed; he was a "psychological emperor and not a real emperor," with real power residing in the people represented by the Bundesrat. Finally, *The Fatherland* asserted the continuity between British policies in the era of the American Revolution and Early Republic and contemporary British policies; Britain was the same enemy in 1914 that it had been in 1814. It conspired with Wall Street to subvert American ideals, and unfairly controlled Ireland.[41]

Again, these were exceptions. Much more common, particularly as the war unfolded, were pro-British editorials, favorable news from London (since the British controlled the cables to America), and condemnation of "hyphenated Americans". It is impossible to determine how effective such propaganda was at changing minds about the war. What is clear, though, is that the language used to describe the war and the demonization of Germans, their supporters, and even defenders of neutrality, emphasized many of the same themes as those found in Wellington House-sponsored books and pamphlets. Moreover, as the United States entered the war and repressive measures drove out alternate voices, the image of an Anglo-American community and identity of interests became the predominant narrative. Oklahoma newspapers, for example, gave prominent coverage to Woodrow Wilson's attacks on "hyphenated Americans," supplementing them with their own supportive editorials, thus conjuring up an image of an "ill-defined enemy within their midst." In James Fowler's words, "the newsmen of Oklahoma became convinced that Germany, with the aid of 'hyphenated-Americans,' conspired not only to subvert the American electoral process but also to destroy American lives by fomenting strikes, by blowing up munitions plants and ships, and by destroying bridges." When President Wilson's shift of emphasis from strict neutrality to "preparedness" attracted dissenters, the *Daily Oklahoman* asked of its German-American correspondents: "If preparedness is good for Germany why is it not good for the United States: Wherein lies the difference? Why this particular attitude? Is it inconsistency? Or Worse? We Wonder."[42]

Aside from newspapers, the British cause won the sympathy of Walter Lippmann and his colleagues on the influential new political magazine, *The New Republic*. At the war's beginning, Lippmann advocated an "aggressive pacifism" that gradually evolved into interventionism. The

sinking of the *Lusitania* underscored that the United States did not
have a sufficient navy to enforce its rights as a neutral nation, but
relied on Britain's. Thus, the choice lay between defending Britain and
building an American navy the size of Britain's. To Lippmann, moreover, the question of neutral rights was not paramount; rather,
American foreign policy must be based on "a vision of the Anglo-
American future." To Lippmann, German submarine warfare was not
the real issue, but a necessary pretext for bringing the U.S. into the war
on the Allied side. By February 1917, he argued that America was an
integral part of the "Atlantic Community," a community that was
endangered by Germany's submarine warfare on the "world's
highway," the Atlantic Ocean.[43] Writing to the British journalist
Norman Angell in March, Lippmann asserted that American entry into
the war presented a unique opportunity to attempt to create a liberal
and ultimately peaceful international order such as Angell had long
advocated. He even asked the famously pacifist Angell to write an
article justifying American intervention on "liberal and international
grounds" in order to help undermine American pacifists' influence.[44]
Atlantic Monthly editor Ellery Sedgwick had similarly asked British
radical A. G. Gardiner, in 1915, to write sympathetic portrayals of
British leaders in Flanders for the American magazine; in 1918
Sedgwick proclaimed his devotion to promoting pro-English feeling in
America.[45]

Once the United States entered the war on Britain's side, American
newspapers more frequently echoed themes of British propaganda.
According to the *Knox County Democrat* (Missouri), Germany had
forced the U.S. into the war by ignoring its rights on the sea. This
theme was echoed by the *Miami Herald*.[46] Both papers, and countless
others, thus echoed the British emphasis on the rights of neutral
nations. Readers of the *Arkansas Gazette* were told to buy Liberty Bonds
in order to defend the United States from "Prussianism," with all of the
connotations assigned to it by G. K. Chesterton:

> Our own cherished institutions, our free government, all that our
> fathers fought for, all that free people prize, is threatened by an
> enemy that would impose his own hateful Kultur on every free insti-
> tution in every liberty-loving land.[47]

The themes of British propaganda were seen, too, both before and after
the United States entered the war, in the way that the German "rape"
of Belgium became a common metaphor in American politics. The

1915 lynching in Marietta, Georgia, of Leo Frank, a convicted rapist whose execution was commuted to life imprisonment following the appearance of exculpatory evidence, was compared by Boston merchants to "bleeding Belgium," and the merchants suggested boycotting Georgia products. According to Milton Ready, this condemnation went far towards winning Georgians to support for Wilson's "preparedness" agenda; Georgians, out of a sense of shame and a desire to reconcile with the rest of the country, began to distance themselves from anti-Wilsonian politics. Similarly, the *Chicago Defender* illustrated a lynching story with a picture of a decapitated head and the caption "NOT BELGIUM – AMERICA."[48] In these examples, the British version of Germany's "Belgian atrocities" had passed to the level of common sense, a metaphor through which to understand domestic controversies.

In order to examine this rhetorical development of an Anglo-American community more clearly, we conducted case studies of two newspapers, *The Atlanta Constitution* and *The Milwaukee Journal*, from the beginning of the war in Europe.[49] Although space permits only illustrative quotations rather than a detailed discussion of these case studies, our findings confirm the gradual triumph of language similar to that found in the Wellington House pamphlets. *The Atlanta Constitution*, edited by Clark Howell, had since the late nineteenth century under Henry Grady championed the New South while supporting such progressive causes as opposition both to lynching and to the domination of public life by big business. The latter cause often (though not of necessity) went hand-in-hand with antipathy to England. The *Milwaukee Journal*, edited by part-owner Lucius W. Nieman since its first month of existence in 1882, maintained a self-image as an independent paper that often championed unpopular causes. Its historian concludes that it "was not the voice of any particular political party or special interest group." It often challenged the views of Senator LaFollette, the leading politician in Wisconsin, and its independence stood out in a city where the other English-language papers supported the Republican Party, and in which a significant foreign-language press, including a German-language and pro-German press, flourished.[50] These two papers began the war with somewhat different leanings; by early 1917, however, both had transformed from critical and ostensibly neutral papers into consistent proponents of an Anglo-American and anti-German imagined community.

At the start of the war *The Atlanta Constitution* maintained a formally neutral perspective, subtly favoring the Allies while not excluding the German point of view. Despite pro-English tendencies, the *Constitution* treated the English position with initial skepticism, which decreased as the war progressed. As criticism towards the English became muted, criticism of Germany grew correspondingly. By the time the United States entered the war *The Atlanta Constitution* was in full support of American intervention and closer Anglo-American ties. There was a marked shift in the language used to describe the war and the demonization of Germans upon the United States' entrance into the war, which emphasized many of the same themes as those found in Wellington House-sponsored books and pamphlets.

Yet this development did not emerge suddenly. As early as 1915, a *Constitution* news story quoting Sir Edward Carson, a former British solicitor-general, implied that the United States had a role to play in upholding international law for the sake of civilization.[51] In the same issue an atrocity report about Germany's Muslim allies throwing babies into fires was based on details related by Lord Bryce. In an editorial on December 24, 1915 the editor spoke strongly against America continuing to wait patiently for the outcome of discussions with Britain concerning neutrality. It is "time to get away from this attitude of beggary," stated the editor.[52] A few months earlier, in a front-page cartoon entitled "Value of Unity," a long line of German troops was marched across Europe while the Allies were distracted with domestic issues. The editor stated that the value of unity is the biggest lesson of the European war, specifically that the Germans were the only ones prepared and unified. Although this statement did not advocate American intervention, it helped to frame a context in which unity and loyalty to the war effort were both celebrated and required.

By the eve of America's entrance in the war, Germany was consistently rebuked for its actions in Belgium on general grounds of humanity and the rights of non-combatants.[53] Two months prior to America's declaration of war, the *Constitution* reported that 18 respectable papers from across the country thought that war with Germany was the only proper American response to resumed submarine warfare.[54] The editorial page continued to echo these themes, writing in March that "America's only justification for entrance into the European holocaust, is that of freedom of the seas and the protection of humanity's rights on the ocean, which have been violated by German U-Boats."[55]

After American entrance into the war such language became much more common, with the themes of Anglo-American civilization and liberty underscored by contrast with German barbarity. When the first Liberty bond drive succeeded beyond anyone's expectations the *Constitution* declared this as "tangible evidence of the degree of unanimity with which the American masses have gone to war for world liberty."[56] These drives were understood to indicate the level of national devotion to the war cause. Bond buyers were also praised for their devotion to the "cause of humanity" and the "cause of world-wide democracy."[57] While espousing such ideals it was not uncommon for the *Constitution* to look back at the war's origins and assign blame to German actions. In direct contrast to the causes that America was fighting for, the editor concludes that "the conduct of German rulers throughout this war...have shown them to be utterly disregardful of truth, honor, or the rights of mankind; and wholly unmeritorious of confidence or trust."[58] By 1918 the terms Prussians and Huns were used interchangeably for the Germans. Before American entrance to the war the most common local complaint was economic, namely the effect of restricted trade on cotton. By the time of American entrance into the war, Wellington House's projected image of Anglo-American dedication to humanity and freedom of the seas, under threat by German barbarism, aggression, and militarism, had found a consistent home in *The Atlanta Constitution*.[59]

At the beginning of the war, the *Milwaukee Journal*, though officially neutral, gave ample scope to the German position, both in news coverage and editorials.[60] Indeed, its articulation of the German position went well beyond that in the *Constitution*, no doubt reflecting Milwaukee's large German minority. Well into 1916, the paper not only championed neutrality over involvement on the Allied side, but often provided direct validation of the German government's perspective. Although the reporting of "hard news" often allowed little scope for slanting, particularly if the paper was to maintain any sort of commitment to the nascent ideal of "objectivity," even here it was possible to defend Germany's conduct. For example, a September 1914 headline on page 1, stretching across two columns, asserted "COMPELLED TO BOMBARD RHEIMS." A smaller subheadline just below elaborated: "Germans Declare French Fired from Ancient City and Retaliation was Necessary – Appalling Destruction Along the Valley of the Aisne."[61] While the subheadline underscored the perspectival nature of the German claim, the more prominent and larger headline effectively endorsed their claim, smuggling "views" into ostensible "news." In short, a potential German atrocity story was reinterpreted as a necessary German response.

A much more common method entailed the reporting of German or pro-German speeches as news. A notable example of this method occurred in October 1914, in the first two columns of page one, in a lengthy report on George Bernard Shaw's remarks on the war. In case any one missed the purport of this story, the subheadline announced that "George Bernard Shaw Makes Some Scathing Remarks About War – Declares England and Germany Are Like Quarrelsome Dogs, Each Determined to Do the Other Incalculable Mischief." While Germany did not come off well in this subheadline, at the very least it took the air out of British claims to have morality on its side. This position was argued effectively in the story itself:

> "England is not at war because Germany made an 'infamous pro-posal' to violate Belgian neutrality," began Mr Shaw. "If it had suited us to accept that proposal we could have found plenty of good reasons. The England that grabbed Ireland, India, and Egypt cannot delude the Germany of Wilhelm II. Our national trick of sanctimonious indignation is simply hypocrisy. Let us therefore drop it."[62]

Shaw continued to criticize the idea that Germany was uniquely mil-itaristic, claiming that "the junker caste of Germany is no better no worse, than the junker caste of England... the German people hate the military caste as do the English people, and for the same reasons."[63] Shaw's remarks, reported at the top of page one (of the Sunday edition), could have two effects. First, they acted to undermine the morality of the British case, so that if Germany was to be seen as an aggressor, then Britain would be as well. Second, and by logical exten-sion, if Britain was to be seen as a moral actor despite its imperial con-quests, then German aggressiveness was equally compatible with international moral standing.

By the time the United States had entered the war, however, the *Milwaukee Journal* became a virtual agent of pro-Allied propaganda, uti-lizing many of the same themes that were on display in Wellington House-sponsored pamphlets, while demanding displays of loyalty on the part of all Americans, particularly those of German descent. Rather than conveying numerous examples, a close examination of a single issue, that of 2 October 1917, will make this point. Although specific stories changed, the themes recurred repeatedly, and a survey of a single issue underscores the totality of the message that confronted the paper's readers. This issue consistently highlighted German atrocities, German militarism, and the determination of the American people to deal effectively with infiltration by German-sympathizers in their midst. Lest anyone imagine simply that war occasioned atrocities on all sides, German attacks were headlined in bold at the top of page one, and emphasized attacks on hospitals, nurses, and wounded. By contrast, attacks on Germany by the allied French appeared lower in the column, with a smaller subhead; positioned thus in the story, France's own attacks on civilians would be seen as a fair response to German provocation, and indeed, the story evoked future French attacks "in retaliation for German aerial attacks on French cities."[64] Nor should anyone imagine that Europeans had merely stumbled into the war. A four-column story with a three-column headline, on page four, was entitled "WHY PRUSSIAN CASTE DECIDED FOR WAR"; this was a news story, not an editorial, and it essentially argued the *primat der innenpolitik* thesis that German war-making was an attempt to stave off a popular uprising. Immediately to the right appeared a column about the University of Wisconsin president's annual address to the faculty, in which readers learned "U.S. AID DECISIVE VAN HISE SAYS: ODIOUS GERMAN DEEDS MUST BE PREVENTED." In the text of his speech readers were treated to arguments that could have been penned in Wellington House, for example that German rulers believed in their culture's superiority, that they were above international law, and that might made right. Even front-page coverage of a local sex scandal mentioned that the perpetrator was a German captain. These are only the most glaring examples in an issue that, both in news and editorial copy, was full of charges against German militarism juxtaposed with Anglo-American commitment to win the war they had only reluctantly entered. In virtually every case, the guilty culprit was not the German people, but its militaristic government; the war was portrayed, therefore, as a war of liberation for the German people as well as the rest of the world.

III

To a large extent, Wellington House's intended messages were reflected in American newspaper coverage of the war. The case studies of the *Atlanta Constitution* and *Milwaukee Journal* reveal a common commitment, by the war's end, to the idea that Germany was a threat to a just and humane Anglo-American international order. More evidence would be needed in order to understand the extent to which British propaganda helped to *cause* the shift in coverage in these two papers by the time of American entrance into the war, and certainly it is not surprising that they would support the Anglo-American side enthusiastically once the United States entered the war, as well as demonizing the pro-German and pro-neutral positions.[65] Moreover, following the war, Anglo-American relations underwent a strain as American isolationism was exacerbated by widespread perceptions that the United States had been tricked into intervention by ubiquitous British propaganda. These perceptions, in turn, jeopardized American intervention in the more dangerous World War II.[66] There is thus no direct line between war-time cooperation and the "special relationship" that evolved under World War II and Cold War conditions. However, by articulating common values and identity, which were contrasted with Germany's barbaric threat to these very qualities, American newspapers and Wellington House propaganda together helped to provide a conceptual framework that could facilitate the emergence of this "special relationship" under more fruitful (or desperate) conditions.

Notes

1 We are grateful to Alice Byrne, Nicoletta Gullace, Thomas Hajkowsi, Fred Leventhal, George Robb, and Marcile Taylor for their valuable comments on earlier drafts of this essay.

2 John Bodnar, "Remembering the Immigrant Experience in American Culture," *Journal of American Ethnic History* 15 (Fall 1995), 3–28; Rudolph J. Vecoli, "The Significance of Immigration in the Formation of American Identity," *History Teacher* 30 (1996), 9–27; Joseph M. Siracusa, "American Policy-Makers, World War I, and the Menace of Prussianism, 1914–1920," *Australasian Journal of American Studies* 17 (1998), 1–30; Priscilla Roberts, "The First World War and the Emergence of American Atlanticism 1914–20," *Diplomacy and Statecraft* 5 (1994), 569–619.

3 *Military Press Control. A History of the Work of M.I.7. 1914–1919.* INF 4/ 1B, National Archives (London).

4 Taylor, *British Propaganda in the Twentieth Century*, 3. More broadly, this paragraph is taken from Taylor, *British Propaganda*, 5–34.

5 See Frederic William Wile, *The German-American Plot: The Record of a Great Failure: the Campaign to Capture the Sympathy and Support of the United States* (London: C. Arthur Pearson Limited, 1915). In their preference for reaching elite opinion, Masterman and Parker embodied contemporary intellectuals' antipathies toward an emerging mass society. See John Carey, *The Intellectuals and the Masses: Pride and Prejudice among the Literary Intelligentsia, 1880–1939* (Chicago: Academy Chicago Publishers, 2002).

6 *Third Report of the Work conducted for the Government at Wellington House* (Very Confidential), p. 6, CAB 37/156/6, National Archives.

7 Gilbert Parker, "The United States," in *Report of the Work of the Bureau established for the Purpose of laying before Neutral Nations and the Dominions the case of Great Britain and her Allies* (Secret), 10, INF 4/5, National Archives.

8 The following is based on a representative, but not a random, sample of 15 of the pamphlets, selected by title in order to uncover as wide a range of themes as possible. For alternative and more thorough accounts, see George Robb, *British Culture and the First World War* (Basingstoke: Palgrave

Macmillan, 2002), 96–128; Nicoletta F. Gullace, *"The Blood of our Sons":
Men, Women, and the Renegotiation of British Citizenship During the Great War*
(Basingstoke: Palgrave Macmillan, 2002), 17–33.

9   Trevor Wilson, "Lord Bryce's Investigation into Alleged German Atrocities
in Belgium, 1914–15," *Journal of Contemporary History* 14 (1979), 369–83. See
also James Startt's chapter in this book.

10 James Bryce, *Neutral Nations and the War* (London: Macmillian and Co.,
Ltd., 1914), 9; G. K. Chesterton, *The Barbarism of Berlin* (London: Cassell &
Co., Ltd., 1914), 8–9.

11 Charles F. G. Masterman, *After Twelve Months of War* (London: Darling,
1915), 12.

12 Masterman, *After Twelve Months*, 6.

13 The doctrines to which Bryce is referring in *Neutral Nations and the War* (1)
are from a book written by General von Bernhardi, entitled *Germany and the
Next War*, and published in 1911.

14 Bryce, *Neutral Nations*, 6.

15 Sir Edward Cook, *Why Britain is at War: The Causes and the Issues* (London:
Macmillian and Co., Ltd., 1915), 24.

16 Both were united in privileging military necessity over the rights of non-
combatants, or denying the distinction between combatant and non-
combatant. For British recognition that their blockade of Germany, on
grounds of military necessity, was equally culpable, see Nicoletta F. Gullace,
"Sexual Violence and Family Honor: British propaganda and international
law during the First World War," *American Historical Review* 102 (1997), 737.

17 Dudley Rawson Stratford de Chair, *How the British Blockade Works* (London:
Sir Joseph Causton & Sons, Ltd., 1916), 7.

18 Archibald Spicer Hurd, *Murder at Sea* (London: T. Fisher Unwin, Ltd, 1916),
7.

19 Bryce, *Neutral Nations*, 3.

20 Bryce, *Neutral Nations*, 12.

21 Cook, *Why Britain is at War*, 24.

22 Dikaios Logos, *An Ordinary Briton's View of the War: An Open Letter to a
Senator of the USA* (London: Darling and Son, Ltd., 1915), 8.

23 Bryce, *Neutral Nations*, 7.

24 H. W. Massingham, *Why We Came to Help Belgium* (London: Harrison and
Sons, 1914), 7.

25 Masterman, *After Twelve Months*, 5.

26 Masterman, *After Twelve Months*, 8.

27 Stephen E. Koss, *Fleet Street Radical: A. G. Gardiner and the Daily News*
(London: Allen Lane, 1973), 148–9.

28 Sir Gilbert Parker, *The World in a Crucible: An Account of the Origins and
Conduct of the Great War* (London: Dodd, Mead and Company, 1915), 342.

29 Chesterton, *The Barbarism of Berlin*, 28–9.

30 James M. Beck, *The Case of Edith Cavell: A Study of the Rights of Non-
combatants* (New York: G. P. Putnams's Sons, n.d.), 41. Beck was a former
Assistant Attorney General.

31 For example, Hurd, *Murder at Sea*, 28.

32 Rene Chambry with a preface by M. le Pasteur Giran, *The Truth About
Louvain* (New York: Hodder & Stoughton, 1915), 8.

33 *German Barbarians: Excerpts from Diaries of German Soldiers* (1914), 1.

34 *German Barbarians*, 6.

35 For the role of American-generated propaganda in winning support of the war, see Harold Lasswell, *Propaganda Technique in World War I* (Cambridge, MA: M.I.T. Press, 1971). For atmosphere of censorship, see, for example, Dale Zacher, *The Scripps Newspapers Go to War, 1914–18* (Urbana and Chicago: University of Illinois Press, 2006); Theodore Kornweibel, "'The Most Dangerous of all Negro Journals': Federal Efforts to Suppress the *Chicago Defender* During World War I," *American Journalism* 11 (1994), 154–68; Mick Mulcrone, "'Those Miserable Little Hounds': World War I Postal Censorship of the *Irish World*," *Journalism History* 20 (1994), 15–24; Jean L. Berres, "Local Aspects of the 'Campaign for Americanism': The *Milwaukee Journal* in World War I," PhD dissertation, Southern Illinois University, 1977.

36 William P. Slosson, *The Great Crusade and After: 1914–1928* (New York, 1930), 10–11, cited in Felie A. Bonadio, "The Failure of German Propaganda in the United States, 1914–1917," *Mid-America: an Historical Review* 41 (1959), 42.

37 For example, "Florida newspapers largely ignored the war in Europe until 1917." C. Peter Ripley, "Intervention and Reaction: Florida Newspapers and United States Entry into World War I," *Florida Historical Quarterly* 49 (1971), 255.

38 Y. D. Prasal, "William Randolph Hearst and Pro-Germanism During World War I," *Indian Journal of American Studies* 17 (1987), 93–100, esp. 94, 96.

39 Odd S. Lovoll, "North Dakota's Norwegian-Language Press views World War I, 1914–1917, *North Dakota Quarterly* (Winter 1971), esp. 78.

40 See Frederic William Wile, *The German-American Plot: The Record of a Great Failure: the Campaign to Capture the Sympathy and Support of the United States* (London: C. Arthur Pearson Limited, 1915).

41 Felie A. Bonadio, "The Failure of German Propaganda," 40–57. See also La Vern J. Rippley, "Conrad Kornmann, German-Language Editor: A Case Study of Anti-German Enthusiasm during World War I," *South Dakota History* 27 (Fall 1997), 108–32. The idea of a conspiracy between Wall Street and England had other proponents, including Tom Watson, leader of Georgia's Farmer's Union and future Georgia senator. See Milton L. Ready, "Georgia's Entry into World War I," *Georgia Historical Quarterly* (1968), 260.

42 James H. Fowler, II, "Creating an Atmosphere of Suppression, 1914–1917," *The Chronicle of Oklahoma* 59 (1981), 202–23, esp. 202, 204, 212. Quotation of *Daily Oklahoman* is from 19 December 1915.

43 Ronald Steel, *Walter Lippmann and the American Century* (Boston and Toronto: Little, Brown and Company, 1980), 89, 93, 111. For an alternate discussion of the *New Republic* in World War I, see Christopher Lasch, *The New Radicalism in America, 1889–1963: The Intellectual as a Social Type* (New York: Alfred A. Knopf, 1965; New York: W. W. Norton, 1997), 181–224.

44 Lippmann to Angell, 1 March 1917, Angell Papers, Box 17, Ball State University, Muncie, IN.

45 Ellery Sedgwick to A. G. Gardiner, 25 March 1915, 4 April 1918, and 18 November 1918, all in the A. G. Gardiner Papers 1/1, London School of Economics.

46 Lawrence O. Christensen, "Popular Reaction to World War I in Missouri," *Missouri Historical Review*, 389; C. Peter Ripley, "Intervention and Reaction," 256.

47 *Arkansas Gazette*, 6 April 1918; quoted in Joseph Carruth, "World War I Propaganda and Its Effects in Arkansas," *The Arkansas Historical Quarterly* 56 (1997), 390.

48 Ready, "Georgia's Entry Into World War I," 260–1; Kornweibel, "The Most Dangerous of all Negro Journals", 156–7.

49 According to Allan Bell, "In testing samples to represent a full year of news copy, those of 6, 12, 18, 24 and 48 days of a year were all adequate... Samples larger than 12 days provided little additional reliability." Bell, *The Language of News Media* (Oxford: Blackwell, 1991), 23. We have, therefore, selected every 27th issue between 28 July 1914 and 22 August 1918, for a total of 13–14 per year. Following this procedure, seven consecutive selected issues would be from, e.g., Tuesday, Monday, Saturday, Friday, Thursday, Wednesday, Tuesday, so that we have avoided the accidents that might arise from giving a particular day too much prominence. See Bell, *Language*, 9–32.

50 Jean L. Berres, "Local Aspects of the 'Campaign for Americanism'"; Harold Davis, *Henry Grady's New South: Atlanta, a Brave and Beautiful City* (Tuscaloosa, AL: University of Alabama Press, 2002).

51 "Duty of Neutrals As Seen By Carson," *The Atlanta Constitution*, 27 Nov 1915.

52 "Getting Us Both Ways," *The Atlanta Constitution*, 24 Dec 1915.

53 "Germany Rebuked for Belgian Acts by United States," *The Atlanta Constitution*, 9 Dec 1916.

54 "Rupture With Germany Seen by American Press," *The Atlanta Constitution*, 1 Feb 1917.

55 "Call of the Navy," *The Atlanta Constitution*, 27 March 1917.

56 "American's Response," *The Atlanta Constitution*, 16 June 1917.

57 "Well Done," *The Atlanta Constitution*, 29 Oct 1917.

58 "Germans and Their Rulers," *The Atlanta Constitution*, 29 Oct 1917.

59 Unfortunately, editor Clark Howell's papers are not very informative on editorial decision-making, though there is an interesting exchange in which Howell commends his son's enthusiasm for serving his country, but urges him not to be too hasty in enlisting at the "first call." Clark Howell, Sr., to Clark Howell, Jr., February 19, 1917; Ms 818, box 3, University of Georgia, Athens.

60 For the Journal's neutrality in the first two years of the war, see Berres, chapter 3.

61 *Milwaukee Journal*, 21 September 1914.

62 *Milwaukee Journal*, 18 October 1914.

63 *Milwaukee Journal*, 18 October 1914. Shaw was, of course, himself of Irish descent.

64 *Milwaukee Journal*, 2 October 1917.

65 In the case of the *Milwaukee Journal*, demands for war-time unity and attacks on German-American alleged disloyalty frequently included denunciations of socialist politics.

66 Taylor, *British Propaganda in the Twentieth Century*, 43; Fred M. Leventhal, "Public Face and Public Space: the Projection of Britain in America before the Second World War," in Leventhal and Quinault, eds., *Anglo American Attitudes* (Aldershot: Ashgate, 2000), 212–26. Leventhal's chapter demonstrates the measures that the British took to repair the damage done by the American reaction to British propaganda in the Great War. See also Leventhal, "Eric Knight's War: the Campaign for Anglo-American Understanding," in Jonathan Hollowell, ed., *Twentieth-Century Anglo-American Relations* (London: Palgrave, 2001), 44–63.

9
Red on the Map: Empire and Americanization at the BBC, 1942–50

Thomas Hajkowski

On Sunday November 20, 1943, after the 9:00 o'clock news, Norman Angell delivered a *Postscript* on the British Empire. He opened by admitting that the Empire was a "strange institution ... puzzling and confusing to foreigners [and] ... even ourselves." While gently admonishing his audience for being "oblivious" to the importance of the Empire in world affairs, Angell touched upon several themes in his talk: the Empire's importance to the war effort, the autonomy of the Dominions, and the necessity of the Empire to global stability and peace after the war. He also devoted much of his talk on the British Empire to relations with the United States. Angell told his audience that America was shedding its traditional hostility to imperialism. The war had proven the importance of the Empire to American, as well as British security. Far from scuppering Anglo-American relations, the Empire would guarantee that the friendship between Britain and the United States was based on mutual respect and interdependence. Imperial defense, Angell said reassuringly, "is necessary to the security of the United States precisely as American power and resources are necessary to our security."[1]

Angell's broadcast reveals both the anxiety of the BBC hierarchy regarding the future of the Empire and the varied associations between Empire and America that developed at the BBC during the Second World War. In the case of the former, the cost of the war and the strain it placed on the imperial system generated concern. Listener research data that suggested widespread ignorance of imperial affairs among the British public only exacerbated worries about the long-term viability of the Empire.[2] In the case of the latter, both political necessity and cultural anxieties caused the BBC to consider programs about the Empire in the context of American military and cultural might. The BBC had to confront American anti-imperialism in programs for domestic listeners and overseas listeners.[3] Further, Britain's economic and military dependence on the United States provoked anxiety at the BBC about the decline of British influence, status, and culture. Finally, the quantity and popularity of American programs on the BBC during the war undoubtedly aggravated concerns about American cultural dominance.

Under these manifold pressures, the BBC redoubled its efforts to include programs on the Empire in its schedules. Beginning in the summer of 1942, the BBC increasingly portrayed Empire as a strong, interdependent, and above all cohesive entity that would insure Britain a prominent place in the post-war world. As Angell intimated in his *Postscript*, imperial power would balance out American power and insure a more equal partnership between Britain and the United States. In addition to maintaining British prestige, if only in the imagination, the BBC used Empire, and the typically "British" values it represented, as a defense against the Americanization of popular culture. Imperial culture, packaged in a compelling form, offered a viable and impeccably British alternative to American entertainment. From 1946–49, the BBC's Drama department produced several serialized adaptations of Victorian imperial fiction: *King Solomon's Mines, Allan Quartermain, Sanders of the River, Captain Kettle, The Four Feathers,* and *No Other Tiger.* The radio renaissance of the imperial adventure story, and the traditional values embodied by the imperial hero, represented, in part, a response to the modernity and materialism of America culture.[4] Examining the BBC's treatment of the Empire as a reaction to American cultural and political dominance underscores the importance of Empire to British national identity and helps to explain the persistence of Empire in BBC programs long after the war. Although the pressing need for propaganda about Empire faded after V-J Day, it continued to be an important element in BBC programming well into the 1950s. The BBC broadcast talks and features on Empire, special programs for Empire Day and Christmas, and tried to represent Empire generally in its schedules.[5]

Before the Second World War, the attitude of the BBC hierarchy towards American broadcasting ranged from contempt to admiration.[6] On one hand, many British broadcasters felt that the American system represented broadcasting at its worst. Driven by the demands of advertisers, American programs were considered vulgar and responsive to the desires, but not the needs, of the listeners. The BBC contrasted its monopoly favorably to the "chaos of the air" produced by commercial broadcasting in the United States. The American radio style – characterized by quickness, precision timing, and informality – was considered unsuitable for British audiences. However, despite a firm belief in the superiority of the British system, there was considerable hand wringing at the BBC over the economic and cultural impact of the American entertainment industry.[7] For its part, the BBC tried to minimize the impact of American cultural imports such as jazz, crooning, and soap operas.

At the same time, aspects of American radio fascinated British broadcasters. It was common for BBC producers and administrators to visit the United States to observe American broadcasting techniques. Program makers, especially those responsible for developing entertainment programs, mined American radio in search of fresh ideas. In the 1930s the comic Eddie Pola produced popular programs for the BBC that parodied American entertainers such as Kate Smith, Al Jolson, and Amos n' Andy.[8] To the disappointment of the Board of Governors, the BBC slowly adopted certain American styles and by the mid-1930s the Corporation began importing programs from the United States. By 1939 British broadcasters could look to America and see an inspiration, a competitor, and a cultural bogeyman.

The BBC hierarchy felt no such ambiguity about the Empire. Reith and most of his lieutenants agreed that broadcasting should play a significant role in binding the Empire together. In 1930 the BBC resolved "that the Corporation should identify itself closely with Empire consolidation."[9] With much fanfare the BBC launched the Empire Service, "a connecting ... link between the scattered parts of the British Empire," in 1932.[10] As the political situation in Europe worsened an increasing number of Empire programs appeared. In 1938, Basil Nicolls, the BBC's program director, warned his department heads "that there should be greater reflection of the Empire in the Home programmes." He suggested a monthly series from the Empire on the lines of the popular talks, *America Speaks*, "as a means of increasing the representation of the Empire."[11]

When the war began in 1939, Empire figured prominently in the BBC's schedules. Government officials rushed to the microphone to praise the loyalty of the Empire and to assure the Home audience of its support for the war effort. Before the end of October, Anthony Eden, then Secretary of Commonwealth affairs, had broadcast three times.[12] The BBC supplemented these ministerial speeches with talks, features, drama, and other creative programming on the Colonies and

Dominions. For the duration of the war, the BBC would expand its presentation of Empire to its domestic listeners, refine its message, and search for new ways to draw audiences to Empire programs.[13]

The war also forced the BBC to significantly modify its relationship with American broadcasting. The ambiguity that characterized the BBC in the 1930s faded and the first three years of the war saw an unprecedented level of cooperation between the BBC and the American networks. A benevolent neutral and potential ally, the government and the BBC considered it important that the British people have a favorable impression of the United States. More importantly, the BBC, with the cooperation of the Ministry of Information (MOI), needed to inform the American public about the struggles of Britain at war. This was the remit of the BBC North American Service (NAS), established in 1940. Forced to compete with American stations for an American audience, the NAS quickly adopted the methods of American broadcasting. Techniques borrowed by the NAS from American broadcasting, such as the "continuity system" (insisting that programs do not overrun their allotted time in the schedule), were eventually adopted by the Home Service.

If NAS was the back door through which American broadcasting came to exert a major influence on British broadcasting, the demands of the war broke down the front door in 1941. In that year Lindsay Wellington, representing both the MOI and the BBC, visited the United States to coordinate Anglo-American propaganda efforts and the relay of American programs to Britain and Europe. These new initiatives pried open the BBC to greater American influence than at any time before the war.[14] British broadcasting became even more vulnerable to American influence after Pearl Harbor. The United States was no longer a friendly bystander but a vital ally. Starting in 1942, the BBC was called upon to provide programs for the thousands of American servicemen arriving in Britain. In May 1942, Olive Shapely began a series of talks on America in the *Children's Hour* and the BBC introduced *Command Performance*, a program organized by the US War Department, into the Forces Programme.[15] In June, the BBC began broadcasting *Let's Get Acquainted*, "to promote understanding and friendship between the members of the American expeditionary force" and the British people, as well as an "American" version of the popular quiz show *Brains Trust*. Finally, in August, Laurence Gilliam, the head of the Features Department, announced to readers of the *Radio Times* several ambitious programs designed to "interpret Britain to America and America to Britain," and "forge strong human links of Anglo-American understanding."[16]

On July 10, in the midst of this wave of American programs, the Directors-General of the BBC, Robert Foot and Cecil Graves, asked the heads of the Talks and School Broadcasting Departments to "examine their autumn plans with the idea of getting into them a reflection of Empire."[17] Yet the Talks Department especially had been highlighting the contributions of the Colonies and the Dominions to the war effort since September 1939 and George Barnes, the Talks Director, replied that "the number of talks by Dominion and Colonial speakers and about the Dominions and Colonies has steadily increased in the last year."[18] In December 1941, both the Colonial and Dominion Offices expressed their approval of Barnes's strategy of stressing "quality over quantity" when it came to talks about the Empire.[19] Why were the Directors-General suddenly pressuring the Talks and School Broadcasting Departments to produce more programs on the Empire? "With increasing contributions from the United States" wrote Foot and Graves, "listeners' interest in the Empire should be stimulated."[20]

One response then, to the Americanization of the BBC, was to reiterate the importance of Empire in radio programs. On one hand, this action was based on American anti-imperialism and the popularity of BBC programs about the United States. Listener research showed that Britons were more interested in hearing about America than the Dominions or Colonies. The BBC's first series of Empire talks, *Dominion Commentary*, was explicitly modeled on the Raymond Graham Swing talks *American Commentary*. Yet the imperial version never attracted as many listeners as the American original.[21] On the other hand, Empire represented a way to reiterate British achievement and values in light of the American invasion of British airwaves. Empire represented British power on a global scale. Empire builders embodied many qualities regarded as typically British – a commitment to service, self-sacrifice, and uncanny leadership ability – but perhaps lacking in Americans. Finally, Empire could be regarded as a uniquely British accomplishment.

The increasing demands on the Talks and Features Departments to produce attractive programs on the Empire led to the formation of a new interdivisional committee for imperial affairs. It included George Barnes (Director of Talks), Laurence Gilliam (Features Director), S. J. de Lotbiniere, (Empire Programme Director), Michael Barkway (NAS) and Tony Rendall (Assistant Controller, Overseas Service). The committee charged Rendall with drafting a statement to serve as the basis of official policy towards the Empire. The memorandum he produced was a systematic statement of the problems the BBC faced in promoting Empire along with a series of proposals for increasing the Empire's representation in the Home Service. Although space does not permit a detailed examination here, three relevant ideas clearly emerge from Rendall's policy paper. First, promoting Empire was not simply a matter of war propaganda, but a long-term commitment to informing listeners and preparing them to make sacrifices for imperial unity. Second, "patriotic pride" could play an important role in stimulating interest in the Empire. Third, American anti-imperialism was a serious problem, particularly the belief that "Empire ... [has] no place in the new post-war world."[22]

In response to Rendall's memorandum, the Talks Department began to develop a new "empire discussion" series titled *Red on the Map*. The BBC Programme Board originally rejected the idea for the series because the Talks producers wanted to include an American critic of Empire in the first installment of the series. When Programme Board balked, Barnes replied that the series required a critic "whose ignorance of the British Empire and its ideals would be at once manifest and plausible." The producers settled on an American in the hopes that criticism of "a British institution" from a "friendly foreigner" would tap into the national pride of the audience. Satisfied with Barnes's explanation, the first installment of *Red on the Map* went on the air with the London correspondent of the *Chicago Sun-Times*, Frederick Kuh, playing the role of critic.[23]

Red on the Map reveals some of the incongruous connections between Empire America in the minds of BBC personnel. Certainly *Red on the Map* represents an attempt by the BBC to rebut American anti-imperialism. Kuh, speaking for the United States, was given the latitude to express his disapproval of the British Empire, but only in order to be gently corrected by the other members of the panel. Barnes prevailed over the Board on the matter of using a hostile American by arguing that criticism of Empire from an American would only encourage a patriotic defensiveness about imperialism. Yet Programme Board's hesitancy to allow an American to critique the Empire raises questions. It is not clear why Programme Board initially rejected the idea of an American critic, but the fact that the BBC had allowed critics of imperialism to broadcast earlier in the war suggests that their objection had more to do with the nationality of the critic than the criticism itself.[24] Given the popularity of American programs, perhaps Programme Board worried that the audience would identify more with the American critic than the British and Australian defenders of Empire.

While the responsibility for promoting Empire fell largely to Barnes's staff, other departments were involved as well, partly because talks, in general, attracted small audiences. Not surprisingly, one of the most highly rated Empire programs of the war came from the Variety Department, founded in 1933. In 1943, Leslie Baily, who had produced a number of popular programs under the title of *Scrapbooks*, approached the Director of the Variety Department about creating a light program to stimulate more public interest in imperial matters. Significantly, Baily framed the program as a response to America, almost exactly as the Directors-General had in July 1942. "The BBC is doing a great deal to promote Anglo-American understanding on the 'common man's level,'" Baily wrote. But:

> are we doing as much to bring our listeners in touch with the life and interests of the common man in the Dominions and Colonies? The ignorance and indifference about the Commonwealth in this country is an evil that broadcasting should tackle.[25]

The result of Baily's efforts was *Travellers' Tales*, a mixture of songs, sketches, and the personal reminisces of Britons who had journeyed throughout the Empire. Due to Baily's determination to keep the program light, it became one of the most popular ever produced by the BBC on the Empire.[26] The first series of *Travellers' Tales* set a record for listeners in its Sunday evening time slot, drawing 14.3 percent of the audience.[27]

Despite its success, the BBC did not renew *Travellers' Tales* or another popular program, *Brush Up Your Empire*. The Corporation also shelved *Red on the Map* after it completed its run of episodes. Rendall fired off a memorandum to Foot, protesting the apparent change of policy and expressing his fear that the BBC was failing to fulfill its responsibility to educate its audience.[28] He need not have worried. Not only did Foot reassure him that the BBC maintained its commitment to fostering imperial unity,[29] but Foot's replacement as Director-General, William Haley, was to be as committed to Empire and the resistance of Americanization as Rendall himself.

William Haley, a newspaperman all his life, came to the BBC in 1943 to become the Corporation's first ever "editor-in-chief." He became Director-General in April 1944 and was to serve in that post until 1952. Although he took the reins of the BBC during a time of tremendous change, he remained committed to the public service ideals that had animated the BBC since the days of Reith. In a press release on the nature of the post-war BBC, Haley claimed "we shall safeguard broadcasting from becoming a glorified jukebox ... [rather] we shall play our part in making this country the best informed democracy in the world."[30] In internal correspondence, he reminded his staff that "the aim of the BBC must be to conserve and strengthen serious listening ... [we] must never lose sight of its cultural mission."[31] In addition to his commitment to instructive public-service broadcasting, Haley's diaries reveal a man painfully aware of Britain's decline, relative to the United States. In August 1949, he wrote, regarding the Labour government's efforts to secure a loan from America: "Bevin and Cripps are off to America next weekend to beg still more dole from Washington. To such straits in four years has this great nation come. England is sick."[32] A year later, he complained of being in a "nihilistic frame of mind." "The nation is going down" he concluded, "values are going down, in the sacred name of equality ... There is no sense left of taking part in national achievement. There is little opportunity left for personal achievement."[33]

In Haley the BBC had a Director-General committed to using the BBC as a tool to educate and raise the cultural tastes of the British public. He fought hard to preserve the BBC's monopoly and opposed commercial broadcasting in Britain. Haley was also acutely aware of Britain's decline and dependency on the United States after the war. In short, he would be a Director-General unlikely to allow the proliferation of American cultural influences in Britain. Indeed, Haley's tenure would prove to be as hostile to America as any period in the BBC's history.[34]

Following D-Day, Haley and his senior staff began to discuss in earnest the future of the BBC. They settled on a plan in which the BBC would be divided into three networks: the Light Programme, a popular entertainment network, the Home Service, which would carry mixed programming, and a high-brow arts network which eventually became the Third Programme. The Light Programme was not to be frivolous, and Haley hoped that the BBC might be able to gradually raise the standards of the network. Nor was the Light Programme to be a conduit for popular American programs. Writing near the end of 1944, Basil Nicolls insisted that all three networks were to be "firmly British in character" and provide "effective resistance to the Americanization of our entertainment."[35] A month later, Haley followed up Nicolls's memo with a directive to all the senior staff on the nature of the post-war service. "It is an important continuing objective of British broadcasting," he wrote "that the programmes should be firmly British in character, and should, by reflecting our national environment and characteristics, have the effect of encouraging and consolidating listeners in their feeling for British speech, culture and institutions."[36] The memo also included a strong condemnation of American cultural influences. His policy, Haley concluded:

> implies a steady, friendly resistance to foreign influences and particularly to the Americanisation of our programmes ... the by-products of this war-time vogue [for American programs] have not been welcome – sham American entertainment produced in Britain, the unnecessary use of American slang, crooning in spurious American accents, and the pursuit of American idioms, sentiments and rhythms.[37]

Haley's memorandum clearly demonstrates his commitment to keeping American programs to a minimum. But Haley's answer to Americanization is not merely the exclusion of foreign material, but also the projection of a vigorous national identity. The BBC had to make "Britishness" as appealing and alluring as American cultural products.

Haley struck similar notes in December of 1945, in a memorandum to Lindsay Wellington, now Controller of the Home Service:

> It is essential that ... the Basic Home Service during 1946 should strike keynotes attuned to the national position and outlook. Those keynotes should be virility, a sense of endeavour, courage exemplified by experience... . We should inculcate a spirit of striving... . We are nowhere near finished in our island or world story.[38]

In suggesting the ways in which the Home Service could stay attuned to the "national outlook," Haley singled out the Commonwealth and Empire. Haley proposed that they be "constantly projected as a great heritage, responsibility, and opportunity without in any way being jingoistic."[39] Haley quite explicitly tied Empire to British national identity – the island story (which was also a world story) – as well as British prestige. This was no more evident than during the British withdrawal from India in 1947. Haley directed the BBC to develop programs commemorating the transfer of power and "the British achievement in India."[40] Despite objections from his producers and words of caution from the historian Reginald Coupland, Haley insisted on maintaining the theme of national accomplishment.[41] Even the India Office, which had serious misgivings about Haley's plans, could not dissuade him from using the BBC to justify and celebrate British imperialism in India.[42]

All of the program departments were responsible for implementing Haley's policies of resisting America and promoting the Empire. In May 1946, the acting Controller of the Entertainment division reported that "it is likely as a matter of policy that we shall endeavour to introduce Commonwealth programmes regularly into our Home Services, both as a service to listeners, and as an overall Commonwealth job."[43] The Variety Department resurrected *Travellers' Tales* in the autumn of 1945.[44] The Talks department, which had always been relied on to try and educate the audience on imperial matters, continued its considerable work after 1945.[45]

At the program level, nothing better reflects Haley's dual mandate to resist Americanization and embrace Empire as heritage and opportunity than Drama Department's adaptations of Victorian imperial fiction: H. Rider Haggard's *King Solomon's Mines* and Edgar Wallace's *Sanders of the River* in 1946, Cutcliffe Hyne's *Captain Kettle* in 1947, A. E. W. Mason's *The Four Feathers* and Rider Haggard's *Allan Quartermain*, in 1948, and Mason's *No Other Tiger*, set in Burma, in 1949. In addition, when the popular detective serial *Dick Barton* took its regular hiatus in 1948 the BBC replaced it with *Adventure Unlimited*, which was "set against a background of tom-toms, pidgin English, flashing knives, and poisoned darts." The hero of the new serial was "tall, red-haired, deep-voiced – an Englishman every bit as fearless as his predecessor [Barton]."[46] The "imperial heroes" of these adventure tales represent different opportunities provided by Empire and reveal different aspects of the national character.[47] *Sanders of the River* relates the tales of District Commissioner Sanders, a man of singular purpose and unparalleled leadership capabilities who has devoted his life to the Empire. In *King Solomon's Mines*, Allan Quartermain demonstrates the economic opportunities of Empire, where an Englishman with a little pluck and derring-do could make his fortune. Harry Feversham, the central character of the *Four Feathers*, represents Britain's military tradition, loyalty, and the redemptive power of Empire.

These programs constituted Drama Department's efforts to do something for the Empire in response to Haley's policy, but do they mirror concerns over the Americanization of British culture? It is significant that the Drama Department chose to do these particular types of programs. During the war, the BBC largely ignored the imperial adventure story.[48] The dominant themes of imperial propaganda during the war were tolerance, cooperation, and mutual benefit. In one affecting broadcast, Learie Constantine, a famous West Indian cricketer, discussed his experiences of racism in Britain.[49] Dramas and features on

Empire focused on the work of education in the Empire, or the eradica-
tion of pests like locusts and the tsetse fly – what John Mackenzie has
called "the empire of peace and economic regeneration."[50] Feversham,
Sanders, and Quartermain represent the Empire of conquest, rule, and
economic exploitation. These were novels written during the heyday of
Empire, when 1/4 of the world was red and Britannia ruled the waves.
These programs were exercises in nostalgia for a simpler time. Writing
about *King Solomon's Mines* in the *Radio Times*, Val Gielgud admitted
that Haggard was "a little out of fashion," but he could not resist
"drawing to this story the attention of all listeners who share my own
weakness for yarns which gave them, or should have given them,
extreme pleasure when they were schoolboys."[51] Two years later,
Gielgud encouraged younger listeners to tune into *Allan Quartermain* "if
only to realise what used to keep their fathers from their homework!"[52]

Another striking aspect to the programs was the stress placed on
their authenticity. These were neither bowdlerized or scrubbed versions
of the books nor were they dubious Hollywood adaptations of British
culture. The Drama Department strove to keep as true to the originals
as possible. Take, for example, the introduction to the first episode of
Sanders of the River:

> We are in a primitive land; a strip of British West Africa ... inhabited
> by a million black folk whose minds are as the minds of children ...
> here dwelt Mr. Commissioner Sanders – Sanders of the River – a
> man who understood the minds of his people, and knowing them,
> loved them.[53]

This is a far cry from Learie Constantine's war-time broadcast on the
racial intolerance he experienced in Britain. Compared to the rest of
the BBC's programming on Empire, which emphasized progress,
benefice, and a better understanding of the non-white population of
the Commonwealth, these sentiments are wholly out of place; but they
are completely loyal to Wallace's novels. The *Radio Times* was similarly
unabashed in promoting Wallace, noting that he took his inspiration
from "the primitive tribes, with ... their childish logic and forest super-
stitions."[54] The BBC revealed a similar desire for authenticity with their
Captain Kettle broadcasts, assuring listeners that "we shall hear the real
Kettle ... and only when it is absolutely essential will the little fire-eater
be 'brought up to date.'"[55]

Finally these programs ought to be considered in light of the general
opposition to Americanization precisely because they are so imperialis-

tic; thus they represent effective opposition to Americanization. The traditionalism and masculinity of these serials (*Sanders* concludes with his eponymous hero leaving Africa, grateful that he did not propose to a lady missionary) stand in stark contrast to post-war films, which attempted to modernize the concept of Empire by "incorporating women... giving attention to American genres and markets... [and] by giving it [Empire] Hollywood associations."[56] This is not to say that every old-fashioned or heritage program produced by the BBC should be read as cultural resistance. But given the directives from Haley, the nostalgic framing of the programs, and the length to which the BBC went to ensure their authenticity, these programs operated as a rejection of American culture. They represent an attempt, if only for a few years after the war, to recreate a popular culture of imperialism because it would be, *de facto*, British.[57]

The BBC maintained its hostile attitude towards American broadcasting well into the 1950s. Programs originating from the United States were given a distinctive British flavor and America featured prominently as a negative example during debates over the BBC monopoly and the introduction of commercial television in Britain.[58] The BBC just as consistently promoted Empire in the years following the Second World War. In addition to a solid helping of talks, features, and variety programs, the BBC broadcast numerous special programs for King George VI's tour of Africa, the transfer of power to India in 1947, and "Colonial Month" in 1949.[59] In 1950 Haley assured the Commonwealth Relations Office that the BBC would continue to do its part to represent the Empire its schedules.[60] His successor, Ian Jacob, oversaw Elizabeth II's Coronation broadcast, "foremost ... a Commonwealth affair,"[61] and during the Suez crisis, when British impotence in the face of American opposition became manifest, the BBC heavily favored the government's pro-intervention position.[62]

In this essay I have attempted to delineate some of the ways in which American economic, political, and cultural power conditioned conceptions of Empire and British national identity. In the case of broadcasting, we can draw several conclusions. First, imperial popular culture was more enduring in Britain than scholars once supposed.[63] With the conclusion of the Second World War, Empire ceased to be a pressing propaganda problem. But the BBC did not radically reduce the representation of Empire in its schedules but instead reiterated its general commitment to doing imperially themed programs. Indeed, imperial culture, at least in broadcasting, enjoyed a revival after the war as the BBC and its listeners rediscovered Empire as a place of opportunity and adventure. Drama Department's serialized plays proved to be quite popular; seven million people tuned in to the first broadcast of *King Solomon's Mines*, while almost nine million listened to the first installment of *The Four Feathers*.[64] Second, anxiety about America and Americanization encouraged some Britons to turn to Empire as a kind of military and political equalizer. Empire, the BBC argued, would enable Britain to remain a great power after the war, a vital, not junior partner to the United States. Finally, imperial culture and the traditional values associated with it – manliness, vigor, courage, and self-sacrifice – were erected as alternatives to the modern consumerist values associated with America. The BBC's ardor for Empire in the face of American political and cultural power reminds us of the importance of the imperial legacy to British national identity, a legacy that continues to affect the British imagination to this day.

Notes

1 Norman Angell, *Postscript*, BBC Written Archives Centre (hereafter BBC WAC), Scripts, Talks, 20 November 1943.
2 R. A. Rendall to George Barnes, 5 May 1942, BBC WAC, R34/350/1.
3 On Empire propaganda to America see Susan Brewer, *To Win the Peace, British Propaganda in the United States During World War II* (Ithaca NY: Cornell University Press, 1997).
4 Recent scholarship suggests a similar relationship in post-war juvenile fiction. See Kathryn Castle, "Imperial Legacies, New Frontiers: Children's Popular Literature and the Demise of Empire," *British Culture and the End of Empire*, Stuart Ward, ed. (Manchester and New York: Manchester University Press, 2001), 146.
5 Programme Policy Meeting, 1 July 1947, Programme Policy Meeting, 29 July 1947, BBC WAC, R34/615/6.
6 Asa Briggs covers America and the influence of American broadcasting intermittently in *The History of Broadcasting in the United Kingdom*, vols. I–IV (Oxford: Oxford University Press, 1995). See also Paddy Scannell and David Cardiff, *A Social History of British Broadcasting* (Oxford: Blackwell, 1991), 292–303. D. L. LeMahieu discusses Americanization and British culture between World Wars I and II in *A Culture for Democracy: Mass Communication and the Cultivated Mind in Britain between the Wars* (Oxford: Oxford University Press, 1988). The most thorough examination of the BBC's response to American broadcasting is Valeria Camporesi, *Mass Culture and the Defense of National Tradition: The BBC and American Broadcasting, 1922 to 1954* (Fucecchio, Italy: European Press Academic Publishers, 2002).
7 Camporesi, *Mass Culture*, 127–9.
8 Ibid., 92–9.
9 Control Board, 3 June 1930, 17 June 1930, BBC WAC, R3/3/6.
10 The quote is from Reith's address during the BBC's first Empire transmission, 19 December 1932. See Gerard Mansell, *Let the Truth Be Told, 50 Years of BBC External Broadcasting* (London: Weidenfeld and Nicolson, 1982), 1–19.

11 Programme Board, 23 June 1938, BBC WAC, R34/600/10.
12 *Listener*, 14 September 1939, 503, 12 October 1939, 702, 2 November 1939, 843.
13 See Thomas Hajkowski, "The BBC, the Empire, and the Second World War, 1939–1945," *Historical Journal of Film, Radio and Television*, 22 (2002), 135–55, Siân Nicholas, "'Brushing Up Your Empire:' Dominion and Colonial Propaganda on the BBC's Home Services, 1939–1945," *Journal of Imperial and Commonwealth History*, 31 (2003), 207–30.
14 Camporesi regards Wellington's meeting as a pivotal moment which "entailed the elimination of the main controls set up before the war to defend British broadcasting from the dangers of Americanization." Camporesi, *Mass Culture*, 139–40. See also Briggs, *The History of Broadcasting in the United Kingdom*, vol. III, *The War of Words*, 368–70.
15 *Radio Times*, 1 May 1942, 3, *Radio Times*, 22 May 1942, 1, *Radio Times*, 12 June 1942, 3, *Radio Times*, 5 June 1942, 3.
16 *Radio Times*, 21 August 1942, 4.
17 "Extract from Programme Policy Meeting," 10 July 1942, BBC WAC, R51/91/1.
18 Barnes to Assistant Controller (Home), 16 July 1942, BBC WAC, R34/350/1. See also Hajkowski, "The BBC, The Empire."
19 Rawdon Smith to Barnes, 30 December 1941, BBC WAC, R51/91/1.
20 "Extract from Programme Policy Meeting," 10 July 1942, BBC WAC, R51/91/1. The BBC also began to track the number of School Broadcasts on America and compare them to the number on Empire. See Assistant Director of School Broadcasting to Barnes, 1 March 1943, BBC WAC, R34/350/1.
21 Barnes to H. R. Pelletier, 2 November 1942, Ibid.
22 Rendall to Barnes, Laurence Gilliam, S. J. de Lotbiniere, and Michael Barkway, 5 May 1942, Ibid. In addition to spearheading the BBC's efforts to promote Empire, Rendall emerged as one of the chief critics of American influence on the BBC. "We must be careful," he cautioned in February 1944, "that we do not become an agent for American cultural propaganda." Similarly, in 1950, Rendall penned a report that concluded, "there can be no doubt that Americanisation has involved a lowering of standards of taste." See Camporesi, *Mass Culture*, 136, 165.
23 For the development of *Red on the Map*, see "Notes of a Meeting Re: Empire Discussions," 1 December 1942, R. A. Rendall to J. B Clark, 28 January 1943, Richard Maconachie to Barnes, 13 February 1943, Barnes to Maconachie, 15 February 1943, Clark to Rendall and Maconachie, 20 February 1943, Ibid.
24 For example, in 1942 the BBC broadcast a series of roundtable discussions on the future of India. See BBC WAC, R51/256/1.
25 Leslie Baily to Basil Nicolls and Kenneth Adam, 16 February 1943, R34/350/1.
26 Notes of a Meeting, 27 September 1948, BBC WAC, R51/93.
27 Baily to Adam, 8 December 1943, BBC WAC, R19/1331/1.
28 Rendall to Robert Foot, 28 February 1944, BBC WAC, R34/350/1.
29 Foot to Rendall, 9 March 1944, BBC WAC, R34/350/1.
30 Briggs, *War of Words*, 652.

31 Haley, Memorandum on Home Programme Policy, n.d. BBC WAC, SC5/32.
32 Haley Diary, 28 August 1949, Churchill Archives Centre, HALY 13/6.
33 Haley Diary, 18 August 1950, Ibid.
34 Camporesi, *Mass Culture*, 167–72.
35 Briggs, *The History of Broadcasting in the United Kingdom*, vol. IV, *Sound and Vision*, 47.
36 Haley to Controllers, 26 January 1945, BBC WAC, R34/420.
37 Ibid.
38 Haley to Lindsay Wellington, 31 December 1945, Ibid.
39 Ibid.
40 Haley to Lord Mountbatten, 15 June 1947, BBC WAC, R34/423.
41 Gilliam, Meeting on India, Notes given by Professor Sir Reginald Coupland, 16 July 1947, Wellington to Haley, 16 October 47, BBC WAC R34/432.
42 On the India Office's objections to Haley's programs for the transfer of power see India Office, L/I/1/965.
43 Acting Controller (Entertainment) to PCD, 30 May 46, BBC WAC, R34/350/1.
44 *Radio Times*, 21 September 1945, 5.
45 Two post series were, *Commonwealth and Empire* and *Enterprise and Achievement*. See BBC WAC, R51/93, *Radio Times*, 24 June 1949, 1.
46 *Radio Times*, 2 April 1948, 5.
47 Robert H. MacDonald, *The Language of Empire: Myths and Metaphors of Popular Imperialism* (Manchester and New York: Manchester University Press, 1994), 81–108.
48 An eight installment adaptation of the *Four Feathers* that had been in preparation for months before the war was broadcast during the autumn of 1939, although there was some concern about the "romantic formula" of the serial. Nevertheless, the BBC's Home Board considered it a success. Home Service Board, 1 December 39, BBC WAC, R3/16/1, Val Gielgud to Peter Creswell, 14 December 1939, BBC WAC, R19/392.
49 According to the *Listener* critic W.E. Williams, "Learie Constantine... did more to shame us out of racial prejudice than anyone else is ever likely to do." *Listener*, 9 September 1943, 304.
50 John M. Mackenzie, "In Touch With the Infinite, The BBC and the Empire, 1923–53" *Imperialism and Popular Culture*, John M. Mackenzie, ed. (Manchester and Dover, NH: Manchester University Press, 1986), 183.
51 *Radio Times*, 20 September 1946, 3.
52 *Radio Times*, 23 January 1948, 7.
53 *Sanders of the River*, BBC WAC, Drama Scripts.
54 *Radio Times*, 20 September 1946, 4.
55 *Radio Times*, 29 August 1947, 5.
56 Wendy Webster, "Domesticating the Frontier: Gender, Empire and Adventure Landscapes in British Cinema, 1945–59," *Gender & History*, 15 (2003), 103.
57 There is a certain irony in the fact that the BBC used, in part, serialized plays to resist the Americanization of its schedules, for the serial play was an American invention, one the BBC refused to utilize until just before the Second World War.

58 Valeria Camporesi, "There are no Kangaroos in Kent: The American 'Model'
    And the Introduction of Commercial Television in Britain, 1940–1954,"
    Hollywood in Europe: Experiences of Cultural Hegemony, David W. Ellwood and
    Rob Kroes, eds. (Amsterdam: VU University Press, 1994), 266–82, Briggs,
    Sound and Vision, 395–6.
59 On the King's tour see Programme Policy Meeting, 18 July 1946, BBC WAC
    R34/615/5, *Radio Times*, 24 January 1947, 3, *Radio Times*, 14 March 1947, 4.
    On "Colonial Month" see *Radio Times*, 17 June 1949, 1, 5, 14.
60 Record of a conversation between Gordon-Walker and Haley, 3 May 1950,
    Public Records Office, DO35/3847.
61 *Radio Times*, 5 May 1953, 5.
62 See Tony Shaw, *Eden, Suez and the Mass Media: Propaganda and Persuasion
    During the Suez Crisis* (London and New York: I. B. Tauris, 1995).
63 For an excellent introduction to this debate see Stuart Ward's introduction
    to *British Culture and the End of Empire*, 1–20.
64 BBC WAC, R9/12/2 and R9/12/3.

Part IV

Americanization and its Discontents

10
Keeping the News British: the BBC, British United Press and Reuters in the 1930s

Siân Nicholas

In May 1931 the news agency British United Press (BUP) offered to supply the British Broadcasting Corporation (BBC) with their overseas news wire services, supplementing the BBC's existing agreement with a consortium of British news agencies led by Reuters. In so doing, it unleashed an eight-year dispute that came to involve the BBC, all the major British news agencies, leading figures in the British press industry, and even the Foreign Office. The BBC's eventual decision during 1936/7 to adopt the BUP news service alongside its established news agency services met with outrage from the other British news agencies, an outrage manifested in a campaign orchestrated by Sir Roderick Jones, chairman and principal shareholder of Reuters, to discredit the BUP in the eyes of the BBC, the government and Parliament. The aspect of the dispute most regularly highlighted was whether a news agency that, despite having "British" in its name, was registered in Canada, and that was widely believed to be a front organization for the United Press of America (UPA), was an appropriate source of news for the British Broadcasting Corporation. Would, in fact, taking the BUP news wires fatally compromise the integrity of British news-broadcasting? This dispute also brought to the surface longstanding rivalries between the British and American international news agencies, and highly vocal concerns about "American" *versus* "British" news values in the 1930s. Thus it encapsulates a range of tensions in Anglo-American media relations in the mid-twentieth century: as a commercial dispute centering on "news" as a commodity; as a cultural dispute about the "national character" of news; and as a wider international dispute about global American media influence in a time of British imperial decline.[1]

The news agencies and the BBC news service

The history of the international news agencies presents a fascinating study in the commodification and globalization of information, refracted through territorial rivalries and competing formulations of national identity.[2] Since the mid-nineteenth century, the three great international news agencies, the British Reuters, the French Havas and the German Wolff, had operated a global cartel (or "news ring") that effectively divided the world's news markets into three spheres of influence: the British Empire, China and Japan (Reuters); Western Europe, French West Africa and South America (Havas); and Central and Eastern Europe and Scandinavia (Wolff). Each agency had exclusive rights *vis-à-vis* the other two agencies to distribute foreign news to all news outlets within these areas, and exclusive rights to gather domestic news from these same outlets for distribution overseas. After the First World War, Havas and Reuters had divided the Wolff overseas markets between them. In the 1920s they welcomed the American news agency Associated Press (a cooperative agency owned by the American press) into the news ring as a junior member, with rights over the USA and related territories. Outside this cartel, a number of smaller-scale private news agencies operated as free agents both domestically and/or internationally. In Britain, for instance, as well as Reuters (formerly a public company, now in private ownership), newspapers subscribed to the Press Association, the domestic news agency representing the British provincial press, to Exchange Telegraph (Extel), a limited general home and overseas news service whose principal attraction was its extensive sports news service run in association with the Press Association, and/or to the small private agency Central News (which specialized in American news). The most successful independent international agency was the United Press of America (UPA), founded by E. W. Scripps in 1907, which operated worldwide in competition with the news ring and which troubled Reuters in particular in the Far Eastern market. In the 1920s a Canadian-registered subsidiary of UPA, British United Press (BUP), began under the management of Herbert Bailey to expand its own international news-gathering operation for the British market. It sold an attractive brand of foreign news that was lighter, more popular in tone and with more human interest than Reuters, and Fleet Street newspapers began increasingly to pick up its news service alongside those of Reuters and the smaller agencies.[3]

The creation of the BBC in 1922 presented an entirely new market for the sale of news. Newspaper interests soon identified the potential competitive threat posed by broadcast news. Throughout the 1920s the combined lobbying powers of the Newspaper Proprietors Association (NPA), representing Fleet Street, and the Newspaper Society (NS), representing the provincial press, ensured that the British Broadcasting Company was prohibited from operating any independent news service of its own, or from broadcasting any news bulletins before the early evening (thus competing with neither the morning nor the evening newspapers). These bulletins were to broadcast only a summary of the news, provided by Reuters from the wires of the four principal British news agencies, Reuters, Extel, Central News and the Press Association, with a copyright acknowledgement to the agencies broadcast at the end. It was only after the granting of the BBC Charter in 1927 that the agencies reluctantly agreed to let the new British Broadcasting Corporation write its own news bulletins, though still only from a digest of material supplied by the agencies, with the broadcast acknowledgment "copyright reserved." Only at the end of 1929 was the BBC's "News Section" permitted to compile bulletins from the agencies' full wire services rather than the pre-selected digest (prompting an expansion of the BBC news staff from two to six).[4] These formal arrangements between the BBC and the British press and the BBC and the news agencies consortium were codified in two agreements, the Agencies Agreement of February 1927 (which specified the terms and conditions of the four agencies' supply of news to the BBC), and the Press Agreement of September 1928 between the BBC, the NPA and Newspaper Society (which detailed the permitted scope and extent of BBC news-gathering and news-broadcasting, including the Agencies Agreement). The Press Agreement was monitored by a Broadcasting Committee consisting of representatives of the BBC, NPA, Newspaper Society and agencies that met irregularly. The close relationship between the various press interests was compounded when in 1930 Sir Roderick Jones negotiated (to considerable personal financial gain) the Press Association's acquisition of Reuters.[5] Thus, when in May 1931 C. F. Crandall, President of the BUP, made his first approaches to be added to the BBC's list of news agencies he was attempting to break into a tight-knit agency consortium that had had a government-sanctioned and press-supported monopoly on supplying news to the BBC since 1922.

Early BUP approaches to the BBC: 1931–34

Crandall's first approach to the BBC, addressed to W. E. Gladstone Murray, the BBC Director of Publicity, was presumably intended as a winning combination of flattery and generosity. It was also careful, at a time when "American"-style news values were widely derided as superficial, sensationalist and far too easily gaining ground in the British popular and pictorial press, to stress the *British* credentials of the agency. Having "watched with admiration the development of your whole broadcasting system – in pleasant and favourable contrast with conditions in Canada and the United States," the BUP (as Crandall emphasized, a "British company incorporated in Canada") wished to offer the BBC a "faster, briefer and better written and more suitable" news service than the current agencies were providing.[6] Several further letters followed, in which Crandall drew attention to successive triumphs of BUP news-gathering in comparison to its rivals. Not having elicited a positive response by these arguments, Crandall then made a direct personal application to BBC Director General Sir John Reith in early 1932 to be given "equal treatment with the other agencies" as a news provider for the BBC.[7] Reith's first response was to refer the application to the NPA and the news agencies, discussing the offer with both Lord Riddell, Chairman of the NPA, and Sir Roderick Jones of Reuters.[8] Meanwhile, the BBC News Section (which had been monitoring the use of BUP material in the British press since Crandall's first approach to them the year before) reported back that BUP's service was in fact not good enough to warrant a change to the status quo. It "tends to sensationalism" (a common signifier for "Americanized," and something that BBC news famously avoided); its much-trumpeted scoops appeared to be, rather, "intelligent anticipations" (something in which BBC news preferred not to deal); and, unlike BUP's Fleet Street clients, the BBC "requires a much higher standard of reliability."[9] No action was therefore taken.

In October 1932 Crandall renewed his request to Reith in more forceful terms, no longer simply asking for equal treatment with the other British agencies, but stressing the BUP's greater impartiality compared to the BBC's current news suppliers (for instance, BUP had no such "entanglements" as Reuters in their relations with Dominion press interests). He again underlined the BUP's British credentials ("entirely British controlled and all its news is either gathered by Britishers direct or passes through the hands of British editors"), and even hinted that the BBC and BUP form some kind of merger.[10] This time, Reith wrote to the BUP specifically declining the offer. One of the reasons for the decision (not passed on to Crandall) was the BUP's "present tie up with the UP of America."[11]

Over the winter of 1932 and spring of 1933 Crandall contacted the BBC daily, forwarding samples of BUP news material that would have been available for the previous day's BBC bulletins had the BBC only been a subscriber, and sending expressions of congratulation whenever BBC news was publicly praised. He itemized particularly newsworthy instances where the BUP wires had scooped the opposition (notably, Adolf Hitler's appointment as Chancellor of Germany in January 1933), and forwarded a letter from Sir Thomas McAra of the NPA confirming that they had "no objection to the British United Press being recognized as a British agency."[12] This bombardment of information seems to have had some effect. In February 1933 the BBC's Director of Talks Charles Siepmann recommended to Reith that the BBC terminate the contracts of Extel and Central (always very much the junior partners in the agency consortium) and bring in BUP instead alongside Reuters and the Press Association.[13] In April 1933 Reith went so far as to refer to the Broadcasting Committee the question of extending the Agencies Agreement to include the BUP. The idea was unanimously rejected, with Sir Roderick Jones apparently threatening to withdraw Reuters and the PA's news service from the BBC altogether – in effect crippling the BBC's entire news-gathering operation – if BUP was included.[14] Crandall, unsurprisingly, protested against the decision. But his appeals to "fair play" and to Reith's better nature ("I resent ... being victimized by competing agencies....") as well as veiled threats (such as the suggestion that the BUP might now become involved in a new English-language news service broadcasting from the BBC's commercial rival Radio Normandie instead) fell on deaf ears.[15] Though Jones's threat was widely considered to be a bluff, Reith was loath to rock the boat for what he still considered to be marginal gains.[16] However, he did make some attempt to assert the BBC's ultimate independence in this matter, pointing out to the Secretary of the Broadcasting Committee (and Reuters' European General Manager) William Murray that "had we been anxious to have the BUP, we should not necessarily have felt that the negative answer given by the other parties would have concluded the matter."[17]

The Ullswater Report and after: 1935–36

Although successive letters from Reith to Crandall in April and July 1934 reiterated that the BBC's attitude to the BUP was unlikely to change in the near future,[18] the BBC's own perception of its news service was undergoing significant change. The extension of its domestic service at both national and regional level, the extension of "eyewitness" reportage to complement agency news, the creation of the

BBC Empire Service in 1932 (for which Reuters, abandoning all pretence of an united agency front, demanded a separate and exclusive financial settlement for providing its news material) and the redesignation of the BBC News Section as a bona fide Department in 1934, all marked a new commitment to the Corporation as a news medium in its own right. Crandall's own renewed approaches saw him offer the BBC's planned new representatives in foreign capitals both facilities and free advice from the BUP's foreign bureaux, criticize the pro-Franco tone of Reuters' despatches from the Spanish Civil War, and point out how many Fleet Street titles now subscribed to BUP alongside the other agencies (i.e. nineteen).[19]

The decision of the 1935 Ullswater Committee on Broadcasting to include as part of its remit the question of the future BBC news service gave the BUP another forum for their application, and the BBC itself new opportunities for rethinking the future development of broadcast news. During its submission to the Committee BUP formally requested that it be considered for supplying news to the BBC on the same terms as "all other British agencies." When the Committee then raised this request in session with the news agencies, Sir Roderick Jones, as their spokesman, was scathing (for reasons which, intriguingly, the shorthand writer in attendance was instructed not to take down).[20] Jones's mysterious evidence clearly did not carry the day. When the Committee reported in February 1936, it unexpectedly appeared to encourage wider BBC news-gathering efforts. Although the Ullswater Report described the current arrangements between the BBC and the agencies as "satisfactory," in a clear reference to the BUP it expressed anxiety that "there should be no bar to variations as future circumstances may require."[21] After its publication Crandall immediately renewed his lobbying efforts, and this time was received more favorably by a BBC clearly emboldened by the Ullswater Report. In particular, John Coatman, the new head of the BBC News Department, recommended that the BBC now adopt the BUP news services, notwithstanding any objections from Reuters. His recommendation was endorsed by the BBC Control Board in March 1936.[22] In a private letter to Jones on 1 April Reith noted that the recommendations from News and Programmes Divisions were so strong that he could no longer put them off.[23] It is clear that the BBC intended to use the agreement with BUP as an opportunity not only to renegotiate the Agencies Agreement with the consortium, but to redraw its entire relationship with the British press.

The BBC's attitude to the quality of BUP news coverage also shifted in BUP's favor during this time. After comparing BUP and Reuters coverage over the summer of 1936, particularly over the Spanish Civil War, Coatman concluded that BUP coverage *did* often appear to be both faster and better than Reuters in its reports, and that it "invariably" gave better "appreciations of the situation." In short, the BUP service was indeed sufficiently valuable to be adopted by the BBC as an additional news source, even in the face of the opposition of the other agencies.[24] At the same time, Sir Stephen Tallents, the BBC's Controller (Public Relations), went so far as informally to solicit opinion from within the Foreign Office as to BUP's reputation. The response was less than flattering to BUP ("the least desirable of all agencies.... a constant source of trouble to the FO on questions of reliability.... always trying to get ahead with the news at the risk of accuracy"[25]), but it significantly stopped short of a recommendation *not* to use. Sir Roderick Jones compounded matters with his own intransigence, first refusing to countenance the bracketing of the name of Reuters with that of BUP in any on-air copyright acknowledgement, then demanding a fantastically high increase in the BBC's annual subscription to Reuters for its home news service (from £6,000 to £18,000 pa). This demand the BBC (already smarting at Reuters' demands for extra fees to provide news from the Berlin Olympics) declined to take seriously.[26] Delays in negotiations were caused by, among other things, the abdication of Edward VIII in December 1936 and Crandall's own absence in Canada in early 1937.[27] Then the BUP service was again formally monitored by the BBC for a month, during which time Reuters again antagonized the BBC, this time with its willfully inadequate supply of news for broadcast from the floods then devastating parts of the USA.[28] However, the decision to adopt the BUP service was reaffirmed by Control Board on 17 April 1937,[29] and by July the BBC and BUP had provisionally agreed to financial terms.[30] In a telling document drawn up in September 1937 detailing the history of the BBC's news agreements, Basil Nicolls, BBC Controller (Administration), went so far as to anticipate the breakdown of all relations with the agencies. He posited a new situation in which the BBC might in the short term rely for news on the BUP, its own contacts, and those "responsible newspapers" (such as *The Times* and *Daily Telegraph*) with which Reith had a cordial personal relationship, before in due course establishing its own news service "on a more or less permanent footing."[31] On 1 November 1937, over lunch at Claridges, Reith informed Jones of the BBC's plans to dissolve the home consortium.[32]

The consortium fights back: 1937–38

While the agencies were not about to let their comfortable domestic monopoly arrangement with the BBC go without a fight, for Reuters in particular the encroachment of BUP represented something far more, a potential body-blow to both its financial security and its international status. The old international news ring had been dissolved when AP withdrew in 1934, leaving in effect a free global market in news. In this new international news market the American agencies had the upper hand, one which AP further exploited by aggressive cost-cutting tactics in markets where it now competed directly against Reuters. Reuters clearly feared ceding ground to a competitor (i.e. BUP) they considered simply a Trojan horse for the continued Americanization of the international news market. Meanwhile, international news was increasingly being seen by governments as a valuable *national* commodity. The leading news agencies in France, Germany and Italy were now in receipt of government subsidies specifically designed to enable them more effectively to spread their respective nations' news across the world, while Reuters itself ("the news agency of the British Empire") had been receiving covert government support since the First World War.

In this new environment Reuters found itself in a particularly invidious position. Its reputation depended on its independence and objectivity. Yet aside from its "concealed" government subsidy – heavily discounted rates to use the British Overseas Wireless Service transmitter at Rugby – it also saw itself as presenting the world "through British eyes."[33] Jones, for one, clearly did not regard this as a contradiction in terms, and indeed saw it as a necessary corrective, for instance, to what he considered the American slant of the American international news agencies. Conversely, its international rivals increasingly targeted Reuters' perceived bias, above all AP, whose Anglophobic general manager, Kent Cooper, considered Reuters to be a tool of British imperial propaganda and an enemy of the kind of free and truthful news he believed had been pioneered by the *American* news agencies.[34] Finally, Reuters' news service itself was failing to meet the needs of its customers. Its typically long despatches were considered inferior to its American rivals' short clear bulletins. Its coverage in the Far East was criticized for its seemingly uncritical pro-Britishness, precipitating, for instance, a long-running dispute with the *Straits Times* of Singapore. Even its coverage of European politics appeared to many to be marred by its partiality: in Germany (where the Foreign Office considered it took far too much on trust from state-subsidized news sources); in Italy (where its chief correspondent on the Abyssinia crisis was the fascist sympathizer J. S. Barnes); and in Spain (where one Reuters correspondent, J. S. Sheepshanks, was posthumously honored by Franco after being killed in the field).[35] Unbeknownst to his fellow Reuters directors, Jones was already actively exploring new ways in which Foreign Office money could be secretly brought in to shore up Reuters' increasingly parlous financial state. Now he mounted a desperate rearguard action to thwart any news agreement between the BBC and BUP.

First, Reuters sought to flex its muscle by again demanding the BBC more than double its current payment for Reuters home news. Then Jones disrupted the BBC/BUP negotiations by passing on detailed allegations of predatory price-fixing by AP and BUP in the South American news market aimed specifically (so Jones claimed) at denying the "British" point of view across an entire continent. This was a highly political development. The BBC was itself in the midst of discussing with the Foreign Office the possible institution of BBC foreign language broadcast service in addition to its (English-language) Empire Service, and, taking no chances, it put negotiations on hold and sent the allegations to Rex Leeper, head of the Foreign Office News Department, for comment.[36] But the formal introduction of the Foreign Office into the equation severely complicated matters – in ways not altogether helpful to Jones. The setting up of a Cabinet Committee on Overseas Broadcasting, headed by Sir Kingsley Wood (Minister of Health and former Postmaster General), from December 1937 to June 1938, initially to address the South America issue, provided a forum in which future government relations with Reuters (in particular financial relations) could be addressed. However, by also including the BBC's potential foreign language services in its remit, it gave the BBC an opportunity to challenge Reuters in turn. While some in the Foreign Office saw a generous settlement on the part of the BBC as a new means of indirectly subsidizing Reuters' foreign news service, for the BBC Nicolls in particular saw this as an opportunity for the BBC to gain financial and possibly even a controlling interest in Reuters.[37] Rather than shoring up Reuters' strength, Foreign Office intervention can therefore be seen as further exposing its weaknesses, as the next few months' negotiations over BUP were conducted under the shadow of the Sir Kingsley Wood Committee.

Over the next few weeks, first informally over a series of luncheons and telephone conversations with representatives of the NPA, Newspaper Society, Press Association and Reuters, then formally on

30 November with a letter of intent to the news agencies in the consortium, the BBC announced their intention to terminate the 1928 Press Agreement and renegotiate the Agencies Agreement to include BUP. It was also made clear that "in the event of a war with the Press" the BBC would go their own way, even to the extent of setting up a news agency of their own. The informal approaches had mixed results. While for instance Esmond Harmsworth and James Henderson apparently promised their support in getting the NPA and Newspaper Society respectively to accept the new arrangement,[38] Jardine Brown came away from a telephone conversation with a representative of the Press Association convinced that "PA are so linked with Reuters that they will do nothing of which Reuters do not approve."[39] The next few weeks saw a succession of increasingly intemperate meetings between agency and BBC representatives at which Jones sought again to mobilize support against the BUP as an unwanted and irresponsible "American" agency.

On 8 December, after a meeting of the Newspaper Society, Arthur Mann, managing editor of the *Yorkshire Post*, leading member of the Newspaper Society, chairman of the Press Association and a director of Reuters, sent a letter to Prime Minister Neville Chamberlain protesting at the BBC/ BUP negotiations (he also sent a copy to Jones, for information).[40] On the 9th the BBC offered Reuters an "all in" annual payment of £17,000 for both home and empire news – only to withdraw it on the same day, after receiving information that the government were themselves about to reconsider the subsidy question.[41] On the 10th there was a fraught and inconclusive meeting of the Broadcasting Committee, at which Tallents and Jardine Brown were taken aback, first to find that the BBC's negotiations with the BUP were leading the agenda, and then, when they were requested to withdraw so that the agencies and press representatives might confer without them. Jones urged the NPA and Newspaper Society to pass a resolution of protest against the BBC-BUP negotiations specifically as being "against the national interest," but rather than go so far, it was agreed instead to arrange a "private personal talk" over luncheon between Colonel Lawson for the Newspaper Society, Sir Esmond Harmsworth for the NPA, Jones, and Reith himself.[42] On the same day, at a separate meeting with William Crozier, editor of the *Manchester Guardian*, and Sir Walter Layton, chairman of the *News Chronicle*, R. S. Lambert, editor of the BBC house journal *The Listener*, was surprised to be warned whether the BBC "at all realize[d] the rod which they were pickling [sic] for themselves if they used the BUP service?"[43] Later that day Reith wrote to Sir Thomas Gardiner (Director-General of the General Post Office) asking if the Sir Kingsley Wood Committee might like to address the issue of the news agencies and the BBC, and in a follow-up letter to Wood himself he went so far as to raise the prospect of a tri-partite arrangement between the government, BBC and Reuters, to circumvent Reuters' current "quite unreasonable" financial demands.[44]

The following week was a busy one for Jones. On 14 December he compiled a confidential *"Addendum"* and list of recent BUP reporting errors for the luncheon, and an *Aide Memoire* ("private and confidential" and "not on any account [to] be quoted, nor must Reuter nor RJ [Jones] be brought into the matter") briefing John Jacob Astor, leading member of the BBC Advisory Committee, against the BUP in preparation for a scheduled meeting on the 17th.[45] On the same day he sent messages to all Reuters representatives in the major European capitals demanding information on the number of full- and part-time BUP correspondents resident there. The information was to be received in London by the following morning, by telephone, and sent immediately to Jones himself, with neither the outward nor inward message to be copied.[46] On the 16th he attended the Harmsworth lunch, to Reith's clear annoyance,[47] though he appears to have largely failed in his main intention. As a result of the lunch, the NPA and Newspaper Society agreed that Reuters and the other agencies should not be party to any new press agreement; negotiations with Reuters were however suspended while the question of subsidy was considered by the government.[48]

In the event, the meeting of 17 December was not held. However, the following couple of weeks saw the pressure turned higher. On 21 December the Reuters Overseas General Manager took the opportunity at the Lobby Correspondents luncheon to "put ... wise" William Ormsby-Gore MP (former Postmaster-General and current Colonial Secretary) about the BBC and BUP, again specifically raising the "national institution" line, and suggesting the Postmaster-General might take an interest in the matter.[49] On 29 December J. C. Moore of BUP "categorically denied" to Jardine Brown that the BUP used its British status as a blind "and ... said that he personally would rather resign than adopt any such attitude." On the 30th, prompted by Reuters, Reith rather weakly suggested the BBC hold another trial in which the BBC paid BUP for their service but did not actually use their material (a suggestion quickly dismissed by Nicolls).[50] On 3 January Nicolls strongly recommended to Reith that the BBC "now regard the issue of the integrity (for want of a better word) of BUP as settled" and award them a ten-year agreement.[51] During a meeting of the Kingsley

Wood Committee on the 4th, it was concluded that BUP was a "well-conducted agency," and that while clearly an offshoot of and dependent on the UP, the Foreign Office was happy to treat it like any other British press agency. A day later the situation was unexpectedly thrown into turmoil once more.[52]

A twist in the tale

On 5 January 1938 Sir Wilfred King of Extel showed Reith a report from Bradstreet's Confidential Agency stating that "the whole of the Montreal stock of BUP is held by the UP Association of New York City with the exception of one share held by Mr Crandall in Montreal." This directly contradicted information received by the BBC from the BUP's Montreal auditor who had certified that Crandall "controls the majority shares of that Company's stock."[53] Although Crandall immediately denied these "slanderous and apparently malicious canards"; and a cable from Deloittes in Montreal appeared to back his story,[54] the BBC then learned that Tom Johnston MP was to raise in parliament the issue of the BBC taking the wire service of the "American-owned" BUP. Questioned by Jardine Brown, King denied that Extel had leaked the information about BUP ownership to the MP, though he acknowledged it "must have come from the same source."[55] On 13 January BUP pre-emptively issued a bulletin to all newspaper editors denying the allegation ("The control of BUP is and always has been entirely in British hands").[56]

The final bombshell was a follow-up cable from Deloittes in London to the BBC. Additional information from Montreal had apparently showed that while Crandall and his Employee Directors did indeed hold a majority shareholding in BUP (51 shares), UPA of New York owned not just the other 49 shares but also "beneficial ownership" of (including potential voting powers over) 21 of the shares registered in Crandall's name. The misleading information given in the previous cable had been given "on instructions of Crandall." Nicolls, previously one of BUP's leading champions within the BBC, found this news "somewhat staggering" and concluded that Crandall had in fact been deceiving them all along as to the BUP's British credentials.[57] The one reassuring fact was that Foreign Office opinion was clear – both Leeper and his superior Sir Robert Vansittart had recommended that the BBC take the service.[58]

On 7 February Johnston asked his question, whether the Postmaster-General was aware that "the British Broadcasting Corporation is or has been in negotiation with the British United Press," that "90 percent of its shares are held by citizens of the United States," and whether he was satisfied that "in the national interest it is desirable that the selection and control of a considerable proportion of the international news supplied to the people of this country should be in the hands of persons who are not British subjects."[59] The Postmaster-General's answer (drafted by the BBC) batted the question away, stressing that the BUP was to be taken on merely as a supplement to other agencies. Meanwhile, in a presumably frosty meeting on the same day between Crandall, Nicolls and Jardine Brown, Crandall ("most anxious ... to remove any doubt from the minds of people in the BBC that there might have been some concealment of essential facts") attempted to argue a distinction between his current *"de facto"* control of BUP as opposed to UP's "potential" control. He announced BUP's intention to form an English company affiliated to the Canadian one to control the BUP service outside Canada – a move designed specifically "to remove beliefs that control of the company is in other than British hands." This, Crandall assured the BBC, had been verbally agreed by all the directors of UPA except E. W. Scripps himself, who was currently "on a yacht." (Unhelpfully, Scripps died suddenly on the yacht later that month, throwing even this move into confusion.) Crandall also conceded that any contract between the BBC and BUP would include a clause by which the BBC would have the right to terminate the contract in the event of BUP's control passing to non-British interests.[60]

Negotiations over the revised Press Agreement went on through February 1938. The final agreement was in many respects still heavily restrictive, for instance still confining the BBC to evening news bulletins only ("save in the case of events of national importance or of exceptional public interest"), but crucially it left out any mention of news agencies – and tellingly, the BBC refused to send a copy of the draft agreement to the agencies even as a courtesy.[61] But again, the new Agreement was put on hold for six months while the government considered what it wanted to do with Reuters. Jones meanwhile maintained his active campaign against the BUP. In May 1938 for instance, he sent Sir Horace Wilson, Chamberlain's confidant and personal advisor on foreign affairs, cuttings demonstrating the dangerous and alarmist nature of BUP journalism, and noting how Reuters had "fortunately" been able to correct the BBC's coverage.[62] The BBC News Department, which resented the implication that they were unable to sift irresponsible from responsible agency material, got its own back during a subsequent visit to Broadcasting House by Sir Horace, by explaining to him the background to Jones's antagonism to BUP, detailing Jones's majority control of Reuters, criticizing his administration ("both personal and dictatorial") and suggesting that any reform of Reuters would probably require his removal.[63] In October Jones met Reith's successor as Director-General, Sir Frederick Ogilvie, "partly a courtesy call, partly for the purpose of opening up consideration of the questions outstanding between Reuters as such, the Agencies as a group, and the BBC." The meeting was not a success, with Ogilvie appearing to have been less than fully cooperative. Strikingly, Jones's new line of attack (arguing that Reuters, as the news agency with the greatest "trustworthiness and responsibility" was entitled both to a considerably higher fee for its service and a greater faith in its reliability than Extel, Central or BUP) put at an end any pretence that Jones was speaking as part of a united British news agency front rather than exclusively in the interests of Reuters.[64] Jones was unaware of a devastating Foreign Office opinion voiced a month earlier that BUP was *not* particularly anti-British, that it was treated by the Foreign Office as any other British news agency, and that Reuters' claims regarding the BUP were ultimately "a fuss over nothing" whipped up by Jones and Sir Wilfred King to scupper the BBC/BUP negotiations.[65]

Munich and after

The Munich crisis was a watershed in British broadcast foreign news coverage. The BBC took the opportunity of the national emergency to institute news bulletins throughout the day, and saw its news audiences increase accordingly. However, the BBC News Department itself felt that the episode had painfully exposed the limitations of the BBC's foreign news coverage both before the crisis itself (in part owing to the BBC's own excessive caution in reporting potentially controversial foreign affairs) and even during it. R. T. Clark, the BBC Home Service News Editor, was highly critical of the coverage of all the news agencies during the crisis, but Reuters most of all. Anticipating the imminent outbreak of war, Reuters had withdrawn most of its correspondents from Germany during the crisis, and found themselves roundly beaten by their rivals (above all the resident US correspondents) in their coverage. Clark therefore recommended adding BUP to the roster of the BBC's agency services at the soonest opportunity.[66]

The dispute was still not entirely played out. The agencies continued to put pressure on Ogilvie, for instance inviting him in February 1939 to an "informal" talk about the BUP with Jones, King, PA Chairman

Samuel Story and Hugh Herbert, General Manager of Central News. Crandall too continued to brief the BBC against Reuters in general and Jones in particular. In December 1938 for instance he informed Jardine Brown that the news agencies consortium had promised BUP an additional payment for its service to them, provided BUP would *not* make it available to the BBC.[67] However, at the end of February Nicolls recommended that the BBC take decisive action at last and sign up BUP without further delay ("This will show Reuters that we mean business. It breaks the Consortium in the sense of breaking the monopoly and it will have a healthy effect all round.") After all, he pointed out, the BBC was the agencies' best customer, but the agencies were artificially united by their hope of getting "an enormous golden egg from the BBC goose." "The moment we sign up BUP and show some independence, I am pretty certain that the junior members of the Consortium will be prepared to break away [from Jones]." Jardine Brown seconded Nicolls's belief, referring to Jones for good measure as a "Fleet Street Hitler."[68] Even so, it was not until 1 September 1939, the day war broke out, that a Special Control Board meeting finally endorsed a five-year contract for the BUP, at a rate of £4,000 pa, with a quality (though not a "nationality") get-out clause. A BUP teleprinter was installed in the BBC News Department a few days later.[69]

Conclusions

On one level this entire episode can be seen as a simple business dispute, an attempt to protect a comfortable monopoly from a destabilizing outside challenge. However, this would be to ignore both the terms in which so much of the discussion was couched (in particular, both the BUP's insistent declarations of its "Britishness" and Jones's equally insistent declarations of its American-ness) and the complex commercial, cultural and political realities underpinning the rhetorical fears evoked by the spectre of "Americanization" in inter-war Britain. For Reuters, at that time under commercial threat globally from both UPA and the Associated Press, and with its worldwide reputation as a British and imperial news agency dwindling, the BUP encroachment on one of its last secure monopolies symbolized something far more than a simple business rivalry. Sir Roderick Jones's decision to invoke political fears of Americanization (to the extent of lobbying government agencies to rule whether American-owned news agencies should be in a position to "influence" the output of a news organization (the BBC) whose reliability was of the utmost political importance) indicates his increasing desperation to protect Reuters' position at all costs against the global spread of American news services. Conversely, the BBC was happy to ignore the issue of Americanization when it suited them. Clearly, they initially felt the BUP were both superfluous to its requirements as a news provider and too "American" (i.e., slick, speedy and speculative) in its news values. These attitudes were to be modified, along with the BBC's own vision of its news service, during the 1930s. But the BBC's "shock" in January 1938 at learning of the BUP's true origins appears somewhat disingenuous, since from as early as 1931 they were clearly aware of ambiguities at the very least in the BUP's status. Significantly, the impact of the revelation that the BUP was indeed, despite its repeated denials, a *de facto* subsidiary of UPA, was far less important for the BBC than the exposing of the inadequacies of both its own and Reuters' news coverage during the Munich crisis. Munich finally convinced the BBC to ignore the consortium and to expand its international news gathering operation, to include – and indeed go beyond – BUP. In 1942 it added AP to its roster of wire services.[70]

The war years would see Jones finally overplay his hand. In early 1941, when his fellow Reuters directors finally learned of the extent of his negotiations with the government, he was forced to resign. The BBC's wartime News Department, on the other hand, would gain in confidence, authority and ruthlessness, as it in its turn deliberately invoked cultural and political fears that American news might set and dominate the wartime news agenda (i.e., to the exclusion of the British war effort) as a means of brokering the expansion of its war reporting operation with the British military.[71] Kent Cooper's history of AP, published in 1941, carried the epigram: "True and Unbiased News – the highest original moral concept ever developed in America and given the world." Ironically, it was in its championing of "true and unbiased news" (arguably by becoming more "American" in its attitude to news) that the BBC would, over the course of the Second World War, establish and cement the uniquely powerful worldwide reputation of "British" broadcast news.

Notes

An earlier draft of this chapter was presented as a paper to the North American Conference of British Studies, Portland, Oregon, October 2003. My thanks to those who commented on the paper then and subsequently.

1 Historians of the BBC and of Reuters have paid little attention to this episode. The relevant volume of Asa Briggs's monumental history of the BBC (*The Golden Age of Wireless*, Oxford: Oxford University Press, 1965)

does not mention it, and Donald Read's history of Reuters gives only a bare outline (see Donald Read, *The Power of News: the History of Reuters 1849–1989* (London: Oxford University Press, 1992), 216, 223–4). However, the BBC's and Reuters' written archives provide a comprehensive picture of events from the two opposing perspectives.

2 See Oliver Boyd-Barrett and Terhi Rantanen, eds., *The Globalization of News* (London: Sage, 1998).

3 See Oliver Boyd-Barrett, *The International News Agencies* (London: Constable, 1980), 120; Read, *Power of News*, 178, 216. For the early history of the United Press Associations see Terhi Rantanen, "Mr Howard Goes to South America: the United Press Associations and Foreign Expansion," Roy W. Howard Monographs in Journalism and Mass Communication Research, No. 2, May 15 1992, Indiana University.

4 For further details, see Siân Nicholas, "All the news that's fit to broadcast: the popular press *versus* the BBC, 1922–45," in Peter Catterall, Colin Seymour-Ure and Adrian Smith, eds., *Northcliffe's Legacy: Aspects of the British Popular Press 1896–1996* (Basingstoke: Macmillan, 2000), 121–48.

5 See Donald Read, "The relationship of Reuters and other agencies with the British press 1858–1984," in Catterall *et al.*, eds, *Northcliffe's Legacy*, 157–8.

6 C. F. Crandall to W. E. Gladstone Murray, BBC Director of Publicity (DP), 20 May 1931; BUP Ltd to BBC, 20 May 1931, BBC Written Archive Centre, Caversham (hereafter BBC WAC) File R28/143/1. In BBC internal correspondence, personnel were sometimes identified by name, sometimes simply by the initials of the post they held. Where possible, I have identified both name and BBC position on first reference in footnotes, and thereafter cited them as they appear on each occasion.

7 Crandall to Sir John Reith, BBC Director-General (DG), 18 January 1932, BBC WAC R28/143/1.

8 See Reith to Charles Siepmann, BBC Director of Talks (DT) 21/1/32, BBC WAC R28/143/1.

9 Memorandum, "The BUP News Service," ns nd (probably J. M. Rose-Troup, BBC Assistant Director of Talks (ADT), February 1932), BBC WAC R28/143/1.

10 Crandall to Reith 20 October 1932, BBC WAC R28/143/1.

11 See ADT to DG 18 November 1932, BBC WAC R28/143/1.

12 See for instance, Crandall to Siepmann, 16 December 1932; Crandall to Reith, 18 March 1933; McAra to Crandall, 15 December 1932, BBC WAC R28/143/1.

13 DT to DG 1 February 1933, BBC WAC R28/143/1.

14 Reith to Crandall, 21 April 1933, BBC WAC R28/143/1.

15 Crandall to Reith, 4 May 1933, BBC WAC R28/143/1. See also Crandall to Reith 24 April 1933 and correspondence through July–August 1933.

16 Reith to Crandall, 21 April 1933, BBC WAC R28/143/1.

17 Reith to William Murray (Reuters) 28 April 1933; and related correspondence, BBC WAC.

18 Reith to Crandall, 13 April 1934, BBC WAC R28/143/2. See also list dated 25 March 1936, R28/143/3.

19 See note in file, BBC WAC R28/143/2.

20 Ullswater Committee: Verbal evidence: minutes, Folio H Ninth meeting 30 May 1935, BBC WAC R4/7/18/5.

21 Ullswater Report, 133.5

22 John Coatman, BBC Chief News Editor (CNE) memorandum, 27 March 1936; BBC Control Board minutes No. 200, 31 March 1936; BBC WAC R28/143/3.

23 Reith to Jones, 1 April 1936, BBC WAC R28/164/1. He offered an olive branch: "It will be a great regret to us if the inclusion of the BUP should be distasteful to you, and because of our past relations I wanted to tell you at once and informally of what we have in mind."

24 CNE to Cecil Graves, BBC Controller, Programmes (CP), 23 July 1936, and 22 September 1936, BBC WAC R28/143/3.

25 Tallents to CP, 3 June 1936 and 15 June 1936, BBC WAC R28/143/3.

26 See Tallents to DG, 5 May 1936; Reith record of meeting with Jones 16 November 1936, BBC WAC R28/164/1; correspondence between Jardine Brown (BBC Business Manager) and Murray (Reuters), July 1936, R28/152/2.

27 See BBC Control Board minutes, No. 276, 13 April 1937.

28 The BBC News Department was particularly shocked by Murray's response to its complaints: "But what would the newspapers say if we let you have a special service?." GNE to Basil Nicolls, BBC Controller, Administration (CA), 29 January 1937, BBC WAC R28/152/2.

29 BBC Control Board minutes, No. 276, 13 April 1937.

30 Under the agreement the BBC would pay BUP £3,000 for the first five years, and £4,000 for the next five, for its full wire service. Moore to Jardine Brown, 7 July 1937, BBC WAC R28/143/3.

31 Nicolls, "The News Agreements," 7 September 1937, BBC WAC R28/79.

32 Reith diary, 1 November 1937, BBC WAC.

33 Read, *Power of News*, 133.

34 See Kent Cooper, *Barriers Down: the Story of the News Agency Epoch* (Port Washington NY: Kennikat Press, 1969 [1942]), passim.

35 Read, *Power of News*, 227. See also Reith diary, 1 Nov 1937: "The FO had said they were sick w Reuters who seemed so much in the hands of foreigners."

36 Control Board minutes, 5 October 1937, BBC WAC. Leeper had a particular interest in the issues raised by BUP's "encroachment," having been the driving force behind the establishment of the British Council in 1934 – as indeed for the BBC did Tallents, former Secretary of the Empire Marketing Board, author of *The Projection of Britain* (1932), and at the time of this dispute Director-General designate of the shadow Ministry of Information.

37 DG to CA 8 December 1937, CA to DG 9 December 1937, R28/164/1. See also memorandum, 28 October 1938.

38 See DG to CA, 19 November 1937, BBC WAC R28/161/1.

39 Jardine Brown record of telephone conversation with Robbins, 12 November 1937; Jardine Brown report of meeting with Robbins, 16 November 1937, BBC WAC R28/164/1.

40 Arthur Mann to Neville Chamberlain, 8 December 1937, Reuters Archive, London (hereafter, Reuters) File R 2 iv a 8.

41 Nicolls to Murray, 9 December 1937, CA to DG 9 December 1937, Reuters R28/164/1.

42 For different accounts of this meeting, see The News Arrangement, BBC WAC R28/161/1, and cf. Report of meeting of Joint Broadcasting

Committee, 10 December 1937, Reuters R 2 iv a 8. Tallents was clearly still bridling about this treatment some months later. See too Reith diary 10 December 1937.

43 See J. R. Scott (chairman of *Manchester Guardian* board, also director of Reuters) to Sir Roderick Jones, 11 December 1937, Reuters R 2 iv b 9.

44 Reith to Gardiner, 10 December 1937; Reith to Sir Kingsley Wood, 13 December 1937, The National Archives, Kew (hereafter, TNA): FO 395/552.

45 Addendum, List of BUP Errors, Aide Memoire, all dated 14 December 1937; Jones to Captain R. J. H. Shaw (*The Times*), 15 December 1937, Reuters R 2 iv a 8. See too Jones to Mann (*Yorkshire Post*), 18 December 1937, I and ii: Reuters R 2 iv b 9.

46 Note for Editor in Chief, initialled HBC, 14 Dec 1937, Reuters R 2 iv a 8.

47 Jones's detailed account of the luncheon (which he circulated to his fellow directors of Reuters) is more emollient than Reith's own long report back to Tallents. See Jones to [various], 16 and 17 December 1937, Reuters R 1 iv b 9, and Jones to Ewing (*Glasgow Herald*), 16 December 1937, Reuters R 2 iv b 9; Reith to C(PR), 16 December 1937, BBC WAC R28/161/1.

48 Control Board minutes, No. 748 and re 739, 21 December 1937.

49 OGM (Reuters) to Jones, 21 December 1937, Reuters R 2 iv a 8. Unfortunately, the Postmaster-General, Ormsby-Gore noted, was "up to the eyes in PO reorganization work" ("chiefly the result of the growing popularity of the telephone") and the government was reluctant to interfere with the BBC and had to be "careful" with Reith.

50 Reith to CA 30 December 1937 BBC WAC R28/164/1, and Nicolls to Reith (?) 31 Dec 1937.

51 Nicolls to Reith, 3 January 1938, R28/156/1.

52 Proceedings of Fourth Meeting of Cabinet Committee on Overseas Broadcasting, 4 January 1938, TNA: CAB27/641.

53 Alex Murray, Accountant Auditor-Trustee (Montreal), To Whom It May Concern, 4 January 1938, BBC WAC R28/156/1; 5 Jan 1938: Sir Wilfred King "in a second SOS visit" to Reith "with more lurid revelations about the BUP." (Reith diary). And see King to Jones, 6 Jan: King had taken copy of BUP accounts to end of 1936 to show Reith ("I think he was a bit surprised!") (Reuters R 2 iv a 8).

54 Crandall telegram to Moore, 10 January 1938; cable from Deloittes (Montreal) to Jardine Brown, 12 January 1938, BBC WAC R28/156/1.

55 Jardine Brown record of telephone conversation with Sir Wilfred King, 13 January 1938, and of telephone conversation with Mr Wills (Manager, Extel), 13 January 1938 (five minutes later), BBC WAC R28/156/1.

56 BUP bulletin to all newspaper editors, 13 January 1938, BBC WAC R28/156/1.

57 Deloittes letter, and Nicolls addendum, BBC WAC R28/156/1.

58 DG to CPR 14 January 1938, BBC WAC R28/156/1.

59 *Hansard*, 7 February 1938, c. 674.

60 Record of meeting between Crandall, Nicolls, Jardine Brown, 7 February 1938, R28/156/1. In fact, Crandall's contrition was short-lived. Just a few days later he was writing to Jardine Brown complaining that a BBC news bulletin reference to "material supplied by the four news agencies" ought to have read "to the four agencies to which the BBC at present subscribes."

A week later he was vigorously criticizing Reuters's European coverage to Major Astor ("nationalistic and frankly tendentious, while the UP, whatever its weaknesses had no political colouring and was as frankly commercial as a grocery business"); and offering to set up more full time BUP men in more European capitals should they make a news contract with the BBC; the BBC also received a report from the *Straits Times* criticizing the "extravagant tribute" paid to Reuters by one MP in the debate on the supply of British news abroad and Reuters itself for monopolizing British news and for refusing to permit a "second British news service … thoroughly reliable, absolutely independent and of worldwide repute" to operate. See Crandall to Jardine Brown, 11 February, 17 February 1938, Moore to Jardine Brown, 18 February 1938, all R28/156/1.

61 See correspondence through February 1938, and Draft Agreement, February 1938; also Tallents to Jardine Brown, 13 April 1938, BBC WAC R28/161/1.
62 Jones to Sir Horace Wilson, 24 May 1938, BBC WAC R28/218.
63 HSNE to CP, 31 May 1938, BBC WAC R28/218; see also BBC memorandum, 28 October 1938.
64 Two notes (marked "Private" and "strictly Confidential" respectively) by Jones of interview with Mr F. W. Ogilvie, 18 October 1938, Reuters R 2 iv a 8.
65 Nash (Foreign Office) to Bowyer (Colonial Office), 20 September 1938, TNA: FO395/577.
66 R. T. Clark, Home Service News Editor (HSNE) to CP, 4 November 1938, BBC WAC R28/218. For further details of Reuters' coverage of the Munich Crisis, see Read, *Power of News*, 227; for more on the BBC's coverage, see Briggs, *Golden Age*, 645–57; Paddy Scannell and David Cardiff, *A Social History of British Broadcasting, Vol I: 1922–39, Serving the Nation* (Oxford: Basil Blackwell, 1991), 125–7, 130–2.
67 BBC WAC R28/156/1. Jardine Brown noted how the BUP and Reuters stories rarely coincided though Crandall was generally "much more circumstantial and explicit."
68 BBC WAC R28/156/1.
69 Special Control Board 1 Sept 1939 No. 560. Fisher (BUP) to Jardine Brown, 5 September 1939.
70 BM to DAB, 16 April 1942, BBC WAC R28/164/2.
71 For more detailed discussion of BBC news during the Second World War, see Siân Nicholas, *The Echo of War: Home Front Propaganda and the Wartime BBC* (Manchester: Manchester University Press, 1996), ch.6, and Nicholas, "War report," in Mark Connelly and David Welch, eds, *War and the Media* (London: I. B. Tauris, 2005).

11
Americanization and its Limits: United Artists in the British Market in the 1930s and 1940s

Peter Miskell

> Motion pictures are silent propaganda, even though not made with that thought in mind at all ... Imagine the effect on people ... who constantly see flashed on the screen American modes of living, American modes of dressing, and American modes of travel ... American automobiles are making terrific inroads on foreign makes of cars [because] the greatest agency for selling American automobiles abroad is the motion picture.[1]

These words were written in 1927 by the general manager of the Paramount Famous-Lasky Corporation. This US film executive no doubt overstated the role of motion pictures in creating export markets for American manufacturers, yet he was by no means alone in holding such a view. In one of the first serious academic studies of the film industry, published in 1933, Howard T. Lewis argued that:

> The American-made picture introduces American ideals, American customs, American habits of thought; it displays American articles of commerce; and it interprets American points of view. To subject millions of people in Germany, France or Italy time after time to this subtle influence could not but have its effect, not only in developing a favourable response to American attitudes of mind, but also in tending to stimulate the desire for American products.[2]

It was not only US film executives or Harvard-based academics who considered the influence of American films to be so important. National governments in both Europe and the United States seemed in

215

little doubt that the international popularity of American films had important political and commercial spin-offs. Between 1925 and 1928 a series of European governments, particularly in those countries whose film industries had collapsed during the First World War,[3] introduced legislation to protect and promote their national film industries and to limit the influence of American pictures.[4] The US government, for its part, used what influence it had with foreign governments in the 1930s and 1940s to keep such protective measures to a minimum.[5] In Britain protective legislation was first introduced in 1927 to ensure that a quarter of all screen time in British cinemas would be filled by British made films.

The effect of the 1927 Films Act on the British film industry has been much discussed by film historians. The legislation certainly stimulated film production in Britain (some of it by American owned firms), but these "British" films were seldom able to compete with American pictures in international markets. Some historians have argued that British film-making in the 1930s was driven by the need to produce a set number of films to meet quota requirements, and that the resulting "quota quickies" were of such low quality that they damaged the reputation of British pictures for years to come.[6] More recently, a number of historians have argued that British films of this period were actually much more popular than had been previously imagined, and that the 1927 legislation had enabled the British film industry to fight back with some success against Hollywood dominance.[7] Recent scholarship, then, has cast the British film industry of the 1930s in a new light, and has reinterpreted the effect of the 1927 legislation. The literature on the film industry, however, continues to be written from a distinctly *national* perspective. This chapter examines the film industry less in terms of competing national industries, but more from the perspective of competing individual firms.

Films were regarded as "agents of Americanization," because they were cultural as well as economic products. The cultural value of films meant that the strength of national film industries was closely bound up with issues of national identity and national expression. Much of the literature on the film industry in Britain has been concerned with the degree to which British policy was successful in reducing the cultural dominance of American films. American interests, as such, have been grouped together under the heading "Hollywood."

Taken together, American films undoubtedly did exert an important social and cultural influence in Britain in the 1930s and 1940s. Yet these films were not created or distributed by national institutions but by individual firms. When we analyze the operations of individual US film *companies* in Britain, rather than treating Hollywood as a homogenous entity, the relative power of American interests can be seen in a different light. By focusing on the activities of United Artists in Britain, this chapter argues that the extent to which one of Hollywood's major companies (albeit one of the smaller majors)[8] was able to act as an "agent of Americanization" in Britain was actually severely constrained. United Artists was at its most successful in Britain in the 1930s when it had a regular supply of British made films to distribute, and access to British cinema screens. To maintain such a position in the 1940s the firm needed to secure a deal with J. Arthur Rank, the dominant figure in the British film industry at that time. Unable to offer Rank as attractive a deal as its larger American competitors, United Artists was effectively left out in the cold, and saw its business decline quite dramatically in the British market.

United Artists (UA hereafter) was not a typical firm. The value of this case study is not that it tells a story that is somehow representative of all US film companies, but that it illustrates just how distinctive individual firms within this industry could be. UA was established in 1919 by a group of four leading film actors / producers as a distribution outlet for their pictures. The company's original objective was not simply to maximize profits, but to provide an alternative means of distribution for film-makers who wished to remain independent of the major film companies. Its aim was to preserve artistic independence in the film industry, and to serve the (financial) interests of independent producers, rather than to function as a purely commercial enterprise. In addition to the films of the four founding members (Mary Pickford, Charlie Chaplin, Douglas Fairbanks and D. W. Griffith), in the mid-1920s UA began distributing the pictures of Sam Goldwyn, Joseph Schenck and Howard Hughes. During the 1930s, as the output of the four founders began to tail off, product was also provided by the likes of David O. Selznick, Edward Small, Walter Wanger and Walt Disney. By this time UA were one of the leading international distributors of motion pictures and a profitable commercial enterprise. Unlike the largest US film companies, UA did not produce its own films, nor did it own or control any chains of cinemas. It was the smallest of the so-called "Big Eight" film companies, but while it did not distribute as many films as its larger competitors, its pictures were mostly high quality productions by some of the most famous names in the industry. In the 1930s UA could best be described as a specialist distributor of prestige pictures, rather than an integrated combine pursuing a strategy of mass production and exhibition.

UA was not the most commercially powerful of US film companies, but it distributed films on behalf of some of the leading producers in the industry. Its pictures were certainly popular with British audiences and, as we shall see, a substantial portion of the company's revenues came from this market. How, then, did the distributor of films such as *A Star is Born, Dead End, Stagecoach* and *Spellbound* actually operate its business in Britain, and to what extent could it be described as an agent of Americanization?

American films and the British Market: a mutual reliance

In the mid-1920s 95 percent of films shown in Britain were of American origin. By any standards it was clear that American pictures dominated the British market. Yet while Britain was one of many countries in which American films were dominant, the British market was actually far more important to US film companies than any other. As Table 11.1 (below) illustrates, Britain accounted for more than a third of foreign revenues generated by American films. This was particularly important because US companies relied heavily on foreign markets for profits. While Hollywood studios were just about able to cover their costs in the domestic market, profits were made with foreign sales. As a source of profit, the British market was more important than any other by the mid-1920s.

Despite the legislation introduced by the British Government in 1927 (and updated in 1938 and 1948), American films continued to fill

Table 11.1   Selected Markets for American Films, 1925

	Percentage of America's Foreign Revenue	Percentage of American Films in Total Films
United Kingdom	35	95
Germany	10	16
Australia and New Zealand	8	95
Scandinavia	6	85
Argentina	5	90
Canada	5	95
France	3	70
Japan	3	30
Brazil	3	75

Source: Lewis, *The Motion Picture Industry*, p. 397.

between 70–75 percent of screen time in British cinemas throughout most of the 1930s and 1940s. British exhibitors continued to rely on American companies to supply the majority of their product, but the extent of American dominance had been somewhat reduced. Over the same period, however, the relative importance of the British market to US companies increased significantly. There were four main reasons for this.

First, the introduction of talking pictures in the late 1920s meant that the demand for American films began to fall away in non-English speaking countries. American firms did subtitle or dub (or occasionally entirely remake) pictures for foreign markets, but subtitled or dubbed films were usually less popular with audiences than those made in their own language. Second, at about the same time as sound films were becoming widespread, legislation designed to protect national film industries was beginning to take effect. In large European markets such as Germany and France, imports of American films were restricted and domestically produced films took up an increased market share. Third, as the 1930s progressed, a number of European markets were effectively closed off to American firms as nationalist governments assumed power. By 1940, with most of Europe under either fascist or communist control, there were few outlets for US films in large industrialized economies. Finally, at the same time as other foreign markets were being lost, the size of the British market was rapidly expanding. Film audiences grew steadily in Britain during the 1930s, but they increased dramatically in the 1940s. (See Figure 11.1 below).[9]

Figure 11.1 Cinema Attendance in Great Britain, 1934–1951

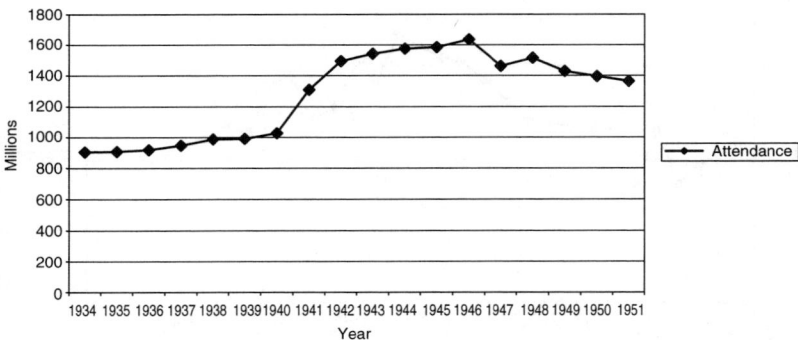

Source: Browning and Sorrell, "Cinemas and Cinema-Going in Britain," *Journal of the Royal Statistical Society* (1954)

The increasing importance of the British market in the 1930s and 1940s meant that American film companies came to rely on Britain as much as British cinema exhibitors relied on American films. The relationship was less one of American dominance, than of mutual dependence. For an illustration of the relative importance of the British market for American companies one need look no further than the output of Hollywood studios. As Mark Glancy has shown, the period from the mid-1930s to the mid-1940s was one "when Hollywood loved Britain." Far from imposing their products indiscriminately on the British market, US film studios made a series of films in this period that portrayed Britain and the British in an extremely positive light. American film-makers in this period were as sensitive to the views of British film censors as they were of the Hays Office.[10]

Evidence from the United Artists archive demonstrates just how reliant on the British market an American firm could be. Figure 11.2 shows the proportion of UA's total revenues coming from foreign markets. As we can see, from the early 1930s to the mid-1940s between 40–60 percent of the firm's income came from outside the US and Canada.[11]

Figure 11.3 shows the particular importance of the British market to UA in the 1930s and 1940s. Until the end of the Second World War, Britain usually accounted for between 60–70 percent of foreign earnings, and for most of the 1930s and early 1940s the British market made up around one third of UA's total revenues.

Figure 11.2 % of United Artists's Total Gross coming from foreign markets, 1919–1950

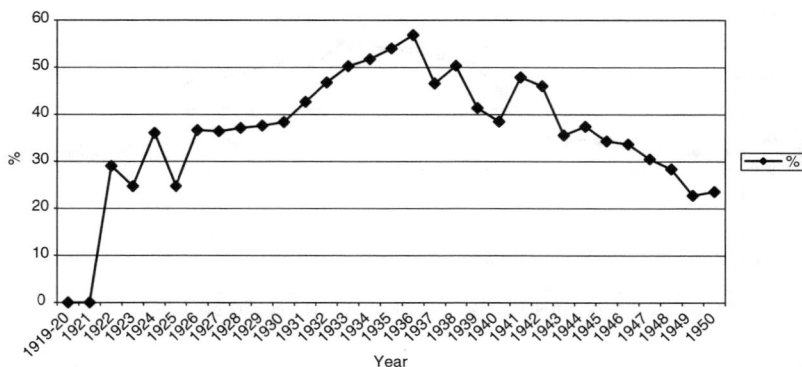

Source: United Artists Balance Sheets

Figure 11.3 Proportion of United Artist's Gross Box Office Revenues coming from Britain, 1931–1950

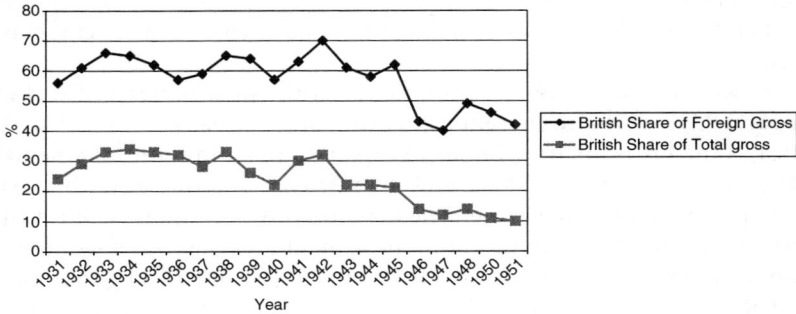

Source: United Artists Balance Sheets

UA's dependence on Britain becomes even more apparent, however, when we look at profits. For most of the period from the 1920s to the 1950s UA failed to cover its costs in the US market alone. It relied on earnings from its foreign markets to bring its figures into the black, and much the most important of these foreign markets was Britain. Figure 11.4, which contrasts UA's total profit with the profit earned in the UK, illustrates just how dependent on the British market this company was. Without Britain, the firm would no doubt have struggled to survive throughout the period.

British film exhibitors were clearly dependent on American films, but with around 30 percent of screen time taken up by British pictures,

Figure 11.4 Profits of United Artists, 1921–1950

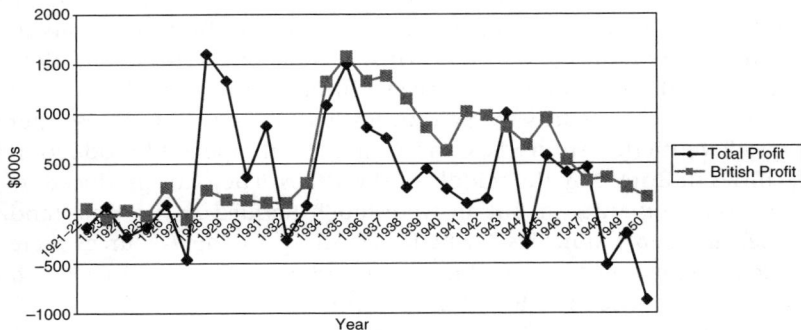

Source: United Artists Balance Sheets and Cabled Foreign Reports

they did not necessarily depend heavily on product from *every* US film company. For UA, however, access to British cinema screens was absolutely crucial if they were to remain in profit. This company depended on the British market rather more than British cinemas relied on it.

As well as illustrating the importance of the British market for UA, figures 11.1–11.4 also present something of a puzzle. Why was it that just as the British market began to expand rapidly in terms of cinema attendance, the performance of UA in Britain in terms of both sales and profits went into decline? The deteriorating performance of UA in Britain during the 1940s was not typical of all US firms, but if we are to understand why the company performed as it did throughout the 1930s and 1940s the limits of Americanization soon become apparent.

Doing business in Britain in the 1930s

The introduction of quota legislation by the British Government in 1927 did not cut off the British market, but it served to increase the level of competition between US firms for access to British screens. As exhibitors were obliged to fill a quarter of screen time with British films, the market share available to US films was significantly reduced between the mid-1920s and the mid-1930s. In addition to the exhibition quota, there was also a distributors' quota which by the mid-1930s meant that 25 percent of all films offered to the market by film distributors needed to be British. Because most US film companies had their own distribution subsidiaries in Britain, this meant that US firms themselves needed to offer British pictures for distribution.

There were essentially four strategies that US companies adopted to deal with the changing environment in Britain in the 1930s. First, a number of US film companies began to produce their own films in Britain. These films counted as "British" under the terms of the 1927 Act provided the filming took place within the British Empire and the majority of labor costs were paid to British subjects. M-G-M, Warner Bros., Twentieth Century Fox and Columbia all operated production facilities in Britain by the middle of the 1930s. The films produced by these US companies in Britain were much derided at the time (and since) as "quota quickies," which according to some sources were screened reluctantly by exhibitors, and often in the mornings when only cleaners were to be found in the auditoria.[12]

A second strategy employed by American companies was to reach an agreement with a British film producer to take over the distribution of their films. As United Artists was a film distribution company, not a producer, this was the course of action it took. UA distributed a small number of Herbert Wilcox films in the early 1930s, before striking a much more important deal with Alexander Korda in 1933. Paramount and RKO also sought distribution deals with British producers in the 1930s. Wilcox and Korda, as two of the most prominent film producers in Britain at this time, found that their talents were much in demand by US companies.

A third strategy used by US firms was to invest in the exhibition sector of the British film industry. By acquiring a stake in the leading British cinema chains, American companies hoped to be able to wield enough influence to gain preferential treatment for their pictures in the British market. By the mid-1930s three major circuits had emerged in Britain: Gaumont-British, Associated British Cinemas (ABC hereafter) and Odeon. Fox bought what it (mistakenly) believed to be a controlling interest in Gaumont-British in the early 1930s – an investment which provided the British circuit with enough capital to install sound equipment.[13] Warner Bros. invested in the ABC circuit, and for much of the 1930s and 1940s the non-British content offered by ABC cinemas was provided almost exclusively by either Warner or M-G-M. In 1935, UA acquired a stake in the Odeon chain, owned at that time by Oscar Deutsch. UA had hoped that its part ownership of Odeon (approximately 25 percent holding) would give it some influence over the circuit booking policy. As we shall see, this did not turn out to be the case.

The final strategy adopted by US companies was to build, acquire or lease a showcase cinema in London's west end. Such cinemas gave US firms control over the way their main feature films were initially released and marketed in Britain. These cinemas at least guaranteed that a company's most important pictures would receive a British premiere, and that they would also attract publicity, press comment and reviews. By generating public interest in their films in this way, US firms were then in a stronger position to rent their pictures to the main circuits. United Artists took out a lease on London's Pavilion Theatre for this purpose in 1934.

The first two of these strategies simply enabled US firms to continue operating in the UK – they were designed to fulfill legal obligations. The third and fourth strategies were intended to increase the bargaining power of US firms with British exhibitors, or to gain direct influence over the decisions made by the largest British circuits. As far as United Artists was concerned attempts to buy influence with British cinema chains met with little success. Their minority holding in the

Odeon chain gave UA little or no influence over booking policy. UA's pursuit of the second of the strategies outlined above, however, did prove to be extremely successful in the 1930s.

In 1933 United Artists signed a contract with Alexander Korda's production company, London Films, to produce two films. The first of the pictures Korda made for UA was *The Private Life of Henry VIII*. This proved to be an unusually popular attraction, and was the first British film to achieve a notable box-office success in the US market in the inter-war period.[14] Korda immediately became a highly sought-after producer, and UA's chairman, Joseph Schenck, quickly signed him up to a 16 picture deal on improved terms. A clear illustration of the importance UA attached to Korda was that as well as a long term contract, he was also offered part ownership of the company "practically [as] a goodwill gift." In September 1935 he became a 25 percent shareholder in United Artists Corporation, without actually investing any of his own money in the first instance.[15]

By securing the services of Korda UA did much more than fulfill their quota requirements in Britain, they placed themselves in a very strong bargaining position with British exhibitors. With around a quarter of all screen time needing to be filled by British films, the leading circuits needed to ensure that they were able to book the highest quality British pictures. As the distributor of Korda's films UA were looked on favorably by British exhibitors, who were reluctant to rely on "quickies" to meet their quota requirements. Korda's pictures, such as *Catherine the Great*, *The Scarlet Pimpernel*, *Sanders of the River* and *The Ghost Goes West*, were lavishly produced epics, with production budgets closer to those of the leading Hollywood releases than the typical British film.[16] Typically based on British characters, and set in Britain (or its Empire), these films were among the most popular of the 1930s with British audiences.[17] Though Korda conceived of them as international pictures, they actually proved far more popular with British audiences than those in the rest of the world.[18] With some of the most sought-after British films on their books (as well as American pictures produced by the likes of Selznick, Zanuck, Goldwyn and Wanger), UA had little trouble getting their product released in Britain. Indeed, by 1940 UA's British manager was explaining to the New York office how he intended to drive a much harder bargain with British exhibitors with regard to the advertising of films:

As far as the supplying free of charge posters, stills, etc., to independents is concerned, this practice I put a stop to in no uncertain fashion already four or five years ago. I am now going to do likewise with the circuits and will let you know how I progress in the matter.[19]

UA's deal with Korda in the 1930s seems to have been a key factor behind their success, in the British market at least, at this time.[20] The arrangement meant not only that UA distributed Korda's films in Britain; however, they were also released in the US. Figure 11.5, below, shows the number of British films released by United Artists in the United States between 1920 and 1950.

This chart illustrates two points. First, it shows that by the 1930s (in contrast to the 1920s) British films were beginning to find their way onto American cinema screens. That an American company should feel obliged to distribute British pictures in its home market suggests that US interests may not have been quite as dominant as is sometimes assumed. Second, the chart seems to follow much the same pattern as UA's profit figures for the period. Profits were at their peak in the 1930s (when UA were distributing Korda's pictures) and fell away in the 1940s (as they had fewer British films on their books). UA's access to British product was not the only factor determining success or failure, but given the importance of the British market for the company's profits, it is something which is worth exploring. The following sections will examine UA's operations in Britain in the 1940s in more detail.

Figure 11.5   No. of British Films Distributed by United Artists in the US Market, 1919–1950

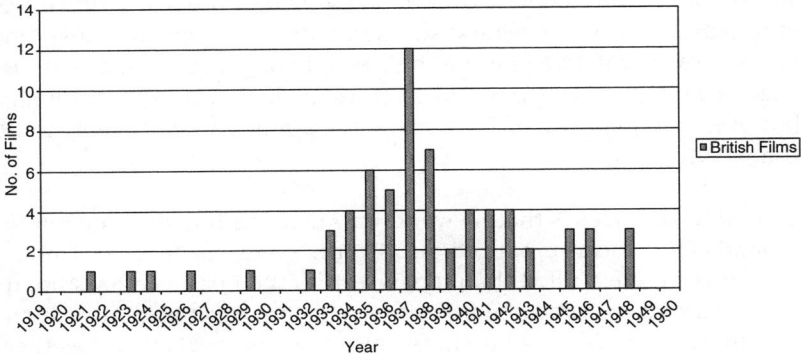

Source: Balio, *United Artists*, appendix 1

War, Rank and concentration in the British film industry

In some ways the war should really have made things easier for American film companies operating in the UK. As the British economy geared itself up for wartime production, a number of film studios were requisitioned and the number of films produced in Britain fell sharply. With fewer British films available, quota regulations were relaxed. Furthermore, increasing cinema attendances meant that the size of the market was expanding rapidly. US companies, then, found themselves operating in a quickly growing market, facing less competition from domestic competitors, and also facing fewer restrictions in the form of government legislation. Yet, for UA, this was a period of declining sales and profits. What went wrong?

One problem was Alexander Korda's exit from the company, after a protracted wrangle, in 1944. Korda had made his last film for UA by 1942, but it took another two years before the company eventually managed to repurchase his 25 percent stockholding.[21] The loss of Korda did not make a significant difference to United Artists box-office revenues in the US, but without a regular supply of British pictures, UA would find things much more difficult in the British market. The situation might have been resolved favorably had Korda's stock been sold to J. Arthur Rank. Rank, as we shall see, was by the early 1940s the key figure in the British film industry. By bringing him into the company, UA would almost certainly have removed any potential problems in terms of supplies of British films or access to British screens. Rank, for his part, was anxious to secure worldwide distribution for his films and saw UA as an appropriate outlet for doing so. In order to achieve this he expressed an interest in purchasing up to 50 percent of UA stock and becoming president of the company. Rank's proposal, which he outlined as part of a general discussion with UA's general manger in Britain, was a tentative one, and he was only prepared to enter serious negotiations if other stockholders consented. Had it gone through, however, the plan would have made UA a much more "Anglicized" company:

> Rank's basic idea is that he wants an American British company to market American produced and British produced films and he is very keen that United should have this as their basic policy stop. If this cannot be agreed he prefers to start new organization with an American producer who shares his views of marketing together American and British films.[22]

The proposal was rejected on the grounds that at least two of the existing stockholders (Pickford and Selznick) were opposed to having Rank as a partner. On hearing that he would not be welcomed in by the other stockholders Rank swiftly dropped his interest in UA and moved instead to build up his own Anglo-American distribution company: Eagle-Lion.[23]

UA was already facing serious difficulties at the time this was taking place. By 1943 the supply of films from its most important producers had dried up. Unable to secure a steady flow of product from the likes of Sam Goldwyn, Walter Wanger, Edward Small and Walt Disney, UA management had been forced to purchase a batch of mostly "B" pictures from Paramount just to get through the 1943–44 season. It did not help that David O. Selznick, who had joined UA as a partner in October 1941, was still yet to deliver a picture, and that Chaplin was threatening to sue him for breach of contract. In the process Chaplin and Mary Pickford also fell out.[24]

Amid the boardroom chaos it was hardly surprising that the approach from Rank did not meet with unanimous approval. Alienating Rank, however, was the last thing UA could afford to do. The loss of Korda, and the failure to replace him with Rank, left UA in a particularly vulnerable position in its most important foreign market. This vulnerability was much increased by the increasing concentration of the film industry in Britain. This process had been ongoing since the late 1920s when the Gaumont-British and Associated British Cinemas film combines were established. These two companies were vertically integrated concerns that controlled the production, distribution and exhibition of films, yet they were far from being all-powerful. The Odeon cinema circuit (approximately 300 cinemas by end of the 1930s) was outside their control in the 1930s, film distribution in Britain was often conducted by American firms, and various British film producers (including Korda's London Films) remained independent. In the early 1940s, however, the situation was to change. In a few short years in the late 1930s and early 1940s J. Arthur Rank came to control a large part of the British film industry. He built Pinewood Studios in 1936, took control of Korda's Denham Studios a couple of years later, and then went on to take a controlling interest in both the Odeon cinema circuit and the Gaumont-British film company. Rank's sudden rise to pre-eminence may have been unexpected, but it left him in a strong position against American companies who needed access to his 600 cinemas. With Warner and M-G-M supplying the ABC circuit, all of the remaining American companies were forced to look to Rank if they wanted a circuit release for their pictures. Rank's bargaining power was to become increasingly apparent to United Artists in the post-war years.

Customs duties, crisis and confrontation

Despite its refusal to invite Rank into United Artists as a partner, the firm had managed to reach an agreement in 1944 to distribute six of Rank's pictures in the US market. By the end of the war, however, UA were beginning to find it difficult to deal with Rank. In 1945:

> An impasse had been reached between Rank and Davis of Odeon and United Artists Corporation Ltd. Meetings were held between Messrs. Rank, Davis and Sears, one of which Mr. Raftery attended.[25]

The meetings were eventually resolved successfully as far as UA were concerned, and the company was provided with sufficient slots in the Odeon and Gaumont circuits for all of its 1946 releases. That both UA's head of foreign distribution (Sears) and its president (Raftery) were required to negotiate personally with Rank indicates how urgent the situation was becoming.

A year later, United Artists were once again facing the very real threat of being shut out of the Odeon and Gaumont circuits.[26] In 1947 Rank visited the United States and began negotiations with three of the five largest US companies (Paramount, RKO and Twentieth Century Fox) for deals whereby Rank's films would be widely distributed in the US in exchange for access to his two British cinema circuits. Without a major cinema circuit of their own in the US, United Artists were in a weaker position than their larger rivals to bargain with Rank.[27] In June 1947 Rank cabled UA's foreign distribution manager, Gradwell Sears, to say that "both circuits are fully booked with pictures which have been chosen in their best interests."[28]

Just as UA were beginning to struggle to get their films a circuit release in Britain, an even greater crisis loomed. In August 1947 the British Government introduced a 75 percent import duty on all foreign films. Their reason for doing so was that Britain had effectively run out of dollars to pay for American films. The American loan Keynes had negotiated the previous year had been all but spent, and 4 percent of it had gone on films. Given the choice between importing films or food, the government opted for the latter, and acted to dramatically reduce the amount of dollars being remitted to US film companies.[29]

The response of the US film companies was to collectively boycott the British market. The boycott held until the British Government was eventually forced to change its policy in 1948. The new policy, introduced by a young Harold Wilson at the Board of Trade, set a maximum limit of $17 million that could be remitted to US film companies each year. In addition to this, Wilson also introduced a new British films quota of 45 percent. The new arrangements were hardly to the liking of US companies, but they were enough to get the boycott lifted.

By the middle of 1948 US film companies found themselves in an extremely difficult position. After a boycott lasting nearly a year, there was a glut of American films ready to pour into the British market. Moreover, the new quota restrictions meant that little more than half of British screen time was actually available to US films. Competition for access to British cinema screens was becoming even more intense and, from the perspective of firms like UA, Rank's position was strengthened yet further.[30] By July 1948 the US companies (under the collective banner of the Motion Picture Export Association) were complaining that Rank was using American films to subsidize his own production. The complaint was based on the (almost certainly well-founded) allegation that Rank was booking popular American films with his own, lower budget, British ones, and treating them as double feature programs.[31] Yet as long as Rank controlled access to the major British circuits, there was relatively little US firms could do to improve their situation. UA's British manager, David Coplan, summed the situation up thus:

> We, in company with other American Companies, are therefore placed in the position where we have little to lose in trying to create an entirely new structure in this country, and by a new structure only one thing can be meant – and that is the creation of a booking arrangement or a booking combination in opposition to the existing big two combinations. ... It is not an overstatement to say that as matters are now, the American industry by its support of the existing factors, is in very point of digging its own grave in England. The very institutions the American industry is supporting seem to be determined to do everything in their power to destroy the hand that is feeding them.[32]

By 1949 UA were beginning to think seriously about by-passing the major circuits altogether, and releasing their films through independent exhibitors only.[33] The vast majority of cinemas in Britain were independently owned, rather than part of a large chain, but there were many drawbacks in pursuing such a policy. The independent halls tended to be much smaller, and the majority of them were second or third run houses (meaning that they were not able to screen new releases until the major circuit cinemas in their area had already done so). The "independent" cinemas UA would have had to release through were those outside of circuit control that were still able to show new releases. In 1949 a survey was made of how much revenue UA could expect to receive from an "independent," as opposed to a circuit, release. The results were not promising:

> Taking an overall position, the actual independents we were able to obtain as against an Odeon Circuit for London and the provincials amounted to 36%, and the actual independents obtained as against the Gaumont Circuit averaged to 44%.[34]

Releasing through independent cinemas instead of the main circuits resulted in UA receiving less than half their expected box-office revenue. Yet even 36% was better than nothing, and by the end of the 1940s this was the situation in which United Artists found itself.

Conclusions

An individual firm like United Artists relied more heavily on the UK market for sales and profits than British cinema exhibitors relied on it. Collectively, of course, the output of US film companies was essential for British cinema exhibitors, and these firms could exert a powerful influence when they acted in unison. Collective action was undertaken by US firms, most notably in 1947–48, but in response to government policies that affected all US firms equally. The effect of J. Arthur Rank's growing market power in the UK was not felt equally by all US firms. Warner and M-G-M, which released films through the ABC circuit, were largely unaffected. For the remaining companies, however, access to cinemas controlled by Rank became absolutely crucial. UA, as one of the smaller US companies with no cinemas of its own, had much less to offer Rank than their larger vertically integrated rivals. Its position was weakened further by the fact that its supply of British-made films from Alexander Korda had just been cut off, and the quality of its American-made films had also declined. In order to strike a deal with Rank in the mid-1940s UA would not only have needed to invite him into the company as a stockholder, he would probably have wanted a controlling interest in the firm. UA might well have been able to reach an agreement with Rank that would have enabled them to operate comfortably in Britain in the 1940s, but in doing so they would have needed to become a much more Anglicized company. In turning down the approach from Rank, UA effectively alienated the key figure in the British film industry and found it increasingly difficult to book their films in British circuits for the remainder of the decade.

American-made films continued to be popular with British audiences throughout the 1930s and 1940s. While British films did become more popular with British audiences as the period progressed, this did not alter the fact that American films were far more commonly seen and enjoyed in Britain than British films were in the US. To many observers at the time, the cultural and commercial dominance of American films did appear to offer clear evidence of "Americanization." On closer examination, however, the interactions between British and American interests are shown to be rather more complex. The size of the UK market, and its relative openness to US products, made it by far the most important foreign market for US firms. This importance meant that American film producers frequently made pictures designed to appeal to British audiences, and seldom produced films depicting the British in a negative light. It also meant that US film companies were willing to make deals with British film producers in order to facilitate access to the British market. In the 1930s, UA allowed Alexander Korda to become a 25 percent owner of the company (on very favorable terms) in order to ensure a suitable supply of British films. They also distributed these pictures in the US, despite the fact that most of them were of limited appeal to American audiences. The failure to make a similar deal with J. Arthur Rank in the 1940s was the key factor behind the crisis facing UA in the British market.

The market power of US film companies in Britain in the 1930s and 1940s was much less apparent than the appeal of American films. To the business historian, the striking feature of the interactions between American and British film companies in this period was not just the dominance of US films, but the strength of the bargaining power held by some British firms in their negotiations with the major US players.

Notes

1 Sidney R. Kent, quoted in Thomas H. Guback, "Hollywood's International Market" in Tino Balio, ed., *The American Film Industry* (Madison: University of Wisconsin Press, 1976), 390.
2 Howard T. Lewis, *The Motion Picture Industry* (New York: D. Van Nostrand, 1933), 398.

3 It is worth remembering that prior to 1914, European films had reached a far wider international audience than American ones. See Gerben Bakker, "The Decline and Fall of the European Film Industry: Sunk Costs, Market Size and Market Structure, 1890–1927," LSE Working Paper, No. 70/03 (February, 2003).

4 For a summary of the types of protective legislation introduced in the largest European markets see Lewis, *The Motion Picture Industry*, 393–433.

5 Guback, "Hollywood's International Market," 393–4; John Trumpbour, *Selling Hollywood to the World: US and European Struggles for Mastery of the Global Film Industry, 1920–1950* (Cambridge: Cambridge University Press, 2002), 63–90.

6 See Rachael Low, *Film Making in 1930s Britain* (London: Allen and Unwin, 1985); Margaret Dickinson and Sarah Street, *Cinema and State: The Film Industry and the British Government, 1927–1984* (London: BFI Pub., 1985).

7 For example, John Sedgwick, *Popular Filmgoing in 1930s Britain: A Choice of Pleasures* (Exeter: University of Exeter Press, 2000); Jeffrey Richards, ed., *The Unknown 1930s: An Alternative History of the British Cinema, 1929–1939* (London: I.B. Tauris, 1998); Ian Jarvie, *Hollywood's Overseas Campaign: The North Atlantic Movie Trade, 1920–1950* (Cambridge: Cambridge University Press, 1992).

8 The eight major film companies in the US are usually divided into the "big five" (M-G-M, Warner Bros., Twentieth Century Fox, Paramount and RKO), and the "little three" (United Artists, Universal and Columbia).

9 See Kristin Thompson, *Exporting Entertainment: America in the World Film Market, 1907–1934* (London: BFI Pub., 1985); Andrew Higson and Richard Maltby, eds., *"Film Europe" and "Film America": Cinema, Commerce and Cultural Exchange, 1925–1939* (Exeter: University of Exeter Press, 1999); H. Mark Glancy, *When Hollywood Loved Britain: The Hollywood "British" Film, 1939–1945* (Manchester: Manchester University Press, 1999).

10 Glancy, *When Hollywood Loved Britain*.

11 The US and Canada were deemed to constitute the "domestic" market according to UA balance sheets.

12 Evidence of the Board of Trade to the Committee on Cinematograph Films (Lord Moyne's Committee) 1936, Public Record Office, BT 55/3, No. 44 p. 9.

13 Robert Murphy, "Under the Shadow of Hollywood," in Charles Barr, ed., *All Our Yesterdays: 90 Years of British Cinema* (London: BFI Pub., 1986), 47–71.

14 Sarah Street, "Stepping Westward: The Distribution of British Feature Films in America, and the case of *The Private Life of Henry VIII*," in Justine Ashby and Andrew Higson, eds., *British Cinema, Past and Present* (London and New York: Routledge, 2000), 51–62.

15 The stock Korda acquired was valued at $650,000, but payment of this was extended over a long period. Tino Balio, *United Artists: The Company Built by the Stars* (Madison: University of Wisconsin Press, 1976), 132–5.

16 Sedgwick, *Popular Filmgoing in 1930s Britain*, 232–5.

17 Sedgwick, *Popular Filmgoing in 1930s Britain*, appendix 3.

18 Karol Kulik, *Alexander Korda: The Man Who Could Work Miracles* (London: W. H. Allen, 1975), 96–114.

19 E. T. Carr to Arthur Kelly, 31 May 1940, United Artists Collection of the Center for Film and Theater Research, State Historical Society, Madison, Wisconsin [UAC hereafter], Series 4F, Walter Gould Papers, box 4, file 11.

20 Tino Balio felt that if Korda had refused to extend his contract with UA in 1935, "UA's future in Britain would have been bleak indeed." Balio, *United Artists*, 134.

21 Balio, *United Artists*, 197–201.

22 Carr to Kelly, 2 December 1943, UAC, Gradwell Sears Papers, box 5, file 7.

23 Geoffrey Macnab, *J. Arthur Rank and the British Film Industry* (London and New York: Routledge, 1993), 77–81.

24 Balio, *United Artists*, 186–201.

25 Memorandum for the Board of Directors, 18 December 1945, UAC, Series 6B, Arthur Kelly Papers, box 2, file 11.

26 A history of United Artists' complaints against Rank was compiled by their British manager in 1949. See David Coplan to Arthur Kelly, 7 February 1949, UAC, Series 6B, Arthur Kelly Papers, box 7, file 7.

27 Balio, *United Artists*, 220–1.

28 Coplan to Kelly, 7 February 1949, UAC, Series 6B, Arthur Kelly Papers, box 7, file 7.

29 See Macnab, *J. Arthur Rank*, 162–87; Robert Murphy, *Realism and Tinsel: Cinema and Society in Britain, 1939–1949* (London and New York: Routledge, 1989), 219–25; Jarvie, *Hollywood's Overseas Campaign*, 213–37.

30 While Rank's bargaining power with US firms had been strengthened *as an exhibitor*, his position as a producer became extremely precarious once the US boycott was lifted. See Macnab, *J. Arthur Rank*, 162–87.

31 Arthur Kelly to David Coplan, 20 July 1948, UAC, Series 6B, Arthur Kelly Papers, box 7, file 5.

32 Coplan to Kelly, 26 May 1948, UAC, Series 6B, Arthur Kelly Papers, box 7, file 6.

33 Kelly to Morton, 8 July 1949, UAC, Series 6B, Arthur Kelly Papers, box 7, file 8.

34 Schroeder to Kelly, 9 August 1949, UAC, Series 6B, Arthur Kelly Papers, box 7, file 8.

12
"Typically Anti-American"? The Labour Movement, America and Broadcasting in Britain, from Beveridge to Pilkington, 1949–62

Tom O'Malley

> Lifestyle was a sensitive issue in socialist culture. Suspicions of revisionists like Crosland, Jenkins and Douglas Jay, centred as much on their urbanity…as their politics (the "left," typically anti-American, dubbed them "jaywalkers").[1]

From 1951 until 1964 the Conservative Party governed the United Kingdom with the Labour Party in opposition. These were years of change in the international and domestic arena. America's dominance as a global superpower, rapidly eclipsing the UK, became clear to all, especially after the Suez affair of 1956. The expansion of consumer culture and growth of affluence amongst working class people, plus the spread of television, helped alter the cultural landscape in the UK.[2]

Historians have noted the existence in these years of anti-Americanism amongst political elites,[3] particularly on the "left," which has been characterized as "typically anti-American."[4] The language used in much public discourse about America in these years contained elements of hostility to American culture and power and a sense of complacency in the UK about the superiority of things British. Were, however, the pronouncements of the "left" on matters of culture "typically anti-American," or is that too one dimensional a summation of the views on American culture held by people on the left of the political spectrum?

This essay opens with some comments on terminology and a brief survey of the complex relationships between America and British culture in the 1950s. It then explores critiques of the American media from both outside and inside the Labour movement in connection with three key points in public debates about broadcasting: the Beveridge Report on broadcasting, 1949–51,[5] the advent of commercial television in 1955,[6] and the Pilkington Commission on broadcasting 1960–62.[7] The essay argues that there are two senses in which it is wrong to characterize the left as "typically anti-American" on matters of culture. Firstly, views in the Labour movement reflected concerns about American culture and television in particular, that were wide-spread in British society, and insofar as members of the Labour movement shared in them, they are more accurately viewed as an expression of the general ambivalence towards US influence in the UK than as a simple expression of crude anti-Americanism.[8] Secondly, the criticisms of the American media within the Labour movement were substantive, relating to real domestic concerns about how broadcasting should operate in post-War Britain; labelling them as "typically anti-American" does not do justice to the seriousness of the issues they raised. Given that America had the world's most developed system of television, it was not surprising that debates about the future of TV in the UK should look to the States for both positive and negative examples of how broadcasting might develop.

Left, right and labour

This essay uses "Labour movement" to cover all those supporting either the Labour Party, the Trade Union movement, the Communist Party of Great Britain (CPGB), or independent socialists such as those allied with the New Left. These people were bound together by an overt commitment to raising the material and cultural living standards of the population. Their views on American cultural influence were not a simple expression of where they stood on the political spectrum within the movement. For example, an individual like Hugh Gaitskell, who favored an Atlanticist foreign policy and was seen as on the right of the party, and a figure like Aneurin Bevan, who for much of the 1950s was seen to be on the left and was more sceptical of the leadership's stance on relations with America and the Soviet Union, could share a similar critique of US cultural influence with the historian E. P. Thompson, who in the early 1950s was an active member of the CPGB. Even the Conservative MP, Selwyn Lloyd, who played an important part in promoting the case for commercial television, was careful to do so in a manner that distanced his proposals from practices in America.[9] As this essay illustrates, a simple left-right, divide cannot do justice to reasons why people inside and outside of the Labour movement raised concerns about the impact of America on British culture. The range and depth of the attitudes towards America in the Labour movement suggest that describing these as "typically anti-American" is an over-simplification.

America in 1950s Britain – the roots of concern

Mark Hampton has pointed out that to "Victorians, the idea of America conjured ambivalent sentiments." It symbolized a possible future but also stimulated fears of "populism, crude informality, commerce and 'anti-culture'." By the late nineteenth century, attacks "on the commercialization of the British press often cited the American example as the dangerous destination to which Britain was heading." This, in spite of the fact that the UK press and journalists drew on US experience in the transformation of the Victorian press into the more readable, popular style of the early twentieth century.[10] Attitudes to mass culture amongst the "English literary intelligentsia" during the early twentieth century were frequently expressed as a hostile response to the emergence of a mass reading public and exemplified elite anxieties about the kind of mass culture for which America stood.[11]

After 1945 America stimulated mixed responses of approval and fear. In Europe, "'Americanisation' was…a source of profound reinvigoration, but also of potential danger, threatening to previous national traditions and cultural institutions." This led members of the intelligentsia to prefer the pull of the Soviet rather than the American model of society.[12] The economic and military decline of the UK relative to the US meant that many were unable to "observe American culture other than with mixed feelings."[13] For example, although Hollywood films dominated British screens, British comedy and war films were most popular amongst occasional filmgoers. Responses to American films were therefore "far from being monolithic," varying "significantly according to gender, age, social background and frequency of attendance."[14]

In an assessment of popular attitudes towards Russia and America in 1953, Mass Observation found only 41 percent of the public "were either 'definitely' or 'mainly favourable' to America." McCarthyism did much to undermine support for America in Britain in the 1950s and anti-Americanism was both "rife" and "present beyond Labour circles."[15] In the 1950s the roots of this lay in "the genuine concerns of people who feared American atomic power, resented US interference in their own country's affairs, including its military and secret intelligence installations, and mistrusted its power and wealth." Fear of American cultural imperialism fostered criticism amongst trade unionists and "worries about the imposition of the ruthless techniques associated with American business."[16]

Recognition of this situation makes it possible to understand the range of attitudes in the British Labour movements towards the US in the period 1949–62. The CPGB was vociferous in the late 1940s and early 1950s in its denunciations of America's cultural influence. This was prompted by the Cold War and the Moscow-led mobilization against American influence in Europe after 1947.[17] The targets chosen by the party, including American horror comics, advertising techniques, music and films were, in a sense, easy ones given the ambivalence about US culture in the UK.[18] As John Callaghan has pointed out, however, the campaign was center-driven within the party and it gradually faded in the wake of the revelations after Stalin's death in 1953. By 1962 the CPGB membership were "not as interested in cultural struggle as the leadership." Equally, official denunciations of jazz as "decadent" did not stop Communists playing and appreciating it in the 1940s and 1950s.[19]

Outside of the CPGB the situation varied. In the Labour Party the Cold War posed the problem for G. D. H. Cole, writing in 1952, of how to "meet the challenge of Communism without accepting the philosophy of Americanism as a substitute."[20] Labour's Atlanticism had preceded the Cold War and the 1945–51 Labour government, led by Clement Attlee, had played a key role in setting up the system of international alliances that dominated the Cold War. Indeed the divisions in the 1950s were often about the demands coming from the Bevanite wing of the Party, which wanted "a certain critical distance from the Atlanticism so enthusiastically embraced by Labour's Front Bench."[21] Thus the political stance of Labour hovered between a mixture of support for American democratic ideals, in the face of the Soviet threat, and a deeper suspicion of American power.

These concerns fed Labour movement responses to the influence of the American media in Britain.[22] In 1946 Michael Foot MP used evidence from campaigners in the US critical of the US media to back a motion in Parliament calling for a Royal Commission on the Press.[23] In 1947 Kingsley Martin, editor of the *New Statesman and Nation*, while attacking the domination of radio and cinema in America by "Big Business," recognized that the media system "in the greatest of capitalist democracies" bred "criticism of government, and without criticism no government can be good."[24] Indeed the criticisms members of the Labour Party and the National Union of Journalists made of the newspaper press in the UK drew not only on a critique of US-style concentration of ownership, but also on criticisms of the influence of advertisers on content and standards which were shared by people from a range of political positions. These concerns certainly were connected with a distaste for American-style advertising culture in the 1950s, but were also criticisms about practices within the press and advertising industries, not simple anti-Americanism.[25]

Beveridge, anti-Americanism and the labour movement

Labour movement attitudes towards US influence were not therefore homogenous and reflected more widely held views in British society. From the outset UK officials and politicians had kept a watchful eye on developments in US broadcasting.[26] Wartime conditions prompted the Cabinet to establish a War Cabinet Committee on Broadcasting in 1944. One major theme of its deliberations was economic. This reflected a fear that in the post-war period the technical superiority of the US plus its commercial interests would lead to the spread of commercial broadcasting around the world and the capture of "European markets, particularly in television."[27] Indeed this fear was well-grounded. In 1947–48, "American media reached their highest point," in terms of their international dominance in film and television. In 1948, 92 percent of the world's TV sets were in the US and only 6 percent in the UK. In 1954, America led the world with 199 sets per thousand in the population.[28] This sense that American companies posed an economic threat to British industrial interests remained a source of criticism of the American media throughout the 1950s, and ran parallel with cultural concerns.

Given the importance of the US as the home of the most advanced system of television, its activities in this field were of interest to the Beveridge Committee on broadcasting, which deliberated on the shape of UK Broadcasting policy between 1949 and 1951. Several members of the Committee visited the US. The Committee did not want sponsored programming in the UK, although three members did advocate allowing advertisements. The majority view was grounded in concerns about control over content and in a perception of the aims of broadcasting:

> We reject any suggestion that broadcasting in Britain should become financially dependent on sponsoring as it is wholly in the

United States, and largely in Canada and Australia. Sponsoring carried to this point puts the control of broadcasting in the hands of people whose interest is not broadcasting but the selling of some other goods or services or the propagation of particular ideas.

In addition the Committee noted the relative failure of educational broadcasting under the US commercially dominated system, in contrast to the situation in the UK.[29] The financial structure of US radio meant, according to Beveridge in a personal note included in the Committee's report, that:

> From the British point of view the broadcasting agencies in America in pursuing public service aims and maintaining standards are fighting against difficulties much greater than those experienced by broadcasters in this country.[30]

One Committee member, Selwyn Lloyd, a Conservative MP, produced a minority report appended to the main report, dissenting from the Committee's main recommendation, that of retaining the BBC's monopoly in broadcasting. He advocated commercially funded competition in television. He visited America and was highly critical of the US model in line with the majority of the Committee's members. The system lacked a public service network, the Federal Communications Commission did not appear to exercise effective control over programme content, and the influence of advertising agencies on content "might well be towards crudity and over commercialisation." He thought advertisements "boring, repetitive" and "too frequent." He did, however, think that in the UK it was not "impossible to devise rules which would make it tolerable."[31]

Lloyd's qualified sympathy for advertising was not shared by six other members of the Committee who appended a document listing 16 reasons against advertising and sponsorship on the grounds that these militated against the social purposes of broadcasting.[32] In making these judgments, based on either the evidence they received or direct contact with American broadcasting, the Committee's members were reflecting views held more widely in society, including in the Labour movement. For members of the BBC's Midland Regional Advisory Council, some of whom had had experience of broadcasting in America, the introduction of commercial broadcasting "would prejudice the efforts of the BBC to maintain high standards."[33] The evidence of low standards appeared, according to the Institute of Incorporated

Practitioners in Advertising (IIPA), to "derive from the distorted picture of commercial radio in America presented by certain American films and novels." Nonetheless, it recognized the force of the critique by suggesting that there "is no reason whatsoever to suppose that British commercial programmes would imitate commercial radio in America."[34]

Another organization with a direct economic interest in the future of broadcasting, and in particular in the music played by the BBC, was the Songwriters Guild of Great Britain. It objected to the BBC's "foreign sound," and that only 23 percent of the Corporation's program time was devoted to work by British composers. The remaining 77 percent "is filled with foreign compositions, principally American." The Guild pointed to the extent to which payments of royalties in dollars to American composers had an adverse affect on the exchange position. It insisted that more encouragement to British writers would "assist in gaining world recognition of their works and increase the chance of enabling such works to earn fees in the dollar area."[35] The economic motive here mixed with the cultural and echoed the kind of anxiety about the economic power of US broadcasting expressed in the deliberations of the War Cabinet Committee on Broadcasting of 1944.

From a more overtly political perspective the evidence from different political traditions exhibited similarities where the issue of US broadcasting was concerned. The Liberal Research Group[36] argued that "the monopoly of the BBC in sound broadcasting and television can no longer be justified." Its own "survey of Liberal Opinion" yielded only 5 percent in favor of "commercial broadcasting, as in the US." Not surprisingly, then, it rejected the American model of "full-scale competitive commercial broadcasting for the UK."[37] The Fabians, a well-established Labour movement policy pressure group, submitted similar evidence. They were more explicit in their critique of American broadcasting. Their objections to commercial broadcasting drew on examples from the US where "advertisers can influence the choice of broadcasters" and where "on examination it is found that the real impact of serious programmes on the American radio audiences is small."[38]

The Labour Party's evidence echoed these critiques of commercial broadcasting and directly confronted the view that sponsored radio in the US was of a higher standard than BBC radio. It pointed out that a "comparison with American radio on the content of entertainment programmes is far from valid for American programmes have a much larger entertainment industry, especially in films, to draw on." The objections to advertising listed by the party included the motives of advertisers "whose primary interest is certainly not the development of good broadcasting" and it believed that BBC programs "that were influenced by commercial interests might make all the programmes from British stations suspect." Additionally Labour noted how the "commanding lead that the BBC had in television before the war is in danger of being lost to America." The question was whether a new corporation needing new resources would help to rectify this situation. Labour concluded that in "these circumstances it may be undesirable to set up a separate corporation for television services."[39]

Thus, for many of those submitting evidence and for the Committee members, America provided both an economic model and a cultural example of how not to develop broadcasting. Critics of the American model represented clearly held views reflecting both cultural and economic concerns. Some were arguably self-interested, like the Songwriters Guild. Others, like the Conservative MP Selwyn Lloyd, the Liberal and Fabian Groups and the Labour Party, held views which were based on grounded criticism of the effects of the US commercial model on the content and purposes of broadcasting.

Commercial TV and Christopher Mayhew MP

Many of these issues resurfaced in the 1950s when concerns about the US model of broadcasting came into play in the debates over the introduction of commercial TV in the UK. Asa Briggs has described the complexity of the debate around the origins of the 1954 Television Act, which brought advertising-funded TV to the UK. The debates reflected divisions within the Conservative and Labour Parties and the political elite over the direction that broadcasting should take. Yet these debates were also proxies, in part, for larger divisions of opinion about the relative merits of state planning and state controlled monopolies versus private enterprise. Thus, references to America in these debates should be filtered through this prism, and when this is done it is difficult to view the debates as containing a significant degree of crude anti-Americanism.[40]

Briggs has recognized that the association in the early 1950s of the US with terms like "consumer society," "admass" or "popular culture" meant "there was to be an anti-American element in the British struggle against the advent of commercial television." Papers like the *Daily Sketch*, the *Daily Express* and the *Daily Herald* showed hostility to commercial television and "used the American handling of the Coronation (of 1953) as a dangerous warning."[41] The left-wing *Tribune* newspaper echoed this criticism of American TV's handling of the Coronation when, in recommending the creation of separate corporations for broadcasting and a devolved BBC, it headlined its article "Break up the BBC – But No Mr Mugs," referring to the chimpanzee who had entertained American viewers during the commercial breaks.[42]

The sense in which the case for commercial broadcasting was damaged by the practice of American broadcasting, something which had been expressed in the IIPA's evidence to Beveridge, surfaced again in the early 1950s. In March 1952, Lord Bessborough, an advocate of a new commercial service, wrote to *The Times* arguing that "There is also no reason why the standards of advertising in American television should be allowed in this country...American standards would certainly not be acceptable in this country."[43] Margery Fry, the academic and penal reformer, echoed this view and wished that "those who advocate the change could be exposed for a week to a non-stop commercialized programme," as she had been during her time in the US in World War II.[44] In June of that year the Conservative Home Secretary, Maxwell Fyfe, argued that Britain could avoid the worst of US broadcast practice because "we are a much more mature and sophisticated people," a sentiment pounced on by the Labour Party's Herbert Morrison as "anti-American." In 1953, "Jules Thorn, Chairman of a British firm of television set-makers, returned from the United States openly hostile to commercial Television."[45]

In this context the ideas of the Labour MP, Christopher Mayhew, perhaps the party's most high profile opponent of the introduction of commercial TV, about the nature of American television can be seen as quite conventional, in that they reflected ideas that went well beyond the Labour movement. Mayhew, "anti-Soviet" and possessing "deep reservations about the cultural influence of America,"[46] campaigned vigorously against the introduction of commercial TV.[47] He was behind the initiative which established the cross party National Television Council (NTC) in June 1953, which determined "to resist the introduction of commercial television into this country and to encourage the healthy development of public service television in the national interest."[48]

In 1953 Mayhew published the pamphlet, *Dear Viewer*. It sold between 40,000 and 60,000 copies and he donated the royalties to the NTC.[49] The US appears frequently in the pamphlet, but always in the context of the problems posed for British culture by practices in American broadcasting. Mayhew took the view, shared by many of his contemporaries, that "the power of TV in our national life will be unprecedented." Its power resided in its capacity to influence "standards of entertainment, art and citizenship." In this context he maintained that commercial TV "would be a real disaster for this country."[50]

Mayhew's argument was that "commercialism ruins standards."[51] In support he described how a play he wrote was cut by 24 minutes when shown in the US to allow for *Lucky Break* cigarette advertisements from the show's sponsor, the American Tobacco Company. However, he argued that "it was not because they were American that the producers" made the cuts but "because they were advertisers, doing their job efficiently."[52] He asserted that there were economic reasons why the introduction of commercial TV would lead to "the gradual swamping of the national characteristics of TV in this country if advertising comes." UK companies with interests in US television would be inclined to show recorded American programs in Britain because these would most likely be cheaper. At the same time, British commercial TV companies would have a preference for making programs that might sell in the American market. If so, they would shy away from those that did not suit American tastes.[53]

Mayhew's rejection of the American model, reflecting widespread concerns about commercial TV, was not based on a rejection of capitalism or commerce. TV should be an "end in itself, and not just a tool for something else. Commerce and industry are vital to our country. We need business men of enterprise and courage – and advertisers too! But let commerce and advertising stick to the sphere where they rightly belong."[54] Thus, this high-profile Labour critique of commercial TV was not simply anti-American, but it was grounded in evidence about the nature and the consequences of commercialism in television which was drawn from the world's most developed system of broadcasting.

Yet there was another, more deep-seated, reason for Mayhew's views, rooted in a longer tradition of cultural discussion. Mayhew was concerned that commercial TV "must play down to the lowest common factor" and after "a time many of us will come to like the programmes which result." This would lead, he believed, to an erosion of intellectual aspirations amongst the population. His objection drew on John Stuart Mill's *Utilitarianism* (1861), which he quotes:

> Men lose their high aspirations, as they lose their intellectual tastes, because they have no time or opportunity for indulging them; and they addict themselves to inferior pleasures, not because they

deliberately prefer them but because they are either the only ones to which they have access or the only ones which they are any longer capable of enjoying.[55]

Mill's emphasis on the need to encourage "high aspirations" in the population was common in the political classes during the 1950s.[56] The problems associated with raising the educational and cultural standards of working people, of encouraging aspiration and valuing quality in life were addressed by Mill in the nineteenth century and again in the 1950s by figures as diverse as Anthony Crosland in the Labour Party, the CPGB activist E. P. Thompson and the independent socialist Raymond Williams. Mayhew wanted to use television to raise the cultural standards of the population; he therefore attacked the American model and the idea of importing it into the UK because it appeared to him to militate against what he thought was the proper purpose of television.[57] Mill's influence was arguably far more significant in framing Mayhew's approach to commercial television than anti-Americanism.

Pilkington and the American model

The critique of America as a model for UK broadcasting, which much of the evidence submitted to Pilkington was based upon, and which represented concerns about its likely impact on the UK, was well expressed by one member of the Committee, Elizabeth Whiteley, who said in an interview conducted many years later, "we all started with the fear that broadcasting in Britain would sink to the level of the United States...we felt we had to resist the American model."[58] Labour movement critiques of the American model during the Pilkington Committee's inquiry into broadcasting, shared ground with this view and other non-Labour movement opinion. A brief review of some of the evidence given to Pilkington illustrates this point.

Sir Kenneth Clark had been the first Chairman of the Independent Television Authority, set up under the terms of the 1954 Television Act to supervise commercial television. Writing in 1961 he felt there was too much TV, with "few things it can do well and these are rapidly becoming exhausted." He argued that "this is what has happened to television in America" where they "do not even try to make one programme better than another."[59] His rather dismissive attitude found some support in the views of Dr Hilde Himmelweit, author of a 1958 study on *Television and the Child*. Writing in 1961 in the context of the demand by ITV for a second commercial channel, she warned against more competition in UK broadcasting by arguing that "studies in the United States show conclusively that the larger the number of channels, the lower the level of programmes at peak viewing times."[60]

A more ambivalent note was struck by the Scottish Nationalist Party, which saw the need for a Scottish Broadcasting Corporation to prevent Scotland being "submerged in a stream of Anglo-American ideas and culture." Yet it also argued that:

> You may receive evidence to say that the content of commercial TV is too "American"...If anything, we approve of the amount of material from the United States. It at least gives our people a viewpoint other than that of London.

Welsh nationalists expressed similar concerns about the influence of English TV on Welsh language and culture. Both the Scottish and the Welsh were responding, in different ways, to the cultural anxieties thrown up by this new and rapidly expanding technology, in much the same way as were other groups in the UK. In all these cases the problem was that an external model of broadcasting posed a perceived threat to an indigenous set of cultural norms.[61]

America provided a warning to the Congregational Union of England and Wales of the dangers of providing "facilities for buying time by religious bodies" and because these facilities were being "exploited."[62] According to the Television and Screenwriters Guild, advertisers in "direct-control of programmes" as in the US, led to a "decline in quality."[63] The "safeguards of the Television Act" had not prevented commercial TV from approximating to the American advertiser-led model, which militated against the educational aims of "any education system," argued the Association of Education Committees.[64] The Council for Children's Welfare wanted a broader range of TV programs to replace the violent Westerns that were "bought comparatively cheaply after they have already paid their way in the States."[65] The National Federation of Women's Institutes wanted less American programs and "a reduction in the amount of violence and crime" on TV.[66] The Viewers' and Listeners' Association wanted a television service "free of those direct importations from the commercial television industry of the United States" and one more "consciously representative of the national attitude."[67]

A similar level of awareness of the problems posed by American TV existed amongst the business community. The Northern Irish National

Union of Small Shopkeepers drew on the US experience to call for the regulation of the "profit element" in broadcasting.[68] Still another commercial interest, the British Home Entertainment Ltd., argued for pay TV to be introduced on the grounds, echoing concerns raised by both the 1944 War Cabinet Committee on Broadcasting and Christopher Mayhew, that "a large proportion of the best viewing time throughout the world is occupied by American-made material." This was because US programs could recover costs domestically before being exported to the UK at a cost below that needed to produce programs in the UK. Pay TV would remedy this by stimulating the UK production sector.[69] Tolvision Limited made a similar argument for its "Tolvision" system, but felt it had to distance itself from the potential charge that it would be a "United Kingdom outlet for American material. In fact it may well be the reverse."[70] The Rank Organisation made an economic case for subscription TV in the UK: "Failure to encourage this will cede to the US world domination in this field as was the case with the film industry."[71]

Labour movement concerns about America, as expressed in evidence to the Pilkington Committee, were very similar to those in the evidence already cited, and were shared by producers' organizations within the cinema and television industries. The CPBG's critique, if more emphatic than some, was using a language easily recognizable as echoing these concerns: "Commercial Television is a frankly money-making concern and the same interests which dominate it have made vast profits out of sensationalism and the exploitation of sex, violence and brutality on the screen and newspapers."[72] Especially amongst the trade unions, the economic argument, a theme which runs throughout the debates of the 1950s, was strong. It was linked to a view of the cultural problems posed by American practices in the UK media. The Trades Union Congress noted that in 1959–60 imported films took up 12 percent of transmission time on ITV and "somewhat less" on the BBC, with a higher proportion in peak time of "foreign-especially American filmed material" of "indifferent quality."[73] A condescending stab at "the apparently low cultural standards of American viewers," as reflected in "too many" of the American imports, was accompanied in the evidence of the Association of Broadcasting Staff, the BBC staff union, by an assertion of the damage done to television by the "transmission of this kind of rubbish," which was "a prostitution of intricate machinery and of the ingenuity of the people who make and maintain it, and to anyone seriously interested in broadcasting of quality, a depressing waste of time and skilled workmanship."[74]

The objection then was to the impact on the UK broadcasting industry of importing cheap product from America. Equity, the actors' union, recognized that the informal quota exercised by the ITA on program imports had prevented commercial TV being "flooded with American productions." The Union asked for both a tightly defined quota and a law-making UK television companies devote money to "genuinely British TV filmed programmes."[75] The Radio and Television Safeguards Committee, an umbrella organization representing employees' organizations in the industry, wanted legislation to resist "strong foreign pressures for increased non-British content," and called for precisely defined quotas of foreign material.[76] The British Film Producers' Association and the Federation of British Film Makers called for quotas. Christopher Mayhew wanted a 15 percent ceiling on US material during "normal viewing" hours.[77]

While the protectionism in these views expressed genuine anxieties about the threat to jobs and culture posed by US industry, some Labour movement evidence to Pilkington was careful to point to more positive aspects of American broadcasting and culture. The politically marginal Socialist Party of Great Britain complained about its inability to get airtime in the UK, in contrast to the US, where SPGB visitors "had several opportunities of stating our case on TV."[78] The Co-operative Union's Parliamentary Committee also recognized that the American programs on UK commercial TV were "not at all representative of the range of the best of American culture and not desirable for our own."[79]

The Pilkington Committee dealt with the issue of American content on UK TV in a manner which broadly reflected the spectrum of views that had been put to them. The Committee started from the fact that the 1950s had seen TV explode onto the cultural scene in the UK. It pointed out that on 1 January 1951 there were 586,000 combined TV and Sound Licences in the UK, but by December 1961 this had risen to 11,658,000.[80] It took the view that "unless and until there is unmistakeable proof to the contrary, the presumption must be that television is and will be a main factor in influencing the values and moral standards of society."[81] It registered the concerns presented to it about the amount of time given over to US material on TV, but also took care to make the distinction which had also been made by the Co-operative Union's Parliamentary Committee. Where foreign material caused concern, "particularly some programmes made in the United States, it was in the main, not that they were foreign, but that their quality was poor."[82] Like Beveridge it noted the difficulty faced by educational TV in the US in trying to remedy deficiencies in the system, which in the

UK were "not the same in degree."[83] It recommended, however, "against the imposition of quotas" to limit the amount of material produced overseas on UK TV and radio. In phrases reminiscent of many of the criticisms which had been put to it, it drew "the attention of the BBC and ITA to the need to keep constantly in mind that the test by which foreign programmes should be accepted or rejected must be of quality, not of price or easy availability; that the broadcaster's duty is to their British audience."[84]

Conclusion

It is tempting to read the variety of critiques of American culture in the 1950s as "typically anti-American," whether they came from the Labour movement, the Conservative Party, the Churches, or academics. And it is understandable to assume that hostility to aspects of American culture as well as a rather complacent sense of British cultural superiority were present across the board in Britain. Yet this is to simplify. Attitudes to America in the UK were various. The Labour movement shared in this variety and many of the pronouncements coming from it were in line with those of people who were not members of Labour movement organizations.

Just as in the nineteenth century the rapid expansion of newspapers led to a range of cultural and political responses,[85] so too did the advent of mass audience television both inside and outside of the Labour movement. These touched on worries about the global influence of American communications as expressed by the War Cabinet Committee in 1944 and from UK business for pay TV in the late 1950s and early 1960s. They reflected anxieties amongst trade unions and professional groups in the industry about how the economic power of US broadcasting was impacting on UK production. The concern about quality was widespread and repeated across the spectrum, shared even by advocates of commercial competition like Selwyn Lloyd and opponents like Christopher Mayhew. Running through these concerns was a critique, from Beveridge to Pilkington, of the model of US broadcasting, and how that model impacted on the material produced for viewers.

The Labour movement therefore shared in a general set of concerns about the role of broadcasting and, latterly of TV, in UK society in the 1950s. Amidst these concerns were worries about the organization of UK broadcasting and the social purposes of broadcasting, which were substantive concerns that led to mounting arguments in which examples from America, the world's most developed system of broadcasting, were bound to be invoked. Labelling socialists' concerns about broadcasting and culture in the UK as "typically anti-American" takes these views out of their contemporary context, simultaneously implies that they stemmed from prejudice, not reason, and fails to do justice to the range and depth of views held by the Labour movement about the future of broadcasting in post-war Britain.

Notes

1 Lawrence Black, *The Political Culture of the Left in Affluent Britain, 1951–1964* (London: Palgrave, 2003), 28.
2 The BBC restarted TV in 1946 and ITV came on the air in 1955.
3 Richard Weight, *Patriots. National Identity in Britain 1940–2000* (London: Pan, 2002), 176. Michele Hilmes argues that attacks on the American system in the UK in the 1920s where American "chaos" stood for "commercial competition" and provided a "rationale for a centralized state appointed control." In so doing, she points to the importance of interrogating the contexts and motives behind such attacks, rather than taking them at face value; Hilmes, "Who We Are, Who We Are Not: Battle of the Global Paradigms," in Lisa Parks and Shanti Kumar, eds., *Planet TV. A Global Television Reader* (New York and London: New York University Press, 2003), 53–73 (quotation from page 59).
4 Black, *Political Culture*, 28, 192. Black hints at the electoral consequences of Labour's stance on culture. He argues that the left's criticisms of popular culture put it out of step with its natural working class constituency, which happily consumed American fashion, pop music, films and, from 1955, American-style commercial TV. While this gap between the elevated cultural ideals of Labour politicians and activists "registered only marginally at the polls" during Labour's 13 years of opposition (1951–64), "the frequently moralistic rhetoric of branch activists and the left generally *could* contribute deleteriously to perceptions of socialism" (italics inserted). For an account which illustrates just how irrelevant cultural issues seem to have been to the reasons for Conservative dominance in this period, and the importance of economics and class in elections see Andrew J. Taylor, "'The Record of the 1950s Is Irrelevant': The Conservative Party, Electoral Strategy and Opinion Research, 1945–64," *Contemporary British History* 17 (Spring 2005), 81–110. Black also discusses the left and culture in his "'Sheep May Safely Graze': Socialists, Television and the People in Britain 1949–64," in Black, *et al.*, *Consensus or Coercion: The state, the People and Social Cohesion in Post-war Britain* (Cheltenham: New Clarion Press, 2001), 28–48.
5 *The Report of the Broadcasting Committee, 1949* (HMSO, London, 1951, cmnd 8116), hereafter *Beveridge; The Report of the Broadcasting Committee, 1949: Memoranda Submitted to the Committee* (HMSO, London, 1951, cmnd 8117) (hereafter *Beveridge: Memoranda*).
6 See Asa Briggs, The *History of Broadcasting in the United Kingdom. Volume IV. Sound and Vision* (Oxford: Oxford University Press, 1979) (hereafter, *Sound and Vision*).

7   *The Report of the Committee on Broadcasting* (HMSO, London, 1962, cmnd 1753, 1974 reprint) (hereafter *Pilkington*); *The Report of the Committee on Broadcasting: Volume II Appendix E. Memoranda submitted to the Committee* (London: HMSO, 1962, cmnd 1819–1) (hereafter, *Pilkington: Memoranda*).

8   Anti-Americanism in the UK "had a distinguished pedigree, and by the late fifties the debate about what critics called "Americanisation" was an old and rather clichéd one. Often they were really arguing about the changing values of the affluent society rather than about Americans and American products themselves." See Dominic Sandbrook, *Never Had it So Good. A History of Britain from Suez to the Beatles* (London: Abacus, 2006), 136.

9   Black, *Political Culture*, pp. 28, 87, and Thompson in index; for Lloyd, see below. For a different discussion of this issue, see Martin Francis, "Review of *The Political Culture of the Left in Affluent Britain, 1951–1964*," *Twentieth Century British History* 15 (No. 3, 2004), 323.

10 Mark Hampton, *Visions of the Press in Britain 1850–1950* (Urbana and Chicago: University of Illinois Press, 2004), 64, 92–3; Joel H. Wiener, "The Americanisation of the British Press, 1830–1914" in Michael Harris and Tom O'Malley, eds., *Studies in Newspaper and Periodical History: 1994 Annual* (Westport, CT, and London: Greenwood Press 1996), 61–74.

11 John Carey, *The Intellectuals and the Masses* (London: Faber, 1992), viii.

12 Malcolm Bradbury, *Dangerous Pilgrimages. Transatlantic Mythologies and The Novel* (London: Penguin, 1996), 431.

13 Ross McKibbin, *Classes and Culture: England 1918–1951* (Oxford: Oxford University Press, 2000), 524.

14 Vincent Porter and Sue Harper, "Throbbing Hearts and Smart Repartee: the reception of American films in 1950s Britain," *Media History* 4 (1998), 188–9; see also Sue Harper and Vincent Porter, "Cinema audience tastes in 1950s Britain," *Journal of Popular British Cinema* 2 (1999), 66–82.

15 Lawrence Black, "'The Bitterest Enemies of Communism': Labour Revisionists, Atlanticism and the Cold War," *Contemporary British History* 15 (Autumn 2001), 41, 53.

16 John Callaghan, "The Cold War and the March of Capitalism, Socialism and Democracy," *Contemporary British History* 15 (Autumn 2001), 17. See also Callaghan, *Cold War, Crisis and Conflict: The CPGB 1951–68* (London: Lawrence & Wishart, 2003), 90. For US attempts to covertly influence European opinion in favor of America in the 1950s see Frances Stonor Saunders, *Who Paid the Piper?* (London: Granta, 2000), and Black, "'The Bitterest of Enemies.'"

17 Willie Thompson, "British Communists in the Cold War, 1947–52," *Contemporary British History* 15 (Autumn 2001), 123.

18 Martin Barker, *A Haunt of Fears. The strange history of the British Horror Comics Campaign* (London: Pluto, 1984); Black, *Political Culture*, 144; Callaghan, *Cold War*, 88.

19 Callaghan, *Cold War*, 98, 113–14.

20 Cited in Black, "The Bitterest of Enemies," 28.

21 John Callaghan, "The Left and the 'Unfinished Revolution': Bevanites and Soviet Russia in the 1950s," *Contemporary British History* 15 (Autumn 2001), 65.

22 Andrew Thorpe, *A History of the British Labour Party* (London: Macmillan, 1997), 114. For an account of the complexity of "left" responses to the Cold War, see Jonathan Schneer, *Labour's Conscience. The Labour Left 1945–51* (London: Unwin Hyman, 1988), especially Chapter 2. The Conservative Party too had problems with American power, particularly around the time of Suez; see Anthony Howard, *Rab: The Life of R.A. Butler* (London: Jonathan Cape, 1987), 239.

23 House of Commons Debates, 5s, Vol. 428, col. 464, 29 October 1946.

24 Kingsley Martin, *The Press the Public Wants* (London: Hogarth Press, 1947), 14–15.

25 Tom O'Malley, "Labour and the 1947–9 Royal Commission on the Press," in Michael Bromley and Tom O'Malley, eds., *A Journalism Reader* (London: Routledge, 1997), 126–58; Black, *Political Culture*, 105.

26 *Beveridge*, 39. For a discussion of how the discourse around America operated, at the level of high policy, in this context, see Hilmes, 53–73.

27 Briggs, *Sound and Vision*, 35, 39, 41, 52n3.

28 Jeremy Tunstall, *The Media Are American* (2nd ed., London: Constable, 1994), 141, 290–1, 293.

29 Briggs, *Sound and Vision*, 301, 304–5, 385, 391; *Beveridge*, 49–50, 100 (for a sympathetic assessment of advertising), 69 and 290 (for Beveridge's views on the problems stemming from commercial influences on the content of US-sponsored programmes).

30 *Beveridge*, 320.

31 Ibid., 306–7.

32 Ibid., 213–26.

33 *Beveridge: Memoranda*, Paper 45, p. 286.

34 Ibid., Paper 111, p. 545.

35 Ibid., Paper 98, pp. 507–8. The Guild was, to some extent, swimming against the tide, for which and a discussion of the rising popularity of US music in the UK see McKibbin, *Classes*, 390.

36 This was a group of three liberals who had been asked by the Liberal Party to submit evidence. Divisions within the party over the future of the BBC meant that the evidence was submitted as a group of individuals. See Briggs, *Sound and Vision*, 357; *Beveridge: Memoranda*, Paper 64, p. 368.

37 Ibid., Paper 64, pp. 379, 381.

38 *Beveridge*, 41 and *Beveridge: Memoranda*, Paper 56, p. 317.

39 *Beveridge: Memoranda*, Paper 59, pp. 345–6.

40 Briggs, *Sound and Vision*. Surprisingly, Black, in *Political Culture*, does not use *Sound and Vision* in his discussion of the origins of commercial TV.

41 Briggs, *Sound and Vision*, 430, 471–2.

42 Des Freedman, *Television Policies of the Labour Party* (London: Cass, 2003), 15.

43 Lord Bessborough, Letter, *The Times*, 25 March 1952.

44 Margery Fry, Letter, *The Times*, 26 March 1952.

45 Briggs, *Sound and Vision*, 431, 893.

46 Black, *Political Culture*, 94–5; Black, "'The Bitterest of Enemies'", 29–30; Freedman, *Television Policies*, 13; Robert Ingham, "Mayhew, Christopher Paget, Baron Mayhew (1915–1997)," *Oxford Dictionary of National Biography*, (Oxford: Oxford University Press, 2004) [http://www.oxforddnb.com/view/article/63222, accessed 20 April 2005].

47 Ibid., 423–45, 885–935.
48 Ibid., 896ff and for the wide range of organizations and individuals who supported the NTC.
49 Black, *Political Culture*, 95; Briggs, *Sound and Vision*, 904, where two separate figures are given. "Sold" may be a little misleading here if it is read as individual purchases, as the cover of this author's copy is stamped: "U.S.D.A.W. With the Compliments of the Executive Council." This implies that NTC affiliates bought in bulk and distributed to their constituencies gratis.
50 Christopher Mayhew, *Dear Viewer...* (London: Lincoln Prager, 1953), 1. There is no pagination in the pamphlet, so, for ease of reference, page references to the text have been calculated, starting where the text of the pamphlet starts with "Dear Viewer" (page 1).
51 Ibid., 2.
52 Ibid., 13.
53 Ibid., 11.
54 Ibid., 22–3.
55 Ibid., 7. Mayhew was quoting from Chapter 2 of the book, for which see, John Stuart Mill, *Utilitarianism*, ed. M. Warnock, (London: Fontana, 1973), 261.
56 Critiques of Mill's influence were developing in the 1950s, and can be seen in Maurice Cowling's *Mill and Liberalism*, (2nd ed. Cambridge, Cambridge University Press, 1990).
57 Hampton, *Visions*, 95; Jeremy Nuttall, "The Labour Party and the Improvement of minds: the case of Tony Crosland," *Historical Journal*, 46 (March 2003), 133–53; Michael Kenny, *The First New Left: British Intellectuals after Stalin* (London: Lawrence & Wishart, 1995), 88–9; Edward P. Thompson, *William Morris. Romantic to Revolutionary* (London: Merlin Press, [1955] 1977).
58 Cited in Jeffrey Milland, "Courting Malvolio: The Background to the Pilkington Committee on Broadcasting", 1960–62, *Contemporary British History* 18 (Summer 2004), 95.
59 Ibid., Paper 232, p. 1113.
60 Ibid., Paper 237, p. 1125.
61 Ibid., Paper 174, pp. 942, 945–6; for Wales see, Jamie Medhurst, "'You Say A Minority, Sir; We Say A Nation': The Pilkington Committee on Broadcasting (1960–2) and Wales," *Welsh History Review* 22 (No. 2, 2004), 305–32.
62 *Pilkington: Memoranda*, Paper 148, p. 866.
63 Ibid., Paper 136, p. 813.
64 Ibid., Paper 138, p. 821.
65 Ibid., Paper 253, p. 1202.
66 Ibid., Paper 261, p. 1231.
67 Ibid., Paper 270, p. 1262.
68 Ibid., Paper 186, p. 967.
69 Ibid., Paper 213, p. 1051.
70 Ibid., Paper 219, p. 1077.
71 Ibid., Paper 230, p. 1103.
72 Ibid., Paper 162, p. 916.
73 Ibid., Paper 269, p. 1256.

74 Ibid., Paper 124, p. 755.
75 Ibid., Paper 128, p. 785.
76 Ibid., Paper 132, pp. 800–1.
77 Ibid., Paper 226, pp. 1093–4; Paper 228, pp. 1099–101; Paper 242, p. 1136.
78 Ibid., Paper 165, p. 926.
79 Ibid., Paper 252, p. 1195.
80 *Pilkington*, 9.
81 Ibid., 15.
82 Ibid., 99.
83 Ibid., 279.
84 Ibid., 101.
85 See Aled Jones, *Powers of the Press: Newspapers, Power and the Public in Nineteenth-Century England* (Aldershot: Scolar Press, 1996), and Hampton, *Visions*.

13

Transatlantic Invasions or Common Culture? Modes of Cultural and Economic Exchange between the American and the British Advertising Industries, 1945–2000

Stefan Schwarzkopf

"Why the British fail to tell their story is a mystery. Stop kicking the Yanks for being progressive and enterprising – take over the tiller and sell as you've never sold before."

Advertiser's Weekly (1945)[1]

"So the old world is invaded – by American movies, American refrigerators, advertising, blue jeans, toothpaste, Rice Crispies and Coca Cola."

Hi Fi Review (1959)[2]

"The Brits have landed! UK TV formats become US hits – Ad agencies out to break America"

The Guardian (2003)[3]

Introduction

This article explores modes of cultural exchange and economic interaction between the American and the British advertising industry since the Second World War. I argue that the advertising industries on both sides of the Atlantic influenced each other to a great extent even before the full globalization of the advertising market in the 1980s and 1990s.

This influence was reciprocal and the complexity of the mutual cultural and economic interaction cannot be subsumed under notions of "Americanization." I attempt to show that Britain was not so much "invaded" by modern American advertising as that the British and the American advertising industries both changed in the course of constant transatlantic encounters. Indeed, large parts of contemporary structures of the global advertising industry are an outcome of these often very competitive encounters.

The article situates the subject of advertising firmly within the media dimension of the transatlantic relationship between Britain and the United States. I argue that advertising agencies and their service products became part of a global media culture much earlier than usually recognized by historians. Throughout the twentieth century, advertisements and commercials produced on either side of the Atlantic became increasingly part of the shared reading, listening, and viewing experience of ordinary American and British media consumers. Moreover, advertising became a medium itself, which created news stories to talk about, conveyed images about the world outside the home and thus formed media users' opinions and ideas.

The dream of a "transatlantic" advertising culture

The growth of American advertising agencies in Europe and other parts of the world after the First World War is a historical fact emphasized by those historians who favor the idea of an "Americanized" commercial Europe.[4] Yet it is important to recognize that this expansion took place in a space defined by powerful local actors, interests and structures, and often against the resistance of these actors and structures. British advertising businesses selectively appropriated elements of new marketing practices they saw at work in American agencies. The level of self-confidence and the outlook and self-understanding of American agencies also underwent significant transformations as they began to compete with local British agencies in London and found themselves drawn into the economic turmoil caused by the 1930–31 depression.

This process of adaptation and hybridization of American advertising cultures in the British context was powerfully promoted by the fact that American agencies had to close ranks with their British competitors in London in the immediate post-war years. In the late 1940s, faced with a Labour Government keen on policies of nationalization and curbing home consumer expenditure, advertising agencies in Britain found themselves in a position in which mainstream political and economic thought began to predict the end of competitive brands and consumer advertising. Moreover, the cultural Cold War fought in Western Europe around ideas of subsistence, austerity, nationalization, competition and consumer sovereignty affected American subsidiaries in London much more directly than their headquarters and bases in the United States.[5]

In these circumstances of the late 1940s, the policy-formulating elites of the British advertising industry created the idea of "American freedom" and constructed an image of a transatlantic social-economic-cultural alliance between British and American marketers. This dream of a common advertising culture entrusted with the task to defend Western freedom was powerfully enacted in London by the International Advertising Conference in July 1951. In that year, the UK Advertising Association hosted a convention devoted to "The Task of Advertising in a Free World." In the week between July 7 and 13, 1951, London experienced an invasion of almost 3,000 advertising men and women from 37 countries who gathered in Westminster's Central Hall to discuss the conference's theme. This theme, which linked advertising to the discourse of freedom and society, ran through all the major addresses and the specialized sessions, which were given titles such as "How direct advertising contributes to the task of selling in a free world," "The contribution of market research in a free world," and "The task and responsibilities of local newspapers in a free world."[6]

The invention of a close connection between commercial advertising and the freedom of western societies pervaded the conference from the very first opening remarks made by the Conference patron, the Duke of Gloucester, who said he believed "that the most important task for all of us is to keep that free world free."[7] The top ranking representatives of the American advertising industry present at the conference, such as Sam Gale and Fairfax Cone, heavily engaged in that debate about advertising and consumer freedom. According to the speech given by Gale, the advertising manager of General Mills (Wheaties) and past chairman of the US Advertising Council, the industry had used the conference to boast that "advertisers can keep the world free."[8] Cone, chairman of the US Advertising Council, was happy to accept the challenge proposed by the representatives of the left on behalf of his British colleagues. Using their experience of successfully selling consumer products, Cone proposed that advertising agencies could successfully "knock out" communist propaganda.[9]

The dream of a closely intertwined Anglo-American advertising industry was an important part of the identity and official ideology of the beleaguered profession of "want-makers" and "hidden persuaders." At a time when both in the US and in Europe critical journalists, social philosophers and left-wing consumer advocates mounted pressure on the industry as a whole, the political and socio-cultural legitimization offered by the Cold War was quite welcome. Consequently, American and British agencies operating in London were involved heavily in political propaganda on behalf of the Institute of Directors, industrial lobby groups fighting nationalization, the Tories and other right-wing economic pressure groups such as Aims of Industry. The British agency Colman, Prentis and Varley, for example, led the PR and advertising campaigns on behalf of the Conservative Party in the 1950s and 1960s while J. Walter Thompson's chairman John Treasure headed the party's advisory committee on election advertising in the 1970s.[10] Thus, while the 1950s heralded a period of American takeovers of British agencies and the subsequent dominance of the British advertising scene by American multinational agency networks, both industries were also tied together by an official ideology that provided a shared professional platform which needed to defend itself against a common enemy made up of burgeoning left-wing consumer criticism and increasingly self-confident neo-Marxist social philosophy. By the late 1950s, however, this shared socio-political identity, which served as a common denominator for an envisaged transatlantic advertising culture, began to lose its power of attraction. The cracks in the dream of a transatlantic advertising culture began to widen as a debate emerged within the British advertising industry about the differences in social *habitus* between Britain and America and the growing impact of American agencies in the UK market for marketing services.

Realities of "Americanization": debate, difference and dilemma

The reality of aggressive takeovers of British advertising firms by American competitors after 1945 seemingly vindicated the view that the US used its economic power in order to redesign Britain's landscape of consumer culture along American lines. The strong growth of American advertising agencies in the British market in the immediate post-war era caused a competitive shakeout which in the eyes of some observers led to the total domination of the UK advertising market by American agencies. In the late 1930s, for example, there was only one American agency (J. Walter Thompson) among the top ten advertising agencies in Britain. All other top-league advertising agencies, such as the London Press Exchange, S. H. Benson, Mather & Crowther, Crawfords or Lintas (Unilever's in-house agency) were British-owned service providers.[11] By 1970 however, there were eight American-based agencies in the top ten, among them JWT, Ogilvy & Mather, Young & Rubicam and Hobson Bates. Before the end of the Second World War there were only five American-based advertising agencies operating in London, among them J. Walter Thompson (Kraft, General Motors, Lux), Erwin Wasey (Goodyear), Lord & Thomas (Palmolive Soap, Wrigley's), and McCann-Erickson (Esso). This number rose to 24 by 1970. In that year, the American newcomers in Britain controlled some 86 percent of the declared billings (turnover) of the top 20 British advertising agencies. The distribution of advertising billings among agencies in Britain thus also supports this story of American concentration and domination of the British market by virtue of high advertising expenditure by large American clients, a game in which British agencies seem to have been on the losing side.[12]

Some of the largest American agency networks began to establish offices in London while the wars in Europe and Asia were still being fought, such as Young & Rubicam in January 1945. In February 1946, Foote, Cone and Belding (American Airlines, Frigidaire) arrived in London.[13] These American agencies, and those that had been in London before the war, embarked on a course of growth through acquisitions of their British competitor agencies. Between 1957 and 1967 alone, American agencies bought 32 British agencies. These sales were often a response by British agencies to being overstretched by the demands of their clients while being undercapitalized and thus incapable of building up business in the United States. In 1961, for example, the British Pritchard-Wood agency sold out to McCann-Erickson; in 1969, the London Press Exchange sold out to Leo Burnett Chicago; in 1971, S. H. Benson was acquired by the New York-based Ogilvy & Mather network, and in 1974, Masius Wynne-Williams sold out to the American D'Arcy-McManus agency. In the early 1970s, Unilever, the largest of all British multinational firms in the consumer goods sector, gradually sold its former in-house agency Lintas to a small New York advertising agency.[14] In the words of the eminent *Times*, the march of American "super-agencies" into the British market was an example for "yet another successful American invasion."[15]

Contemporary students of the industry, however, such as the sociologist Jeremy Tunstall, challenged this impression of an all-out American takeover of British advertising. In his 1964 study on the inner life of London advertising agencies Tunstall observed that American agencies employed preciously few American staff but instead sent their British staff for training to New York and other American commercial centers. This employment and training policy helped international agencies adapt to British conditions the American experience of "doing the ads."[16] One of these conditions, which made it difficult if not impossible to impose American styles of advertising and marketing in the new television era on British society, was that advertising regulations in the UK were much stricter than in the United States.

One of the most striking differences between the British and the American understanding of what was *de rigeur* or not in advertising was the British dislike of aggressive and directly comparative text in advertisements which put two brands against each other ("knocking copy"). British advertising before the 1980s was far less aggressive and "pushy" in its sales effort but also far less informative about "hard" facts and more driven towards conveying atmosphere and a soft image of the product.[17] This insistence on "image" instead of facts or direct sales messages was eventually brought to the United States and global markets by the charismatic English advertising man David Ogilvy, who set up his agency in New York in 1948. In the 1960s and 1970s, Ogilvy and his advertising network Ogilvy & Mather became the vanguard of the idea of the "brand image" which advertising had to create in people's mind.[18]

Another difference between British and American advertising cultures was that in the US, television advertising mainly existed in the form of "sponsored programming," where the advertiser would create and pay for an entire program, such as a "soap opera" or a game show. This system of advertising-sponsored television was inherited from the system of sponsored radio programs which emerged in the US between the 1920s and 1940s.[19] The 1954 Television Act in the United Kingdom, in contrast, specifically rejected the system of sponsored programming for fear of advertising and commercial interests influencing the content of television programs. While this distinctive cultural and regulatory gap between American and British broadcast advertising remained in existence throughout the 1950s, the early 1960s noticed a decisive change with US advertisers being less willing to buy and sponsor whole programs. Instead, advertisers in America began to buy more advertising "spots" of the type produced in Britain, thereby moving more towards the British TV advertising system. The British, in turn, began to allow some association between program and commercials by making it possible for advertisers to order a commercial next to a specific program.[20]

On the surface, therefore, British advertising appears to have come under threat from American takeovers and the growing international presence of American agency networks in the post-war period. And yet, the exchange and interaction that took place between America and Britain with regard to advertising cultures was much more complex. The transatlantic media and advertising reality saw an increasing convergence between the British and the American advertising systems. Moreover, the distinctly "British" understanding of advertising as the conveyance of "atmosphere" and brand image slowly began to make inroads into Madison Avenue.

This new Anglo-American equation which emerged in the 1950s and 1960s not only provided for a gradual convergence of two media and advertising systems. It also provided the background for the perpetual assertion of cultural difference. American and British advertising professionals still perceived their counterparts as "the other." Where British agency staff traveling to New York perceived hard-nosed salesmen with fake Texan smiles, American agency staff condemned the British as aloof yet disorganized colonial masters. The near impossibility of making American and British ways of advertising and salesmanship work in the respective countries without intermediate "cultural translation" of sales messages was summed up by David Duncan, the former Head of Research of the British market research company Attwood's. When asked how he assessed the differences between American and British cultures of consumption in the post-war era, Duncan replied: "The Americans were [behaving as] competitive conformists and the British as co-operative individualists."[21]

At some moments, the "othering" of Americans and America by British advertising professionals took the shape almost of an ethnological discourse. In the early 1950s, for example, a series of pamphlets by the Dollar Exports Board explained the characteristics of the American market to the British exporter in terms of a business and consumer ethnography.[22] The second brochure issued by the Board in 1950 on American advertising and sales promotion practices included a detailed drawing of a typical American "High Street" on which British consumer goods would have to compete. This drawing of an idealized heart of American post-war consumer modernity laid out how chain stores, variety stores, specialized shops, banks and recreation centers in an American town offered a great number of sales points and distribution channels.[23] The pamphlet's text explained: "This is the shopping centre of a North American town. The distributor's job is to keep goods flowing into the many varied retail outlets. The British exporter can get his goods into the flow by arousing consumer demand for them." This pamphlet and a number of other publications by the Dollar Exports Board and its Advertising Advisory Council, the Federation of British Industries, the British Export Trade Research Organisation (BETRO), or the trade journal *Advertiser's Weekly* attempted to explain to British manufacturers how firmly the "habit of buying by brand" was enrooted in American consumer culture, how American advertising agencies helped the manufacturer in finding and interpreting vital market information, how American consumers deciphered advertisements and how the American manufacturer viewed advertising not as expenditure, but as investment.[24]

The post-war British advertising discourse used "America" and "American" as a synonym for "the other" which needed explanation and cultural translation.[25] An impressive source for this insistence on the "otherness" of American commercial cultures is the remarkable incoherence between the external and internal communication of the then largest British advertising agency London Press Exchange (LPE). In its communication to the public and potential clients, LPE always stressed the fact that its organizational facilities and research services were on a par with what American agencies were offering to their clients. One advertisement issued by the LPE in 1960 claimed that the sheer breadth of different services the agency offered from its numerous offices around St. Martin's Lane and St. Martin's Square had turned this area of London into the "English Madison Avenue." The advertisement continued: "We have always admired American ideas about the proper scope of advertising agency service. In fact, we have not only admired it – since the 1920s we have been giving it to our own clients."[26] The image of an agency keeping up-to-date with trends in American advertising was underpinned by LPE's acquisition of the New York-based advertising and market research agency Robert Otto Inc. in 1962.[27]

The internal communication which took place within the agency at the same time, however, conveys the picture not of an advertising agency embracing the American advertising world but of an agency asserting its "essential" difference from everything "America" stood for. In particular, the letters and travel reports which appeared in the LPE house magazine *In and out the Lane* speak a language far removed from the agency's official admiration of American advertising practice. One of these travel reports, appearing in 1959, tells the story of Angus Shearer's business trip "Among the Status Seekers."[28] The Englishman Shearer described America as a foreign land where he was offered coffee instead of tea and where outside New York, English visitors were still a novelty. Although he found that the English were generally welcome ("the uppercrust American is often a great Anglophile"), he also assured his colleagues back home that the Americans were not in the least better at the job of advertising: "They probably think they are. But they don't really know very much about the standards of advertising we have in this country and I think most of them would be quite surprised to see how advanced we are in many techniques."

The travel reports submitted by LPE staff to the house magazine also show that some people felt rejected by their American colleagues and business partners on the grounds of different notions of professional masculinity. American advertising executives placed great value on a methodical and sales-oriented approach as an attribute of the "manliness" of someone working within a corporate environment. English businessmen, on the other hand, ran into the danger of being perceived by their American counterparts as disorganized, "arty" and decadent for attitudes which would have been understood as part of a gentlemanly culture within the British context.[29] The indifferent politeness encountered by Shearer in 1959, for example, is entirely missing in a travel report that appeared in 1964. Here, an English LPE staff member travels to New York to visit a client but is told by the American: "Don't ever wear suede shoes to this office again. I regard them as a sign of English decadence." Life in the US is described by this Englishman as governed by the three principles of "conformity, simplicity, uniformity." New York subway trains were allegedly dirty even by London standards and money seemed the key to everything: "it breeds togetherness," not contempt as in England.[30]

A similarly "gendered" approach to the differences between American and British marketing and salesmanship cultures was used by an anonymous contributor to the government- and industry-sponsored market research journal *Markets and People* in 1951.[31] As a member of the British Export Trade Research Organisation (BETRO) who had just returned from London to New York, this contributor felt that the British businessman was too naïve and "far too gentlemanly in his approach to selling" compared to the structured and disciplined sales organization of most American companies. However, this tentativeness, he argued, "the almost feminine uncertainty" of the British manufacturer, could also be an advantage on the world markets in the light of the often misdirected zeal of the American school of salesmanship.[32]

The general picture of mutual "otherness" of English and American advertising cultures in the post-war period is confirmed by the experiences of the young Joan Bakewell, who later became a famous journalist and BBC presenter. Bakewell began her career as a copywriter for the American McCann-Erickson agency in London in the early 1950s. At McCann, her tasks included the "translation" of package inserts for American cosmetic and hygiene products such as "Tampax" from their American version into "proper English." According to Bakewell, American top managers would regularly fly in from New York in order to convene with local English managers. Due to their different dress codes, accents and habits, the "merrican" agency personnel would be looked at by young English staff as "aliens."[33]

There were therefore limits to the growth of American advertising in its new "colony," the United Kingdom. The resilience of British culture, the regained competitiveness of larger British agencies as well as the difficult economic conditions of the mid-1960s began to check the seemingly irresistible advance of American advertising agencies in London. Symptomatic of this was the failure of J. Walter Thompson London to acquire the large advertising account of Ford in 1961 when it lost the battle against the British agency London Press Exchange.[34] This episode in some sense preluded the slow decline of JWT as the world's largest advertising agency since the 1960s. JWT's famous and very successful approach to advertising – a design based on the perceived uses of a product, a slogan, a photo of a movie star, a pack shot and an explanatory advertising text – came to be seen as stale, stencilled and boring during a decade that witnessed the rise of a new transatlantic breed of highly creative advertising wizards such as Helmut Krone, William Bernbach and Leo Burnett.[35]

At the same time, British agencies began to react to the increased American competition in London by putting more and more emphasis on creativity, on engaging in strategic mergers and on forming international networks themselves. Throughout the 1960s, a number of middle-sized and large British advertising agencies, such as the London Press Exchange, Lonsdale-Hand and Peacock formed strategic partnerships with or bought North American, European, Asian and African agencies or set up entirely new agencies in these parts of the world at considerable cost. Like the London Press Exchange, other large British agencies initially focused their growth strategy on the former Empire markets (India, South Africa, etc.) and only moved to the United States in the mid-1960s.[36] This kind of international growth of British agencies and the mergers between American and British agencies made some industry observers suspicious that British agencies would lose their identity and simply join the growing ranks of "faceless Anglo-

American animals."[37] These voices recognized that for many British agencies the only chance to survive was to be independent, individualistic and different from the efficient yet "run-of-the-mill" campaigns delivered by many of their larger American competitors who could boast the functional integration of largely systematized, in some cases even standardized services.[38] The last part of this article shows how British advertising agencies rigged the British market for advertising services against the American newcomers and used an emphasis on creativity and strategic acquisitions in order to make inroads into the American market, thus changing American conceptions of advertising.

Beyond dreams and ideologies: the ironies of America's new global reality

Throughout the post-war period, British advertising agencies and their executives influenced New York's Madison Avenue and American advertising. The above-mentioned David Ogilvy started as an account executive with the London agency Mather & Crowther in the early 1930s. In 1938, Ogilvy was sent to New York to learn the "American way" of advertising. After the war in spring 1948, the large British agency S. H. Benson and Ogilvy's old agency Mather & Crowther agreed to contribute to a fund which helped Ogilvy to set up his own agency right on Madison Avenue under the name of Ogilvy, Benson & Mather. A great number of people doubted Ogilvy's ability to survive with his new and rather small venture amidst the heated competition between the largest advertising agencies of the world. Indeed, Ogilvy himself noted in his autobiography that American advertisers went for the biggest agencies simply because this type of service provider with a complete set of sub-departments could better meet the needs of large clients. In the words of Ogilvy, it was the focus on creatively challenging advertising campaigns which helped his agency survive. Ogilvy's venture into American advertising became so successful that he eventually acquired Mather & Crowther London in 1964 and S. H. Benson's agency in 1972 to form Ogilvy & Mather (O&M).[39]

What is more, in the two decades after his risky start-up in New York, Ogilvy's agency in New York became the hot spot for the development of marketing innovations which revolutionized post-war advertising, such as the idea of the "brand image." Ogilvy's advertising became mainly concerned with establishing the most favorable image, the most sharply defined personality for a brand through creative advertising design. By drawing on the idea that brands needed to be connected in consumers' minds with a distinctive face or character (such as "the man in the Hathaway Shirt" or Commander Whitehead of the Schweppe's advertisements), Ogilvy directly took on Doyle Dane Bernbach (DDB), the miracle agency of America's 1960s advertising "creative revolution."[40] Yet, unlike his great American rival Bernbach, the Scotsman Ogilvy always believed that apart from being creatively challenging advertising had to be based on "scientific" grounds by testing and measuring audience response in great detail. The irony in this is that Ogilvy first adopted this scientific view on advertising design in the US when working in the late 1930s for George Gallup's Audience Research Institute at Princeton. Upon his return to his Mather & Crowther home agency in London, Ogilvy's new "American" views clashed with the older establishment at the agency, embodied by the poet, typographer and book designer Sir Francis Meynell. In the 1960s, this clash between the "artistic" and the "scientific" understanding of advertising resurfaced under new auspices with the American Bernbach now spearheading the camp of artistic creativity against the austere "scientification" of advertising looming from across the Atlantic.[41] The Bernbach-Ogilvy controversy which gripped the transatlantic advertising community in the 1960s thus disrupts the idea of "American advertising" as a homogenous and hegemonic practice.

Just at the time around the end of the 1970s and the early 1980s when the transatlantic power relationship between British and American advertising began to stabilize in favor of American agency networks, a number of structural changes in global marketing began to take place. These developments once again point at the co-evolution between advertising and media systems. Slowly, yet inexorably, these changes made the American advertising industry surprisingly vulnerable to a wave of aggressive takeovers planned and executed in the City of London. These structural changes were characterized by the arrival of global satellite TV and niche-market specific television stations, such as the music channel MTV launched in 1981. At the same time, the rise of Rupert Murdoch's News Corporation signalled the emergence of global media empires. Accordingly, there was an incentive for advertising agencies to match the growth in global media companies by forming globally active media buying units which gave advertising agencies and their clients increased bargaining power over media outlets. By the same "global" token, companies such as Coca-Cola, Procter & Gamble, and Unilever, began to overhaul the way they conceptualized target markets. These companies had understood themselves as international actors that played different games in independent national markets. The socio-demographic and cultural convergence in consumer markets in the 1970s and 1980s challenged these consumer goods giants to adopt a truly global outlook. This, in turn, favored agencies which understood themselves as building *global* instead of merely internationally active British, German, American or Japanese brands. In the words of the media analyst Neil Blackley, the new type of agency that was required served as the "meat in the sandwich between giant consumer products companies and giant media companies."[42]

The prime example of a British agency which benefited from these structural changes of the global marketplace and which forced the American advertising community into a soul-searching debate over the cultural bases of advertising designs was Saatchi & Saatchi. Founded in London in 1970 by the two sons of an Iraqi-Jewish textile merchant, the Saatchi agency expanded through an aggressive acquisitions policy. In 1975, the Saatchis secured a reverse takeover of the London branch of an American agency – Compton – which catapulted them to the top end of the British agency rankings. Two years later, the Cambridge and Harvard-trained finance genius Martin Sorrell joined the Saatchis as their Director of Finance and helped the brothers exploit the London Stock Exchange as a major source of capital to fund further acquisitions, which finally brought a number of old and established British agencies into the hands of the Saatchis.[43] This growth policy led to a surprising British invasion of Madison Avenue with Saatchi & Saatchi purchasing a whole number of large American agencies since the early 1980s. The "invasion" began in 1982 when Compton Communications, the fourteenth largest advertising agency in the world, was taken over by the Saatchis for more than $30 million. In 1986, the takeover of Ted Bates Worldwide (the third largest American advertising agency) made the Saatchi & Saatchi group the largest in the world. By 1983, the US side of Saatchi & Saatchi handled more American "No.1 brands" than any other agency in the United States. The Saatchi empire was based on a new understanding of the *financial* character of advertising agencies. While American agency networks tried to grow mainly through winning new and larger clients, it was these two British art connoisseurs who introduced the idea of an agency as a "cash-cow" which could be milked in order to fund the acquisition of competitor agencies, management consultancies, PR agencies and even banks.[44] This purely "monetary" definition of advertising agencies puzzled a great number of American agency owners. In the heyday of the Saatchi acquisition tour in the US, a senior American advertising executive commented: "I used to love the Saatchis. I thought they were really neat. But now they've turned into monsters."[45]

Not only did this takeover strategy make two British advertising wizards the uncrowned kings of the 1970s and 1980s global advertising world – beside the British-born David Ogilvy, who by then was still actively involved in the running of his own advertising empire O&M. Moreover, one of the purchased American agencies, Ted Bates, had been the home agency of Rosser Reeves, America's most famous advertising copywriter after the Second World War. Reeves' 1961 classic *Reality in Advertising* had given rise to the idea of the USP. This principle taught advertisers in the western world how to successfully use the appeal of a well-defined product benefit – a "unique selling proposition" – in advertisements. The Saatchis based much of their marketing philosophy on the idea of the USP as well as on a new type of "British" creativity, which tended to be more sophisticated, ironic and at times aggressively shocking in comparison to much of the 1970s American advertising creation.[46]

This new emphasis by Saatchi & Saatchi on creativity was embedded in yet another marketing innovation: global market segmentation and the idea of "world brands." In the early 1980s, marketing consultants and academics such as Theodore Levitt of the Harvard Business School came to the conclusion that the globalization of world markets favored large, multinational enterprises which could offer standardized, high-quality products at the lowest price. The theory further predicted that this would in turn result in a global convergence of consumer tastes. This homogenization of consumer preferences for certain products again made it possible for international advertising agencies to segment markets not according to national differences but on a truly global scale, where a Japanese, an American and a French middle-class family of a certain income would be expected to prefer similar products. The deep irony of this is that it was a British agency, Saatchi & Saatchi, which first executed this quintessentially American marketing philosophy.[47]

The slow transformation of advertising agencies from craftsmen-led workshops in the 1950s and 1960s to objects of investment strategies in the 1980s was finally concluded by the former Head of Finance at Saatchi & Saatchi, Martin Sorrell. He left his bosses in 1985 and acquired a major stake in a Kent-based manufacturer of shopping trolleys called Wire and Plastic Products (WPP) in order to gain access to the stock market. Sorrell's coup was to use this small workshop for the acquisition of the American-owned J. Walter Thompson group at a cost of $566 million in 1988. Only one year later, Sorrell's WPP bought the then fifth-largest agency group in the world, Ogilvy & Mather. By the end of 1989, the British-owned WPP group topped the world ranking of advertising agencies. Today, WPP is the world's second largest marketing group with a pre-tax profit of £669 million (ca. $1.25 billion) and an ever-expanding portfolio of marketing communications agencies, including JWT, Ogilvy & Mather, Young & Rubicam, Grey Global, and Hill & Knowlton PR.[48]

This factual listing of growth and achievements hardly reveals the sense of turmoil and shock these acquisitions left behind in the global advertising scene, which until then was firmly in the hands of large and established American agencies. The same charge that had been levied against the American agencies in the post-war years was now thrown at the third British newcomer after David Ogilvy and the Saatchis. The purely financial approach of investors such as Sorrell to the advertising industry left American advertising professionals worried about the national and creative "soul" of their agencies on Madison Avenue.[49] Thus, the same kind of market-driven globalization of advertising once started by American agencies now returned and threatened to take away the American sense of superiority in matters of marketing and selling. What is more, Sorrell's new ideal of professional specialization within agencies challenged the traditional American way of looking at advertising agencies as organizations. While post-war American agencies worked on the idea that agency owners were the ultimate leaders of agencies both in terms of financial strategy and creative output, Sorrell radically separated both spheres and did not get involved in the creative side of campaign planning. Seeing themselves more as investors and detached facilitators who provided creative opportunities for talented designers, the "Sorrell generation" of 1980s agency managers afforded the emergence of a so-called "second wave" of highly creative British agencies which eventually undermined the established American Madison Avenue system of global advertising. Today, small and "edgy" British advertising workshops such as Abbot Mead Vickers, Bartle Bogle Heggarty, Leagas Delaney, Yellowhammer, Mother and St. Luke's are preferred by Masterfoods, Anheuser-Bush, Unilever, Levi's, Coca-Cola, British Telecom, Adidas and other global brands for their creativity and flexibility in reacting to the swift changes especially in the market of the modish and media-savvy teens and twentysomethings.[50]

Conclusion and implications

While in the 1950s and 1960s the United Kingdom experienced several waves of American agency networks taking over large parts of the British advertising industry, the 1970s and 1980s experienced a radical turning of the tables. By the end of the 1980s, British agencies managed for the first time to break the pre-eminence of US-owned agencies over global advertising. This pre-eminence, as shown above, was always built on rather shifting ground and the "imagined" American advertising and market Empire seemed to have enjoyed a life in mere fantasy as much as it doubtlessly did in reality.

The evidence presented above substantially undermines Jeremy Tunstall's and Victoria de Grazia's theses of Britain and Europe as the dependency of an American media and marketing empire. The extreme closeness and similarity of the British and the American advertising systems as noticed by both authors allowed the British advertising world to successfully challenge the American dominance which did exist in various sectors of the industry at certain points in time. Eventually, this process of competition and counter-challenge led to the global rise of British agencies and British agency owners began to make inroads into the American market for advertising services. Similar developments took place throughout the 1980s and 1990s in other sectors of the media world with Rupert Murdoch and Conrad Black demonstrating similarly expansionist approaches.

The thesis of an "Americanized" British advertising industry is therefore challenged by three considerations. Firstly, a whole number of globally significant innovations in advertising creation, campaign planning and market research have British origins (brand image, global market segmentation). Secondly, over the last two or three decades, skilful and aggressive London-based investors have bought up large parts of the American advertising industry. This development, referred to as the "British invasion," provided the role model for other non-American investors in the global advertising sector. Today, UK-owned (WPP), French-owned (Publicis) and Japanese (Dentsu) advertising groups stand side by side with American marketing conglomerates (Omnicom, Interpublic). Thirdly, the decline of traditional forms of mass marketing since the 1970s, the global media revolution in the 1980s and the rise of fast-changing niche markets in the same period opened up opportunities for London-based, small and creative advertising and PR workshops, which today compete directly with the large and established US advertising agencies. This in turn allowed British notions of advertising creativity to regain centre stage. In the last three decades or so, the United States went through a period characterized by an influx of this "British" approach to advertising, which puts more emphasis on notions of creativity and the use of irony in advertising messages. In this changed environment, American advertising professionals saw themselves exposed to subsequent waves of "creative revolutions" which challenged the traditional approach of research-based and often formulaic advertising designs.

These developments took place within the framework of a continuous and reciprocal Anglo-American encounter of commercial cultures which complicates notions of an outright American dominance of global marketing and media communications. Rather than being subjected to subsequent waves of "Americanization," British agencies have always taken part in defining a common, transatlantic advertising culture. Both American and British professional identities in marketing and the creative industries emerged as a result of a constant yet often hidden conversation between the industries on both sides of the Atlantic. In this hidden conversation, advertising practitioners often struggled to mark and defend boundaries of national and professional identities against an influx of elements that were able to undermine the perceived stability of their respective national advertising cultures.

Notes

1 Norman Flood, "Americans Out-told and Out-sold Us," *Advertiser's Weekly* (June 28, 1945), 516.
2 Eric Salzman, "A Mise en Scène for Disgruntled Americans," *Hi Fi Review* 2:2 (February 1959), 47–9, 52–3.
3 *Guardian*, headline of the Media Supplement, August 11, 2003.
4 Victoria de Grazia, *Irresistible Empire: America's Advance through Twentieth-Century Europe* (Cambridge, MA: Belknap Press, 2005), 226–83; Harm Schroeter, "Die Amerikanisierung der Werbung in der Bundesrepublik Deutschland," *Jahrbuch für Wirtschaftsgeschichte* (1997), 93–115; Alexander Schug, "Wegbereiter der modernen Absatzwerbung in Deutschland: Advertising Agencies und die Amerikanisierung der deutschen Werbebranche in der Zwischenkriegszeit," *Werkstatt Geschichte* 12 (2003), 29–52; Harm Schroeter, *Americanization of the European Economy: a Compact Survey of American Economic Influence in Europe Since the 1880s* (Dordrecht: Springer, 2005), 111–20.
5 LPE Organization Intelligence Centre, *Advertising and the Labour Party* (March 9, 1964), History of Advertising Trust Archive (henceforth HAT), LPE 3/3/2; Anthony Crosland, "A socialist view of advertising," *The Journal of Advertising*, 1 (1963), 7–22; "Socialists accuse advertising," *Advertiser's Weekly* (September 6, 1951), 391; Ralph Harris and Arthur Seldon, *Advertising in a Free Society* (London: Institute of Economic Affairs, 1959),

42–5; Stefan Schwarzkopf, "They Do it with Mirrors: Advertising and British Cold War Consumer Politics," *Contemporary British History* 19 (2005), 133–50.

6 *The International Advertising Conference (Great Britain) 1951* (London 1951), HAT, Advertising Association collection, AA 15/5.

7 *International Advertising Conference*: 1, 5; "Flags are out for 40 Nations: Royal Welcome for 2600 Conference Delegates," *Advertiser's Weekly* (July 5, 1951), 3; conference report in *Advertiser's Weekly* (July 10, 1951), 2.

8 Speech by Gale, *Advertiser's Weekly* (July 12, 1951), 84 and *Daily Mail* (July 10, 1951), 3.

9 See *International Advertising Conference*: 9–11.

10 Richard Kisch, *The Private Life of Public Relations* (London: MacGibbon & Kee, 1964), 32–3; Allan Potter, *Organized Groups in British National Politics* (London: Faber & Faber, 1961), 323–33; Dominic Wring, "Political Marketing and Party Development in Britain: a 'Secret' History," *European Journal of Marketing*, 30 (1996), 92–103; Dominic Wring, *The Politics of Marketing the Labour Party* (Basingstoke: Palgrave, 2005), 48–50; "Obituary: John Treasure," *Admap* (April 2004), 49.

11 On Benson and Mather & Crowther see Stanley Pigott, *OBM: A Celebration. One Hundred and Twenty-Five Years in Advertising* (London: Ogilvy Benson & Mather, 1975); on Lintas see Len Sharpe, *The Lintas Story* (London: Lintas, 1964).

12 Douglas West, "Multinational Competition in the Advertising Agency Business, 1936–1987," *Business History Review* 62 (1982), 467–501; Douglas West, "The Growth and Development of the Advertising Industry Within the United Kingdom, 1920–1970" (Ph.D. diss., University of Leeds, 1984), 189ff.; William Leiss *et al.*, eds., *Social Communication in Advertising: Consumption in the Mediated Market Place* (London: Routledge, 2005), 372; Sean Brierley, *The Advertising Handbook* (London: Routledge, 2002), 69.

13 *Advertiser's Weekly* (January 11, 1945), 47; *Advertiser's Weekly* (August 29, 1946), 473.

14 James O'Connor and John Crichton, *Fifty Years of Advertising – What Next?* (London: Advertising Association, 1967), 13; West "Multinational Competition"; Jeremy Tunstall, *The Advertising Man in London Advertising Agencies* (London: Chapman & Hall, 1964), 224–6; David Jeremy, *A Business History of Britain, 1900–1990s* (Oxford: Oxford University Press, 1998), 481; *Advertiser's Weekly* (October 3, 1958), 5; *Campaign* (July 5, 1985), 29–31; *Campaign* (January 30, 1970), 7; "Advertising Agencies Reforge Old Links," *The Times* (July 5, 1971), 18.

15 "Why Madison Avenue Moved In," *The Times* (June 26, 1969), 25.

16 Tunstall, *Advertising Man*, 34.

17 Tunstall, *Advertising Man*, 63; see also Labour Party, *Opposition Green Paper: Advertising* (London: Labour Party, 1972) which criticizes advertising for not being informative enough.

18 "New British Ad. Agency Opens in New York," *Advertiser's Weekly* (June 17, 1948), 495; David Ogilvy, *Confessions of an Advertising Man* (London: Longmans, 1964).

19 See Lawrence Samuel, *Brought to You By: Postwar Television Advertising and the American Dream* (Austin: University of Texas Press, 2001), 3–7.

272   *Anglo-American Media Interactions, 1850–2000*

20   "Why Trend in Network TV is to Multiple Sponsorship," *Mediascope* (August 1960); E. P. H. James, "Commercial TV in Britain," *Printer's Ink* (July 5, 1957); Graham Murdock, "Embedded Persuasions: The Fall and Rise of Integrated Advertising," in Dominic Strinati and Stephen Wagg, eds., *Come on down? Popular Media Culture in Postwar Britain* (London: Routledge, 1992), 202–31; Tunstall, *Advertising Man*: 87–8.

21   Interview with David Duncan on February 1, 2006. Attwood's was founded by the former Head of Research at JWT's British Market Research Bureau, Bedford Attwood, and became renowned in the 1950s for the development of TV audience measurements (TAM).

22   The series was called *Dollar Sales*. Copies are at the British Library and in the papers of the Dollar Exports Board at the Modern Records Centre, University of Warwick (GB 0152 MSS.200/DEC).

23   Dollar Exports Board, *Dollar Sales: Advertising and Sales Promotion. A Practical Guide to the Advertising and Merchandising of British Goods in the USA and Canada* (London: Dollar Exports Board, 1950), 10f.

24   British Export Trade Research Organisation, *Distributing Goods in the USA: Report on Distribution Margins and Practices, Illustrated by Case Studies* (London: BETRO, 1952); "American Market Supplement," of *Advertiser's Weekly* (March 23, 1950); "American Market Supplement, No. 2" of *Advertiser's Weekly* (December 28, 1950). The articles in these two supplements were written by American specialists on market research, packaging and product design, consumer psychology, and supermarket retailing.

25   "Anglo-U.S. Advertising Committee: Advice for Exporters," *The Times* (September 30, 1949), 6.

26   "The English for Madison Avenue is St. Martin's Lane," *The Times* (November 28, 1960), 11.

27   See *The LPE Reporter* 3 (Spring 1963), 16, at HAT, LPE 3/4/1; *In and Out the Lane – IAOTL* 3 (1962), 30; "New Trends in Advertising Industry," *The Times* (February 27, 1962), 16.

28   *IAOTL – In and Out the Lane* 1 (September 1959), 14–17, at HAT, LPE 3/2/1.

29   On notions of masculinity in the creative and manufacturing industries see Michael Roper, *Masculinity and the British Organization Man since 1945* (Oxford: Oxford University Press, 1994), 23–33, 132–9; Sean Nixon, *Advertising Cultures: Gender, Commerce, Creativity* (London: Sage, 2003), 95–115; Sean Nixon, "Advertising Executives as Modern Men: Masculinity and the UK Advertising Industry in the 1980s," in Mica Nava *et al.*, eds., *Buy this Book: Studies in Advertising and Consumption* (London: Routledge, 1997), 103–19; Tunstall, *Advertising Man*: 65–70, 193–8.

30   "Let's do the Madison," *IAOTL – In and Out the Lane* 9 (1964), 18–21.

31   *Markets and People* had started in 1946 as the *BETRO Review*, the journal of the British Export Trade Research Organisation (BETRO).

32   "Thinking Out Loud," *Markets and People* (March 1951), 10–11.

33   Interview with Joan Bakewell, July 13, 2004 and Joan Bakewell, *The Centre of the Bed* (London: Hodder & Stoughton, 2003), 127–9.

34   See John Pearson and Graham Turner, *The Persuasion Industry* (London: Eyre & Spottiswoode, 1966), 9–35; Sean Nixon, "Apostles of Americanization? J. Walter Thompson Ltd., Advertising and Anglo-American Relations, 1945–67," *Journal of British Studies* (forthcoming).

35 James Webb Young, November 11 1963 (interview transcript), Hartman Center, Duke University (NC), JWT Archive, Sidney Bernstein Papers, Box 1. For the "creative revolution" in 1960s American advertising see Lawrence Dobrow, *When Advertising Tried Harder. The Sixties: The Golden Age of American Advertising* (New York: Friendly Press, 1984); Warren Berger, *Advertising Today* (London: Phaidon, 2001), 45–81; Clive Challis, *Helmut Krone. The Book. Graphic Design and Art Direction (Concept, Form and Meaning) After Advertising's Creative Revolution* (Cambridge: Cambridge University Press, 2005). For JWT's difficulties with the creative challenges of the 1960s, see West "Growth and development": 211–19.

36 By the late 1960s, S. H. Benson had invested more than £700,000 into its overseas growth and the London Press Exchange had opened branches in South Africa, Rhodesia, South America, India, and Zambia. See "New Trends in Advertising Industry: Growth of World Agency Service," *The Times* (February 27, 1962), 16; *LPE Reporter* 3 (1963), at HAT LPE 3/4/1; *IAOTL – LPE Staff Magazine* 8 (1962), 12–30, at HAT LPE 3/2/8; *S. H. Benson Nigeria, 1965–67*, at HAT, OM (L) 19; Philip Stobo, "Advertiser's Push," *The Times* (March 4, 1965), 13.

37 *Advertiser's Weekly* (May 16, 1969), 28.

38 For this essential difference see Alfred Chandler, *Scale and Scope: The Dynamics of Industrial Capitalism* (Cambridge, MA: Harvard University Press, 1994), 389–92 and Michael Porter, *The Competitive Advantage of Nations* (Basingstoke: Palgrave, 1998), 239–47.

39 Mark Random, "Benson Agency Keeps Growing at 68," *Advertising Age* (April 17, 1961); *The Economist* (November 21, 1964), 907; John McDonough, "Ogilvy & Mather Worldwide, Inc." in John McDonough and Karen Egolf, eds., *The Advertising Age Encyclopedia of Advertising* (New York: Fitzroy Dearborn, 2002), Vol. 2: 1161–7; "O&M Success Story," *The Times* (May 5, 1966), 21; Derek Hollier, "The Agency Takeover Game," *Advertiser's Weekly* (September 29, 1972), 26–7; Ogilvy, *Confessions*: 24–45.

40 David Ogilvy, *Ogilvy on Advertising* (London: Pan, 1983), 9–16; Leiss, *Social Communication*: 145; Brierley, *Advertising*: 140–1; David Aaker, *Building Strong Brands* (London: Simon & Schuster, 2002), 69–71.

41 For the Meynell-Ogilvy and the Bernbach-Ogilvy controversies over advertising as "art," "science" or "salesmanship," see David Ogilvy, "A New Deal for our Clients" (Typescript, February 9, 1939), at HAT; Francis Meynell, *My Lives* (London: Bodley Head, 1971), 229–32; Hazel Warlaumont, *Advertising in the 60s: Turncoats, Traditionalists and Waste Makers in America's Turbulent Decade* (Westport, CT: Praeger, 2000); Martin Mayer, *Madison Avenue, USA* (New York: Harper, 1958); Denis Higgins, *The Art of Writing Advertising: Conversations with William Bernbach, Leo Burnett, George Gribbin, David Ogilvy, Rosser Reeves* (Lincolnwood, IL: Contemporary, 1965); Philippe Lorin, *Five Giants of Advertising* (New York: Assouline, 2001).

42 Neil Blackley, *The Global Advertising Marketplace* (London: James Capel, 1988), 38. For the new geostrategic outlook of agencies in the 1980s see Armand Mattelart, *Advertising International: The Privatisation of Public Space* (London: Routledge, 1991), 1–30.

43 "Saatchi Moves into US," *The Times* (March 16, 1982), 15; "Saatchi & Saatchi: Fast Expansion," *The Times* (May 5, 1982), 18; "The Rise and Rise of the New Brits," *The Times* (September 27, 1984), 14.

44   The "Saatchi story" is told by Philip Kleinman, *The Saatchi & Saatchi Story* (London: Weidenfeld & Nicholson, 1987); Ivan Fallon, *The Brothers: The Rise & Rise of Saatchi & Saatchi* (London: Hutchinson, 1988); Alison Fendley, *Commercial Break: The Inside Story of Saatchi & Saatchi* (London: Hamish Hamilton, 1995); Kevin Goldman, *Conflicting Accounts: The Creation and Crash of the Saatchi & Saatchi Advertising Empire* (New York: Simon & Schuster, 1997).

45   "The Taking of Madison Avenue," *Campaign* (June 9, 1989), 40.

46   Jeremy Tunstall, *The Anglo-American Media Connection* (Oxford: Oxford University Press, 1999), 118–25; Leiss, *Social Communication*: 372–408; Patricia Tisdall, "The Saatchi Agency – An Advertisement for Success," *The Times* (April 12, 1976), 20.

47   R. C. Endicott, "Global Media," *Advertising Age* (December 19, 1988), 21–7; Saatchi & Saatchi Company Ltd. *Annual Report Year Ending September 30 1982* (London: Saatchi & Saatchi, 1983), 10–17; Torin Douglas, "Satellite TV Could Bring 'World Brands'," *The Times* (January 23, 1984), 14; D. A. Leslie, "Global Scan: The Globalization of Advertising Agencies, Concepts and Campaigns," *Economic Geography* 71 (October 1995), 402–26; Theodore Levitt, "The Globalization of Markets," *Harvard Business Review* (May/June 1983), 2–11; "The Return of the Global Brand," *Harvard Business Review* (August 2003), 1–3.

48   Joseph L. Bower, *WPP – Integrating Icons to Leverage Knowledge.* Harvard Business School Case Study, HBS No. 9-396-249 (1997); "Split Personality Which Made JWT Vulnerable," *Campaign* (July 3, 1987), 18–19; "How David Ogilvy Ate His Words," *Financial Times* (May 17, 1989), 24; William Phillips, "Ad Finitum: WPP and the Death of a Sector," *Admap* (March 1991), 13–18; Randall Rothenberg, "Brits Buy up the Ad Business," *New York Times Magazine* (July 2, 1989), 14–19.

49   Stefano Hatfield, "Getting Americans to Appreciate this World-Class Brit is a Tall Order," *The Independent*, Media Weekly, (April 10, 2006), 19; "The Taking of Madison Avenue," *Campaign* (June 9, 1989), 40–4.

50   Special supplement commemorating the twentieth anniversary of AMV, *Campaign* (November 21, 1997); Stefano Hatfield, "London's New Gold Rush," *Creativity* (May 1, 2002); "Watch Out, Giant Agencies: Boutique Creative Shops like Nitro are Winning Some Big Clients," *New York Times* (April 4, 2005), 6; Nixon, *Advertising Cultures*: 40–55; Nixon, "Advertising Executives," 111; Randy Jacobs, "United Kingdom," in McDonough and Egolf, *Encyclopedia of Advertising*, Vol. 3: 1585–94.

14
From High Culture to Hip Culture: Transforming the BBC into BBC America

Christine Becker

"If you're an American flipping through hundreds of channels and you come across us, you're probably thinking, 'hmmm, BBC America, that'll be some nice Jane Austen piece'. Then there's me with a big dildo."[1]

– British comedian Graham Norton

In a 2003 television ad campaign for BBC America, a group of American twenty somethings offer testimonials extolling the greatness of the cable channel's hit BBC import, *The Office*. "It's willing to take a risk in a way that no American show is willing to," says one. "It's so real, that it was kind of shocking," says another. "It's over the edge of what would be acceptable at a normal American network." One might easily mistake this as a commercial for HBO, since the ad pinpoints the primary traits of 'quality TV' associated with the prosperous pay-cable outlet: it's risky, it's 'real', it's not network TV. This is an intriguing connection, in fact, as the hip, maverick identity established in this commercial diverges notably from what the BBC brand has historically signified in the U.S. Indeed, prior to the emergence of BBC America in the late 1990s, few Americans would have connected the BBC with HBO; PBS would have been the most likely association. Further, the material that BBC America has presented to the U.S. differs significantly from what the BBC has sent over to American television in the recent past.

BBC America was launched in the U.S. in March 1998 as a cable channel funded by both subscription fees and advertising. It was a joint venture with Discovery Networks; Discovery put up $100 million in start-up costs for the channel and handled all ad sales, while the entertainment channels division of BBC Worldwide, a commercial subsidiary of the BBC, purchased and supplied the programming. While the majority of programs featured on BBC America originally aired on BBC1 or BBC2 in Britain, the channel also buys shows from Channel 4 and independent producers like Endemol. With a programming schedule dominated by lifestyle reality shows (*Changing Rooms*, *What Not to Wear*, *Cash in the Attic*), contemporary comedies (*My Hero*, *Coupling*, *The Office*), classic comedies (*Fawlty Towers*, *Monty Python*), crime dramas (*The Vice*, *Murder in Mind*), talk shows (*Parkinson*, *So Graham Norton*), and daily live airings of BBC World News, BBC America reached an estimated 40 million television homes in the U.S. by early 2005.[2] While this number represented less than half of the total number of television households in the States, it is actually an impressive figure given that the channel aired only on digital cable and satellite line-ups in this period, and this total surpassed even HBO's reach.[3]

BBC America began garnering significant media attention in 2003, riding the success of *The Office*. Scores of articles about the channel appeared in American newspapers at this time, with television critics raving about the superiority of the channel's programming, especially in comparison to what was viewed as a dearth of quality American network fare. Thus, in only five years, BBC America rocketed from an obscure digital cable channel to what the trade paper *Broadcasting and Cable* called "a beacon for programming trends," battling the vaunted HBO for the crown of network superior.[4] How did BBC America find such success so quickly? Further, how exactly has the BBC's identity been transformed in the U.S. through the development BBC America, and why did the corporation decide to forge this new path in the States across the turn of the century?

In this chapter, I will first discuss how the particular marketing and programming choices made by BBC America in its inaugural half-decade separated the new channel from the traditional BBC brand identity in the U.S. I will then argue that this reorientation was the result of two primary goals for BBC America's parent corporation: first, simply to succeed on American television and thus generate revenue for the BBC, revenue necessary for survival in the competitive multi-channel global television marketplace; and second, more indirectly, to help the BBC maintain its current operational and funding structure in anticipation of its potential 2006 Royal Charter renewal, fighting off attempts to drastically alter the corporation. Finally, I will end the chapter with a discussion of how the ongoing globalization of media industries and contents has been a central factor in the success of this transnational channel.

The BBC-PBS connection

As Jeffrey Miller has argued, the BBC has historically staked its reputation on a divergence from and cultural superiority to mainstream American network television, and the exportation of British shows to the U.S. has played a central role in perpetuating that reputation. Miller places these exports within an historical legacy of cultural exchange between America and Britain in order to illustrate the long-perceived cultural perception that "British cultural artifacts are better than American ones" and that American "[t]elevision was merely the newest frontier in which a cultivated British sensibility might help civilize the wilderness."[5] This cultivated sensibility has largely been oriented around shows and series with historical and literary ties, including *Brideshead Revisited* and *The Forsyte Saga*, and even, to some extent, comedy shows such as *Monty Python*.[6] Traditionally, American institutions like PBS and sponsoring corporations like Mobil tied themselves to these programs, the BBC, and "Britishness" itself in order to elevate their cultural standing in the U.S. When cable arrived in the 1980s, the cable channel A&E (Arts & Entertainment) similarly and successfully adopted BBC programming as a way to elevate its brand identity above typical cable fare, especially the many reruns of network programming on competing channels. *Time* cultural critic James Poniewozik dismissively described the stereotypical American fan of this era of BBC programming thusly:

> [These viewers are] buttered-scone Anglophiles who have supported middlebrow imports like *Ballykissangel* and *Masterpiece Theatre* through pledge drive after pledge drive: those self-hating televisual Tories who cling to genteel dramas and dotty, dated comedies as a Union Jacked bulwark against American TV's tendency to be so crude, so commercial...so American.[7]

Drawing on Herbert Gans' more academic distinctions among so-called taste cultures, it can be said that BBC programming became identified in America as part of "upper-middle culture," as television to be consumed along with foreign films and the *New Yorker*.[8] Similarly, in her study of British literary adaptations, Sarah Cardwell describes the BBC adaptations as taking on the identity of "a 'haven' within the televisual,"[9] and

in America, this haven was defined by drawing on high culture connotations of literary sensibility and elite tastes to distinctly separate BBC –
and PBS – fare from mainstream low and middlebrow culture that otherwise filled American television screens.

As these descriptions illustrate, the BBC has historically defined itself
comparatively to mainstream American broadcasting, and as broadcast
historian Michele Hilmes has shown, the corporation has done so since
its beginning days to validate its own existence as a publicly funded,
non-commercial broadcaster.[10] Partly to justify charging every television set owner in Britain a substantial license fee, the BBC has had to
prove that its programming has higher cultural value than American
programming and that this value could only come from a non-
commercial system. The traditional method for proving this was to
create a rhetorical high culture-low culture split between BBC programming and American programming, with the exportation of literary
dramas and classic comedies into America public television as a way to
perpetuate that split on America's own screens.

With the arrival of BBC America in the late 1990s, I do not believe
that these aims to bolster the BBC's reputation changed; it is quite
clear, however, that the BBC's strategies to support this reputation
were transformed, as illustrated by BBC America's particular marketing
and programming choices. In fact, rather than perpetuating this traditional separation between American and British TV and correspondingly between the low and the high, with BBC America the corporation
managed to mesh the national identities of British and American television and the low and the high, while still presenting the BBC as the
superior program producer due to its unique organizational nature.

Transforming the BBC into BBC America

When BBC America first launched in limited distribution, it was pro-
grammed in the mold of the PBS-identified reputation of the BBC, with
literary adaptations and classic cult sitcoms predominant. In fact, an
October 1998 review of the channel complained that, "As it stands
now, its content is too much like a public television station – and a
second-rate station at that."[11] Quite facetiously, BBC America's then-
CEO Paul Lee more recently remarked, "Six years ago, the typical BBC
America viewer would have been a 54-year-old man in a bowler hat,
probably gay and didn't know it."[12] More seriously, he described elsewhere, "At first...the BBC America brand was pretty stuffy and close to
PBS,"[13] and "People told me, 'The only things you can do are what

you've already made a success of...Mysteries, classic dramas, maybe the more conservative sitcoms from PBS.'"[14] Lee and his colleagues realized quickly, though, that following these old rules in the new digital cable and satellite world would only doom them to failure. Thus, by early 2000, BBC America had begun to transform itself away from the old BBC image in America, shaping itself into an entity that was, as Paul Lee described, "closer to the new Beetle than to the Jaguar: vibrant, contemporary, different."[15] Indeed, the model of a successful cable channel in the early twenty-first century was no longer A&E, as it had been in the 1980s. It was now HBO and MTV leading the way toward success, and the desired target demographic, especially for the more costly digital cable channels, became younger and hipper.

As a result, BBC America began to explicitly distance itself from the traditional BBC brand in America, intending to attract an audience quite different than the stereotypical "buttered-scone Anglophile" *Masterpiece Theater* crowd. In one notable example, a spring 2004 BBC America commercial for the channel's Mystery Monday line-up began with a voice-over declaring, "It's no mystery; BBC America is the place for new crime shows." This tagline clearly recalls the long-running PBS series *Mystery!*, which presents episodes of shows like *Poirot* and *Rumpole of the Bailey*, and the stylized contemporary dramas of violent urban crime featured in the Mystery Monday line-up were quite far from the witty, literary whodunits that have typically made up the *Mystery!* series. Just as the Monday night line-up was no *Mystery!*, BBC America was no PBS.[16]

I'd like to delve more deeply into the specific traits of BBC America's brand at this point and explore how this image has been geared towards staking out a distinctive place within the cluttered American multi-channel line-up. Specifically, I want to show how in trying to define an image based around markers of hip quality rather than high culture, BBC America has drawn on "three Rs": risks, realism, and refinement.

First, in his many interviews with the press about the channel's early success, former CEO Paul Lee invariably focused on the idea of creative risk-taking by BBC America. For example:

- "We definitely like to take risks, and when you take risks your chances of creating a hit increase."[17]
- "Shows like *The Office* and *Curb Your Enthusiasm* take creative risks. They represent a different way of making television. The same sophisticated upscale audience that HBO attracts has also found

BBC America, FX, Bravo and other networks that take creative risks."[18]

- "HBO succeeded by tapping an audience that wanted risks, and BBC America plays to the same audience."[19]

The risks he refers to here run the gamut from explicit language, often heard during episodes of *So Graham Norton*, to graphic sex and violence, with the explicit cop drama *Wire in the Blood* advertised in commercials as "the most shocking two hours of television," to simple creative innovation, often credited to unconventional shows within traditional genres, like the sitcom *The Office*.

Even some of BBC America's advertisements went the risky route. A January 2002 ad campaign for BBC America was halted after the ads were rejected by potential outlets for displaying bad taste. One presented a clip from *So Graham Norton* depicting the host with a sex toy and containing the tagline, "Don't bother calling. We're sorry already." Matt Smith, creative director for the agency that produced the ad, responded to the controversy with a revealing comment: "What's interesting about this rejection was that it told me we'd captured what BBC America was all about. We're being provocative because normal BBC programming is provocative and [our American programming] is not."[20]

In this vein, BBC America explicitly separated itself from traditional network television, as well as from the traditional BBC image, and aligned with those cable channels identified with hip, quality programming, such as HBO. In fact, even when Lee didn't actually use the word "risk" in an interview, he still managed to imply that because BBC America was not beholden to the same standards and formulas as network television, it could be much more innovative:

- "We're not dependent just on whether eyeballs are going to be there the next second. We're making shows audiences are going to remember. In television today with so much competition, memorable shows shine much more brightly than they used to...The 100 channel universe puts more value on great content."[21]
- "The key is to be seen as a destination for creativity, especially when audiences are getting bored with traditional television."[22]
- "Look at the stars of American TV of the last few years. They are Tony Soprano, Ozzy Osbourne, Vic Mackey from *The Shield*, Larry David from *Curb Your Enthusiasm*, and now David Brent. They're all anti-heroes. Our research told us five years ago that Americans were

getting bored of what they call 'cookie-cutter' TV – the 'Honey, I'm home' comedies – and so it's proved."[23]

It is quite easy to read between the lines of this latter quote – the stars he cites were borne by cable television, and the "Honey, I'm home" comedies he references are certainly representative of network television. According to Lee's rhetoric, the networks are incapable of taking risks because of their heavy dependence on advertising; because of its parentage, BBC America is not as beholden to these limits.

A second distinguishing element of BBC America's inaugural brand translated this creative risk into realism. An *American Demographics* article on BBC America referenced a series of focus groups conducted by Discovery Networks, which found that "most of the focus-group participants said they appreciated BBC America's realistic approach."[24] What "realistic approach" exactly means is unclear, but that phrase certainly describes the many lifestyle reality shows on BBC America, touted by critics for their presentation of "unvarnished portraits of the lives of real people" and frequently contrasted with the American versions of the same shows on the basis of authenticity.[25] *Entertainment Weekly* fittingly praised a set of cop dramas on BBC America for their character depth, represented by the fact that they "rarely feature anyone who would make it past the 8 x 10-glossy stage at an American TV audition."[26]

Indeed, similar to the risk rhetoric, one notion circulating throughout BBC America's promotion during this period was that their shows were more genuine and authentic in content than mainstream network television because of their relative distance from the commercial world. The fictional show most connected with this particular rhetoric of realism was *The Office*, as it was frequently praised for using its mockumentary format to avoid the artificial manipulations of typical American sitcoms – such as the laugh track and the contrived and predictable "setup-development-payoff gag structure"[27] – resulting in a depiction of what the BBC America website touted as the "excruciating truth about the world of nine-to-five."[28] BBC America executive Kevin Reilly described *The Office* in just this vein: "Workplace comedies are a staple of TV. Unfortunately, most office comedies have all the reality leeched out of them."[29] Similarly, another BBC America "man-on-the-street" commercial for *The Office* contained the following testimonials:

- "*The Office* has characters that you know, people that you've seen. These are people that you actually work with in your offices."

- "None of them look like actors. They don't look like cast members of *Friends*."
- "It feels real. It feels more real than, you know, any real reality show."

The underlying tone of the commercial, especially underscored by the sneering reference to *Friends*, is that only by circumventing the traditional mechanisms of commercial television production can such a realistic show be produced.[30]

A final thread of rhetoric surrounding BBC America's identity was intriguingly tied to an old BBC definition, and this is the idea that BBC America provides programming of refinement, or programming which can better your life and uplift your cultural sensibilities. Only rather than tying refinement to the circumstance of bringing high culture material into an otherwise low culture wasteland, as in the past Reithian ideal, this updated version of refinement takes low culture texts and lifts them to a higher plane of cultural value. In this sense, BBC America's programming publicity openly acknowledged that its shows trafficked in some of the same low genres as mainstream American television; it just claimed to do them better and with greater cultural value. For instance, whereas network reality shows have been endlessly criticized for humiliating and degrading their participants, not to mention their viewers, BBC America's reality shows were touted as vehicles for improvement and enrichment. If, as a *New York Times* editorial described, "the [reality] genre has always been a slightly sour cocktail of exploitation, voyeurism and humiliation,"[31] BBC America presented its reality shows as an amiable elixir of civility, collective participation, and enrichment.

And if *The Office* was the ideal show to define BBC America's rhetoric of realism, *Faking It* best highlighted the channel's tropes of refinement. *Faking It* was a reality show in which a participant was given a month to adopt an identity wholly unsuited to her personality and experience, with the assistance of an expert in that field, and then tested herself to see if she could "perform" that identity well enough to fool other experts (e.g., a classical musician performs as a hip-hop DJ, a fry cook tries to pass as a professional chef, an insurance salesman becomes a stunt man). Despite the obvious potential for it, *Faking It* was not about showcasing the participant's inadequacies, putting them in a position to be humiliated, or mocking their failures, the approaches most often identified as low culture tendencies of network reality shows. Instead, *Faking It* focused on the complexities of the struggle to adopt a different identity and on the heartfelt partnerships that developed between the training experts and the participants. A *Village Voice* review perceptively described the perception left by *Faking It* in contrast to the typical makeover reality show:

> Makeover shows have spread across the airwaves like a plague, constantly mutating into ever more virulent strains. But the British series *Faking It*...goes beyond mascara and haircuts, wallpaper and floor treatments. Instead of Queer Eye-style tips on how to rub in hair gel or 'zhuzh' your jacket, *Faking It* heads for more sticky, uncharted territory: career, craftsmanship, identity.[32]

In essence, the viewer learned about class boundaries, cultural stereotypes, and human nature from *Faking It*, viewing societal processes and personal achievements rather than surface outcomes and material gains.

Similarly, the show *Life Laundry*, in which a host forces participants to discard the worthless belongings they have accumulated in their homes over the decades and the emotional baggage that goes with them, was heralded by the BBC America website as "more than just a makeover show" and a "show that will literally change your life."[33] This latter slogan could only apply "literally" to the show's participants, but the ad strongly implied that *Life Laundry* could improve the viewer's life by extension, through teaching the audience how to rid their lives of both material and emotional clutter. I believe that this message of refinement and betterment was exactly the impression that BBC America was hoping that viewers would take away from all of their reality shows in this period. While these programs may have fallen under the same generic umbrella as network reality shows, cable reality shows, and even American adaptations of the same shows, the channel wanted to convey the impression that what it offered was not just another makeover show or just another personality competition. Only BBC America's versions served a genuine function of potentially improving a viewer's everyday life.

The bottom line for what BBC America tried to become through these marketing strategies was well summarized by former CEO Paul Lee in praising one of the channel's ad agencies: "They made us look cool but high quality."[34] And cool but high quality is an apt definition for most of America's successful cable channels. In fact, one could even see BBC America's early 2000 programming as a crystallization of nearly all of the prominent cable television trends in America at the time: the channel offered HBO-style edginess, TLC's lifestyle reality, FX's gritty police dramas and USA's light-hearted ones, Comedy Central's topical sketch comedy, and CNN-style news. This success subsequently gained the attention of the broadcast networks. As the influential trade paper *Variety* described in late 2004, "Broadcast execs are scouring for potential primetime programming the ever-rotating lineup at BBC America,"[35] a fact which Paul Lee continually stressed during his tenure as CEO:

- "Five years ago people said to us watch the big networks, copy the broadcast networks because you'll never be relevant if you don't. Now they are the ones paying closer attention to us, and some of the other cable networks, because we are the ones taking the risks."[36]
- "Far from us taking notes on what big broadcast networks are doing, we're flattered they are watching us closely."[37]
- "People search harder for programming that stands out. The big analog networks are looking over their shoulders at us."[38]

This was rather hyperbolic publicity rhetoric, since the networks have looked over their shoulders at all of cable and not just the relatively small BBC America. But it was part of a strategy labeled "public relations success" by the *New York Times*, since BBC America had succeed by 2003 in attaining a level of media attention that certainly outstripped its subscriber reach.[39] And it reached this level by following the contemporary model for success in the cable and satellite landscape in the U.S.: developing a rhetoric of hip quality oriented around risk, realism and refinement, and thereby separating the channel's identity from the traditional network model of commercial, conservative, mass-oriented aims. The channel's British identity then acted as a distinguishing supplemental factor to mark it as unique within the huge sea of competing cable and satellite channels.

How BBC America served the BBC

While these strategies served as means to success in the States for BBC America, I also believe that their impact was intended to reverberate back toward Britain. By the late 1990s, the BBC was already looking toward its potential 2006 charter renewal and considering how to argue for the maintenance of its basic structure and license fee support. The BBC was taking on considerable criticism at the turn of the millennium for allegedly abandoning its founding public service principles and highbrow programming in favor of "dumbed-down" shows that merely duplicated the offerings of the many commercial terrestrial and satellite channels flooding the nation. It was especially accused of becoming "too American" in direction, which translated into being concerned with mass popularity rather than cultural edification and public service.

If it hoped to retain its position as a license fee-supported public corporation, the BBC had to argue that it had not turned its back on its public service principles, and in fact, only a large-scale public broadcaster like the BBC could truly provide popular, high quality programming with cultural value in the contemporary multi-channel, commercial-dominated world of global broadcasting. Greg Dyke, the former Director-General of the BBC, said exactly this in a November 2003 speech, and in doing so, echoed the same rhetoric evident in the construction of BBC America's brand:

> Far from being a barrier to the success of commercial enterprise, we can be the catalyst for competition, for quality and creativity... Being publicly funded gives us freedom to take risks, to be creative and to ask awkward questions. That is something we should all treasure and if we lose it we do so at our peril.[40]

He also added proudly that the BBC "manages to be more popular than its commercial counterparts" in Britain, thus underscoring that only the publicly funded BBC could provide programming that is both culturally valuable and popular.[41] This delicate combination was exactly what BBC America insisted it maintained, and its success in America's own cable and satellite backyard could be used as proof of the BBC's superiority over the very programming it was accused of parroting. The two Golden Globes awarded to *The Office* in February 2004 must have been a dream-come-true for the BBC in that regard, since the show defeated the most highly acclaimed American sitcoms. In fact, this victory was referenced in the BBC's 2004 governance proposal as evidence that the BBC had become a global leader in television.[42]

In fact, BBC America became so successful in this period that it was nearly a victim of that success. In addition to the critical praise it received, the channel also provoked measurable criticism back in England. Some questioned why the BBC should be chasing ratings and profits outside of its own borders, while others offered that if the

BBC could run an international commercial channel so successfully, perhaps the corporation could operate successfully at home without the license fee system. Rivals to the BBC also complained that it was unfair for the BBC to benefit from both internal, guaranteed public funding and external commercial funding, and to use its dominant domestic market position, earned via a license fee contributed by nearly all British citizens, to compete internationally.[43]

These criticisms extended to BBC America's highly successful parent company, BBC Worldwide, and in late 2004, the BBC held an internal review to consider selling off its international commercial arm. There was speculation that BBC Worldwide would sell for as much as $3.6 billion, with suitors including Time Warner, Bertelsmann, and Disney,[44] but the corporation ultimately decided not to sell. The BBC's judgment was that BBC Worldwide and its ancillary commercial operations were in fact enhancing the public service value of the license fee, by exploiting fully the BBC's assets and thereby bringing valuable profits back to the corporation, profits that were helping to prevent increases in that fee. In a speech declaring these findings, BBC Director-General Mark Thompson explained, "The review has concluded that we do have a duty to derive as much commercial value as we can out of the intellectual property created by licence-fee investment." He further defended the BBC's indispensable integrity in the midst of exploding global commercialism:

> Despite its eccentricities and failings, [the BBC] remains one of the greatest – some might say the greatest – force for cultural good in the world...Its programme-making heritage – its conviction, its commitment to talent and to giving that talent the time to get things right, its commitment to gratuitous quality (in other words, quality over and above what you would need to provide to make a programme fit for commercial purpose) – this heritage is what the emerging on-demand world is crying out for. The future is heading towards, not away from, the BBC.[45]

It is quite striking how closely these ideas conform to the publicity rhetoric that surrounded BBC America, thus illustrating how valuable the channel's success in the U.S. could be for the corporation and its larger aims.

In fact, the parallels between the BBC's charter-renewal arguments and BBC America's publicity rhetoric at this time were numerous. To those who accused the BBC of abandoning its high culture aims by fos-

tering commercially successful shows, then-BBC2 controller Jane Root
responded:

> Read between the lines and they want a BBC that is timid, small and
> under-funded; shrunk in ambition and lacking in impact; appealing
> to those already in the know...A polite, almost embalmed public
> service...Look at PBS in the states – if you can find it. It has no real
> salience, no impact.[46]

After once again distinguishing this old PBS-identified BBC image from
its new image, likely so as not to appear elitist or out-of-touch with the
ordinary license fee-paying public, she then argued that *The Office*,
which began its life on BBC2, was indeed public service broadcasting
because of its high-risk unconventionality, meaning that despite its
acknowledged quality, a commercial broadcaster likely would not have
developed the show:

> Four out of five comedies struggle. Comedy is expensive. The BBC
> spent 18 million pounds on this riskiest of genres last year. Hardly
> surprising that commercial channels aren't exactly queuing up to
> have a go. It's a classic example of market failure but comedy falls
> outside the definitions of public service. That worries me. If the
> 40-year history of BBC2 has taught us anything, it's that we should
> reject narrow notions of public service broadcasting. We should
> choose broad over niche. Bold over meek. Alive over embalmed.[47]

Further, Paul Lee's repeated insistence on how BBC America blazed a
trail for American networks to follow illustrates that the corporation
was trying to prove that it was most certainly not becoming
Americanized; instead, it was the American networks that had to play
catch-up with the more innovative BBC. This is in part why I believe it
was crucial for BBC America to reshape the corporation's identity in
the U.S. and offer America shows within popular, mainstream genres
instead of the stereotypical upper-middlebrow, PBS-style programming.
Rather than opening itself up to questions of irrelevance and elitism by
continuing to highlight "stuffy" and "embalmed" shows, the BBC tried
to prove on American soil that it could do what the American networks do, only better, and only with its operational structure left
intact.

In this sense, the BBC tried to use its transnational success in order to
shore up its national control. And in just about every regard, starting

with its very name, BBC America is a transnational entity. Its programming structure presents a hybridity of British programs with American-style scheduling and flow, as even its BBC-originated programs are interrupted by commercials.[48] And in addition to airing British shows in the U.S., BBC America also began commissioning original programs specifically for American audiences in 2003, such as the garden makeover show *Ground Force America*. Similarly, and much to the consternation of many of its fans,[49] *Faking It* began replacing the original British soundtracks for the show with American-accented voiceovers. Finally, despite Paul Lee's insistence that the channel's programmers were "cherry-picking the best of what the BBC is producing and putting it all on one channel,"[50] BBC America has not actually provided what anyone might truly consider the best of the BBC or of British television in general. For example, none of the documentaries for which the corporation has become so internationally respected have appeared, and many innovative British sitcoms and dramas have never been included in the programming line-up.

The reasoning behind these circumstances can be found in a statement by David Bernath, vice-president of programming for BBC America: "We are a mainstream American channel, so our shows need to appeal to an American audience."[51] As the *New York Times* further explicates, "That means references to British culture can't be too parochial and the accents can't require subtitles…The trick, it seems, is to spot cultural distinctions that are different enough to seem exotic yet not so strange that they actually seem foreign."[52] Thus, the expressed intent here is to create a truly transnationally oriented, rather than solely nationally defined, television channel. It is not simply the BBC airing in America; it is BBC America.

Conclusions

While BBC America clearly tried to market itself as a new entity, there were some crucial similarities with the BBC's past identity in the U.S. As Jeffery Miller describes in reference to the U.S. popularity of *Monty Python's Flying Circus* in the 1970s:

> As was the case with other imported shows from *The Avengers* to *Upstairs, Downstairs*, difference itself – or the varying utterances of otherness – was attractive, especially to an audience angry with or weary of the cultural norms that were the sources of American comedy. That attraction was heightened by the fact that [*Monty*

Python] appeared almost exclusively on television stations operating outside the norm of commercial American broadcasting.[53]

This description could easily be applied to BBC America: its shows were attractive as an "other" to mainstream American television, and they appeared industrially outside the norm of the commercial networks. While this is exactly what HBO has done as well – sell itself as an alternative for those who are too smart and sophisticated for network fare – this is also reminiscent of the traditional *Masterpiece Theater* image of the BBC image or even *Monty Python*'s combination of wacky, sometimes racy humor (i.e. risks) and highbrow references (i.e. refinement).

However, a crucial distinction between past and present is that BBC America has tried to portray itself as a hybrid of the best of British and American television and has marketed its superiority on that basis, rather than pinning its identity on being uniquely British, much as past BBC programming in America did. This might explain the constant references to previous BBC fans in the U.S. as bowler-wearers or "tea-sipping Anglophiles,"[54] as well as the presence of young, urban–identified Americans in its ad campaigns and the many allusions to HBO. While the national identity of the BBC may have represented high Anglo culture to Americans in the past, the transnational identity of BBC America represents hip global culture in the present.

Thus, BBC America has indeed become "a beacon for programming trends," as this circumstance echoes an ongoing development within globalized media in the twenty-first century, where national borders between programming and production are increasingly blurring. While this has been happening for some time in the rest of the world, given the growth of satellite distribution and the dominance of American television abroad, it is only now encroaching onto American screens. American producers are looking abroad for new reality and game show formats, the networks and cable channels are adopting British sitcom and drama formats in increasing numbers, and transnational production companies like Endemol and FreemantleMedia are producing shows for American television. Further, even the American seasonal scheduling model is starting to shift to one more common to international programming, particularly the BBC, with the growth of limited-run series premiering throughout the calendar year. BBC America has thus also represented an attempt to capitalize on these increasingly invisible lines between national origins, identities and methods in global and American television. David Bernath describes, "We don't think of Coldplay as a British group; it's just a group. We don't go to 'Harry Potter' and think of it as the British thing. [Hopefully] in 2008 people will say, 'Did you see that thing on BBC America?' and they don't even think of it as British."[55]

However, if this were to happen it would represent a seismic shift from the resolutely nationalistic past of American television. BBC America does represent an exception, albeit still a rare one, to the historic rule that U.S. television is always U.S.-produced television. Further, NBC's rather disastrous remake of the BBC's *Coupling* in Fall 2003 received as much press for its British origins as for its controversial content, since many post-cancellation reviews compared it negatively to the original.[56] For its part, BBC America heavily publicized the fact that it was airing the original episodes of *Coupling* at the same time that NBC was airing the remake. Importantly, they highlighted most strongly the fact that it was a hip quality sitcom, not simply that it was British. In this manner, BBC America was clearly trying to push toward acceptance within the home-grown tradition of American television while still posing itself as superior because of its risks, realism and refinement, in addition to its Britishness. While I don't foresee this transnational trend in U.S. television moving much beyond BBC America in the near future, it is at least indicative of the fact that the American television networks are feeling the impact of international competition, yet another factor they never had to deal with prior to the digital age. And the BBC has furthered its international efforts, launching other global channels, including BBC Canada, BBC Japan, and BBC Prime, which airs in parts of Europe, Africa and the Middle East.[57]

Ultimately, while BBC America did not topple the mighty U.S. networks in the first half of the 2000s, it did at least thrive financially and rhetorically within the heavily competitive cable and satellite market. I also believe that the channel's U.S. prosperity and the success of channels like it will have an impact on present and future BBC charter discussions. At the very least, BBC America did succeed in affecting the image of the BBC in the U.S. Then-CEO Paul Lee said in November 2003, "Research that we've done backs up the view that Americans now see the BBC and Britain as young, funny, maybe a little eccentric, but definitely someone you'd like to meet at a party."[58] In fact, an ideal representative of this description, Graham Norton, was invited to the party: he signed a two-year contract in 2003 with American cable channel Comedy Central.[59] Somehow I doubt that Jane Austen would have received the same invitation.

Notes

1 Quoted in Steven Pratt, "In the Picture – Remade in America," *Northern Echo* (September 20, 2003), 11. Retrieved February 15, 2004, from ProQuest.

2 Maria Esposito, "BBC America Overtakes HBO," *C21Media.net* (July 20, 2004). Retrieved July 20, 2004, from www.c21media.net/common/print_detail.asp?article=21196.

3 According to Nielsen Media, there were about 109.6 million television households in the U.S. in early 2005 (see www.nielsenmedia.com/newsreleases/2004/04-05_natl-UE.htmg). An estimated 24 million households were subscribed to satellite services, and out of the approximately 70 million cable-subscribing households, 24 million were subscribed to digital cable tiers (see www.forbes.com/personaltech/2005/01/05/cx_de_0105cable.html). Finally, as of early 2005, HBO reached about 28 million subscribers, though HBO's subscriber totals frequently fluctuate across the year, as viewers subscribe for particular shows, such as *The Sopranos*, and then cancel the service when those shows are on hiatus.

4 Allison Romano, "At the Helm of a Programming Pacesetter," *Broadcasting and Cable* (November 3, 2003). Retrieved February 5, 2004, from http://www.broadcastingcable.com/article/CA333168?display=People.

5 Jeffery Miller, *Something Completely Different: British Television and American Culture* (Minneapolis, MN: University of Minnesota Press, 2000), 20, 178.

6 Miller offers an especially astute reading of *Monty Python*'s success on PBS on pages 127–38.

7 James Poniewozik, "Anarchy from the U.K.: A different British invasion is under way as BBC America imports shows that are anything but stuffy," *Time* (Jun 5, 2000), 48. Retrieved February 15, 2004, from ProQuest.

8 Herbert Gans, *Popular Culture and High Culture: Revised and Updated Version* (New York, NY: Basic Books, 1999). See especially 106–10.

9 Sarah Cardwell, *Adaptation Revisited: Television and the Classic Novel* (Manchester and New York: Manchester University Press, 2002), 81.

10 Michele Hilmes, "Who We Are, Who We Are Not: Battle of Global Paradigms," in Lisa Parks and Shanti Kumar, eds., *Planet TV* (New York and London: New York University Press, 2003), 53–73.

11 Ryan K. Johnson, "BBC America Comes to Cable," *Ryan's British TV Show Reviews* (posted October 8, 1998). Retrieved January 24, 2004, from www.eskimo.com/~rkj/weekly/aa100598.htm.

12 Quoted in Caryn James, "It's Brash, It's British, It's Not PBS," *New York Times* (March 8, 2004). Retrieved March 28, 2004, from http://www.nytimes.com/2004/03/28/arts/television/28JAME.html. Paul Lee left BBC America and became the president of ABC Family in summer 2004.

13 Quoted in Romano.

14 Quoted in Poniewozik.

15 Quoted in Poniewozik.

16 Of course, both of these identities are artificially constructed discourses – just as PBS has aired plenty of lowbrow British comedies, BBC America's countless reruns of Changing Rooms should taint its hip quotient. But again in both cases, reality has been overshadowed by successful image-

building, and these multiple images have served key rhetorical purposes on both sides of the ocean.

17 Quoted in Clark Humphrey, "The English Channel," *MISCmedia.com* (September 4, 2000). Retrieved January 23, 2004, from www.miscmedia.com/9-4-00.html.

18 Quoted in Jack Myers, "BBC America Establishes a Solid Beachhead in U.S.," *Jack Myers Report* (October 10, 2003). Retrieved January 24, 2004, from www.jackmyers.com/pdf/10-10-03.pdf.

19 Quoted in Charles Goldsmith and Emily Nelson, "Golden Globes May Help BBC America Expand Audience," *Wall Street Journal* (January 27, 2004), B1. Retrieved February 15, 2004, from ProQuest.

20 Quoted in Alicia Griswold, "BBC Ads Rile Media," *Adweek* (January 14, 2002), 6. Retrieved February 15, 2004, from ProQuest.

21 Quoted in Myers.

22 Ibid.

23 Quoted in John Naughton, "Situation Vacant," *Radio Times* (November 8, 2003), 34–5. Retrieved May 25, 2004, from LexisNexis Academic.

24 Cristina Merrill, "Absolutely Fabulous," *American Demographics* (January 2000), p. 27. Retrieved February 15, 2004, from EBSCOhost.

25 Quote from Merrill. See also Erin Oates, "Re: To Kassidy," *BBC America.com Home Improvement Discussions Message Board* (January 29, 2004). Retrieved February 15, 2004, from bbcamerica.com. http://discussions.bbcamerica.com/forum.jspa?forumID=14.

26 Ken Tucker, "Cream of the Crop," *Entertainment Weekly* (May 28, 2004), 112.

27 Christopher Sieving, "The Office," *PopMatters* (February 10, 2003). Retrieved February 3, 2004, from www.popmatters.com/tv/reviews/o/office.shtml.

28 www.bbcamerica.com/genre/comedy_games/the_office/the_office_about.jsp

29 Quoted in Mark Sage, "NBC To Make U.S. Version of *The Office, Press Association News* (October 16, 2003). Retrieved February 16, 2004, from LexisNexis Academic.

30 Even creator-star Ricky Gervais opted for reality rhetoric when discussing the show with an American newspaper: "Just for that half hour, I hope [viewers] suspend their disbelief and feel that they are eavesdropping on these people. I hope they don't think of me as an actor, but they do sort of think, 'I wonder what Brent's doing now,' because I watch and go, 'I wonder if he's at work.' Just for a minute, you want to think that he exists." Quoted in Robert Wilonsky, "Back to Work," *Dallas Observer* (November 25, 2004). Retrieved December 15, 2004, from LexisNexis.

31 Editorial Desk, "Losing Touch With Reality," *New York Times* (February 21, 2004), 14. Retrieved February 21, 2004, from nytimes.com.

32 Joy Press, "My Brilliant Career," *Village Voice* (November 18, 2003), 48. Retrieved March 3, 2004, from LexisNexis Academic.

33 http://www.bbcamerica.com/genre/home_living/life_laundry/life_laundry.jsp.

34 Quoted in Justin M. Norton, "BBC Taps 2 Shops," *Adweek* (March 12, 2001), 10. Retrieved February 15, 2004, from ProQuest.

35 Denise Martin, "Yank execs take a Peep at BBC Americas offerings," *Variety* (December 6–12, 2004), 31. Retrieved December 15, 2004, from LexisNexis Academic.

36 Quoted in David Teather, "BBC Has the Last Laugh in US," *The Guardian* (January 5, 2004). Retrieved January 23, 2004, from www.guardian.co.uk/business/story/0,3604,1115991,00.html.
37 Quoted in Romano.
38 Quoted in Myers.
39 James.
40 Quoted in "Dyke: Americans Don't Get the BBC," *C21Media.net* (November 25, 2003). Retrieved November 25, 2005, from www.c21media.net/features.
41 Ibid.
42 "Building Public Value: Renewing the BBC for a Digital World," 40. Retrieved June 30, 2004, from http://www.bbc.co.uk/thefuture/pdfs/bbc_bpv.pdf.
43 For good summary of some of these criticisms, see Tim Webb and Miranda McLachlan, "BBC Worldwide Has to Change; The Only Question is How," *Independent on Sunday* (September 26, 2004), 6–7. Retrieved December 15, 2004, from LexisNexis Academic.
44 "A BBC Unit May Be Headed For The Block," *Business Week* (September 20, 2004), 57. Retrieved December 15, 2004, from LexisNexis Academic.
45 Mark Thompson, "The NS media lecture (7 December 2004)," *New Statesman* (January 1, 2005). Retrieved January 11, 2004, from LexisNexis.
46 Quoted in Ed Waller, "Root: Comedy is Public Service," *C21Media.net* (February 11, 2004). Retrieved February 11, 2004, from www.c21media.net/news/detail.asp?area=5&article=19204.
47 Ibid.
48 The only exception is BBC World News, which airs live without commercial interruptions.
49 See http://discussions.bbcamerica.com/forum.jspa?forumID=39.
50 Quoted in Dirk Smillie, "The British Are Coming – To U.S. Cable," *Christian Science Monitor* (September 11, 1998). Retrieved January 30, 2004, from www.csmonitor.com/durable/1998/09/11/p57s1.htm.
51 Quoted in James.
52 James.
53 Miller, 130.
54 James. Incidentally, according to BBC America.com's message boards, the channel has alienated a segment of its fanbase by not objecting to these disparaging descriptions of its Anglophile viewers. There has also been a considerable outcry in response to BBC America's cancellation of the soap opera *EastEnders*. Channel spokespeople say that the removal was due to low ratings, while angry fans point out that *EastEnders* didn't draw too much less than the many repeats of daytime lifestyle reality shows do. I would point out the fact that the show does not fit into the channel's risks-reality-refinement strategy, thereby stressing that this may also have been a key factor in its cancellation.
55 Quoted in James.
56 *Coupling* lasted for only four episodes on NBC, following a substantial publicity campaign.
57 "BBC has cunning plan for Japan with Blackadder," *The Guardian* (October 9, 2004). Retrieved December 15, 2004, from LexisNexis.
58 Quoted in Naughton.

59   Andrew Wallenstein, "Brit Hit Norton Joins Comedy Club in U.S.," *Hollywood Reporter* (September 24, 2003). Retrieved May 27, 2004, from www.hollywoodreporter.com/thr/.article_display.jsp?vnu_content_id=1985 07

Index